EXPERT SYSTEMS IN BUSINESS AND FINANCE

John Wiley
SERIES IN INFORMATION SYSTEMS

Editors

Richard Boland
Case Western Reserve University

Rudy Hirschheim
University of Houston

EXPERT SYSTEMS IN BUSINESS AND FINANCE
Issues and Applications

Edited by

Paul R. Watkins
and
Lance B. Eliot

University of Southern California, Los Angeles, USA

John Wiley
SERIES IN INFORMATION SYSTEMS

JOHN WILEY & SONS
Chichester · New York · Brisbane · Toronto · Singapore

Copyright © 1993 by John Wiley & Sons Ltd,
Baffins Lane, Chichester,
West Sussex PO19 1UD, England

Other Wiley Editorial Offices

John Wiley & Sons, Inc., 605 Third Avenue,
New York, NY 10158-0012, USA

Jacaranda Wiley Ltd, G.P.O. Box 859, Brisbane,
Queensland 4001, Australia

John Wiley & Sons (Canada) Ltd, 22 Worcester Road,
Rexdale, Ontario M9W 1L1, Canada

John Wiley & Sons (SEA) Pte Ltd, 37 Jalan Pemimpin #05-04,
Block B, Union Industrial Building, Singapore 2057

Library of Congress Cataloging-in-Publication Data

Expert systems in business and finance : issues and applications /
    edited by Paul R. Watkins and Lance B. Eliot.
        p.   cm. — (John Wiley series in information systems)
    Includes bibliographical references and index.
    ISBN 0-471-91967-5
    1. Expert systems (Computer science)   2. Business—Data
processing.   3. Finance—Data processing.   4. Information storage
and retrieval systems—Business.   5. Information storage and
retrieval systems—Finance.   I. Eliot, Lance B.   II. Series.
HF5548.2.E963   1992
658′ . 05421—dc20   91–33804
                                                                    CIP

British Library Cataloguing-in-Publication Data

A catalogue record for this book is available from the British Library

ISBN 0-471-91967-5

Typeset in 10/12pt Baskerville from author's disks by Text Processing Department,
John Wiley & Sons Ltd, Chichester
Printed and bound in Great Britain by Biddles Ltd, Guildford and King's Lynn

CONTENTS

LIST OF CONTRIBUTORS

Chidanand Apte   *Thomas J. Watson Research Center, IBM Research Division, P. O. Box 218, Yorktown Heights, NY 10598*

Susan Athey   *Computer Information Systems Department, Colorado State University, Fort Collins, CO 80523*

Stanley F. Biggs   *Director of Ph.D. Program, College of Business, University of Connecticut, Storrs, CT 06268*

Edward Blocher   *Chair, Department of Accounting, University of North Carolina, Carroll Hall, CB3490, Chapel Hill, NC 27514*

Carol E. Brown   *College of Business, Oregon State University, Bexell Hall 200, Corvallis, OR 97331-2603*

George S. Cole, Esq.   *793 Nash Avenue, Menlo Park, CA 94025*

Lance B. Eliot   *P. O. Box 30041, Long Beach, CA 90853-0041*

James Griesmer   *Thomas J. Watson Research Center, IBM Research Division, P. O. Box 218, Yorktown Heights, NY 10598*

Se June Hong   *Thomas J. Watson Research Center, IBM Research Division, P. O. Box 218, Yorktown Heights, NY 10598*

Rodger Jamieson   *Director, Information Technology Research Centre, School of Information Systems, University of New South Wales, P. O. Box 1, Kensington, New South Wales, AUSTRALIA 2033*

Maurice Karnaugh   *Thomas J. Watson Research Center, IBM Research Division, P. O. Box 218 , Yorktown Heights, NY 10598*

John Kastner   *Thomas J. Watson Research Center, IBM Research Division, P. O. Box 218, Yorktown Heights, NY 10598*

David King   *Comshare, Inc., 9600 Great Hills Trail, Austin, TX 78759*

George Krull, Jr.   *Grant Thornton, 1700 Prudential Plaza, Chicago, IL 60601*

Meir Laker   *Thomas J. Watson Research Center, IBM Research Division, P. O. Box 218, Yorktown Heights, NY 10598*

Thomas J. Martin   *Vice President, C.P. Test Services-Valuco, Inc., 234 Sandford Avenue, Kearny, NJ 07029*

Eric Mays   *Thomas J. Watson Research Center, IBM Research Division, P. O. Box 218, Yorktown Heights, NY 10598*

Leif Birger Methlie   *Institute for Information Systems Research, Norwegian School of Economics and Business Administration, Hellevn. 30, N-5035 Bergen-Sandviken, NORWAY*

Robert R. Moeller   *Director, Internal Audit, Sears Roebuck & Co., 1045 Ridge Avenue, Evanston, IL 60202*

Daniel E. O'Leary   *Editor, International Journal of Intelligent Systems in Accounting, Finance and Management, School of Business Administration, University of Southern California, Los Angeles, CA 90089-1421*

Mary Ellen Phillips   *College of Business, Oregon State University, Bexell Hall 200, Corvallis, OR 97331-2603*

Alan Rowe   *School of Business Administration, University of Southern California, Los Angeles, CA 90089-1421*

Kenneth A. Scalf   *Prentice-Hall Professional Software, 2400 Lake Park Dr., Smyrna, GA 30339*

Mallory Selfridge   *Computer Applications Research Center, Department of Computer Science, University of Connecticut, Storrs, CT 06268*

William T. Tener   *27042 La Paja Lane, Mission Viejo, CA 92691*

Efraim Turban   *Professor, Department of Information Systems, 1250 Bellflower Boulevard, Long Beach, CA 90840-8506*

Paul R. Watkins *Director, Advanced Technologies in Information Systems Program, School of Business Administration, University of Southern California, Los Angeles, CA 90089-1421*

Stephen V. N. Yates *Grant Thornton, New York, NY, (212) 599-0100*

SERIES FOREWORD

In order for all types of organisations to succeed, they need to be able to process data and use information effectively. This has become especially true in today's rapidly changing environment. In conducting their day-to-day operations, organisations use information for functions such as planning, controlling, organising, and decision making. Information, therefore, is unquestionably a critical resource in the operation of all organisations. Any means, mechanical or otherwise, which can help organisations process and manage information presents an opportunity they can ill afford to ignore.

The arrival of the computer and its use in data processing has been one of the most important organisational innovations in the past thirty years. The advent of computer-based data processing and information systems has led to organisations being able to cope with the vast quantities of informations which they need to process and manage to survive. The field which has emerged to study this development is *information systems* (IS). It is a combination of two primary fields, computer science and management, with a host of supporting disciplines, e.g. psychology, sociology, statistics, political science, economics, philosophy, and mathematics. IS is concerned not only with the development of new information technologies but also with questions such as: how they can best be applied, how they should be managed, and what their wider implications are.

Partly because of the dynamic world in which we live (and the concomitant need to process more information), and partly because of the dramatic recent developments in information technology, e.g. personal computers, fourth-generation languages, relational databases, knowledge-based systems, and office automation, the relevance and importance of the field of information systems has become apparent. End users, who previously had little potential of becoming seriously involved and knowledgeable in information technology and systems, are now much more aware of and interested in the new technology. Individuals working in today's and tomorrow's organisations will be expected to have some understanding of and the ability to use the rapidly developing information technologies and systems. The dramatic increase in the availability and use of information technology, however, raises fundamental questions on the guiding of technological innovation, measuring organisational and managerial productivity, augmenting human intelligence, ensuring data integrity, and establishing strategic advantage. The expanded use of information systems also raises major challenges to the traditional forms of administration and authority, the right to privacy, the nature and form of work, and the limits of calculative rationality in modern organisations and society.

The Wiley Series on Information Systems has emerged to address these questions and challenges. It hopes to stimulate thought and discussion on the key role information systems play in the functioning of organisations and society, and how their role is likely to change in the future. This historical or evolutionary theme of the Series is important because considerable insight can be gained by attempting to understand the past. The Series will attempt to integrate both description—what has been done—with prescription—how best to develop and implement information systems.

The descriptive and historical aspect is considered vital because information systems of the past have not necessarily met with the success that was envisaged. Numerous writers postulate that a high proportion of systems are failures in one sense or another. Given their high cost of development and their importance to the day-to-day running of organisations, this situation must surely be unacceptable. Research into IS failure has concluded that the primary cause of failure is the lack of consideration given to the social and behavioural dimensions of IS. Far too much emphasis has been placed on their technical side. The result has been something of a shift in emphasis from a strictly technical conception of IS to one where it is recognised that information systems have behavioural consequences. But even this misses the mark. A growing number of researchers suggest that information systems are more appropriately conceived as social systems which rely, to a greater and greater extent, on new technology for their operation. It is this social orientation which is lacking in much of what is written about IS. The current volume, *Expert Systems in Business and Finance,* provides an overview of expert systems that explicitly joins issues of technological integration with the organizational, human, security and legal factors which ultimately determine their success or failure. Watkins and Eliot bring together insights from the leaders in the field and blend the best of theoretical understanding with a breadth of practical experience to produce an important guide to the development of effective expert systems.

The Series seeks to promote a forum for the serious discussion of IS. Although the primary perspective is a more social and behavioural one, alternative perspectives will also be included. This is based on the belief that no one perspective can be totally complete; added insight is possible through the adoption of multiple views. Relevant areas to be addressed in the Series include (but are not limited to): the theoretical development of information systems, their practical application, the foundations and evolution of information systems, and IS innovation. Subjects such as systems design, systems analysis methodologies, information systems planning and management, office automation, project management, decision support systems, end-user computing, and information systems and society are key concerns of the Series.

Rudy Hirschheim
Richard Boland

PREFACE

This book was conceived for the purpose of presenting issues and of identifying opportunities that are or should be of interest to those who are evaluating, researching, developing or have a particular interest in applied artificial intelligence, especially expert systems.

Expert systems have gone through a series of developmental stages in the past few years and are now being viewed as a somewhat stable technology for use in business, finance and accounting information systems. With any "new" technology, there exist growing pains and issues that require identification, discussion and attention with the intent to improve the technology and increase the real and derived benefits from its use in the particular domain(s) of interest.

Although there are many issues and opportunities that could be discussed in any volume such as this one, we have identified four major themes or issues that we believe are crucial for successful utilization of the technology in the research, development and implementation phases. These four themes are: (1) Issues in the Design and Integration of Expert Systems, (2) Issues in the Modeling of Human Judgment for Expert Systems, (3) Issues in Validation, Auditability and Security of Expert Systems and (4) Legal Issues, Training Effects, Resource Planning and Public Accounting Expert Systems.

PART I ISSUES IN THE DESIGN AND INTEGRATION OF EXPERT SYSTEMS

Expert systems were originally conceived and implemented as stand alone systems, particularly in areas such as medicine, geology and so on. As expert systems have become commonplace in business organizations, the need to integrate these systems with conventional computer-based systems has become increasingly important. This section of the book consists of five chapter dealing with the areas of integration and design.

Chapter 1: Expert Systems Integration with Computer-based Information Systems

This chapter provides an overview of the integration issues and describes major modes of integration and reviews areas in which integration might be most applicable. A feature of this chapter is an extensive bibliography of references which are useful for researching this area.

Chapter 2: Conceptual Issues in the Integration of AI/ES with Conventional Information Systems

This chapter presents the argument that the major issues in integration are not technical such as databases, languages and so on but conceptual, organizational and methodological. This chapter attempts to emphasize the desirability of careful conceptual planning and development of a sound methodology in order to facilitate smoother integration efforts.

Chapter 3: Building Computerized Financial Advisors: The User Model and Human Interface

An area that is often neglected in information systems design and development is the human interface and the user model. This is also the situation with many expert systems and decision support systems projects. This chapter presents issues, ideas and examples of how a properly designed user model and human interface design can enhance the usability and effectiveness of intelligent support systems.

Chapter 4: Experiences with Object Centered Modeling of Financial Marketing

This chapter describes development efforts for a prototype system, FAME, which provides a method of integrating problem solving expertise for financial marketing. The basic approach utilized in this prototype is an object centered one and as a result a methodology is described which may be useful in integrating knowledge into other problem domains.

Chapter 5: Integration of Intelligent Technologies into Conventional Information Systems: Key Issues, Opportunities and Potential Pitfalls

As a capstone chapter, this material presents a framework which considers both technical issues in integration and the organizational, problem solving and environmental issues. A views model is proposed which looks at integration from a number of views or perspectives including systems such as MIS, DSS and so on.

PART II   ISSUES IN THE MODELING OF HUMAN JUDGMENT FOR EXPERT SYSTEMS

Originally expert systems were conceived as a means of capturing human expertise and representing this expertise in a system which would perform at the same level or higher levels of the expert. Many systems being developed today in business and finance are ones in which human expertise is minimal. These systems are knowledge intensive concerned with codification of existing procedural knowledge. There are, however, many applications which require the elicitation and acquisition of human expertise and the subsequent representations of this expertise in the system. This section presents three chapters which focus on the cognitive side of expert systems.

Chapter 6: The Meta Logic of Cognitively Based Heuristics

Heuristics are increasingly being used for complex problem solving activities expecially in domains where problems are ill-defined and variable are inter-dependent. As expert systems are applied to these kinds of managerial problems, means must be found to develop efficient and effective solution techniques. This chapter relates cognitive processes to efficient search strategies for problem solving. Cognitive mapping, judgmental processes, composite concepts, analogical reasoning, neural networks and other topics are discussed in context of managerial problem solving support.

Chapter 7: Performance Modeling: A Cognitive Approach to Building Knowledge-Based Systems

This chapter is based on the observation that in practice cognitive approaches to developing knowlege based systems are scarce. One suggested reason for this observation is that more emphasis is placed on technical development rather than on problem analysis and human cognition. This chapter develops a methodology of human performance modeling and demonstrates the methodology through development of a prototype expert system for financial advising, SAFIR.

Chapter 8: The Architecture of Expertise: The Auditor's Going-Concern Judgement

This chapter examines the nature of knowledge utilized by expert auditors in assessing going concern judgments of client firms. The chapter proposes that a cognitive model of an expert auditor requires knowledge in a variety of domains and that such a model would be significantly different from traditional expert systems. A prototype system is described which was developed utilizing the proposed methodology.

PART III ISSUES IN VALIDATION, AUDITABILITY AND SECURITY OF EXPERT SYSTEMS

Often validation, auditing and security concerns are given low priority in development of expert systems due to time and financial pressures. This section consists of six chapters which discuss the issues and methods underlying verification, validation, auditability and security of expert systems.

Chapter 9: Verifying and Validating Expert Systems: A Survey

This chapter provides definitions and a basic conceptual structure for understanding verification and validation. The chapter provides an extensive survey of literature and other sources to provide perspective on the verification/validation issues. An extensive bibliography is also a feature of the chapter.

Chapter 10: Expert Systems in Auditing

This chapter reviews the current research and development activities for expert systems in auditing. Discussion of issues underlying these R & D efforts are discussed.

Chapter 11: Expert Systems: Auditability Issues

This chapter discusses the issues facing an auditor or audit firm who must understand control procedures and assess the control risk of an expert system which is used for a financially significant application.

Chapter 12: Perspectives on Auditing Operational Knowledge Based Systems

This chapter provides perspectives on and guidance for the auditor involved in the audit of operational knowledge based systems. The chapter sets audit objectives for the review, outlines risks in the environment and discusses internal control considerations. The gathering of audit evidence and the development and use of audit tools and techniques applicable to the audit of a knowledge based system are also discussed. Future issues and research areas are also addressed.

Chapter 13: Expert Systems for Computer Security

This chapter discusses ways in which expert systems may be used to help assure security in complex information systems environments such as LANs, telecommunications and mainframe-distributed processing.

Chapter 14: Issues in Expert Systems for Security

This chapter extends the prior chapter by focussing on the relevant issues for research and development of systems appropriate for maintaining secure computing environments.

PART IV   LEGAL ISSUES, TRAINING EFFECTS, AND FINANCIAL AND RESOURCE PLANNING APPLICATIONS OF EXPERT SYSTEMS

This section consists of a variety of chapters dealing with issues ranging from legal and training to actual production systems in accounting and finance domains.

Chapter 15: Legal Issues in Applied Artificial Intelligence

Applied artifical intelligence, expert systems, offer new technology to apply to a variety of existing problem domains. This chapter focuses on issues which may arise in the distribution and development of such systems. This chapter raises issues on how the law will treat this broad domain of intelligent systems and the manner in which potential disputes may be resolved.

Chapter 16: Training and Performance Effects of A Knowledge-Base System for Analytical Review.

This chapter reports the results of a study of auditors' analytical review judgments. The results show how the auditor's risk assessments and performance in the evaluating the inherent risk and bankruptcy risk of two audit cases were affected by the presence of a knowledge-based system in training. Conclusions based on the study are offered regarding the use of expert systems both as a practice aid and a training tool.

Chapter 17: Survey of Expert Systems for Resource Planning

This chapter describes a variety of resource planning expert systems in areas of manufacturing and administration. The potential benefits of these systems are described and attention is directed to the manner in which they help improve effective use of resources by managers.

Chapter 18: A Survey of Expert Systems Used in the Practice of Public Accounting

The practice of accounting includes sub-domains of tax, auditing and consulting. This chapter describes some of the systems used in accounting practice and the benefits, problems and opportunities that arise from their use.

Paul R. Watkins
Lance B. Eliot

Part I
ISSUES IN THE DESIGN AND INTEGRATION OF EXPERT SYSTEMS

Part I

Chapter 1

EXPERT SYSTEMS INTEGRATION WITH COMPUTER-BASED INFORMATION SYSTEMS

Efraim Turban
Lumpkin College of Business, Charleston, ILL

There is no magic in expert systems; they are like any other technique developed and applied to the advancement of information systems. However, one can obtain significant benefits by using expert systems as effective means to build unique applications either by the use of free-standing systems or by integrating this technology into existing information systems environments. This chapter surveys the major modes of such an integration and reviews the potential application areas. Finally, an extensive bibliography is provided.

1.1 INTRODUCTION

The commercialization of expert systems (ES) started in the late seventies and the early eighties. The vast majority of systems developed during the first five years of this period were completely independent systems. The entire knowledge of the systems was included in the ES's knowledge base. The major purpose of these systems was to provide consultation in a narrow domain.

Toward the mid-eighties it became apparent that expert systems can also be used as an integral part of a larger computer-based information system (CBIS). Such an integration could set off an explosion in both ES and in CBIS in general.

Much attention has been given to the integration of ES and Decision Support Systems (e.g. Bonczek *et al*, 1981, Holsapple and Whinston, 1985 and Turban and Watkins , 1986). Recent experiences, however, indicate that ES are being integrated into a wide range of other CBIS resulting in substantial benefits. Many people appear to advocate the integration of ES (and other artificial intelligence (AI) products) with conventional CBIS in order to increase the usefulness of the latter. Some even believe that ES can revolutionize the way that corporate users manipulate information.

Expert Systems in Business and Finance: Issues and Applications. Edited by P.R. Watkins and L.B. Eliot
© 1993 John Wiley & Sons Ltd.

Also, many ES often need to formulate and execute conventional information systems (IS) applications as a subtask (e.g. access databases and retrieve information).

Many articles have been written on various aspects of integration (e.g. see list at the end of this chapter). Yet, it is not clear to the unsophisticated reader (especially managers) what integration is, or what types of conventional IS are the prime targets for the integration with ES.

The purpose of this chapter is to address these issues. Specifically, the chapter presents a definition of integration and then the benefits of integration are summarized. The targets of the integration are divided into three categories: databases, model management, and factory automation. Finally, an extensive bibliography is provided.

1.2   WHAT IS SYSTEMS INTEGRATION?

Before exploring the issue of integration it is worth while to discuss its meaning. The vast majority of papers devoted to integration avoid this issue. The fact is that there are several types of integration which should be considered when an integration is planned for.

The integration of computer-based systems means that rather than having separate hardware, software and communications for each independent system, these systems are integrated into one facility. An integration can be at the development tools level or it can be at the application system level. There exist two general types of integration: functional and physical.

Functional integration implies that different support functions are provided as a single system. For example, working with electronic mail, using a spreadsheet, communicating with external databases, creating graphics representation and storing and manipulating data, can all be accomplished at the same workstation. The user can access the appropriate facilities through a single, consistent interface, and can switch from one task to another and back again. Lotus 1-2-3 is an example of functionally integrated development software.

Physical integration refers to packaging of the hardware, software and communications features required to accomplish functional integration. Physical integration includes several components and it appears in several configurations.

Several physical integration approaches exist, the major ones are shown in Figure 1.1 and are summarized next.

(a) Access approaches
According to this approach, ES development tools, and/or application programs, can access standard applications or development software.
Three subcategories exist here: single processor, multiprocessor, and networking.

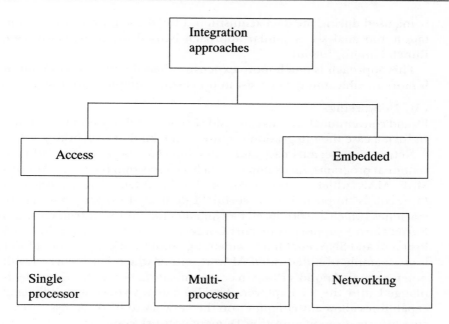

FIGURE 1.1   Integration approaches

(1)   Single processor
This simple and most common approach relies on ES software and traditional software, operating on the same processor. With this approach, traditional programs and databases are callable from knowledge systems and vice versa.

An example of such an integration is the availability of LISP and/or PROLOG as a single processor with conventional languages. Hewlett Packard's (HP) AI System is a good illustration. This system integrates LISP, FORTRAN, C, PASCAL and HP-UX (a version of UNIX). As a result, programmers can edit, compile, test and debug FORTRAN, C, and PASCAL programs incrementally and interactively, using either LISP or UNIX, without ever leaving the LISP editor.

This approach is not so expensive, and the processor can be highly utilized, but it is not as powerful as the following approaches.

(2)   Multiprocessors
According to this approach, different software packages are operating on different processors within the same machine. LISP Machine Inc. was the first vendor to produce a machine with both LISP and UNIX processors. Texas Instruments is currently using a similar approach. The different packages communicate with each other. While UNIX is

being used during the data acquisition, LISP is used for data representation and analysis. A similar approach is used by Xerox Corp. (see Runch-Hindin, 1986b).

This approach is much more expensive than the previous one but it is more flexible and it can assist in processing complex jobs faster.

(3) Networking

ES and conventional systems can reside in completely different machines. In such a case the integration requires some kind of networking.

Networking permits easy and quick interface between ES and conventional programs. An example of such a connection is General Motor's MAP. MAP, which is the acronym for Manufacturing Automation Protocol, is supported by powerful AI dedicated workstations. These machines (which are produced by Symbolics Inc., Texas Instruments, and Xerox Corp.) support Transport Control Protocol, Ethernet, Internet Protocol and SNA, enabling a wide range of networking. TI's Explorer is an example of a dedicated AI workstation which is networked with other systems. Apollo's Domain communication board, for example, is plugged into the TI Explorer. The Domain's virtual demand-paged capabilities allow any computer on the network to store, access, or execute information on any other Domain-network computer, as if it were on its own.

(b) Embedded Systems

In this approach the ES software is embedded in a conventional IS program. This approach can be considered as the "second generation" of integrated ES and conventional systems. It embeds value-added ES capabilities in conventional programs. The users see a single application that they can work with. There is no distinction between the ES and the conventional parts.

An example of an embedded development tool is GURU (from Micro Data Base Systems, Inc.). This package embeds an ES shell and a natural language processor (another AI product) in an environment that supports integrated spreadsheets, text processing, relational DBMS, graphics, report generation, communication and business computing (for details, see Runch-Hindin, 1986b).

Embedded systems are usually more efficient than systems that provide an access of ES to conventional systems and than the networked systems.

In building integrated systems the physical structure may become an extremely important factor. While embedded systems may seem to be desirable they are more difficult or more expensive to construct. There are more standard components that can support the access approaches, resulting in savings of time and/or money. The selection of an appropriate integration mode is outside the scope of this chapter. However it certainly should be considered in the design phase of an integrated project.

1.3   THE BENEFITS OF THE INTEGRATION

Before addressing the specific areas of integration, let us summarize its potential benefits. In general, the integration of ES with conventional CBIS is aimed at enhancing the capabilities of the latter, which may result in cost reduction or increased efficiency. The specific benefits are summarized here along two dimensions: benefit in the construction of systems and benefits in systems' use. Table 1.1 provides a summary of the major benefits.

The benefits listed in Table 1.1 are those resulting from adding ES to CBIS. However, Expert Systems can also benefit from adding CBIS to ES for the following reasons:

(a)   The capabilities of ES shells can be improved by adding features from conventional systems.
(b)   Even though ES is easily structured by using symbolic processing, it may need, like a human expert, to conduct some computations and analysis. In an integrated system we can do it easier and faster; there is no need to transfer information to another system.

TABLE 1.1   Some Benefits of ES Integration with CBIS

Benefits in construction (system development)	Improves the construction of the database
	Permits symbolic representation of data
	Short cuts development time
	Makes explicit assumptions and relationship in models
	Permits modeling situation with in exact input data.
	Speeds up the systems design
	Expedites programming
	Provides consistent design
	Provides better security measures
Benefits in use (system application)	Improves the operations and maintenance of the database
	Validates the input data to CBIS
	Improves accessibility to large databases
	Improves model management
	Improves sensitivity analysis
	Speeds up simulations
	Enables friendlier dialog
	Provides explanations
	Acts as a tutor
	Enables more applications
	Makes applications more useful and "intelligent"
	Reduces maintenance cost
	Refines the query system
	Improves the chance of IS implementation
	Validates, diagnoses and interprets the results of CBIS

(c) CBIS can be used to improve the construction of the knowledge base (e.g. by using simulation)
(d) Many ES are of limited use because they cannot be easily tied into the corporate database. Thus, ES are restricted in many cases to small, departmental applications. An integrated ES-CBIS system may solve this problem.
(e) The experience in building conventional CBIS, including DSS, can be transferred to the construction of ES.

These benefits can be significant and, in many cases will clearly justify the cost of the integration.

1.4   AREAS OF INTEGRATION

In the previous sections we defined the concept of integration and described the potential benefits. In the forthcoming sections we will describe some specific areas of integration. Expert systems have been integrated with almost all types of computer-based information systems, ranging from databases to robotics. In many of the areas the integration is still in experimental stages, however, in others there are successful integrated systems in operation. Some of the integrated systems are very large; others are very small. The integrated systems can reside in all types of hardware, from small to very large and from standard to wholly dedicated. Some of the systems include two or more traditional CBIS and one expert system, others include several ES and one or more traditional systems. Finally ES may also be integrated with other AI technologies (e.g. natural language processors and computer vision). It is impossible to deal with all these integrations in one chapter. We have elected to discuss here only three major areas of integration: databases, model management, and CIM.

1.5   ES INTEGRATION WITH DATABASES

Tying expert systems to databases, especially large ones, is one of the most critical and rewarding areas of ES integration. There are several goals and several physical modes of such integration.

Organizations, private and public, are continuously collecting data, information and knowledge (all are referred to here as "information") and storing it in computerized systems. The updating, retrieving, use and removal of this information become more complicated as its amount increases. At the same time the number of individuals that are interacting with this information increases due to networking, end-user computing and reduced cost of information processing. Working with large databases is becoming a difficult task which requires considerable expertise. Without database access it is difficult to use ES in large MIS applications, ranging from factory automation to credit card authorization.

Expert systems can make the management of databases simpler. One way to do it is to enhance the database management system (DBMS) by providing it with an inference capability. Al-Zobaidie and Grimson (1987) provide three possible architectures of such a coupling. They also explain how the efficiency and the functionality of the DBMS can be enhanced. The contribution of ES in such a case can be further increased if it is coupled with a natural language processor (NLP). For a description of a database, DBMS, ES and NLP integration see Harris (1987).

Another purpose of ES/DBMS integration is to improve the knowledge management of the ES's knowledge base. As ES became increasingly complex and diverse, the need for efficient and effective management for their growing knowledge base is apparent. Al-Zobaidie and Grimson (1987), proposed an enhanced ES to deal with such situations. The ES will have a special DMBS which can be used to manage its knowledge base.

Another way of looking at ES/database integration is shown in Figure 1.2. In this figure the expert system is shown to receive data from one or more of four resources, one of which is a database. Furthermore, that expert system may feed information back to the database and other sources. Such information flow may need to be managed. Such management may be provided by enhancing the ES with a conventional DBMS.

In addition to the enhanced DBMS and the enhanced ES discussed earlier, it is possible to integrate the ES and the DBMS via a network. Such an

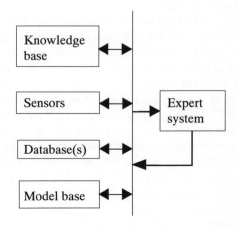

FIGURE 1.2   Sources of ES information

integration is discussed in Section 1.2 and by Al-Zobaidie and Grimson (1987).

Difficulties in tying ES to large databases has been a major problem even for large corporations (e.g.: Boeing Aircraft, American Express). CBIS can be used to improve the construction of the knowledge base (e.g. for strategy. For example, such a system can advise a casual user on how to conduct a simple search or it can guide the more experienced user in accessing difficulty organized databases. In all, it can make an online system transparent to the user. For details see Kehoe (1985) and Hawkins (1988).

1.6   MODEL MANAGEMENT

The integration of ES and databases become a top priority of many organizations. Integrated systems have been moved from the research lab to vendors' products and to fielded systems. Data's major complementary component, however, the quantitative model, is lagging behind in terms of ES integration. The topic has attracted significant academic attention in recent years (e.g. see: Blanning 1988b, Fedorowicz and Williams, 1986, Elam and Konsynski, 1987, because the potential benefits could be very substantial. However, it seems that the practical implementation of integrated ES/database systems is fairly difficult and slow.

Three interrelated subtopics are being investigated: The construction of models (formulation), the use of models (analysis) and the interpretation of the output of models. The quantitative models are primarily in the areas of managerial decision making. More specifically these are management science, statistical and financial models.

(a)   The Construction of Models
The construction of models for decision making involves the simplification of a real world situation so that a simplified representation of reality can be made. Models can be normative or descriptive and they are being used in various types of DSS or other CBIS. Finding an appropriate balance between simplification and representation in modeling requires expertise. Also, the definition of the problem to be modeled, the attempt to select a prototype model (e.g. linear programming), the data collection, the model validation and the estimation of certain parameters and relationships are not simple tasks. For example, data may be tested for suitability to certain statistical distribution (e.g.: does the arrival rate in queuing follow a "Poisson distribution"). The user may be guided by an ES through such a test, so an appropriate model may be selected.
(b)   The Use of Models (analysis)
Once models are constructed they can be put to use. The application of

models may require some judgmental values (e.g. setting an alpha value in exponential forecasting). Also, experience is needed to conduct a sensitivity analysis as well as to determine what constitutes a significant difference (is project A really superior to B?). Expert systems can be used to provide the user with the necessary guidelines to use models. In addition, the ES can conduct a cause–effect analysis.

(c)   Interpretation of The Results

Expert systems can provide interpretation and explanation of the models used and the derived results. For example, an ES can trace anomalies of data. Furthermore, sensitivity analysis may be needed or translation of information to certain format may be desired.

Current work on ES is done occasionally along these three subtopics, or parts of them. For example, Courtney *et al.* (1987) developed an expert system for problem diagnosis. Zahedi (1987) developed a system for model selection. Elam and Konsynski (1987) show, via examples, how future model management systems will work when supported by ES.

However, most experimental ES are being developed, not according to these categories but according to the type of mathematical model used. Then, some portions of one or more of the above three subtopics are being exercised. For example, interpreting the results of simulation (e.g. see Mellichamp, 1987), use of forecasting model or setting up the queuing model. A representative list of models is given in Table 1.2 with appropriate references.

TABLE 1.2   *Representative expert systems in quantitative Models*

Topic	References
Decision theory	Ko and Lin (1988), Lehner and Donnel (1984)
Financial models	Kosy and Wise (1984), Turner and Obilichetti (1985)
Forecasting	Feng-Yang (1988), Kumar and Cheng (1988)
Mathematical programming	Goul *et al.* (1985), Murphy and Stohr (1986)
Project management	Hosley (1987), Sathi *et al.* (1986)
Queuing	Hossein *et al.* (1987)
Simulation	Daukidis (1987), Ford and Schroer (1987), Hill and Roberts (1987), Kuipers (1986), O'Keefe and Roach (1987), Oren (1987), Reddy (1987), Shannon (1985), Zeigler (1985)
Statistics	Hand (1984), Gale (1986), Marcoulides (1981)
Strategic Planning	Goul *et al.* (1986), Lee and Lee (1988)
System Dynamics	Wu (1988)

1.7   INTEGRATION WITH THE DIALOGUE (INTERFACE) SUBSYSTEM

Expert systems may be integrated with the interface sub-system so that the human–machine dialogue will be conducted faster and better. Expert systems are being used today as front-ends to many application and development software packages. For example, HAL is being used to front-end Lotus 1-2-3 and CLOUT to front-end R:Base 5000. For details on this role of ES see Hardman (1985), Harris (1987), Ishikawa (1987), and Sawaragi *et al.* (1986b).

1.8   INTEGRATION WITH DSS

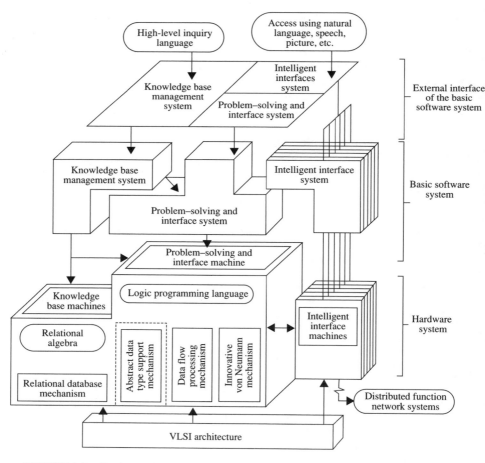

FIGURE 1.3   *Basic configuration image of the fifth-generation computer systems (Reproduced by permission of Japan Information Processing Development Center)*

As shown earlier ES can be integrated with any of the DSS's major components (Database, model base, and the dialogue subsystem). Such an integration can improve the construction and/or operation of the integrated component, thus making the DSS better. However, researchers have advocated the design of a fully integrated ES/DSS. (e.g., see: Henderson, 1987,

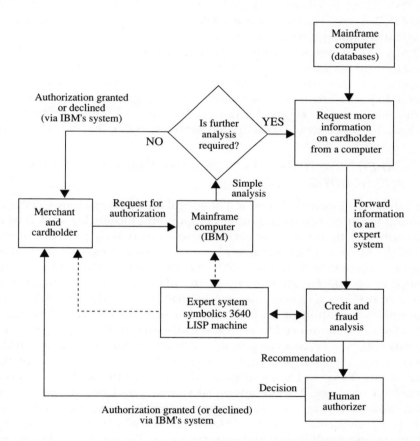

FIGURE 1.4   American Express authorizer's assistant. The merchant requests authorization from the mainframe computer. The computer checks the credit availability and performs a simple analysis (e.g., checking the cardholder's normal charging pattern). If no further analysis is needed, the authorization is either granted or declined. If further analysis is necessary, the computer collects more information about the cardholder from another mainframe computer. The initial and new information is forwarded to a rule-based expert system, which was developed with ART (from Inference Corp.). The expert system may request more information from the cardholder if necessary: then it provides a recommendation to the human authorizer (who uses an IBM 327 X terminal). (Based on information provided by Inference Corporation and American Express.)

Bonczek *et al.*, 1981, Holsapple and Whinston, 1985, Kowalik, 1986, Lee and Lee, 1988, Luconi *et al*., 1986, Sawaragi *et al.*(1986b), Scott Morton, 1986, Sen and Biswas (1985), Shen (1987), Turban and Watkins, 1986, and Teng *et al.* (1988).

Such an integration, which appears under several different names (ES/DSS, XDSS, intelligent DSS, DSS/ES, EDSS), can increase the effectiveness of DSS as well as enable the use of DSS to solve rather complex problems.

The integration of DSS and ES can take various forms. Several conceptual designs of such systems are presented by Turban and Watkins (1986). Other designs are shown in Figures 1.3 and 1.4.

Figure 1.3 displays the basic configuration of the Fifth Generation project. Several Expert systems are providing the intelligent capabilities to the various components. Figure 1.4 portrays American Express Authorizer's Assistant. In this case the DSS and ES components complement each other.

1.9   EXPERT SYSTEMS IN FACTORY AUTOMATION: CIM, FMS, AND ROBOTICS

The automated factory is composed of several different machines, material handling facilities, robots and other components. Orders for work flow in constantly and therefore it is necessary to continuously plan the operation of the factory. An expert system(s) can be used to execute such planning in conjunction with some DSS and the robots. The planning will attempt to coordinate all activities of the plant, to achieve efficiency in the use of resources, to maximize productivity, to meet delivery dates, etc.

Another application of ES is in the area of error recovery. The automated factory is monitored by several sensors and other detecting devices. The data collected here can be interpreted by an ES. Such interpretation will detect errors (or even potential errors) in the operation of any of the components. Next, an ES can diagnose the cause of the problem and recommend a recovery. A more advanced system could be integrated with robots which will execute the necessary *Support Systems.* Expert Systems have been connected to CAD/CAM systems, sensory systems and several manufacturing applications software packages. For further information see Eldeib (1987), Falster (1987), Gero (1985), Herrod and Rickel (1987), Kusiak (1988), and Mellichamp(1987).

1.10   CONCLUSIONS

In this chapter we showed the extent to which ES are being integrated with other CBIS. Such an integration improves both the functionality of CBIS and their efficiency. In addition, the integration can help the construction process of both CBIS and ES as well as the capabilities of ES.

An increased number of organizations are developing ES which are embedded in various types of information systems. These companies recognize that ES can dramatically increase the usefulness of the overall systems. Furthermore, ES helps a variety of complex large systems that have resisted traditional software techniques. To do this, it has become important that ES run on the machines and use the software interfaces that are employed for conventional computing.

The integration with databases is probably in a more advanced stage than any other integration. On the other hand, the integration with model bases could have the greatest impact on the manner in which modeling and quantitative analysis are being used. This topic, however, is still far from a large scale commercialization because of implementation difficulties.

Significant progress, but still on a small scale, has been made in the areas of CAD/CAM, robotics and CIM as well as in the area of software development.

REFERENCES AND BIBLIOGRAPHY

Al-Zobaidie, A., and Grimson, J.B., (1987) "Expert Systems And Database Systems: How Can They Serve Each Other?" *Expert Systems*, Feb.

Archibald, I.G., *et al.*(1985), "Bridging The Generation Gap: Expert Systems As Part of Large Scale Computer Systems", *R and D Management*, April.

Binbasioglu, M., and Jarke M. (1986), "Domain Specific DSS Tools for Knowledge-Based Model Building", *Decision Support Systems*.

Blanning R.W. (1987), "A Framework For Expert Model Base Systems", *National Computer Conference*.

Blanning, R.W. (1988a), "Sensitivity Analysis in Hierarchical Fuzzy Logic Models", *Proceeding 21st HICSS*, Hawaii, Jan.

Blanning R.W. (1988b), "The Application of Artificial Intelligence To Model Management", *Proceedings, 21st HICSS*, Hawaii, Jan.

Bonczek, R.H., Holsapple, C. and Whinston, A. (1981), "Foundations of Decision Support Systems", Academic Press, New York.

Booker E. (1984), "Computers Help You Win The Game", *Computer Decisions*, Sept.

Brodie M. L. and Mylpoulos J. (1986), *On Knowledge Base Management Systems: Integrating Artificial Intelligence and Database techniques*, Springer-Verlag, New York.

Cats-Baril W.L., and Huber G.P. (1987), "Decision Support Systems for Ill-structured Problems: An Empirical Study", *Decision Sciences*, Summer.

Chester J.A. (1985), "Is MIS Ready For The Explosion?", *Infosystems*, 4.

Courtney J.F. Jr. *et al.* (1987), "A Knowledge-based DSS For Managerial Problem Diagnosis", *Decision Sciences*, Summer.

Davis, D.B. (1986), "Artificial Intelligence Enters The Mainstream", *High Technology*, July.

Dean, B. (1988), "Toward an Expert/Decision Support System in Business Venture", in Turban and Watkins (1988).

DeBalogh, F. and Turban, E. (1988), "Integrating Expert Systems Tools into a PC-based logistician's workstation Concept: Demonstration Applications using EXSYS.", University of Southern Calif., Los Angeles; ISSM; DSSL Report L87-4.

Doukidis G.I. (1987), "An Analogy on the Homology of Simulation and Artificial Intelligence", *Journal of Operations Research Society*, Aug.

Elam, J.J. and Konsynski, B. (1987), "Using AI Techniques To Enhance The Capabilities of Model Management Systems", *Decision Sciences*, Summer.

Eldeib, H.K. (1987), "A Methodology For Optimal Design, Planning, Integrating CAD, Expert Systems and Operations Research Techniques", paper presented at TIMS/ORSA metting, New Orleans, May.

Ernst, C.J. (1984), "A Relational Expert System For Nursing Management Control", Human Systems Management, **4**.

Falster, P. (1987), "Planning and Controlling Production Systems Combining Simulation and Expert Systems", *Computers in Industry*, **8**.

Fedorowicz, J. and Williams, G. (1986), "Representing Modeling Knowledge In An Intelligent Decision Support Systems", *Decision Support Systems*, **2**(1).

Feng-Yang, K. (1988), "Combining Expert Systems and the Bayesian Approach To Support Forecasting", *Proceeding, 21st HICSS*, Hawaii, Jan.

Ford, D.R. and Schroer, B.J. (1987), "An Expert Manufacturing Simulation System", *Simulation*, May.

Gale, W.A. (1986), *Artificial Intelligence and Statistics*, Addison-Wesley, Reading, Mass.

Gero, J.S., (ed.) (1985), *Knowledge Engineering in Computer-Aided Design*, North-Holland, Amsterdam.

Goul, M., Shane, B. and Tonge, F. (1985), "Designing the Expert Component of a Decision Support System", Paper delivered at the OESA/TIMS meeting, San Diego.

Goul M. *et al.* (1986), "Using a Knowledge-based Decision Support System in Strategic Planning Decisions: An Empirical Study", *Journal of Management Information Systems*, Spring.

Hand, D.J. (1984), "Statistical Expert Systems: Design", *The Statistician*, **33**, (10) 351–369.

Hardman, L. (1985), "Expert User-friendly", *Systems International*, Apr.

Harris, L.R. (1987), "The Nautral-language Connection; An AI Note", Information Center, Apr.

Hawkins, D.T. (1988), "Applications of AI and Expert Systems for On line Searching", *ONLINE*, Jan.

Henderson, J.C. (1987), "Finding Synergy Between Decision Support Systems and Expert Systems", *Decision Sciences*, Summer.

Herrod, R. and Rickel, J. (1987), "The Industrial Automation—AI Connection", *Texas Instrument Technical Journal*, Winter.

Hill, T.R. and Roberts, S.D. (1987), "A Prototype Knowledge-based Simulation Support Systems", *Simulation*, April.

Holsapple, C.W. and Whinston, A.B. (1985), "Management Support Through Artificial Intelligence", *Human Systems Mgt.*, No. 2.

Hosley, W.N. (1987), "The Application of Artificial Intelligence Software to Project Management", *Project Management Journal*, Aug.

Hossein, J. *et al.* (1987), "Stochastic Queuing Systems, An AI Approach", *DSI Proceedings*.

Hsu, C. and Skevington, C. (1987), "Integration of Data and Knowledge in Manufacturing Enterprises; A Conceptual Framework", *Journal of Manufacturing Systems*, **6**, Apr.

Ishikawa, H. (1987), "KID, Knowledge-based Natural Language Interface For Accessing Database Systems", *IEEE Expert*, Summer.

Jarke, M. and Vassiliou, Y. (1984), "Coupling Expert Systems with Database

Management Systems", *Artificial Intelligence Application for Business*, In Reitman, W. (ed.), APLEX Publishing Corporation, Norwood, New Jersey.

Jenkins, M. (1987), "Intelligent Databases and NIAL", AI Expert, May.

Juris, R. (1987), "Look for Smart Systems", *Computer Decisions*, Jan.

Kandt, K. (1988), "On Building Future DSS", *Proceedings*, 21st HICSS, Hawaii, Jan.

Kehoe, C.A. (1985), "Interfaces and Expert Systems For Online Retrieval", *Online Review*, Dec.

Keim, R.T. and Jacobs, S. (1986), "Expert Systems: The DSS of the Future?", *Journal of Systems Management*, Dec.

Kerschberg, G. (ed.) (1986), *Expert Database_Systems*, The Benjamin/Cummings Pub. Co., Menlo Park, CA.

King, D. (1985), "Bridging the 4th and the 5th Generations: Linking Relational Databases with Expert Systems", DSS 85, *Transactions*, April.

Knickerbacker, C. (1984), "Integrating AI and Unix Applications", *Systems and Software*, Nov.

Ko, C. and Lin, T.W. (1988), "Multiple Criteria Decision Making And Expert systems", In Turban, E., and Watkins, P. (eds.), *Applied Expert Systems*, North-Holland, Amsterdam.

Kosy, D. and Wise, M. (1984), "Self-explanatory Financial Planning Models", *Proceedings, The National Conference on Artificial Intelligence*, Los Altos, CA., William Kaufman.

Kowalik, J.S., (ed.) (1986), *Coupling Symbolic and Numerical Computing in Expert Systems*, North-Holland, Amsterdam.

Kowalski, R. (1984), "AI and Software Engineering", *Datamation*, Nov.

Kuipers, B.J. (1986), "Qualitative Simulation", *AI Journal*, Sept.

Kumar, S. and Cheng H. (1988), "An Expert System Framework for Forecasting Method Selection", *Proceedings, 21st HICSS, Hawaii*, Jan.

Kuratani, Y. (1986), "The Intelligent Decision Support Systems: Synthesis of a Decision Support System and an Expert System", Vol. 2 of: *Proceedings, 7th International Conference on Multiple Criteria Decision Making*, Kyoto, Japan, Aug.

Kusiak, A. (ed.) (1988), *Artificial Intelligence, Implications for CIM, IFS*, Springer-Verlag.

Lee, J.K. and Kang, B.S. (1988), "Intelligent Production Planning System Using The Post-Model Analysis Approach", In Turban, E., and Watkins, P., (eds.), *Applied Expert Systems*, North- Holland, Amsterdam.

Lee, J.K. and Lee, H.G. (1988), "Integration of Strategic Planning and Short-term Planning: An Intelligent DSS Approach By The Post-Model Analysis Approach", *Decision Support Systems*.

Lehner, P.B. and Donnel, M.L. (1984), "Building Decision Aids: Exploiting the Synergy between Decision Analysis and Artificial Intelligence", paper presented ORSA/TIMS, San Francisco, May.

Liebowitz, J. (ed.) (1988), *Expert Systems Applications To Telecommunications*, Wiley, New York.

Luconi, F.L. *et al.* (1986), "Expert systems: The Next Challenge For Management", *Sloan Management Review*, **27**, (4).

Mannino, M.V. *et al.* (1988), "Knowledge Representation for Model Libraries", *Proceedings 21st HICSS*, Hawaii, Jan.

Mantelman, L. (1986), "AI Carves Inroads: Network Design, Testing and Managements", *Data Communications*, July.

Manuel, T. (1985), "The Pell-Mell Rush into Expert Systems Forces Integration issue", *Electronics*, July.

Marcoulides, G.A. (1981), "An Expert Systems For Statistical Consulting", *DSI proceedings.*

Mellichamp, J.H. (1987), "An Expert System for FMS Design", *Simulation*, May.

Michalowski, W. (1986), "Multi-person Decision Support with Knowledge Base Systems", in Sawaragi *et al.* (1986).

Moad, J. (1987), "Building a Bridge to Expert Systems", *Datamation*, Jan.

Murphy, F. and Stohr, E. (1986), "An Intelligent Support For Formulating Linear Programming", *Decision Support Systems*, **2**(1).

O'Keefe, R.M. and Roach, J.W. (1987), "Artificial Intelligence Approaches to Simulation", *Journal Operations Research Society*, August.

Oren, T.I. (1987), "Quality Assurance Paradigms for AI in modelling and Simulation", *Simulation*, Apr.

Pedersen, K. (1988), "Connecting Expert Systems and Conventional Programming", *AI Expert*, May.

Pope, S.T. (1985), "Unix and AI", *Systems International*, Apr.

Rauch-Hindin, W. (1986a), "AI Shapes Up For Mainstream Use", *Mini-Micro Systems*, Aug.

Rauch-Hindin, W. (1986b), "Software Integrates AI, Standard Systems", *Mini-Micro Systems*, Oct.

Reddy, R. (1987), "Epistemology of Knowledge-based Simulation", *Simulation*, Apr.

Sage, A.P. *et al.* (1986), "An Interactive Knowledge Support System With Imperfect Information: Toward A Microcomputer Implementation of ARIADNE", in Sawaragi *et al.* (1986b).

Sathi, A. *et al.* (1986), "CALLISTO: An Intelligent Project Management System", *AI Magazine*, Winter.

Sawaragi, Y. *et al.* (1986a), "A Human-friendly Interface System For Decision Support", in Sawaragi *et al.* (1986b).

Sawaragi, Y. *et al.* (eds.) (1986b), *Toward Interactive and Intelligent Decision Support System*, Vol. 1 of the *Proceeding of the 7th International Conference on MCDM*, Kyoto, Japan, 1986. Springer-Verlag, Berlin.

Scott Morton, M. (1984), "Expert Decision Support Systems", a paper presented at the special DSS conference, Planning Executive Institute and Information Technology Institute, New York, May 21–22.

Sen, A. and Biswas, G. (1985), "Decision Support Systems: An Expert Systems Approach", *Decision Support Systems*, (1).

Shannon, R.E. (1985), "Expert Systems and Simulation", *Simulation*, June.

Sheldon, S. (1987), "Knowledge Management in Decision Support Systems", *Decision Support Systems*, **3**, (1).

Shen, S. (1987), "Knowledge Management in Decision Support", *Decision Support Systems*, **3**, Jan.

Simon, H.A. (1987), "Two Heads Are Better Than One: The Collaboration Between AI and OR", *Interfaces*, July–Aug.

Stix, G. (1986), "MIS Bets On Smart Nets", *Computer_Decisions*, Dec.

Stock, M. (1987), "Cooperating Expert Systems Distribute AI", *Digital News*, Feb.

Sviokla, J. (1986), "Business Implications of Knowledge-based systems", *Data Base*, **17** (4), Part I, and **18** (1))Part II.

Teng, J.T.C. *et al.* (1988), "A Unified Architecture for Intelligent DSS", *Proceedings, 21st HICSS*, Hawaii, Jan.

Turban, E. and Watkins, P. (1986), "Integrating Expert Systems and Decision Support Systems", *MIS Quarterly*, June.

Turban, E. and Watkins, P. (1988), *Applied Expert Systems*. North Holland.

Turban, E. (1993), *Decision Support and Expert Systems.* 3rd edn. Macmillan.

Turner, M. and Obilichetti, B. (1985), "Possible Directions In Knowledge-based Financial Modeling Systems", in *DSS '85 Transactions,* Providence, RI., TIMS.

Vedder, R. and Nestman, C.H. (1985), "Understanding Expert Systems: Companion to DSS and MIS", *Industrial Management,* Mar.–Apr.

Wu, Wenhua (1988), "An Integrated System Based on the Synergy Between System Dynamics and Artificial Intelligence" *Proceedings, 1988 International Conference of the Systems Dynamics Society,* La Jolla, CA July.

Yasdi, R. (1985), "A Conceptual Design Aid Environment For Expert Database Systems", *Data & Knowledge Engineering,* June.

Zahedi, F. (1987), "Qualitative Programming for Selection Decisions", *Computer and Operations Research,* **14** (5), 395–407.

Zeigler, B.P., ed. (1985), Expert Systems and Simulation models, *Proceedings, University of Arizona,* Tucson, Nov. 18-19.

Zualkernan, I., *et al.* (1986), "Expert Systems and Software Engineering: Ready for Marriage?", *IEEE Expert,* Winter.

Chapter 2

CONCEPTUAL ISSUES IN THE INTEGRATION OF AI/ES WITH CONVENTIONAL INFORMATION SYSTEMS

Thomas J. Martin
C.P. Test Services, Inc., Kearny, NJ

Serious conceptual issues remain in the integration of artificial intelligence/expert systems with conventional information systems. The issues before us are not technical (databases, languages, etc.), but organizational and scientific. Expert systems built for business, finance and accounting applications must resemble either the conventional systems in these application areas or the routine problem-solving tasks to simplify the integration task. A unified user interface between the AI/ES application and the conventional application must exist. Finally, the methods and methodologies used to design and implement AI/ES and conventional information systems need to converge. Projects are under way to make progress on all of these issues, with the result being a smoother integration.

2.1   INTRODUCTION

The conventional wisdom is that expert systems (AI/ES) will flourish and prosper to the extent that these systems are integrated with conventional information systems. Martin and Oxman (1988, p.111) write

> ...many of the most valuable applications of expert system technology are those in which expert systems access databases used for other purposes or link to other types of software or systems. Many important applications in the future will combine conventional data processing with expert system technology.

Schorr and Rappaport (1989, p.xv) stated in a similar vein

> ...knowledge-based systems are being integrated with both database systems and conventional procedural programs on conventional platforms. Making this

Expert Systems in Business and Finance: Issues and Applications. Edited by P.R. Watkins and L.B. Eliot
© 1993 John Wiley & Sons Ltd.

integration transparent, enabling the result to perform well, and refining applications that truly complement corporate databases will provide the discipline's primary challenges over the next few years.

In other words, there are few conceptual issues associated with the integration of AI/ES with conventional information systems; the technology is now available to bridge the gap; it is time to get down to the business of building thousands of these integrated systems.

On the other hand, there are lingering signs that make me doubt that progress on the technical issues of integration removes the barriers to AI/ES penetrating the corporate world. Feigenbaum, *et al.* (1988, p.46) wrote

> ...there are still no well-defined guidelines for managing knowledge engineering projects...why can't expert systems be developed in a traditional manner?

Hoffman (1988, p.62) pointed out

> [a]ll experts differ, and all domains of expertise differ; so, too, will all expert systems development projects differ.

These quotes and other remarks in the same vein create feelings of unease in senior MIS executives, who now account for more than half the purchases of expert systems tools in the market (Harman, 1989, p.5). These quotes demonstrate that there are still serious conceptual issues that remain before AI/ES are easily integrated with conventional information systems.

2.2   AI/ES IN BUSINESS, FINANCE AND ACCOUNTING (BFA)

This chapter addresses issues in expert systems in business, finance and accounting. This distinguishes the set of potential issues to be discussed from those relating to expert systems in the large. The characteristics of business needs and problems in the world of BFA are markedly different from manufacturing, military or scientific needs and problems. The financial sector accounts for a small percentage of AI vendors' business today and the applications of AI described in the literature are usually geared toward manufacturing. In (Martin and Zickefoose, 1989), I describe the various characteristics that have made financial applications different and more difficult that other applications. These are briefly:

- A mismatch exists between the tools and languages required for AI/ES and the equipment and skills in place in the BFA sector of the economy.

- The approaches that have evolved in building AI/ES reflects the engineering and scientific approach of experimentation and prototyping. This approach is at odds with the methodology of controlled systems development adopted by the BFA sector.
- Turnkey expert systems targeted at the BFA community do not have good commercial track records, in part because companies have found that a generic representation of knowledge is not as useful as their own.
- AI/ES is viewed as a higher risk endeavor than a conventional information system without the commensurate return. In the sectors of BFA, this perception is stronger than other sectors, because AI/ES project risk is even higher and the promised return assumed to be lower. Much of the knowledge in BFA domains is more difficult to represent than, say, manufacturing or science. Financial knowledge lacks the precise statement of qualitative relationships that lends itself to AI/ES representation. The elusiveness of knowledge results in longer-lasting projects that may offer less because of the low value of the knowledge.

A review of some AI applications may, however, lay the ground work for a discussion of conceptual issues.

2.3 SUCCESSFUL AI/ES IN BUSINESS, FINANCE AND ACCOUNTING

The series of application papers collected in [11] are revealing in their presentation of the issues that remain unsolved. In the Manufacturer's Hanover Trust (MHT) system called TARA, Byrnes *et al.* (1989, p. 73) wrote

> ...many technological and psychological hurdles had to be overcome. The major psychological hurdles were gaining interest among traders with widely varying styles; holding this interest with a rich, yet logical and responsive user interface; and, finally, teaching traders how to use this higher-level tool to enhance their personal trading strategies.

Issues the MHT team called *psychological* are, in fact, conceptual. How do experts interact with a system? Does the interface play a role in encouraging the interaction and what sort of interface do experts require? What is the role of an expert system vis-a-vis a group of experts?

Hart in the discussion of Syntel, (1989, p. 65) noted

> ...the need for a principled approach for dealing with missing data, default assumptions, and imprecise knowledge [and an] overall control scheme has to be data driven like the standard spreadsheet applications which are so familiar to business users. However, data-driven approaches can lead to serious inefficiencies when used on large knowledge bases.

Hart's remarks, part of his discussion of the needs that led to the creation of a specific language underlying Syntelligence's AI/ES products in banking and insurance, are particularly revealing in terms of uncovering issues. Hart addresses the issue of the interface, by alluding to AI/ES which behave like spreadsheet applications. He addresses both the interface and interaction subjects raised by the MHT team.

The Chase personal financial planning system described by Kindle *et al.* (1989, p. 55) reveals that the system test and validation period stretched more that 2 years to bring a complex AI/ES to market. Not only is the test and validation period protracted, but, as the paper points out [p. 58],

> Flavors [the old object-oriented dialect of Lisp offered by Symbolics Inc.] alone, however, did not offer features generally required in the information system industry, particularly the financial community.

The authors confirmed that the support for AI/ES in the financial community by vendors is weak. Hart (1989, p.63) states flatly that

> ...the existing technology was poorly matched to the demands of the selected financial applications...our design response led to a new architecture that departs sharply from the rule- and frame-based architecture that dominates...expert systems today.

These remarks by several teams who have deployed successful applications reveal that many barriers exist to creating AI/ES for business, finance and accounting. The quotes show that conceptual issues had to be confronted and surmounted by each team in the course of delivering the system. The cost of resolving the issues were enormous; the fastest project of the three, TARA, still took four people close to two years! Unless the techniques these teams created are institutionalized and packaged, then AI/ES will never be anything but an intellectual pursuit. By identifying several of the conceptual issues associated with the projects, I can lay out an agenda for developers and vendors who seek to specialize in AI/ES in business, finance and accounting for the years ahead.

2.4 CONCEPTUAL ISSUES

I see the following as the conceptual issues that exist in the integration of AI/ES into conventional information systems:

- We lack a prescriptive approach to the design and implementation of suitable user interfaces.
- AI/ES requires a unifying methodology to marry successfully with conventional information systems.

- Specific advances must be made to create useful AI/ES for business, finance and accounting.

2.4.1 User Interfaces

The early advances of AI/ES brought with it not just superior reasoning power, but superior means of interacting with users. Text-based, single-screen conventional information system interfaces did not convey the higher degree of information and knowledge to users effectively. At the U.S. Environmental Protection Agency, its formal guidelines for AI/ES published by the Office of Solid Waste and Emergency Response as System Life Cycle Management Guidance, Part 3, present the ability *...to simplify the user/computer interaction* as one of the two key benefits of AI/ES technology. User interfaces, therefore, are integral to the development of successful, useful AI/ES.

At present, however, the technology of multiple windows, mice, natural language facilities and explanation lack a unifying approach to the problem of design. As Byrnes *et al.* said in the prior quote, holding the interest of the user with the right interface was a major barrier in the acceptability and utility of TARA. As conventional information system interfaces become richer and borrow from the technology once used only in AI/ES, the problem will be relieved only in some degree. Some of the AI/ES technology is supported by X Windows, OSF/Motif, SAA CUA and the other new graphical user interfaces. If this technology were all that were necessary, however, then the Macintosh would have become the dominant platform for AI/ES a long time ago. Providing useful explanations from the expert system, aimed at the various classes of users, developers and maintainers, is still an area of research. Expert systems without these capabilities are still built routinely, and then shelved.

2.5 CONCLUSION

These are some of the fundamental conceptual issues that stand between integration of AI/ES with conventional information systems. I chose these because they are all tractable issues. Work is proceeding on all these fronts with resolution in sight. The development of user interfaces across platforms in the future will accelerate the integration process. Developments in object-oriented methodologies have brought the standard design methodologies a good deal of the way towards serving the purposes of AI/ES developers. Integration means more than providing an SQL interface between an expert system tool and conventional database management system: developers are being made to facilitate the right kind of integration.

REFERENCES

Byrnes, E. Campfield, T. and Conner, B. (1989), "TARA: An Intelligent Assistant for Foreign Traders", *Innovative Applications of Artificial Intelligence*, Cambridge, Mass:AAAI Press.

Feigenbaum, E. McCorduck, P. and Penny Nii, H. (1988), *The Rise of the Expert Company*, New York:Times Books.

Harmon, P. (1989), "Where Does the U.S. Expert Systems Market Stand Now?", *Expert Systems Strategies*, 5(1):1–13.

Hart, P. (1989), "Syntel(tm):An Architecture for Financial Applications", *Innovative Applications of Artificial Intelligence*, Cambridge Mass.:AAAI Press.

Hoffman, R. (1988), "The Problem of Extracting the Knowledge of Experts from the Perspective of Experimental Psychology", *AI Magazine*, 8(2): 53–67.

Kerschberg, L. and Dickinson, J. (1988), "FINEX: A PC-based Expert Support System for Financial Analysis", *Managing Expert Systems*, Reading, Mass:Addison-Wesley Publishing.

Kindle, K. Cann, R. Craig, M. and Martin, T.J. (1989), "PFPS: Personal Financial Planning System", *Innovative Applications of Artificial Intelligence*, Cambridge, Mass:AAAI Press.

Martin, J. and Oxman, S. (1988), *Building Expert Systems*, Englewood Cliffs, NJ: Prentice-Hall.

Martin, T. and Zickefoose, M.B. "Expert Systems in the Financial Services Industry", *Spectrum Information Systems Industry Applications*, Cambridge, Mass:Arthur D. Little Decision Resources.

Pearl, J. (1988), "Evidential Reasoning Under Uncertainty", *Exploring Artificial Intelligence*, Palo Alto, CA:Morgan Kaufmann Publishers.

Schorr, H. and Rappaport, A. (1989), "Preface", *Innovative Applications of Artificial Intelligence*, Cambridge, Mass:AAAI Press.

Shoham, Y. and Goyal, N. (1988), "Temporal Reasoning in Artificial Intelligence", *Exploring Artificial Intelligence*, Palo Alto, CA:Morgan Kaufmann Publishers.

Chapter 3

BUILDING COMPUTERIZED FINANCIAL ADVISORS: THE USER MODEL AND HUMAN INTERFACE

David King
Execucom Systems Corporation, Austin, TX

The flood of information has heightened the desire for computerized assistance with decision-making and problem-solving processes. The type of assistance needed at the managerial level is characterized quite succinctly by Edward Rensi (1988), President and CEO of McDonald's USA:

> In the business environment, quick access to critical data is essential to making the correct decision. Although quick access to data currently exists in most corporations, computer assistance usually stops at this point. The near future, however, promises a computer management system that will not only give the executive raw information, but will also monitor profit plans, pointing out any deviations as soon as they occur, determine possible causes of these deviations, project their effects, and recommend options to take to resolve these problems... (Of course), the final decision will and should always be made by the manager or executive.

In this chapter, we will explore some of the conceptual and technical issues surrounding the development of a system which automates the abilities of a high level strategic planner or financial analyst.

3.1 INTRODUCTION

Everywhere and everyday, corporations confront accelerating change—change brought about by mergers and acquisitions, by the growth of global market places, and by the quickening pace at which competitors come and go (Peters, 1987). In many corporations a response to the *chaos* created by these changes has been the elimination of entire layers of staff, especially at the middle management level. The feeling is that not only does this hold the bottom line, but it also reduces organizational complexity and improves productivity by shortening the lines of communication

Expert Systems in Business and Finance: Issues and Applications. Edited by P.R. Watkins and L.B. Eliot
© 1993 John Wiley & Sons Ltd.

between (1) those who do the work, (2) those who do the planning, and (3) those in control (Harmon, 1985; Keen, 1988). One of the overall impacts of these changes and reductions is that senior management—from executive officers to senior managers to their consulting staff—has less time and fewer human resources with which to make decisions. It also means that senior management is required to monitor, digest, access, and understand an increasing volume of information. Paraphrasing Lee Iacocca, one of the major problems facing corporations today is that senior management has too much information. *It dazzles them and they don't know what to do with it.*

The question is, *What type of system can or will provide the type of management support required to support the decisions envisioned by the CEO of McDonald's previously cited?*

Historically, corporations have utilized database management systems (DBMS) and decision support systems (DSS) to manage, monitor, understand, and interpret corporate performance. It has been the role of the DBMS to serve as a collection point for corporate data and to provide tools for describing past and present status. DSS, on the other hand, have been used to examine the future, i.e., to assess the impacts of potential decisions, to evaluate alternative courses of action, and to measure trade-offs among different situations. But DBMS and DSS are the tools of the *planner* or *analyst.* Among researchers working in the area of *executive support,* it is generally agreed that the activities, requirements, skills, and personal work-styles of executives are sufficiently rare to require a new form of information technology to deal with these tasks (Rockhart, 1988). This technology goes by the name of *Executive Information Systems* (EIS).

The present generation of EIS are basically PC-based, windowing frontends to mainframe DBMS and DSS. The staple of these systems are customized, summary status reports and graphs which are used to monitor variances from planned performance. The major form of analysis provided by these tools is *drill-down. Drill-down* enables the executive to peruse the detailed data underlying the summarized report. Output from a sample EIS is shown in Figure 3.1. This particular system, which was developed by Execucom, is a bit unusual. Not only does it display summary information (here in graphic form), but it also provides a *computer generated explanation* of the results (a feature we'll discuss later). Like other EIS, however, it provides virtually no support for automatically monitoring complex variations or trends, for determining the implications of results, or for recommending suggested courses of action. These tasks are still the domain of the planner or analyst.

In order to provide automated support for these tasks, what needs to be automated is the *knowledge* of the planner or analyst; both domain knowledge and knowledge about how to use analytical tools. It's this knowledge which enables the planner or analyst to:

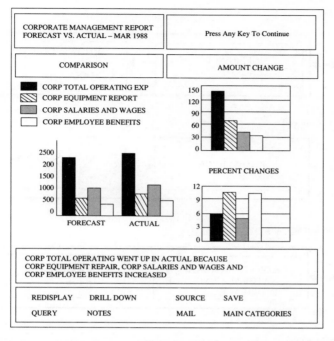

FIGURE 3.1   Sample screen from an executive information system

- determine which data to investigate and monitor
- determine which tools to use in describing and analyzing the data
- perform the requisite analyses
- interpret and understand the analytical results
- suggest recommended courses of action

In other words, the type of system we need to create is a computerized staff assistant or advisor (Keen, 1983).

For purposes of discussion, we call the system a *Computerized Financial Advisor* (CFA). It's a *financial* advisor because in most corporations financial data still form the basis for measuring corporate performance and for deciding among alternative courses of action. The development of a CFA can and is proceeding in a variety of ways. Among the alternative approaches being taken are:

- Expert Systems (ES) in specific financial domains
- Intelligent Frontends (IFE) serving as interfaces to more conventional analytical tools

Expert systems

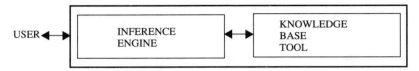

Intelligent front end

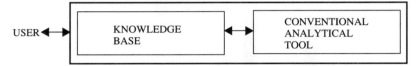

Conversational advisory system

Intelligent agents

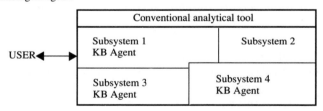

FIGURE 3.2   Computerized advisors—some alternatives

- Conversational Advisory Systems (CAS) based on natural language inter-faces built around knowledge-based systems
- Intelligent Agents (IA) used for monitoring events and performing automated tasks based on those events.

The diagrams in Figure 3.2 summarize some of the architectural differences among the approaches. From the figure, we can see that all of the approaches substitute a knowledge-based system for the role of the advisor. What distinguishes them is the type of knowledge embedded in the system, the user model underlying the system and the interface between the user and the system. In the discussion which follows we consider each approach and its distinguishing characteristics. Throughout the discussion we focus on the question, *How easily can the system be adapted to the skills and needs of senior management?*

3.2   A SAMPLE PROBLEM

Before we actually consider some of the ways in which a CFA can be created, let's clarify some of the tasks we'd like a CFA to handle. Consider, for example, a fast food corporation. At the base of the corporation are retail outlets. Point of sales figures are reported from these outlets to regional headquarters, which in turn are reported to corporate headquarters. Suppose at the end of a given reporting period (e.g., a month or quarter) the corporate figures show a drop in revenues. The obvious questions that come to mind are, *Why did this occur? Is it due to a particular region? And, if so, is it caused by rising expenses or declining sales?* Now, suppose after thorough examination of the detailed figures, the corporation determines that it's due to rising expenses in a particular region (e.g., food costs in the western region) *Is the problem serious? If expenses continue to rise, what will be the impact*

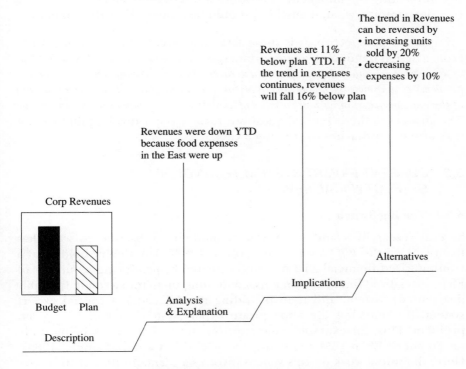

FIGURE 3.3   Sample problem for senior management

on the bottom line at the end of the year? To answer these questions various projections are made using *what if* and trend analysis. Suppose these latter computations reveal that by the end of the year the bottom line will be substantially impacted. The corporation would like to know the best approach. *Do they need to attack the expense side directly or will small changes in prices suffice?* Again, *what if* and *goal seeking* can be used to answer these sorts of questions.

This example is fairly representative of the type of data and problems faced by senior management. In Rockhart and Delong's (1988) seminal study of EIS, a quick review of existing systems reveals that almost all of them are used to monitor and determine the causes of corporate performance. At the foundation of this process is a consolidated report, reviewed by management on a daily, weekly, monthly, or quarterly basis. The basic steps used in analyzing the data in these reports are illustrated in Figure 3.3. Briefly, the steps depicted in the figure include:

(1) describing and monitoring the changes in key variables
(2) interpreting or explaining the causes of these changes
(3) projecting the impact of the continuation of these changes
(4) determining what, if anything should be done to alter the changes.

From our perspective, it is these tasks that are at the heart of a CFA. From a design standpoint, an important question to be answered is, *What type of knowledge is required to perform these tasks? Is it knowledge about the specific problem? Is it knowledge about how to perform the tasks? Or is it some combination of these in conjunction with other types of knowledge like common sense reasoning?* The answers to these general questions form a major dividing line among the various approaches to creating a CFA.

3.3   CURRENT EXPERT SYSTEM TECHNOLOGY: A STEREOTYPICAL REVIEW

3.3.1 The Big Switch

Several researchers and practitioners implicitly subscribe to what has been labeled the *Big Switch* theory (Waltz, 1982). The theory holds that a computerized financial advisor can be created by producing a number of ES in specialized financial domains, combining them into a single (possibly distributed) system, and then providing the *big switch*, a special expert system, for selecting the appropriate expert system to handle a given problem. This, for example, characterizes some of the work being done on Financial ES at IBM's Los Angeles Scientific Center (Gongla, 1988). Here, the initial work on this system involves a formalization of strategies espoused in Porter's (1980; 1985) work on competitive advantage.

Outside of IBM, there are a number of corporations employing ES to perform a variety of tasks in the financial arena. Unlike the IBM system, most of these systems are not combined into larger systems. The tasks performed by these independent ES include such things as financial statement analysis, portfolio management, insurance underwriting, stocks and bonds trading, credit and loan review, and investment planning, to name just a few examples. For interested readers, a description of a number of these systems can be found in Blanning (1987), Rauch-Hindin (1988) and Leinweber (1988). While we will not consider particular systems in detail, ES dealing with cash flow analysis (O'Leary, 1987) and pricing strategies are of particular import for problems like the consolidated analysis described above in the sample problem.

3.3.2 Shell Technology

Typically, ES applications both within and outside the financial area are constructed and run using an ES shell. Shells run the gamut from complex commercial toolkits such as Intellicorp's KEE to more rudimentary, rule-based commercial systems such as VP Expert to proprietary or *home grown* shells often based on AI programming languages such as Lisp or Prolog. Regardless of their complexity, nearly all shells contain tools for encoding knowledge, an inference engine for reasoning with this knowledge, an explanation facility for tracing the system's line of reasoning, and an interface for handling dialogue between the builder and the system and between the user and the system.

In most shells knowledge is encoded in a language which is very similar to a standard programming language, so that the interface between the builder and the system is much like a programming environment with specialized editors, debuggers, etc. Because of the complexity of many of these languages and because most experts are not programmers, a knowledge engineer often acts as a communication link between the domain expert and the system, converting the expert's language into the system's language. The process of transferring and transforming problem-solving expertise has come to be viewed as a critical bottleneck in the development of ES. This bottleneck has been discussed in detail elsewhere (Buchanan *et al*, 1983; Jungduck and Courtney, 1987; King, 1987) and will not be dealt with in this discussion. Instead, we are concerned with the interface between the user and the application created by the expert and the knowledge engineer. Whether the CFA appears in the form of a *big switch* or as series of independent ES is really not crucial. What is crucial to the ES approach is the explicit assumption that the most important element of the system is a large store of *domain specific* knowledge. It's this knowledge that is the key to locating important variables, interpreting results, and recommending alternative courses of action. If access is required to external data or computational procedures, the access typically occurs from the internal knowledge structures used to represent the domain expertise. For instance, a rule or demon in a frame can be used to activate financial computations or *what if* situations when needed.

3.3 User Interface

Most ES applications in the financial area appear to users in one of two forms. First, there are those systems which present the user with a questionnaire or business form where a large number of data items are requested from the user at one time. Good examples of this form of interface are the insurance and banking applications produced with Syntelligence's SYNTEL language (Reboh and Risch, 1986) and APEX's financial planning product called PlanPower (for an informal discussion of the product see Garson, 1988). More frequent, however, are those financial ES where the user is confronted by a machine-driven interview or question-and-answer session. A good illustration of this type of interface is found in the ExperTax system from Coopers and Lybrand (Shpilberg *et al*, 1986). This system provides guidance and advice, through issue identification, to authors and tax specialists in preparing tax accruals for financial statement purposes. During a session, the auditor or tax specialist is asked to answer a series of questions which are presented one at a time. Responses typically require the user to make a selection from a fixed set of choices. A typical question might be something like, *What is the client's bad-debt write-off method for tax purposes? Is it Specific charge-off or Reserve method?* During the Q and A process, the user has the option of answering the question, asking the system *why* the question is being asked and then continuing, skipping the question altogether, or creating a special note for future reference and then continuing. Based on the user's response, the machine decides what conclusions to draw and what questions to ask next. At the end, the user is presented with a written report of issues and conclusions, as well as a log file of the questions and answers and all notes taken.

While ExperTax is based on a proprietary shell technology, it is typical of many of the applications created using micro-based ES shells. Other applications, such as those created with products like Texas Instrument's Personal Consultant or Paperback Software's VP Expert, provide other niceties. For example, instead of typing an answer, the user simply employs the cursor control keys (i.e., up, down, left, and right arrow keys) to make a selection among the fixed choices. Also, at the end of the session, the user can ask *how* a particular conclusion was inferred and what would happen to the conclusions if one of the data values were changed (*what-if*).

Regardless of whether the interaction takes place through a business form or question-and-answer session or whether the system has certain features present or absent, from a *stereotypical* view, the man–machine model on which the ES are based is essentially the same. In almost all of them a shell is used to create a stand alone machine expert that offers diagnoses, problem solutions, and/or recommendations in a fairly narrow domain. While the user initiates a session, the dialogue is almost wholly machine driven, with the user's role reduced to answering questions when, and only when, the system requires data input to draw its conclusions. The user's role is reduced to that of data gather or collector. Of course, in the final analysis the user has the options of ignoring or modifying the conclusions produced by the machine. Roth *et al.* (1987) have called this model of interaction the *prosthesis model.* Here, the machine is seen as a replacement or remedy for a deficiency in the user. It's based on the assumption that the machine expert is required because the task or problem is beyond the skill of the current user.

3.3.4 Some Underlying Problems

ES applications are almost wholly *expert centered.* In developing an ES, the focus is on getting the *reasoning right* from the expert, while the eventual non-expert users are relegated either implicitly or explicitly to a role of secondary importance. If one reads any of the standard texts on how to build an ES, for example Harmon and King (1985), he'll find that most of the discussion deals with how to create a *valid* system. The fallacy is that even if the system is perfectly valid, this doesn't mean that all of its ills will be cured. A system can be perfectly acceptable to the expert, yet when it is used by a naive, inexperienced, less experienced, hostile, or intolerant user, it inexplicably fails. Although the knowledge is there, it's not in a form which the user can or is willing to use (Langlotz and Shortliffe, 1984; Cleal and Heaton, 1988).

Although not in the financial realm, an experimental study by Roth *et al.* (1987) illustrates some of the problems that are encountered when users take a back seat to the expert. In this study, technicians were presented with a series of *machine breakdowns* whose causes were known to the experimenters. An ES was provided for troubleshooting the problems. The ES had been developed and tested for over a year. The ES ran in *question-and-answer* mode where the technicians had the options of asking the system for clarification or explanation and for backtracking to a previous question so that they could change their answers. Because the source of the machine breakdowns were of known origin, the correct solution path was also known. The results indicated that regardless of the skill level of the technician the known solution path was rarely followed. With inexperienced technicians, the system often produced the incorrect solution or basically no solution at all. With experienced users, the system usually produced the correct solution; however, during the session, the system often went off the correct solution path and had to be corrected by the technician (either through backtracking or restarting the system). As they put it, successful performance depended on the ability of the technician to apply knowledge of the structure and function of the device and sensible trouble shooting approaches. This was necessary to follow underspecified instructions, to infer machine intentions, to resolve impasses, and to recover from errors that led the machine off track. Once the machine expert was off track, it could not recover by itself. The burden to detect and recover from deviations fell on the human.

The reasons for the above outcomes are varied, although many can be traced to the underlying model on which ES applications are based. In fact, stereotypical ES are likely to encounter a variety of problems:

Language: Because the input and output language of the application is often couched in terms and concepts only understood by a professional or application expert, entry errors, misobservations, or misinterpretations are likely to occur, especially with the untrained, casual, or novice user (Basden, 1984). Consider, for example, the expert TAXADVISOR developed at the University of Illinois and described by Schwartz (1988). Schwartz notes that, a professional tax advisor or accountant would understand such terms as gifted assets, trusts, term life insurance, transfer taxes, probate, and so on, and would understand the concepts and implications associated with these terms. However, the average consumer does not understand their meaning.

Control: Even if instructions are very elaborate or are computed on-the-fly, they are bound to break if followed in a rote fashion. In any system, it is difficult to build in mechanisms that cope with novel situations, that adapt to special conditions or contexts, or that recover from human errors or bugs in the instructions. When control of the interaction is solely up to the machine, the user has virtually no resources to redirect the actions to account for these unanticipated conditions.

System state: In order to use a tool, the user must know its boundaries and limits—capabilities, side effects, preconditions, postconditions, etc. Question and answer dialogue provides the user with little to determine the state of the system. The burden of remembering the state of the device and the historical flow of the dialogue (observations and hypotheses) is left up to the user.

Communication level: When questions and answers form the basis of communication, the system knowledge is at very low level of detail. At this level, the machine has very little understanding, nor any way of determining, the user's intentions, goals, or plans which may be at the core of the task or problem to be solved. A simple example of the differing levels of communication can be found in the *what if* command present in most DSS. At one level, a user might ask: *What if the unit price equals $1.50 instead of*

$1.00? This is the standard level of communication understood by most DSS, although it is usually stated in mathematical terms. At a higher level, however, a truly knowledgeable DSS could answer queries of the sort: *What will be the effect on revenues if we lease our equipment rather than buy?* In a question and answer dialogue, the level of communication tends to be lower than either of these.

User capabilities: Users of ES are treated as if they fall in the same static category, possessing the same skill, knowledge, intentions, and goals. Developers of other types of software systems (e.g., word processing, databases, etc.) have long recognized that the range of users is much wider, and in some cases have also recognized that the user is able to learn and adapt to the system. In ES, if learning is considered at all, the focus is on the system's ability to expand and modify its knowledge of the domain, not the user's ability to improve his performance.

System goal: In current ES, the emphasis is on achieving known and clearly defined solutions. For many tasks, however, human experts aren't required to produce solutions to well-defined problems. Instead, they're asked for conceptual guidance—to provide contextual information, to focus attention on important topics, to help predict outcomes, and to criticize the solutions offered by others (Coombs and Alty, 1984). In a nutshell, they're required to act as advisors.

Who's the Expert: When the users of an ES consider themselves to be experts, one often finds the advice or solution offered by the system being overridden. This is what happened in the Heuristic Programming Project at the Stanford University Department of Medicine and Computer Science (Langlotz, 1984). There, developers found that oncologists frequently ignored or substantially altered the treatment advice offered by the ONCONION ES, even when the physicians only disagreed slightly with the system's suggestions. In part, this result occurred because highly trained specialists, like physicians, often feel that they are as knowledgeable as the system and can prove it by coming up with a better solution. They also feel that if they take the system's advice, they are relinquishing control of the situation. The experiences are not unlike those reported by Garson (1988) when she noted that stockbrokers were *selectively* resistant to programs like ES that took information or autonomy away from them. They weren't resistant, however, to computer systems that brought them timely information.

There is a range of ES toolkits that provide developers with the capabilities to create a variety of interfaces. It's just that a number of the simpler shells, especially those of the MYCIN class, encourage machine-directed question and answer interfaces. The arguments are not meant to imply that ES are not valuable tools. They've proved to be valuable in a variety of circumstances, especially for application professionals. They also contain various components and features which are necessary for the development of any advisory system. Included are tools for (Leinweber, 1988):

● event-driven or data-driven processing
● discovering complex, generalized data patterns
● dealing with uncertain, incomplete, and inconsistent data
● explaining reasoning processes

The arguments do suggest, however, that in their current form, ES are not well suited for senior management. Among other things, the focus of ES is too narrow, the language they speak is not the language of the executive, and they provide the user with very few ways to explore alternative scenarios or issues.

3.4   INTELLIGENT FRONTENDS

As noted in the introduction, many of the problems and tasks facing senior management have been routinely addressed by planners and analysts with more conventional DBMS, DSS, statistical analysis packages, and spreadsheets. Unlike ES shells, what these analytical systems have is a general set of computational procedures, reporting facilities, and routines for investigating alternative scenarios. In comparison to ES representation schemes, the various capabilities of these systems are better understood, as evidenced by the large body of users. What these systems don't have, however, is the ability to capture symbolic knowledge and to reason with this knowledge.

Several attempts have been made to add, or at least interface, capabilities with these conventional tools. A number of efforts have been made to combine knowledge-based reasoning with DBMS (Kershberg, 1984). In the same vein, VP Expert and Guru are products which combine the features of an ES shell, a database (or file system) and a spreadsheet. At Execucom, we have prototyped changes in the IFPS modeling language and compiler/solver so that users can create knowledge bases in equation form (much like standard IF/THEN rules). Because most corporate data resides in databases, planning models, statistical models, statistical models, and spreadsheets, it is important to be able to reason with these data in a *logical* fashion. Yet, the addition of an ES component still doesn't give the analyst the ability to capture his knowledge of *how to use the tool.* That is, how to automatically determine what procedures to use, what analyses to perform, how to interpret the results, and how to make recommendations. *Knowledge of use* is a prerequisite for building advisory systems. This is where the work done on *Intelligent Frontends* (IFE) comes into play. IFE, also known as "smart systems" (Gerstein, 1987), have a built-in representation of their own functionality (Jackson and Lefrere, 1984), i.e., the system knows how to solve certain problems and how to interpret results. The aim of an IFE is to enable the user to make more effective use of the conventional software package behind the *frontend* (Cleal and Heaton, 1988).

3.4.1 Elements of an Intelligent Interface

Cleal and Heaton (1988) outlines the basic capabilities needed by an IFE to accomplish its tasks. Included are the abilities to:

- carry on a dialogue with a user
- produce a specification of the user's problem
- use the specification to generate instructions for running the underlying package
- interpret the results produced by the analysis.

Outside the world of decision support, IFE have been used to assist:

- ecologists building Fortran simulations—ECO (Cleal and Heaton, 1988)
- designers developing logical circuits—CADHELP (Cullingford *et al.*, 1982)
- novice users of the Unix operating system—Unix Consultant (Wilensky, 1982).

In the world of decision support, most of the work on intelligent interfaces has been done in the area of statistical analysis. A recent discussion by Remus and Kotteman (1986) describes the basic elements of an IFE to a statistical package. The system, which they call an *Artificially Intelligent Statistician,* can parse queries, locate necessary data, select appropriate statistical tests, handle statistical issues such as out and multicollinearity, and finally produce output which minimizes biasing effects. Although their system has yet to be implemented, they envision the *AIS* being able to deal with a wide range of problems facing senior management. Some typical problems, along with the type of output they anticipate, are provided below:

Scenario 1: The sales manager asks the system to compare the sales figures in the Boston sales office with those in the Chicago office. The system would retrieve the appropriate data, display it graphically in a bar chart, and automatically perform various statistical tests to determine the significance of the differences between the two groups. It would also handle any statistical problems that it encountered (e.g., outlier data). Finally, it would report the results of its tests (e.g., there is a greater than 95% chance that the median sales in Chicago over the past year were $500 higher than in Boston).

Scenario 2: The same sales manager wants to know why the differences in sales between the two offices exists. Using a historical database of sales figures, the system would regress the figures on a variety of other factors. Based on the results of this analysis, it might report that it's due to the sales commission structure. It might also project what it thinks the differences will be in the future with and without changes in commissions.

The system envisioned by Remus and Kottemann is an extension of the work done earlier by William Gale (1986) at Bell Labs. Gale and his colleagues developed a system called REX, which served as a specialized frontend to the regression procedures found in the *S* statistical package. Using a question and answer format, REX guided the user through the process of regression analysis by testing assumptions, suggesting possible data transformation when assumptions were violated, interpreting intermediate and final results and instructing users in statistical concepts (Gale, 1986). From the decision-maker's point of view, what is important about an IFE is that allows him to concentrate on what he wants to do rather than on how he is going to do it. Assuming that the system has the capability to parse a natural language query (a point we will discuss later), all the user has to do is pose his query in a language that is comfortable to him and the system has knowledge to do the rest (a task that is easier said than done). More specifically, the system has built-in knowledge of how a component analyst or planner would use the system.

3.4.2 Some Alternative Representations

As with other knowledge-based tasks, various representational techniques can be used to create intelligent interfaces between users and conventional systems. Without going into too much detail, we note some of the possibilities:

Rules: Here, what the analyst or planner knows is represented by a large number of situation-specific rules. The consequences of the rules represent the system commands and procedures for accomplishing specific analyses, while the ante-cedents represent the prerequisites for carrying out those analyses. Although there are no existing analytical systems which employ this scheme, Jackson and Lefrere (1984) used a rule-base to build a prototype, intelligent frontend to the Wordstar program.

Frames: A frame consists of a series of slots. Slots are akin to fields in a database, except that they're much richer data structures; slots consist of various facets. Some of the facets hold data values; others reference procedures which are activated when certain actions are taken on the data facets. These procedural facets are called *demons.* For example, an IF-ADDED demon fires a procedure when a value is added to a slot. Again, in an intelligent interface, the value facet of the slots in a frame are used to represent the system's knowledge of the user's intentions, goals, requests, etc., while the demon facets are used to represent the analyst's or planner's knowledge of what activities or analyses to perform to satisfy the user. The REX interface employs this sort of representation scheme.

Procedural Networks: This is really a collection of diverse schemes used to represent plans for carrying out tasks. Many of these schemes have their origin in Hewitt's (1970) PLANNER language, Winograd's (1972) work on natural languages, and Sacredotti's (1977) Noah program. The issues and representational schemes used to deal with planning tasks are often illustrated with the *robot world.* In this world, a robot is given the task of moving a series of blocks around on a table. In order to perform these tasks, the robot must construct a plan which consists of a series of actions, each defined by a set of preconditions (e.g., to move a block, the robot first has to grasp it) and a set of postconditions (e.g., when a block is moved, it is no longer in the old location and now has a new location). The plan is executed in a backward chaining fashion. Advisory systems can be viewed in the same light.

The system can be viewed as a robot who is given a high-level request by the user. It's the robot's job to develop a plan for carrying out the task and then to execute that plan. Again, the plan consists of a series of preconditions (e.g., the user's intentions or goals, necessary data, analytical assumptions which must be fulfilled, etc.) and a set of postconditions (data transformations, changes to the database, actual analytical results, etc.). To date, procedural representations have not been used very extensively in the decision support arena. One exception is the REX system which, in addition to frames, also employed an *agenda* to schedule various tasks carried out by the system. Procedural representations were also used in the CADHELP and Unix Consultant systems noted above.

While there are differences among the representational schemes, they all share a *common planning* mentality. Whether we call them consequences of rules, demons of frames, or postconditions of procedural networks, we are basically talking about the analytical procedures used by an expert analyst or planner to solve a particular problem. In the same vein, whether we label them antecedents, data facets, or preconditions, we are still talking about the contextual information needed to perform the analysis.

3.4.3 Gap Between Theory and Practice

Leinweber claims (1988) that one equation is worth a *thousand rules*, implying that it is easier for a user to build and understand a model or database than it is to build an ES. An IFE opens up the world of equations to a larger class of users including decision-makers and senior management. They do this by supporting mixed-initiative dialogue.

In such a dialogue, both participants can independently offer suggestions while controlling the actions of the other. In systems of this sort, the user begins the action by making a request or stating a goal. The system responds, warning the user of possible problems, asking the user for clarification, providing answers to their requests, and suggesting further analyses. The user then responds to the system's output. This back-and-forth banter continues throughout the session.

In comparison to the type of model and interface supported by the stereotypical ES, this type of dialogue gives the user more control, allows him to focus on the problems at hand, and allows him to converse at a level he understands. In all fairness to ES, however, there is a wide gap between the theory of an IFE and actual practice: most IFEs suffer the same problems as ES.

Most IFEs do not support natural language dialogue, although they would like to. In reality, they tend to rely on the question and answer dialogue used in most ES. Similarly, while IFEs are designed to interface with systems which possess a broad range of capabilities, in practice they have only been used to frontend systems with narrow sets of capabilities—even narrower, in most instances, than the capabilities found in the typical ES. REX is a case in point. Instead of frontending all the procedures in the underlying statistical package, it can only be used for the regression procedures. The reason for this narrow focus is simple. It takes too much knowledge, both domain and common sense, to handle the range of problems that the typical user of these systems wants to attack.

Finally, as in an ES, the users of an IFE cannot modify the knowledge base on which the system is built. If, for instance, the users of REX don't like the tactics or procedures used to interpret results, there is no way to modify the frames and agenda underlying this advice. This means that if an organization has a certain way of analyzing data, there's no way for them to modify the knowledge base to reflect these practices.

The experiences of researchers and practitioners working the area of natural language provide ample evidence of the difficulties in building systems with mixed-initiative dialogue. In the next section, we examine some of the broader issues involved in carrying on natural language conversations in advisory systems and describe why there may be inherent barriers to building IFEs.

3.5   CONVERSATIONAL ADVISORY SYSTEMS

3.5.1 Some Basic Beliefs

The proponents of natural language processing hold a couple of widely held beliefs which have a direct bearing on the development of a computerized (financial) advisor. First, until computers can process natural language, the population of users will remain circumscribed. The biggest obstacle in teaching major portions of the general population to use computers is that users have to learn to speak the language of the computer and not vice versa. Included within this population is senior management. Second, the development of advanced knowledge-based systems, such as computerized advisors, critically depends on natural language comprehension. The only real way for users to express their intentions in a declarative rather than procedural fashion, and for a computer to understand these intentions, is by utilizing natural language processing. Sowa (1984) summarizes this latter position in the following manner:

> For most people, natural language is the primary means of thinking, learning, and communicating. No other means is as general or flexible. Menus are good for selecting options, but they are awkward for expressing relationships. Mathematical equations are good for relationships but they cannot express commands. Programming languages issue commands but they cannot ask questions. Query languages ask questions but they cannot give explanations. Only natural language can serve all the functions of human communication within a common flexible framework.

Paradoxically, there is a catch to this latter belief. The catch is expressed in a variety of ways:

> World knowledge is the key to language understanding. (Schwartz, 1988)

> Robust natural language understanding cannot occur in the absence of a knowledge-base concerning the relevant subject area. (Schank, 1985)

> Communicating in natural language is an activity of total intellect. (Hendrix, 1985)

> [Even in a simple database] knowledge rather than data is needed to interpret natural language queries and to answer many such queries. (Koa, 1988)

In other words, the development of knowledge-based systems requires natural language processing, while the development of a natural language processor requires a knowledge base.

In part, the paradox explains the difficulties often encountered in simply sticking a natural language interface on the frontend of an existing expert system or knowledge-based system. Some of the difficulties were experienced in the development of Lucy (Wroblewski and Rich, 1988), a natural language frontend applied to an advisory system for doing statistical analysis.

As the developers of Lucy noted, it was almost as difficult to create a (semantic) map, worded in the natural language, the knowledge base as it was to develop the knowledge base in the first place. The problem was never ameliorated, because the knowledge base was under constant revision. They further indicated that it might have been better to develop the two hand-in-hand so that problematic mappings could have been *debugged* before the knowledge base developers forgot the meanings of the various entities in the knowledge base. Indeed, the suggestion was taken to heart when the team of developers came up with a new frontend called Luke, which creates the knowledge base and natural language mappings at the same time.

3.5.2 The Range of User Utterances

For the sake of discussion, let's assume that an advanced system, such as a computerized advisor, requires natural language processing and that natural language processing in turn requires knowledge. What types of knowledge are essential to handling the dialogue between the user and the system? One way to answer this question is to look at studies of the types of vocabulary, grammar, and utterances which a natural language interface must handle. One study which is often cited is Tennant's (1980) analysis of the PLANES system, a prototype natural language frontend to a relational database of aircraft flights and maintenance. Another less known study is Malhotra's (1975) investigation of the utility and feasibility of an English language question-answering system to support management. What studies of this sort show is that a substantial proportion of the utterances typed at a natural language interface are (1) grammatically deficient, and (2) outside the range of information in the system. The following series of hypothetical requests made by a decision-maker interested in examining various pricing strategies is illustrative of the types of utterances found in these studies:

(1) Have you got the costs and sales figures?
(2) What are our unit costs?
(3) How much did we make last year?
(4) What's our margin?
(5) That doesn't look right, are you sure?
(6) Ok, what about the year before?
(7) Before that?
(8) If we up the margin by 5%, what's our break-even volume?
(9) What if it's 3%?

(10)   Now try 10%.
(11)   Which do you recommend?
(12)   Let me see the balance sheet.

These examples touch very briefly upon some of the ambiguities (word senses, pronoun references, etc.) and types of statements (requests, commands, declarations, etc.) that a natural language processor must deal with. A summary of the variety of the kinds of user utterances (requests and statements) occurring outside the range of information provided by a typical query system is provided below:

Requests
● for information about the database
● about the meaning of certain words in an answer
● for the system to verify one of its answers
● consisting of multiple queries
● for advice
● for explanations.

Statements
● referring to previous statements made by the system or user
● informing the system of user preferences
● modifying previous input
● shifting focus of the discussion from one topic to another
● of a miscellaneous or obscene nature.

Overall, the results of these studies show that the users of a natural language interface expect the system to be able to carry on an intelligent conversation regardless of its actual capabilities.

3.5.3   What Does It Take to Converse?

Looking at the above summary, we can readily discern that a tremendous variety of knowledge is required to handle mixed-initiative dialogue simply because there is virtually no way to predict the user's course of action. This is why robust natural language interfaces are so hard to develop. At a minimum, a natural language system requires:

● Linguistic knowledge about words and grammar
● Domain knowledge about the specific topic of conversation
● Common sense knowledge about the world around us (e.g. in the example above, knowledge about *time* constitutes common sense knowledge)
● Knowledge about the user, especially his intentions and goals.

It is this latter knowledge which is particularly helpful in disambiguating the user's utterances.

Generally, a user enters into a dialogue with a computer with specific purposes in mind: (1) to receive assistance in solving a problem; (2) to learn whether the machine has access to a particular piece of information and to have the machine tell us what it is; (3) to get the machine to perform a specific action; or (4) to have the machine explain its actions or some piece of information (Levin and Moore, 1977). Knowing the user's purpose helps the computer interpret the utterance because it helps establish expectations about what is likely to be said next and what shifts in focus are likely to occur. Also, it helps the system determine the type of response it should make.

If the utterance is a non-sequitur, then the computer should be able to acknowledge it and carry on (Cleal and Heaton, 1988). If a request or utterance shows that a user is confused or working with incorrect presuppositions, then the system probably needs to back up and re-explain itself or, at least, correct the user. Even when the utterance is a simple request for information, the computer still needs to attend to all its nuances.

For example, if a user commands, *Show me the sales figures for the past five years*, he probably doesn't want to see a simple listing of the figures. At a minimum, he wants the figures shown by year. Similarly, if the user asks, *Do you have the expense figures for the current year?*, then a simple *yes* or *no* probably won't do. In short, the system needs to provide cooperative responses (Kaplan, 1982; Kao, 1988). If the natural language processor only possesses linguistic knowledge, it is impossible to provide responses of this nature.

3.5.4 Architecture of a Conversational Advisory System

Within the financial and decision support arena there seems to be a renewed interest in natural language frontends. For example, a recent news announcement indicated that the Dow Jones New/Retrieval Service was turning to a natural language frontend running on a Connection Machine in an effort to reduce the complexities faced by users of the service. The popularity of HAL, Lotus Corporation's natural language interface to the 1-2-3 spreadsheet, is also indicative of this interest. A variety of other prototypes have also been developed. One is Blanning's (1984) Merlin system which serves as a natural language frontend to a traditional DSS. Another example is the Intelligent Financial Quote System (Sobrowski and Tischlu, 1988), a Prolog-based interface to a general purpose *financial data system* designed for *traders*. With the interface, a trader can make natural language requests of the following sort: *Let me know when stock XYZ hits 128.*

With the exception of the natural language facility running on the Connection Machine (which is an outgrowth of a long tradition of work by Waltz), HAL and the prototypes mentioned above are basically keyword systems. Developing a keyword interface that can handle a fairly wide range of utterances in a circumscribed domain is a fairly easy task. Practically, any book on Prolog programming provides the basic procedures for constructing this type of interface (for example, Schildt, 1987). But keyword systems rest on the beneficence of the user. That is, they all assume that the user will only input complete and meaningful statements.

Obviously, this means that keyword systems are incapable of carrying on dialogue with the user. The same can also be said of other more sophisticated systems. Virtually none of the commercial natural language interface products has this capability. In general, commercial natural language products are designed for portability so that they can interface with any database regardless of its specific content. But portability precludes domain-specific knowledge and knowledge about the user's intentions.

Among the commercial products currently available, only those developed by Cognitive Systems have the capability to carry on a *conversation*. Cognitive Systems is a commercial offshoot of Schank's AI group at Yale. For quite some time, Schank's former and current students have been developing natural language systems that attempt to understand dialogue (primarily in written form) by determining, among other things, the goals and intentions of the dialogue participants (Cullingford, 1986; Wilensky, 1983; Dyer, 1983). The commercial efforts of Cognitive Systems reflect this tradition.

Recently, Cognitive Systems has focused on the development of *Conversational Advisory Systems* (CAS). To distance themselves from the developers of ES, Schank and his followers have defined a CAS as a simulation of a person with a moderate level of knowledge: enough knowledge to provide advice to a novice or infrequent user (Schank and Schwartz, 1985; Schwartz, 1988).

One example of a CAS is TIBS, an integrated small business accounting system with a conversational interface. The developers contend that, as more knowledge is added to the system, it will have the capability to provide the executive with an MBA-level advisor on his *desktop* (Schank and Schwartz, 1985). Other examples of CAS are the LeCourtier and Streetsmart systems which provide consumers with advice on financial investments. LeCourtier offers advice on Belgian stocks. The kinds of input with which it can deal are illustrated by the following sequence of user statements (Schwartz, 1988):

(1) I want to buy stocks
(2) Should I buy SGB?
(3) What does alpha mean?
(4) Show me all the companies with alphas less than 3.
(5) Which have net profits greater than 200 million?

(6) Do you recommend bonds?
(7) Why?

In the same vein, Streetsmart offers advice on NYSE stocks from the view-point of five investment strategies. The type of conversations it can handle are shown below (Cognitive Systems, 1987):

(1) I'd like to use the STEADFAST strategy.
(2) How am I doing?
(3) What do you think of my portfolio?
(4) What do you think of IBM?
(5) What do you think, HIGHRETURN (note: HIGHRETURN is another strategy)

Both sequences indicate that a CAS is capable of handling not only standard database queries but also questions about advice and explanation and shifts in user focus.

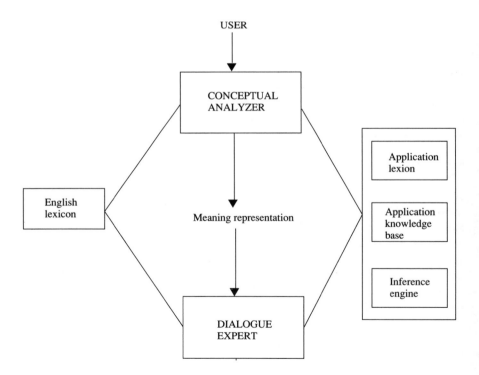

FIGURE 3.4   Architecture of a conversational advisory system (Adapted from Schwartz, 1988)

How are conversations of this sort carried out? The general architecture underlying a CAS is shown in Figure 3.4. As the figure indicates, it is the job of the conceptual analyzer to produce an internal knowledge representation of the user's utterances. The representation, used by Schank and his followers, is called *conceptual dependency* and is well documented in a number of places (Schank and Reisbeck, 1981). A large number of other schemes are also possible (for detailed discussions the reader is referred to Allen, 1987). Once the representation is produced, it is the task of the dialogue handler (also known as a goal monitor) to track the conversation and produce responses. The architecture confirms the supposition that a broad range of knowledge, including domain specific knowledge, is required to produce advice in a conversational fashion.

3.5.5 What If A Computer Could Converse Like You and Me?

For senior management the benefits of CAS are obvious, less training being one. The executive can carry on a dialogue with the system in much the same way that he or she converses with a human advisor or staff assistant. There is no need to learn a new language. Another benefit is that fairly complex ideas and requests can be stated in simple terms. For instance, a question like, *Which is the best pricing strategy?* is easy to state in English, even though it requires a tremendous amount of behind-the-scenes knowledge and computation to answer.

As strong as these benefits seem, there are still limits and drawbacks to natural language processing. The fact of the matter is, *You can't talk to a CAS like you talk to a human advisor.* For one thing, you have to type at a CAS; you can't talk to it. But this is a minor irritant. Executives have shown that they are willing to type if the need is strong enough (Cross, 1988). For instance, many executives show no hesitancy in using e-mail systems, even though they require typing. But even if CAS could understand speech, the current generation is still in its infancy and has a number of important limits. Some of these are described below:

One sentence at a time: Like the natural language interfaces to databases, CAS only deal with a single sentence at a time. This means that problems or thoughts of interest must be broken down into a series of individual steps or statements. Although the steps are not as tedious as those used in producing procedural algorithms, they can be involved, especially if you're not sure what you want.

Imagine the process of producing some table of interest. It may take a series of queries to produce exactly the *right* table. The problem with natural language is that you're often not sure as to how you produced the results. It's easy to lose the flow of the conversation. You just can't ask the machine, *Now, how did I do this?* or *Where are we?* or *Is there a better way to get these results?* If you want to produce the same results again, you may have to repeat a long series of queries, even though there may be a very simple set of formal commands for doing so.

Producing the desired response: As long as the interface is responding the way we think it should, everything is fine. But what if the answer or results are incorrect or not quite what you want? How do you debug the output? Obviously, the only thing you can do is change the words or syntax.

For quite some time, the developers of natural language interfaces have been aware that users have difficulties in determining the syntactic and semantic limits of the system. This is why the interfaces handle questions like, *What do you know?* or *What do you know about Table XYZ?* It's also why some of the developers created alternative modes of input like *natural language menus* so that users can't input incorrect words or statements, but these features only handle part of the problem. Just like a formal language, you can have a syntactically and semantically correct statement but your logic can be wrong; you can enter a perfectly legal statement, yet the results that are produced are not what you want. For novice and inexperienced users, the process of debugging a natural language query, though occasionally humorous, can often be frustrating.

Only one domain at a time: CAS are like ES. They can do only one thing well. As their architecture indicates, they are only designed to work within a specific domain. If they worked in multiple domains, they would be virtually impossible to develop (at least at the present time). They rely quite heavily on the fact that the user's input is restricted to a set of narrow topics. Even when the domain is restricted, it is still much harder to develop a CAS than it is to develop an ES (time quotes for various activities are provided by Schank and Schwartz, 1985). The reason is apparent.

In CAS an ES is only one of the components. The fact that CAS are restricted to single domains also implies that it may be impossible to develop a *conversational* interface (not natural language frontend) to an *Intelligent Frontend* (IFE). An IFE allows the user to work in multiple domains, because the conventional system to which it is attached does so. To carry on a conversation with the user, the interface would have to have built-in knowledge of all these domains. This is beyond the current capabilities of existing natural language systems, although we should note that there are efforts currently underway to develop large knowledge base systems with encyclopedic knowledge and common sense reasoning (Lenat *et al.*, 1986).

All of these limits pinpoint the fact that talking to a CAS is not like talking to a human advisor or assistant. With the human advisor or assistant, it is his or her job to understand what the executive wants and to produce the requested information or advice. If the results are not the desired ones, then it is the assistant's job to correct them—not the executive's job. If the executive asks for something outside the realm of the assistant's expertise, then the executive can readily turn to another assistant for advice or the assistant, himself, can do so.

3.6 INTELLIGENT AGENTS

While there are differences among the three approaches discussed thus far, they all encourage the illusion that the system is anthropomorphic. Regardless of whether the machine is an expert or simply an advisor, all of the systems lead the user to believe that they are engaging in a dialogue with a human. An intelligent agent is also based on an anthropomorphic metaphor, i.e. a *software robot*. In this case, however, the user doesn't engage in a dialogue with the system.

Instead, the agent acts as the user's representative, bringing important events to the user's attention and performing (specified) actions on the user's behalf. In terms of functionality, agents share an important characteristic with *intelligent frontends*. That is, they provide the means to capture an advisor's or assistant's *knowledge of use*. The difference is that instead of *hardwiring* this knowledge into the system, the planner, analyst or staff assistant is given a language for embedding this knowledge himself. Another difference is that unlike experts which possess a large store of knowledge, an individual agent is a small entity that only knows how to do one or two things well. The way in which an agent is surfaced to the user is also much more transparent. In fact, in many cases the user of the application is really unaware of the agent's existence.

In a moment we will illustrate the use of agents with a prototype system we're developing at Execucom. The prototype, which is called a *smart spreadsheet*, is designed to help executives automatically monitor data patterns and carry out prescribed plans of analysis based on the patterns. Before we describe the prototype, we briefly consider the notion of an *agent* in more general terms.

3.6.1 Agents Defined

The concept of an *agent* is a direct descendant of John McCarthy's *advice taker*. The term agent was coined in the middle sixties by Selfridge. What both researchers had in mind was a system entity that, when given a goal, could carry out the appropriate computer operations and could ask for and receive advice when stuck. An agent would be a "soft robot" living and doing its business within the computer's *world* (Kay, 1984). Woods (1987; 1988) has used the concept of intelligent agents as a focal point for the design of larger knowledge based systems. To Woods, an intelligent agent is basically a knowledge based system which is perpetually engaged in a cybernetic loop of perceiving things, reasoning about them, and *taking actions.* The pervasive power of these agents is found in their procedural attachments. As Woods (1988) states,

> The kinds of intelligent computer agents that are needed for a variety of tasks are very much like intelligent organisms trying to get along in the world (trying to find enough food, stay out of trouble, satisfy basic needs, etc.). The most valuable service played by an internal knowledge base for such an organism is to answer such questions like *"What's going on out there? Can it harm me? How can I avoid/placate it? Is it good to eat? Is there any special thing I should do about it?..."* The roles of knowledge for an intelligent agent are very similar. The basic goals of food collection and danger avoidance are replaced by goals of doing what the user wants and avoiding things that the machine has been instructed to do. However, the fundamental problem of analyzing a situation in order to determine whether it is one for which there are procedures to be executed or one to be avoided are basically the same.

Agents have been used in a variety of prototypes and products in a number of different ways. Some examples are listed below:

- Hewlett-Packard's New Wave development environment contains an entity which they call the *agent.* Agents are basically command files that can run in the foreground or background and perform a range of services. An example is an agent that can automatically update graphs and written reports as the underlying data on which they are based changes.
- A number of *Trader's Workstations* use intelligent monitors to track changes in stock prices. Monitors are basically agents that work in the background. When changes in prices conform with some predefined pattern, the monitor pops up to inform the trader (Leinweber, 1988; Sobkowski, 1988).
- The NewsPeek demo developed at MIT's Media Lab (Brand, 1987) is a selective, semi-automatic newspaper that knows the personal preferences of the reader. It's based on the idea of an inquisitive robot that selectively browses the Dow Jones News Retrieval Service, Nexis, XPress, the wire services and television news on behalf of the reader.
- Researchers at the University of Pennsylvania (Kalita, 1988) have developed a system which assists the secretary of an academic journal by keeping track of the submission of referee's reports. Underlying the system is a set of agents which monitor schedules and deadlines.
- At MIT, Malone *et al.* (1986) have created a facility for filtering and categorizing e-mail messages. The facility immediately informs the user of messages he considers urgent, deletes messages the user considers to be superfluous and places other in various folders depending

on their content. The agent which performs these tasks in the background is known as an *Information Lens*.

What these examples appear to have in common is that agents are used often as monitors which perform various actions depending on the nature of the events they have been assigned to watch.

3.6.2 The Use of Agents in Executive Support

Theoretically, intelligent agents can serve a multitude of purposes in an EIS. The role of monitor, however, appears most promising. Regardless of whether an executive is viewed as a *problem-worker* or a *decision-maker*, one of the primary roles of the executive is that of *monitor* (Mintzberg, 1973; Anthony, 1965). Executives spend a sizable portion of time scanning a variety of internal and external data in search of opportunities and problems. Indeed, the vast majority of EIS have been developed to monitor organizational performance and, in many cases, the activities of competitors (Rockhart and DeLong, 1988).

The way in which *monitoring* is accomplished in existing EIS is that the EIS builder specifies results (variances) which the organization considers, *a priori*, to be *unusual*. Any time an unusual result appears in a screen display, the result is highlighted in some fashion (e.g. the figure is shown in red). While this eliminates the time needed to consider each piece of information to determine if it is unusual, it still forces the executive to interpret the results and infer what they portend for the future. The raison d' être for monitoring a situation, however, is not simply to detect or highlight the result. At a minimum, monitoring is an integral part of a feedback loop in which desired results or plans are compared to actual results in order to detect differences so that remedial action can be taken.

The monitoring tools provided by existing EIS generators are incapable of assisting the executive throughout the entire loop, because the monitoring facilities they provide lack procedural attachments. Given a strong set of procedural attachments— compatible with those in other knowledge based systems—agents or monitors could certainly be designed to automatically describe *what had happened* and *why* to draw various conclusions and to make various recommendations. In other words agents can potentially form the foundation for a *computerized assistant*. It isn't that the agent is an expert; instead, it is simply a software entity that acts on our behalf.

3.6.3 An Example

To illustrate the potential use of agents in an EIS, we will consider a simple prototype which we call a *smart spreadsheet*. Actually, the prototype is based on a *modeling* paradigm rather than a *spreadsheet* paradigm and is part of a much larger system which runs on Sun Workstations. A major component of the prototype is a facility which we label *monitors*. Within the spreadsheet, monitors serve as user-defined agents that look for data patterns and can carry out various activities once the patterns occur.

To understand how the monitors function, let's return to the sample problem described at the beginning of the discussion (recall Figure 3.1). To simplify the example, suppose the fast food corporation is made up of two regions, West and East, and that the revenue figures for the consolidated corporation are those shown in Figure 3.5. Looking at this figure, we find that revenues are down. Immediately, a couple of questions come to mind. Is *the problem corporate-wide or is it due to a single region?*, and *What are the primary factors contributing to the downfall?*

In the prototype a detailed explanation of the difference in *Corp Revenues* from *Budget* to *Actual* can be obtained automatically by clicking on the value in the *Actual* column and then selecting *Explain* from the *Analyze* menu (Figure 3.6). The resulting explanation is displayed in Figure 3.7; it indicates that the difference is due to increase in Food Expenses for Region 1. As noted earlier, this *Explanation* facility already exists in some of our other products (e.g. IFPS and Executive Edge), although the interface

---

Model : Corp.mod

File   Edit   Build   Display   Solve   Plot   Analyze   Help

		A	B	C	D	E	F	G
		Budget	Actual	Variance				
1	Unit Price	1.25	1.25	0.00				
2	East Food Expenses	50.00	75.00	25.00				
3	East G & A	10.00	12.00	2.00				
4	East Wages	40.00	40.00	0.00				
5	East Expenses	100.00	127.00	0.00				
6	East Units Sold	60.00	160.00	27.00				
7	East Sales	200.00	200.00	0.00				
8	East Revenues	100.00	73.00	-27.00				
9	West Food Expenses	60.00	65.00	5.00				
10	West G & A	10.00	9.00	-1.00				
11	West Wages	50.00	50.00	0.00				
12	West Expenses	120.00	124.00	4.00				
13	West Units Sold	240.00	240.00	0.00				
14	West Sales	300.00	300.00	0.00				
15	West Revenues	180.00	176.00	-4.00				
16	Corp Expenses	220.00	251.00	31.00				
17	Corp Sales	500.00	500.00	0.00				
18	Corp Revenues	280.00	249.00	-31.00				
19								
20								

Cursor : B18   Value: East Revenues + West Revenues

FIGURE 3.5   Spreadsheet of consolidated corporate results

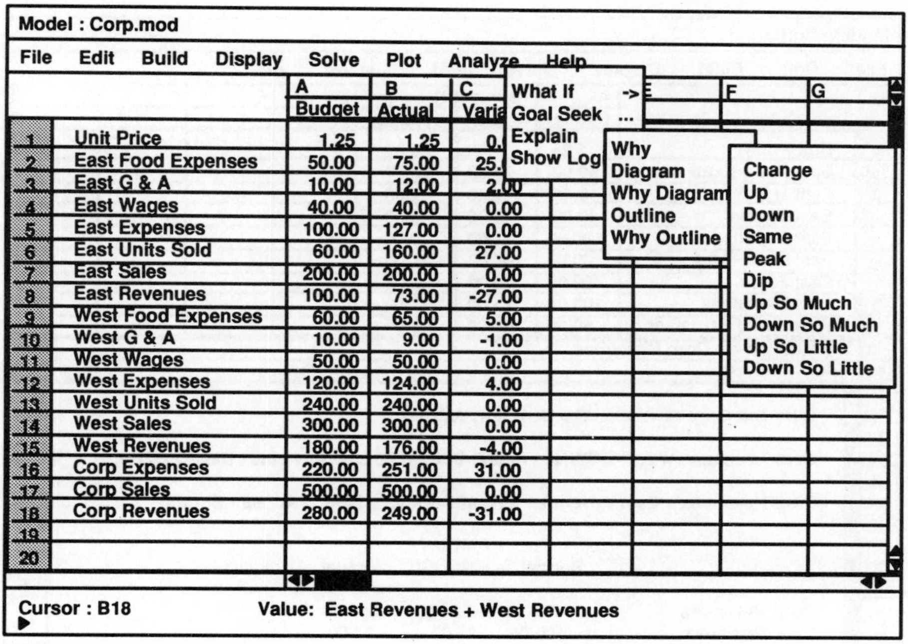

Model : Corp.mod

| File | Edit | Build | Display | Solve | Plot | Analyze | Help | | |

	A	B	C	What If → E	F	G
	Budget	Actual	Varia	Goal Seek ...		
1 Unit Price	1.25	1.25	0.	Explain		
2 East Food Expenses	50.00	75.00	25.	Show Log	Why	
3 East G & A	10.00	12.00	2.00		Diagram	Change
4 East Wages	40.00	40.00	0.00		Why Diagram	Up
5 East Expenses	100.00	127.00	0.00		Outline	Down
6 East Units Sold	60.00	160.00	27.00		Why Outline	Same
7 East Sales	200.00	200.00	0.00			Peak
8 East Revenues	100.00	73.00	-27.00			Dip
9 West Food Expenses	60.00	65.00	5.00			Up So Much
10 West G & A	10.00	9.00	-1.00			Down So Much
11 West Wages	50.00	50.00	0.00			Up So Little
12 West Expenses	120.00	124.00	4.00			Down So Little
13 West Units Sold	240.00	240.00	0.00			
14 West Sales	300.00	300.00	0.00			
15 West Revenues	180.00	176.00	-4.00			
16 Corp Expenses	220.00	251.00	31.00			
17 Corp Sales	500.00	500.00	0.00			
18 Corp Revenues	280.00	249.00	-31.00			
19						
20						

Cursor : B18   Value: **East Revenues + West Revenues**

FIGURE 3.6   Explaining corporate results

in this prototype is substantially different. Readers interested in a detailed description of the facility are referred to King (1986).

The problem with deriving the explanation in this manner is that it requires the user—in this case the executive—to locate the variances of interest and to know something about the various menu picks available in the system. As one alternative, we can place a *monitor* on the cell(s), row(s) or column(s) of interest and then have the monitor not only highlight the cell but also activate the explanation or any other task for that matter.

To establish a monitor in the spreadsheet, the application builder (analyst, planner, etc.), first selects the cell(s) of interest. Next, the *F*2 key is typed (in reality the key sequence is different). At this point, the monitor dialogue box shown in Figure 3.8 appears. This allows the application builder to establish two values against which the cell value (or each of the values in a row, column or block) is compared.

If the first comparison is true, then the cell value will be displayed in italics; if the second is true, then the cell value will be displayed in bold. The syntax for comparisons is like the syntax for SQL *where* clause. In this example, we are attaching a monitor to the *Percent Variance* column and highlighting in bold those cell values outside a 10% range (i.e. not in (-10..10)).

Model : Corp.mod

| File | Edit | Build | Display | Solve | Plot | Analyze | Help |

		A	B	C	D	E	F	G
		Budget	Actual	Variance				
1	Unit Price	1.25	1.25	0.00				
2	East Food Expenses	50.00	75.00	25.00				
3	East G & A	10.00	12.00	2.00				
4	East Wages	40.00	40.00	0.00				
5	East Expenses	100.00	127.00	0.00				
6	East Units Sold	60.00	160.00	27.00				
7	East Sales	200.00	200.00	0.00				
8	East Revenues	100.00	73.00	-27.00				
9	West Food Expenses	60.00	65.00	5.00				

Explanation of: Corp Revenues

| File | Analyze |

WHY DID Corp Revenues GO DOWN IN Actual?

Corp Revenues WENT DOWN in Actual BECAUSE East Revenues DECREASED.

Corp Revenues = East Revenues + West Revenues FOR 2, Actual - Budget

	Budget	AMOUNT CHANGE	Actual
Corp Revenues	280.00	-32.00	249.00
East Revenues	100.00	-27.00	73.00

FIGURE 3.7   Explanatory text produced by "Explain"

When the dialogue box is closed, the spreadsheet appears as shown in Figure 3.9. Thus, when the executive looks at it he or she will see *unusual* results shown in bold. Of course, in this case, values defined in this way can be problematic or pleasing (i.e. revenues below -10% versus those above 10%).

So, in addition to the *Percent Variance* column we have also added an *Alert* column which shows those values that are *OK*, those that are *Problems* and those that are *Looking Good* (this is done with an IF/THEN/ELSE test). If the displays had been in color, we might have used three separate colors to denote the differences.

Thus far, the display is essentially the same as any EIS. More important than the ability to highlight a cell, however, is the ability to attach a *Script* to the monitor. In our prototype this is done by typing in the name of the *Script* at the bottom of the monitor dialogue box in Figure 3.8. Figure 3.10 displays the *Script* associated with this monitor. In the prototype, the script language we use is fairly primitive. Basically, it's modeled after Apple's HyperCard product, although the objects and actions are unique to the prototype. Without going into detail, the language revolves around a set

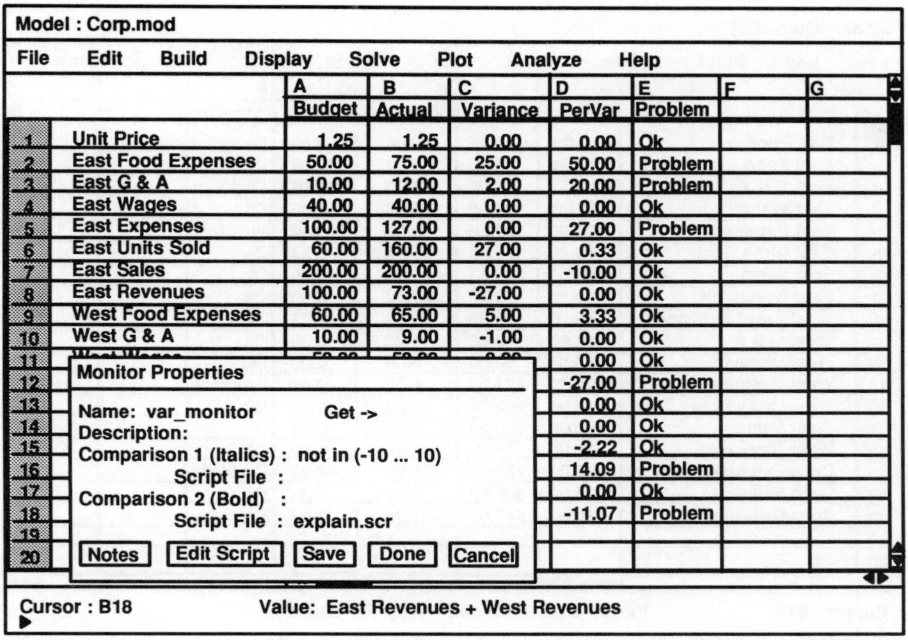

Model : Corp.mod

| File | Edit | Build | Display | Solve | Plot | Analyze | Help |

	A Budget	B Actual	C Variance	D PerVar	E Problem	F	G
1 Unit Price	1.25	1.25	0.00	0.00	Ok		
2 East Food Expenses	50.00	75.00	25.00	50.00	Problem		
3 East G & A	10.00	12.00	2.00	20.00	Problem		
4 East Wages	40.00	40.00	0.00	0.00	Ok		
5 East Expenses	100.00	127.00	0.00	27.00	Problem		
6 East Units Sold	60.00	160.00	27.00	0.33	Ok		
7 East Sales	200.00	200.00	0.00	-10.00	Ok		
8 East Revenues	100.00	73.00	-27.00	0.00	Ok		
9 West Food Expenses	60.00	65.00	5.00	3.33	Ok		
10 West G & A	10.00	9.00	-1.00	0.00	Ok		
11				0.00	Ok		
12				-27.00	Problem		
13				0.00	Ok		
14				0.00	Ok		
15				-2.22	Ok		
16				14.09	Problem		
17				0.00	Ok		
18				-11.07	Problem		
19							
20							

Monitor Properties

Name: var_monitor   Get ->
Description:
Comparison 1 (Italics) : not in (-10 ... 10)
          Script File :
Comparison 2 (Bold) :
          Script File : explain.scr

[Notes] [Edit Script] [Save] [Done] [Cancel]

Cursor : B18   Value: East Revenues + West Revenues

FIGURE 3.8   Dialog box for creating monitors

of global variables (e.g. *curvar* and *endrow*), user-defined local variables (e.g. ?X), objects (e.g. models and explanations), actions (e.g. show), and standard control logic. The control logic also permits *chaining* processes similar to the *forward* and *backward* chaining found in an ES. The language can be used to alter the values in an object or to activate other objects. Within the language a distinction is made between the *activation* of an object and the *display* of an object. For example, the statement *model xyz* brings the model into memory, while the command *show model xyz* displays it in a spreadsheet window.

In our prototype scripts are activated in a couple of ways. First, the user can select one of the *unusual* cells and type *F3*. When this is done the underlying script is invoked. In this case, the user will be presented with a dialogue box informing him that *Revenues are under budget* and asking whether or not he wants to see an *Explanation*. Assuming that the user selects *OK*, the explanation will then be shown along with a plot of *expenses* or *revenues* depending on which variables were determined to be most important in the explanation.

The second way to invoke a monitor script is to access the *Alarm* menu at the top of the spreadsheet window (see Figure 3.9). A model can have

Model : Corp.mod							
File Edit Build Display Solve Plot Analyze Help						● Alarms	

		A	B	C	D	E	F	G
		Budget	Actual	Variance	PerVar	Problem		
1	Unit Price	1.25	1.25	0.00	0.00	Ok		
2	East Food Expenses	50.00	75.00	25.00	-50.00	Problem		
3	East G & A	10.00	12.00	2.00	-20.00	Problem		
4	East Wages	40.00	40.00	0.00	0.00	Ok		
5	East Expenses	100.00	127.00	0.00	-27.00	Problem		
6	East Units Sold	60.00	160.00	27.00	0.33	Ok		
7	East Sales	200.00	200.00	0.00	-10.00	Ok		
8	East Revenues	100.00	73.00	-27.00	0.00	Ok		
9	West Food Expenses	60.00	65.00	5.00	3.33	Ok		
10	West G & A	10.00	9.00	-1.00	0.00	Ok		
11	West Wages	50.00	50.00	0.00	0.00	Ok		
12	West Expenses	120.00	124.00	4.00	-27.00	Problem		
13	West Units Sold	240.00	240.00	0.00	0.00	Ok		
14	West Sales	300.00	300.00	0.00	0.00	Ok		
15	West Revenues	180.00	176.00	-4.00	-2.22	Ok		
16	Corp Expenses	220.00	251.00	31.00	-14.09	Problem		
17	Corp Sales	500.00	500.00	0.00	0.00	Ok		
18	Corp Revenues	280.00	249.00	-31.00	-11.07	Problem		
19								
20								

Cursor : B18	Value: East Revenues + West Revenues

FIGURE 3.9   Values highlighted by variance monitor (NB: strike outs added for demonstration purposes)

multiple monitors attached to it. Any time one of these goes off, the alarm appears at the top of the spreadsheet. When the user selects this menu he is shown a list describing all the monitors which have been *fired*. When the user picks one of the entries on this list, the accompanying script is activated.

What the prototype currently lacks is the ability to automatically invoke scripts. It is not too hard to imagine the problems that might arise if scripts could be activated automatically. Suppose an executive decides to browse one or more spreadsheet displays where each display has 5 or 10 monitors *going off* simultaneously. The question is, *In what order should the scripts be invoked?*, and *What happens if the scripts compete for the same resources or require divergent actions on the part of the user?* It is the same set of questions that arises with any distributed AI system (Huhns, 1987). These questions have been addressed in a variety of ways. We will simply note that we have examined and are prototyping a variety of strategies. Some of those we have considered include:

● Multi-agent planning strategies (Sacredotti, 1977; Wilensky, 1983; Hahn and Jarke, 1988).
● Blackboard Architectures (Nii, 1986a, b).

```
TextEdit : explain.scr
Dialog "Revenues are under Budget. Do you
wish to see an Explanation?
 button "Ok"
 button "Cancel"
end {dialog}

if Dialog = 1
then
  show explain Corp Revenues
  if exptop = "East Revenues"
    then
      set currow East Sales [Budget]
      set endrow East Revenues [Actual]
      show plot (type = 3d)
    end
  if exptop = "West Revenues"
    then
      set currow West Sales [Budget]
      set endrow West Sales [Actual]
      show plot (type = 3d)
    end
if exptop = "East Expenses"
    then
      set currow East Food Expenses [Budget]
      set endrow East Wages [Actual]
      show plot (type = 3d)
    end
  if exptop = "West Expenses"
    then
      set currow West Food Expenses [Budget]
      set endrow West Wages [Actual]
      show plot (type = 3d)
    end
end {if dialog}
```

FIGURE 3.10   Sample script

- Defeasible Reasoning (Covington, 1988).
- Taxonomic Lattices (Woods, 1987; 1988).

The *smart spreadsheet*, illustrated above, is simply one example of how intelligent agents can be used to automate the activities of an analyst or planner and to present them to an executive in a familiar form. In this case what the executive sees is a report with a set of highlighted values. All the executive has to know is that by clicking on some value of interest he will either be presented with a set of options for further analysis or some pre-determined analysis will automatically be performed.

3.6.4 Catering to the Style of the Executive

The WIMP interface (windows, icons, mice and pointing) around which the prototype is built is easy to learn and encourages the development of applications which require minimal action on the part of the user. In this case all the executive has to do is point. However, because the spreadsheet is active, the interface in the prototype also allows the executive to perform more detailed analysis (e.g. goalseeking), if he so desires. Of course, not everyone is enamored with the *desktop* metaphor. Experiences have shown that EIS needs to be flexible enough to conform to the workstyle and habits of the executive.

In the consolidation problem, for instance, some executives might prefer to see an organization chart with each box in the chart containing a revenue figure and appearing in a different color to indicate whether revenues are above or below plan. Others might want to see a summary report where various elements in the report are *hot buttons* linked to more detailed display analyses. Still others might not want to be bothered with a display at all, unless the revenues were deemed to be problematic; in which case, the agent assigned the task of monitoring the revenues would send them a memo through e-mail.

In the final analysis, what is required to create *individualized* systems of the type described above is a script language which enables development of *hypertext* or *hypermedia* systems with agents (i.e. embedded expert or knowledge based systems that can be automatically invoked). The assumption has been that script languages with this capability will be simpler for application builders to use than the languages used to develop expert systems. However, while a script language with these capabilities certainly allows development of *individualized* systems, there is no reason to believe that they are any easier to use than the programming languages found in an ES shell.

In fact, there is some evidence that they may be harder to use and possibly harder for commercial vendors to develop. Daniel Goodman, who has written a number of guides to the HyperCard product, has noted that because of the complexities of the HyperTalk language very few *original* HyperCard stacks have been developed. Alan Kay, an ardent proponent of *agents*, has commented that an *agent is harder to engineer than an expert system.*

3.7 CONCLUSION

In 1945 Vannevar Bush proposed the development of an information system which could store and access an individual's books, records, and communications with exceeding speed and *flexibility*. The device, based on micro-file technology and a precursor to modern hypertext systems, was meant to serve as an enlarged, intimate supplement to the individual's *memory*.

Today, as then, researchers and practitioners are still pondering the development of such systems. The current systems, however, have taken the form of computerized assistants or advisors with the added capabilities of analyzing the decisions facing us, presenting us with suggested courses of action and determining the probable consequences of these actions. Computerized assistants with encyclopedic knowledge are clearly a thing of the future. To date, what we have been able to develop is some mockups like Apple Computer's *Knowledge Navigator* and MIT's *Conversational Desktop* (Brand, 1987) and some prototypes and products which work in very specialized domains.

In this chapter we have considered four approaches to tackling the problem of building a *Computerized Financial Advisor*: financial expert systems, intelligent frontends, conversational advisory systems and intelligent agents. In comparing the approaches, the discussion focused on the *ease* with which the various approaches could be used to create applications for senior management. Applications of this sort, like any application, require a number of features to ensure *ease of use*. In this discussion we have been primarily concerned with the following factors:

- Does the application allow the executive to define problems and tasks in a language and at a level with which he is familiar?
- Does the application allow the executive to deal with a broad range of issues and topics or is it domain-specific?
- Are the contents and limits of the application readily apparent?
- Is the application controlled by the system or does it permit mixed-initiative dialogue?

Throughout the discussion we have treated the approaches as if they were separate paradigms. This was done in an effort to highlight the position of these approaches on the above factors—to indicate some of their benefits and drawbacks as a foundation for a computerized advisor for senior management. It would be convenient if the approaches were actually that separate, then we could easily pinpoint their positions with respect to these factors and choose the one that appeared most promising. In reality this can't be done.

The work being done on each of the approaches is too intertwined. Knowledge representation and reasoning are at the base of all these approaches. The work being done on monitors employs some of the representation schemes used in natural language and intelligent frontends. Systems are being created which allow users to establish monitors with natural language commands. Intelligent frontends are actually expert systems which emulate an expert who knows all the intricacies of analytical tools. The result is that prototypes and products are now appearing that combine all of these technologies. A good example is the *Trader's*

Workstation (Leinweber, 1988) that uses several innovations: windowing display technology; monitors; C-routines for real-time computations and communications; the CLIPS ES shell for doing reasoning in a forward chaining mode; and neural nets for doing pattern analysis. The fact that these approaches are becoming so intertwined is simple to understand. Their aims are ambitious. The problems they attack are so complex that they can't be solved by wearing blinders. Clearly, no single approach or paradigm has all the answers.

REFERENCES

Allen, J. (1987). *Natural Language Understanding*, Benjamin Cummings, Menlo Park, Calif.

Anthony, R. (1965). *Planning and Control Systems: A Framework for Analysis*. Division of Research, Harvard Business School.

Basden, A. (1984). On the Application of Expert Systems, in *Developments in Expert Systems* (Ed. M. Coombs), pp. 59–76, Academic Press, New York.

Blanning, B. (1984). Conversing with Management Information Systems in Natural Language, *Communications of the ACM*, **27**, 201–207.

Blanning, B. (1987). A Survey of Issues in Expert Systems for Management, in *Expert Systems in Business* (Ed. B. Silverman), pp. 24-39, Addison-Wesley, Reading, Mass.

Brand, S. (1987). *The Media Lab: Inventing the Future at MIT*, Viking, New York.

Buchanan, B., D. Barstow, R. Bechtel, J. Bennett, W. Clancey, C. Kulikowski, T. Mitchell and D. Waterman (1983), Constructing Expert Systems, in *Building Expert Systems* (Eds. F. Hayes-Roth, D. Waterman, and D. Lenat), pp. 127–168, Addison-Wesley, Reading, Mass.

Carbonnell, J. (1985). The Role of the User Modelling in Natural Language Interface Design, in *Applications of Artificial Intelligence* (Ed. S. Andriole), Petrocelli Books, Princeton, NJ.

Cleal, D. and N. Heaton (1988). *Knowledge-Based Systems: Implications for Human-Computer Interfaces*, Ellis Horwood Books, Chichester, England.

Coombs, M. and J. Alty (1984). Expert Systems: An Alternative Paradigm, in *Developments in Expert Systems* (Ed. M. Coombs), pp. 135–158, Academic Press, New York.

Covington, M., D. Nute and A. Vellino (1988). *Prolog Programming in Depth*, Scott, Foresman and Company, Glenview, Ill.

Cross, T. (1988). *Knowledge Engineering: The Uses of Artificial Intelligence in Business*, Brady Books, New York.

Cullingford, R. (1986). *Natural Language Processing*, Rowman and Littlefield, Towata, NJ.

Cullingford, R., M. Krueger, M. Slefridge, and M. Bienkowski (1982). Automated Explanations as a Component of Computer Aided Design Systems, *IEEE Transactions on Systems, Man and Cybernetics*, **2**, 168–182.

Dyer, M. (1983). *In-Depth Understanding*, MIT Press, Cambridge, Mass.

Gale W. (1986). REX Review, in *Artificial Intelligence and Statistics* (Ed. W. Gale), pp. 173–228, Addison-Wesley, Reading, Mass.

Garson, B. (1988). *The Electronic Sweatshop*, Simon and Schuster, New York.

Gerstein, M. (1987). *The Technology Connection*, Addison-Wesley, Reading, Mass.

Gongla, P. (1988). Doing Strategic Information Management: How an Expert System Can Help, Invited Paper, *Conference on Computers in Business Schools:*

Keeping Pace with Change, University of Calgary, Alberta, Canada.

Hahn, U. and M. Jarke (1988). A Multi-Agent Reasoning Model for Negotiation Support, in *Organizational Decision Support Systems* (Eds. R. Lee, A. McCosh, and P. Migliarese), Elsevier, Amsterdam.

Harmon, P. and D. King (1985). *Expert Systems: Artificial Intelligence in Business*, Wiley, New York.

Hendrix, G. and Sacredotti, E. (1985). Natural Language Processing: The Field in Perspective, in *Applications of Artificial Intelligence* (Ed. S. Andriole), Petrocelli Books, Princeton, NJ.

Hewitt, C. (1970). *PLANNER: A Language for Manipulating Models and Proving Theorems in a Robot*, Research Report AI 168, MIT.

Huhns, M. (1987). *Distributed Artificial Intelligence*. Morgan Kaufmann, Los Altos, Calif.

Jackson, P. and P. Lefrere (1984). On the Application of Rule-Based Techniques to the Design of Advice Giving Systems, in *Developments in Expert Systems* (Ed. M. Coombs), pp.177–200, Academic Press, New York.

Jungduck, K. and J. Courtney (1987). *Applications of Knowledge Acquisition Techniques to Decision Support Systems*, Working Paper, Business Analysis and Research, College of Business Administration, Texas A&M University.

Kalita, J. and Shende, S. (1988). Automatically Generating Natural Language Reports in an Office Environment, *Proceedings Second Conference on Applied Natural Language Processing*, Association for Computational Linguistics, Austin, Texas, pp. 178–185.

Kaplan, J. (1982). Cooperative Responses from a Portable Natural Language Query System, *Artificial Intelligence*, **19**, 165–187.

Kay, A. (1984). Computer Software, *Scientific American*, **251**, 52–59.

Keen, P. (1983). *The On-Line CEO: How One Executive Uses MIS*, Unpublished working paper, Micro Mainframe, Inc.

Keen, P. (1988). *Competing in Time: Using Telecommunications to Competitive Advantage*, Ballinger, Cambridge, Mass.

Kershberg, L. (1984). Expert Database Systems. *Proceedings of the First International Conference on Expert Database Systems*, Kiawah Island, South Carolina, October.

King, D. (1986). ERGO: An Explanation Facility for Decision Support Systems, *Proceedings of the 6th International Workshop on Expert Systems and Their Applications*, Vol. II, Avignon, France, pp. 991–1011.

King, D. (1987). Knowledge Acquisition in Intelligent Decision Support Systems: A Case for Natural Language, *Transactions of Seventh International Conference on Decision Support Systems*, San Francisco, pp. 115–117.

Langlotz, C. and E. Shortliffe (1984). Adapting a Consultation System to Critique User Plans, in *Developments in Expert Systems* (Ed. M. Coombs), pp. 77–94, Academic Press, New York.

Lenat, D., M. Prakash and M. Shepard (1986). *CYC: Using Common Sense Knowledge to Overcome Brittleness and Knowledge Acquisition Bottlenecks, AI*, **VI**, Winter, 65–85.

Leinweber, D. (1988). Finance, in *Expert Systems and Artificial Intelligence* (Ed. T. Bartee), pp. 33–60, Howard Sams and Company, Indianapolis, Ind.

Levin, J. and J. Moore (1977). Dialogue-Games: Metacommunications Structures for Natural Language Interaction, *Cognitive Science*, **1**, 395–420.

Malhotra, A. (1975). Knowledge-Based English Language Systems for Management Support: An Analysis of Requirements, *Advanced Papers IJCAI-4*, Sept., pp. 842–847.

Malone, T., K. Grant, K. Lai, R. Rao and D. Rosenblitt (1986). Semi-Structured Messages are Surprisingly Useful for Computer-Supported Coordination,

Proceedings of CSCW'86, Conference on Computer Supported Cooperative Work, December, Austin, TX, pp. 102–114.

Mintzberg, H. (1973). *Nature of Managerial Work,* Harper and Row, New York.

Nii, P. (1986a). The Blackboard Model of Problem Solving, *AI,* **VII,** Summer, 38–53.

Nii, P. (1986b). Blackboard Systems Part Two: Blackboard Application Systems, **VII,** Conference Issue, 82-106.

O'Leary, D. (1987). An Expert System for Cash Flow Analysis, in *Proceedings of the First Annual Conference on Expert Systems in Business* (Eds. J. Feinstein, J. Liebowitz, H. Look and B. Silverman), pp. 183–190, Learned Information, New York.

Peters, T. (1987). *Thriving on Chaos,* Alfred Knopf, New York.

Porter, M. (1980). *Competitive Strategy,* Free Press, New York.

Porter, M. (1985). *Competitive Advantage,* Free Press, New York.

Rauch, W. *A Guide to Commercial Artificial Intelligence,* Prentice-Hall, Englewood Cliffs, NJ.

Reboh, R. and Risch, T. (1986). SYNTEL: Knowledge Programming Using Functional Representations, *Proceedings of Fifth National Conference on Artificial Intelligence,* August, pp.1003–1007.

Remus, W. and J. Kotteman (1986). Toward Intelligent Decision Support Systems: A Proposal for an Artificially Intelligent Statistician, *Proceedings of the Nineteenth Hawaii International Conference on Systems Sciences.*

Rensi, E. (1988). Computers at McDonalds, in *Senior Executives Speak Out* (Eds. J. McLimore and L. Larwood), pp. 159–169, Harper and Row, New York.

Rockhart, J. and D. DeLong (1988). *Executive Support Systems,* Dow Jones-Irvin, Homewood, Ille.

Roth, E., K. Bennett and D. Woods (1987). *Human Interaction with Intelligent Machines,* R&D Paper 87-1C6-HUSCI-P5, Westinghouse R&D Center, Pittsburgh, PA.

Sacredotti, E. (1977). *A Structure for Plans and Behavior,* Elsevier North-Holland, Amsterdam.

Schank, R. and C. Reisbeck (1981). *Inside Computer Understanding,* Lawrence Erlbaum, Hillsdale, NJ.

Schank, R. and S. Schwartz (1985). The Role of Knowledge Engineering in Natural Language, in *Applications of Artificial Intelligence* (Eds. S. Andriole), Petrocelli Books, Princeton, NJ.

Schildt, H. (1987). *Advanced Turbo Prolog,* McGraw-Hill, New York.

Schwartz, S. (1988). *Applied Natural Language Processing,* Petrocelli Books, Princeton, NJ.

Shpilberg, D., L. Graham and H. Schatz (1986). ExperTax: An Expert System for Corporate Tax Planning, *Expert Systems,* **3,** July.

Sobrowski, I. and F. Tischler (1988). An Intelligent Financial Quote System, *AI Expert,* April, 38–46.

Sowa, J. (1984). *Conceptual Structures,* Addison-Wesley, Reading, Mass.

Tennant, H. (1980). *Evaluation of Natural Language Processors,* Tech. Rpt. T-103, Coordinated Science Lab, University of Illinois, Urbana.

Tennant, H. (1981) *Natural Language Processing,* Petrocelli Books, New York.

Waltz, D. (1982). State of the Art in Natural-Language Understanding, in *Strategies for Natural Language Processing* (Eds. W. Lehnert and M. Ringle), pp.3–36, Lawrence Erlbaum Associates, Hillsdale, NJ.

Wilensky, R. (1982). Talking to Unix in English: An Overview of UC, *Proceedings of the Second Annual Conference on Artificial Intelligence,* Pittsburgh, PA.

Wilensky, R. (1983). *Planning and Understanding,* Addison-Wesley, Reading, MA.

Winograd, T. (1972). *Understanding Natural Language,* Academic Press, New York.

Woods, W. (1987). Knowledge Representation: What's Important About It?, in *The Knowledge Frontier* (Eds. N. Cercone and G. McCalla), pp.44–79, Springer-Verlag, New York.

Woods, W. (1988). Knowledge Representation, in *Expert Systems and Artificial Intelligence* (Ed. T. Bartee), pp. 147-176, Howard Sams and Company, Indianapolis, IN.

Wroblewski, D. and E. Rich (1988). Luke: An Early Experiment in Early Integration of Natural Language Processing, *Proceedings Second Conference on Applied Natural Language Processing*, Association for Computational Linguistics, Austin, TX, pp. 186–194.

Chapter 4

EXPERIENCES WITH OBJECT CENTERED MODELING OF FINANCIAL MARKETING

Chidanand Apte, James Griesmer, Se June Hong,
Maurice Karnaugh, John Kastner, Meir Laker, Eric Mays
Thomas J. Watson Research Center, Yorktown Heights, NY

4.1 INTRODUCTION

One primary goal of our group in IBM Research is to advance the state of methodologies for the building, maintenance, and usage of very large knowledge based systems. To this end, it is our strong belief that such advances are stimulated by building fully functional prototypes for real world problems that are complex enough to challenge the existing technologies. Many problems in business and financial decision making belong to this category. Building computer based problem solving and support systems for these problems has motivated interesting advances in more traditional fields such as operations research and decision support systems. More recently, interesting advances are being made to knowledge base technologies motivated by this class of business problems (Harmon and King, 1985). Our recent work on the FAME project is one such effort. This system is a fully functional prototype of a semi-automated problem solving consultant in the domain of financial marketing. Building this system posed many interesting problems, the resolution of which required us to make many enhancements and advances in various techniques associated with the areas of knowledge based systems.

This chapter emphasizes and details our experiences with modeling knowledge for a computer based problem solving consultant in the domain of financial marketing. Financial marketing presents a standard class of problem solving activities that are fairly common in the marketing environments of companies that produce capital equipment. Successful solving of these problems requires combining a wide latitude of skills with a vast repository of market data (past, current, and projected). Typically, such problems are tackled today by experienced human experts in conjunction with popular computational tools such as spreadsheet packages and database

Expert Systems in Business and Finance: Issues and Applications. Edited by P.R. Watkins and L.B. Eliot
© 1993 John Wiley & Sons Ltd.

systems. The advent of knowledge base technology makes it possible today to build systems that automate a larger portion of the problem solving activities. We have been experimenting successfully in the past few years with this technology to build a prototype system, FAME (Kastner *et al.*, 1986; Mays *et al.*, 1987), that provides integrated interactive problem solving expertise for financial marketing. In this chapter, we present our experiences with the FAME knowledge bases, and present our strategy for the engineering and acquisition of knowledge bases required for large scale expert systems.

4.2   THE FINANCIAL MARKETING APPLICATION

Financial marketing as an activity is pursued mainly by manufacturing companies that are in the business of producing capital intensive goods, i.e., goods that have extremely high monetary values. These range from items such as jet aircraft and ocean liners to very large mainframe computer systems. The buyers of such goods have not only to be convinced that the goods address and solve some requirements of the buyers in a technical sense, but that the acquisition of these goods does not adversely impact some of the financial constraints of the buyers. The manufacturing companies that produce these goods therefore have an additional burden of coming up with the attractive financial mechanisms that may be employed by a customer to acquire these goods. Financial marketing therefore is an activity that determines an offering which is most beneficial to a customer within an agreed set of financial parameters. Needless to say, the item must also satisfactorily address the customer's technical requirements and be competitive with other similar offerings in the marketplace. (Helfert, 1982) and (Beers, 1983) discuss in detail many of the issues related to financial marketing. This process is usually extensively supported and carried out by the manufacturer's marketing teams.

One of the more challenging aspects of financial marketing is the necessity for marketing proposals to be supported with extensive arguments for the proposal to sell. There are usually no well defined criteria for determining the best solution for the problem. This area is characterized by the lack of single answers, even from a single seller's viewpoint. It therefore becomes very important to be able to strengthen one's proposal by providing appropriate justifications and alternatives.

Financial marketing is knowledge intensive in nature. That is, not only does successful financial marketing require good marketing and financial skills, it also requires skill in mapping the products being marketed onto the customer's requirements, and the ability to combine all aspects of the problem into meaningful, efficient actions, utilizing a vast amount of market data on products and services, historical trends, competition, and the customer's corporate financial profile. Given the high volume of information, problem solving has to very frequently deal with incomplete or uncertain scenarios. This naturally gives rise to the assumption based multiple solutions. It therefore becomes very important to have convincing arguments to support these solutions. The FAME system that we have been evolving since early 1986 is a knowledge based advisory system that helps in the preparation of comprehensive financial marketing recommendations for the mainframe computer business. It helps a user in the interactive construction of a customer's financial profile, and subsequently, in designing marketing proposals. It offers a variety of automated services that can be utilized for generating competitive proposals, explanations, information walk-throughs, and related tasks.

4.3 BUILDING MAINFRAME COMPUTER MARKET KNOWLEDGE BASES

Computer based problem solving in financial marketing requires the modeling of a vast amount of expertise that exists in this field. Instead of attempting to capture this expertise in a collection of production rules, as the classical expert systems approach would suggest, we have attempted to focus upon building a deeper symbolic model of the domain. This shift in emphasis on the domain model rather than the surface expertise is motivated by the premise that a comprehensive symbolic description of domain objects and their inter-relations will provide a much more powerful base upon which a variety of expert problem solvers may reside.

This shift in emphasis towards a particular representation is supported by our initial experience with building a small prototype expert system for financial marketing in an OPS5 framework, FAME/IDV (Kastner *et al.*, 1986). This system consisted mainly of OPS5 rules along with supporting LISP functions for database manipulation, graphics handling, and some numerical computations. All of the system's control and interference processes were encoded in rules. Even with its limited scope, FAME/IDV required a large rule base of close to 800 OPS5 rules. For solving a fairly straightforward problem in financial marketing, approximately 3000 rule firings occurred and used in excess of 11 000 working memory elements. The relative magnitudes of these numbers indicated a very important point; the largest component of the system in its course of solving problems was its working memory. However, in traditional rule based systems, that component usually has the weakest representational structure. We required an alternative representation that would allow us to model this component in a more structured fashion.

4.3.1 K-Rep: The Modeling Framework

For knowledge representation, we have been experimenting with an object centered knowledge representation mechanism, K-Rep (Mays *et al.*, 1988), which views knowledge as a collection of objects in a structured inheritance network, very much influenced by, and in the style of, Kl-One (Brachman and Schmolze, 1985). K-Rep provides a mechanism for representing the very common and most natural styles of objects and their interconnections using the fundamental algebraic relations of subsumption and attribution. The primary object in K-Rep is called a concept. Concepts may be specializations of other concepts, in which case the more specific concept inherits from the more general. Attributive information about concepts is given via a binary relation (called a role relation) to some other concept. Thus one can form fairly complex descriptions, since the roles of concepts may in turn be other (complex) concepts, as well as numbers, strings, and arbitrary Lisp objects. K-Rep also provides a facility for performing definitional classification on new concepts. Based on the role relations of a new concept the classifier places it in the most specific and most general place with respect to specialization of existing concepts. Using the classifier one can perform a restricted pattern match by creating a new concept corresponding to the pattern, classifying the new concept, and retrieving those concepts which are its specializations.

Figure 4.1 illustrates in a very simple fashion the style in which knowledge is modeled in K-Rep. The class of mainframes manufactured and marketed by IBM may be represented by the object, IBM mainframes. A role, price, on the IBM mainframes object, points to an inequality object, > 0 (in K-Rep terminology, an object pointed to by a role is the value-restriction on that role). Another generic object, 3090-400E, is represented as a sub-concept of IBM mainframes, denoting a particular type of model that is an IBM mainframe. This sub-concept will subsume all of its super-concept's properties (in K-Rep terminology, inheritance). Furthermore, the 3090-400E sub-concept may have its own set of roles that can be either specializations of inherited roles (as in price) or be new definitions (as in the maintenance terms and conditions role). Although a role may point to just one object, the full semantics of a role's value restriction may reside in a object-role network reachable through that pointed object (as in the maintenance terms and conditions role). The object XYZ's 3090-400E #15 is an instantiation of the generic 3090-400E object, that is, it represents a specific instance of an IBM 3090-400E mainframe that presumably is owned and operated by XYZ Corporation. An individual object possesses the same inheritance and role-definition properties as any generic object.

K-Rep is a robust knowledge representation service, enabling the building of extremely large knowledge bases that can be efficiently manipulated

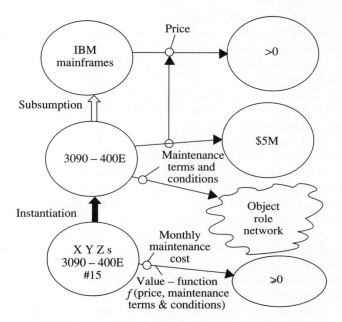

FIGURE 4.1   Representing knowledge in K-Rep

(i.e., computationally fast). Other useful features of K-Rep that help in the building of large yet practical knowledge bases include multiple knowledge base management, role-value caching, facet definability, reverse inheritance, integrated rule based programming and database integration. Mays *et al.*, (1988) describes this knowledge representation service in greater detail.

Utilizing an object centered knowledge representation service like K-Rep for modeling financial marketing enabled us to capture fairly complex domain structures and their inherent abstractions and aggregations in an elegant fashion. This object centered modeling enables efficient access to tremendous amounts of inter-related knowledge that is typically required for producing detailed arguments and justifications for problem solving steps. As we pointed out earlier, this requirement is of premier importance in the domain of financial marketing and was a prime motivation for moving from our earlier rule based prototype.

4.3.2 The Modeling Methodology

Encoding knowledge about a domain in an object centered knowledge representation framework is a crucial task, in the sense that this knowledge encoding process essentially builds an abstract model of the domain. No known automatic knowledge acquisition techniques exist that guarantee the efficient and complete building of such models. Our approach to knowledge acquisition has been to focus upon building powerful interactive utilities that assist the process of knowledge engineering. We will therefore focus first on how we identified and transformed domain knowledge into an object-role network. We will then describe various aspects of computer based tools that assisted this effort.

Various types of objects that play a major role in financial marketing were identified, and their interconnections were studied. Relations between various objects were developed using only the two fundamental algebraic relations of subsumption and attribution. Classifying the domain in terms of objects allowed us to quickly build hierarchies and taxonomies of objects by their different classes. These classes included, but were not limited to, financing mechanisms, manufacturers, products (past, present, and future), customers, financiers, etc. as relevant to the market of mainframe computers. Subsumption allowed us to build abstractions of these classes. This categorization not only makes it easy to build such knowledge into a computer using structured inheritance networks, it also allows acquisition of such knowledge from experts via either a knowledge engineer and/or computer based acquisition tools.

We will go into some detail here to describe how we went about modeling one particular sub-domain in financial marketing, that of computer acquisition financing. We choose this sub-area because it shares many ideas with many other corporate financing methods, and is therefore well understood; it also happens to be a more public knowledge driven sub-domain within IBM's financial marketing domain. In general, when a corporation acquires a capital item, it has available to it a variety of financing methods for executing the acquisition. The corporation may pay for the item entirely in cash by drawing upon its liquid assets. This is a common form of financing an acquisition that we all know about, outright purchase. Alternatively, the corporation may borrow money from a lending institution to finance the acquisition, or go in some kind of an installment payment agreement with the manufacturer, which is generally known as a financed purchase. A popular method of financing for acquisitions by corporations is leasing, which is essentially a long term rental agreement between a lessor (typically the manufacturer or a third party) and the lessee (the corporation that will actually be using the machine). However, depending upon various factors including the item's first ship date and its monthly lease payment, the Internal Revenue Service and the FASB (Financial Accounting Standards Board) may view a lease agreement as either a true lease or a conditional sale. A model of financing methods that is available at any given time for a given kind of a product can be built and captured in an

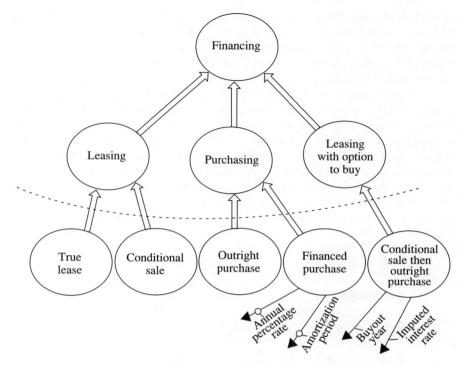

FIGURE 4.2   Modeling mainframe computer financing

object centered representation very succinctly. Figure 4.2 illustrates how this was done in the FAME system. Again an abstraction hierarchy was drawn out based upon commonalities and disjunctions amongst the various financing methods that are generally available for financing computer acquisitions. The types of roles that were attached to this class of objects were attributes that can be utilized in computing the impact of a financing method on the corporation's cash flows, profit and loss statements, and various financial ratios. For example the financed purchase object would have roles including annual percentage rate and amortization period, while conditional sale then outright purchase would have roles including imputed interest rate and buyout year.

The next step in building the model is tying in the computer financing mechanisms with some other relevant objects in the domain. In the computer mainframe market, typically the mainframe manufacturer or marketeer will present proposals tailor-made to satisfy some customer's requirements for mainframe computing. The financing method therefore needs to be tied in two ways. The first tie-in would be with the marketing proposal, which will link the financing to a specific mainframe product, and thereby allowing instantiation of financing terms and conditions. The second tie-in would be with the customer, which would allow instantiation of objects/roles that denote how the specific proposal impacts a variety of the customer's financial numbers, some of which may be of concern to the customer and some not. A detailed illustration of this tie-in is indicated in Figure 4.3. Note that this picture now is that of a more comprehensive model that encompasses a seller of mainframe computers, a buyer of mainframe computers, and the resulting financial ramifications, both to buyer and seller. Another powerful feature of object centered representations that is well put forth in this illustration is that of self-containedness. That is, all relevant financial computations are all present in this small object-role network as function value-restrictions of appropriate objects. This makes the model very self-descriptive. In the FAME system, a

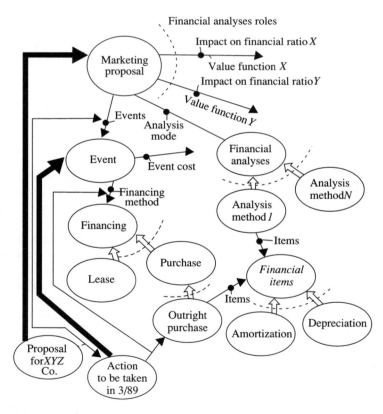

FIGURE 4.3   Modeling financial ramifications of a mainframe acquisition

variety of expert problem solvers reside on top of this particular structure that we have illustrated. These range from financial planners and analyzers to explanation generators.

Our experience indicates that such models can be very powerful in their use and easy to maintain. We successfully modeled the vast domain of the computer mainframe market using this approach. Experiments suggest that there indeed is a knowledge modeling discipline, which forces one to examine the domain world and succinctly model it using K-Rep's enforced semantics.

Tightly coupled with knowledge engineering is the requirement for some form of computer based support for knowledge acquisition. The success of fully automated knowledge acquisition (e.g. self-learning) tools has been quite limited to date. Our experience with the FAME system indicates that even semi-automatic support in the form of advanced graphical interfaces for browsing and editing knowledge bases can be a powerful medium for both the managing and use of very large knowledge bases. Other experiences (Abrett and Burnstein, 1987; Boose, 1986) also indicate this to be the case. In this spirit, we have been evolving an approach to develop object centered interfaces on advanced workstations that allow a structured retrieval of all knowledge stored in the knowledge bases that support FAME. This technique eases tasks such as maintaining very large knowledge bases and their use as an educational medium. In this activity we are developing and extending capabilities similar to those reported in Hypertext systems (Conklin, 1987) and systems such as XCON-in RIME (Soloway *et al.*, 1987).

Knowledge acquisition and maintenance are important issues for knowledge based systems, even more so when we deal with very large knowledge bases. Hypertext systems have traditionally taken the approach that by fully exploiting the more advanced features that are available on today's high resolution bit-mapped monitors and fast desk top computers, one can build fairly powerful interfaces to large amounts of stored data. These interfaces have had the goal of providing access to large databases with very much the ease and flexibility one has when using large dictionaries and encyclopedias. We have taken the view in FAME that providing such interfaces to large knowledge bases not only makes them easy to use, but also makes maintenance and modeling of the knowledge in them very amenable.

We have been successfully using an object-centered interface to FAME's knowledge bases for both knowledge engineer and end user. This interface has very little syntax associated with it, other than having the capability to present objects from a knowledge base on a screen, using certain presentation mechanisms that allow these objects, even when appearing on a screen in many different ways, to be selectable by a user as a unit object. By selecting objects on a screen, the user (whether a knowledge engineer or a end user) may be allowed to carry out a variety of activities, all controlled by essentially where the object is located in the underlying knowledge base. Thus the user may traverse or browse through the knowledge base by reaching out through the object's subsumption and attribution links. This link-driven traversing is extremely powerful for browsing large pieces of non-linear organizations, which is exactly what large knowledge bases are. This philosophy also provides a single coherent interface to knowledge bases that relies upon the semantics of the underlying object-role network, rather than some forced artificial interaction. As Figure 4.4 illustrates, such interfaces allow users to open windows at random into the knowledge base, thereby permitting a structured retrieval of all related knowledge that supports the objects in the initial window.

This object centered browser was used to good effect when knowledge was being acquired and engineered into the FAME knowledge bases. It was extremely easy to identify sub-areas in the knowledge bases in which objects needed to be added, modified, copied, or deleted. Specialized methods associated with these objects were provided for these operations that could

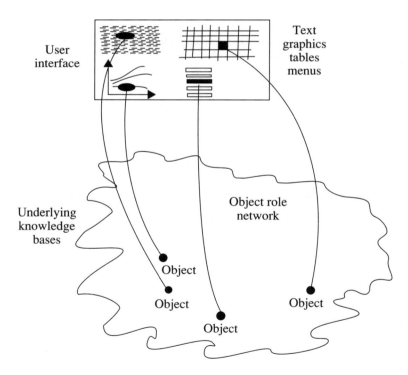

FIGURE 4.4   Object centered interfaces

be dynamically invoked by selecting objects on a screen. This methodology turned out to be an extremely powerful semi-automatic knowledge acquisition and maintenance support tool.

4.4 DISCUSSION

The model of the mainframe computer market that currently drives FAME consists of well over 2000 complex objects connected in a K-Rep network. By complex objects, we mean that typical objects usually have multiple inheritance links, and in addition their roles themselves are restricted by other complex objects. By keeping the types of links allowable in this network to just two different algebraic relations, it has been very easy to build tools and support programs that aid in the acquisition and maintenance of objects in this knowledge base.

Our modeling methodology allowed us to develop an adequate model of the mainframe computer market. This comprehensive model has permitted us to build intelligent planning, control, and problem solving in FAME. An important issue in building large heterogeneous knowledge based systems is that of planning and control. It becomes crucial to dynamically plan problem-solving sequences in the presence of incomplete information to achieve some goals. For this it is important that we can build pattern-directed models that will drive this activity. We have been experimenting with a framework called KROPS (Daly *et al.*, 1988) that allows a RETE net based (Schor *et al.*, 1986) pattern matching of K-Rep based models. In the area of automated problem solving, we have had some interesting results using search based techniques and qualitative reasoning mechanisms. For a large and complex domain such as financial marketing, using the purest forms of search algorithms like the A* are just too inefficient. We have been experimenting with using alternative heuristic search control techniques to achieve rapid search termination (Karnaugh and Min, 1988). This has resulted in very positive performance in our domain. Intelligent problem solving in financial marketing requires one to reason symbolically and heuristically about quantitative relations and the mathematics that governs these. We have been evolving techniques for qualitative reasoning about financial arithmetic and employing these in automated sensitivity analyses (Apté and Hong, 1986; Apté and Dionne, 1988).

We have reached a stage where the experimental prototype of FAME has received sufficient positive feedback from select experts of the potential user community. An effort has begun to plan the transfer and solidification of the prototype into a field usable system.

Systems like the FAME represent an emerging class of very large heterogeneous knowledge based systems. Such systems, with multiple developers and users, pose their own peculiar types of problems. We will be addressing some of these issues to make this class of systems of more practical mainstream use.

ACKNOWLEDGEMENTS

We would like to thank the Advanced Marketing Education group of the IBM US Marketing & Services division for partially supporting this effort.

REFERENCES

Abrett, G. and M. Burnstein (1987), The KREME knowledge editing environment, *Int. J. Man-Machine Studies*, **27** 103–126.

Apté, C. and R. Dionne (1988), Building Numerical Sensitivity Analysis Systems Using a Knowledge Based Approach, *Proceedings of the IEEE CAIA-88*; 371–378.

Apté, C. and S.J. Hong (1986), Using Qualitative Reasoning to Understand Financial Arithmetic, *Proceedings of the AAAI-86* August, 942–948.

Beers, H.S. Jr. (1983), *Computer Leasing*, Lifetime Learning Publications.

Boose, J. (1986), ETS: A system for the transfer of human expertise, J. Kowalik, editor, *Knowledge Based Problem Solving*, pp. 68–111.

Brachman, R. and J. Schmolze (1985), An Overview of the Kl-One Knowledge Representation System, *Cognitive Science*, **9**, 171–216.

Conklin, J. (1987), Hypertext: An Introduction and Survey, *IEEE Computer* (September), 17–41.

Daly, T., J. Kastner, and E. Mays, Integrating Rules and Inheritance Networks in a Knowledge-Based Financial Marketing Consultation System, *Proceedings of the HICSS-88*, January.

Harmon, P. and D. King (1985), *Artificial Intelligence in Business*, John Wiley and Sons.

Helfert, E. (1982), *Techniques of Financial Analysis*, Richard D. Irwin, Inc.

Karnaugh, M. and R. Min. (1988), *Mainframe Equipment Planner: A Case of Industrial Strength Search*, IBM Research Division RC 13558.

Kastner, J., C. Apté, J. Griesmer, S.J. Hong, M. Karnaugh, E. Mays, and Y. Tozawa (1986), A Knowledge-Based Consultant for Financial Marketing, *AI Magazine*, **VII**(5), 71–79.

Mays, E., C. Apté, J. Griesmer, and J. Kastner, Organizing Knowledge in a Complex Financial Domain, *IEEE Expert*, **2**(3), 61–70.

Mays, E., C. Apté, J. Griesmer and J. Kastner, Experience with K-Rep: An Object Centered Knowledge Representation Language, *Proceedings of the IEEE CAIA-88*, 62–67.

Schor, M., T. Daly, H.S. Lee, and B. Tibbitts (1986), Advances in Rete Pattern Matching, *Proceedings of the AAAI-86*, pp. 226–232.

Soloway, E., J. Bachant and K. Jensen (1987), Assessing the Maintainability of XCON-in-RIME: Coping with the Problems of a VERY Large Rule-Base, *Proceedings of the AAAI-87*, pp. 824–829.

Chapter 5

INTEGRATION OF INTELLIGENT TECHNOLOGIES INTO CONVENTIONAL INFORMATION SYSTEMS: KEY ISSUES, OPPORTUNITIES AND POTENTIAL PITFALLS

Paul R. Watkins
Daniel E. O'Leary
University of South Carolina, Los Angeles, CA

Applied artificial intelligence technologies such as expert systems, natural language processing, intelligent databases and neural nets are receiving considerable attention in both the academic and professional communities. Much of this attention has focused on the exploration and development of expert systems to support decision making and problem solving. This chapter describes a views model for evaluating integration issues in intelligent technologies.

5.1 INTRODUCTION

A recent study by O'Leary and Watkins (1989a) showed a wide variety of application areas being addressed through the use of expert systems technology by Fortune 1000 firms. Much of the early expert systems development has focused on standalone systems which are self-contained and independent of any existing conventional management information systems (MIS)/decision support systems (DSS) in the organization. With the wide availability of expert systems shells, the trend toward standalone expert systems development is expected to continue, primarily through means of end-user development on microcomputers. Concurrent with the continued development of standalone systems is the desirability of integrating not only expert systems, but other derived artificial intelligence technologies into conventional information systems in organizations. Note that the conventional information system may be defined as any existing (non-intelligent) information systems technology, regardless of the hardware delivery mechanism such as PC's, Mainframes, Minis, Distributed Networks, and so on.

Expert Systems in Business and Finance: Issues and Applications. Edited by P.R. Watkins and L.B. Eliot
© 1993 John Wiley & Sons Ltd.

Turban and Watkins (1986) present a framework for the integration of expert systems and decision support systems. While this framework serves as a general basis for considering expert systems and decision support systems integration and presents arguments describing the synergistic benefits of ES/DSS integration, it does not address many of the specific issues that concern integration of intelligent technologies with conventional information systems. Also implicit in the Turban, Watkins (1986) article is a rather singular definition of integration which focused on hardware and software issues.

The focus of this chapter is to consider problem solving/decision making as the key motivation for the existence of conventional information systems and the augmentation/enhancement of these systems with intelligent technologies. In order to effectively support and enhance problem solving and decision making, the appropriate data, information and knowledge must be made available. Thus, this chapter develops a conceptual model for augmenting current conventional technologies in support of decision making/problem solving by considering the integration of knowledge provided by several types of intelligent systems such as knowledge based systems, expert systems and neural nets. The characteristics of each of these technologies (both conventional and intelligent) are described both independently and from a point of view of integrating these technologies into conventional information systems. The concept of integration is further developed and expanded from that of prior studies into a views model which provides a more comprehensive perspective of the integration issues.

The chapter is organized as follows: the subsequent section provides a conceptual framework of the environments of information systems and the attributes that might be considered most relevant in systems integration. Next the conceptual views model of integration is described and a discussion is presented of data, information and knowledge. The concluding section of the chapter provides a summary set of issues, opportunities and pitfalls which potentially derive from the integration effort.

5.2   CONCEPTUAL MODEL OF INFORMATION SYSTEMS INTEGRATION

Information systems in most organizations can be viewed from a variety of perspectives. Figure 5.1 presents a perspective that shows the various external and organizational boundaries of a typical information systems environment.

5.2.1   General Characteristics

Of primary importance within the boundaries are the task/problem domain and the decision making domain. The task and the decision making activity,

INDUSTRY/COMPETITIVE/OTHER EXTERNAL ENVIRONMENT

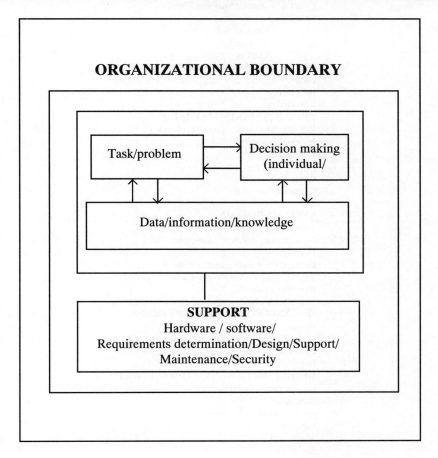

FIGURE 5.1   Components of conventional information systems environments

to a large extent, determine the kinds of data, information and knowledge required to solve a particular problem or to make a reasonable decision. As is known from prior information systems research, the database is crucial to effective information systems support for decision making. (Note at this point information systems are described in a generic sense without delineating between various components such as MIS, DSS and so on.) Somewhat secondary to the three major systems components—task problem domain,

PROBLEM/TASK DOMAIN:
General business domain/problems
Specific domain:
>   Operational
>   Planning
>   Control

DATA/INFORMATION/KNOWLEDGE:
Data
Information
Knowledge

DECISION MAKING DOMAIN:
Routine, structured vs unique, complex
Judgment support
Delegation
Monitoring
Conflict resolution
Consensus building
Training/technology transfer

SYSTEMS DOMAIN:
Transaction processing systems - TPS
Management information systems - MIS
Decsions support systems - DSS
Executive support systems - ESS
Knowledge based systems - KBS
Expert systems - ES
Neural nets - NN

ORGANIZATIONAL ENVIRONMENT:
Power
Control
Goal Congruence
Political

DESIGN/IMPLEMENTATION/SUPPORT:
Requirements determination
Design
Implementation
Support
Maintenance
Security
Auditability

HARDWARE DOMAIN:
Standalone PC's, workstations
Networked environments
Distributed environments
Large, central computing: minis, mainframes

SOFTWARE DOMAIN:
User view
Designer view
Maintainer view
Management (not necessarily the user) view
Developer view: software engineering issues

FIGURE 5.2   *Key attributes for consideration in information technology integration*

decision making domain and data/information/knowledge domain—is the support domain which includes the software, hardware, requirements determination/design, support, maintenance, security and other systems design/implementation/support components.

5.2.2 Detailed Characteristics: A Views Model

Figure 5.2 expands the components in Figure 5.1 to include more detailed attributes of the information system. These attributes are not intended to be exhaustive of all the attributes of an information system but rather to focus on attributes that are of key importance as the integration of various types of systems is considered. As seen in Figure 5.2, eight major categories of attributes are presented. These groupings of attributes represent views from which the integration of conventional and intelligent technologies can be discussed. View 1 is the problem/task/decision domain. This domain is considered from the classic Gorry, Scott-Morton (GSM) (1971) framework.

View 1: The Problem/Task/Decision View

The GSM framework provides a starting point for considering the task/problem and decision making attributes which may require support by an information system. As shown in Figure 5.3, the GSM framework shows structured, operational control type task/decision environments in the upper left hand corner of the diagram and unstructured, strategic planning decisions in the lower right hand corner of the diagram. As has been discussed previously in the literature, different levels of tasks and decision making require different kinds of information systems support. Originally, Gorry and Scott-Morton (1971) suggested that the information character- istics of interest for effective systems design are source, scope, level, time horizon, currency, require accuracy, frequency of use. Thus, these charac- teristics of information would likely differ among structured, operational tasks and unstructured, strategic tasks. This basic framework has been useful in providing perspective for management information systems (MIS) and decision support systems (DSS). MIS were conceptualized to be more apropos to support the problem domains represented by the upper left hand triangle of Figure 5.3 and DSS were conceptualized to be more apro- pos to the problem domains represented by the lower right hand triangle. Although basic characteristics of information were provided in the GSM framework, they are not completely sufficient for many problem domains and tasks. Thus in the next section we provide a discussion of View 2: The Data/Information/Knowledge View.

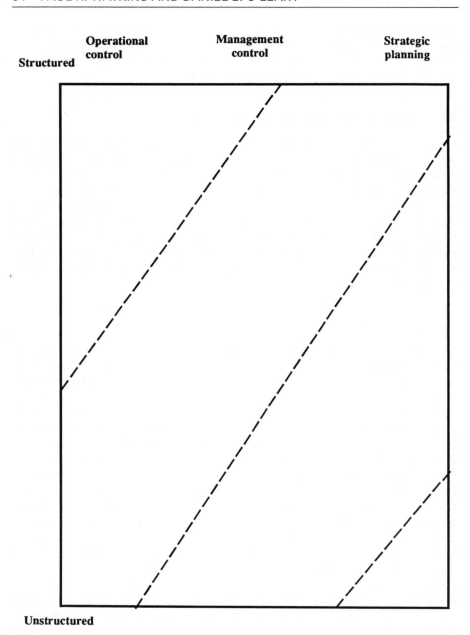

FIGURE 5.3   Integration View 1: Problem/Task/Decision View

View 2: Data/Information/Knowledge View

Definitions of data and information are fairly well known in the information systems literature. Table 5.1 presents general definitions for data, information and knowledge. The distinction between information and knowledge is important for several reasons. First, in view of the GSM framework above, information alone may be insufficient for supporting a give class of problems/decisions in the framework. For example, consider movement from the upper left hand corner of Figure 5.3 to the lower right hand corner of the figure in view of data/information/knowledge requirements for the following items:

- Operational, structured decisions may require more numeric, data driven approaches (e.g., linear programming) whereas unstructured, strategic planning decisions may require more symbolic knowledge and less data.
- Operational, structured decisions may be more data intensive, and require structured static knowledge (e.g., accounts receivable) whereas strategic planning, unstructured decisions may be more expert knowledge intensive (mergers and acquisitions or R&D planning).
- Operational, structured decisions may require more well defined and predictable data and knowledge whereas unstructured, strategic planning decisions may require less well defined, unpredictable knowledge necessary to solve the decision problem.
- Operational, structured decisions typically utilize stable data and knowledge (e.g., approaches to accounting for accounts receivable) whereas unstructured, strategic planning decisions may only have available unstable knowledge (mergers and acquisitions) necessary to solve the decision problem.

TABLE 5.1   *Definitions for data, information and knowledge from a systems point of view*

Data
Data are basically facts, primarily numerical in nature, which form the basis of much of the contents of databases in business organizations.

Information
Transformed data into a form that is useful to the decision maker and/or organization. Information may be items input into or developed by the system which may be helpful for decision making but may often suggest isolated or unrelated situations or facts.

Knowledge
Applies to the understanding of a set of facts or principles or of information. Thus knowledge transcends facts and information and provides a means of intelligently utilizing the facts and information in decision making.

"She has acquired much information but has little knowledge"

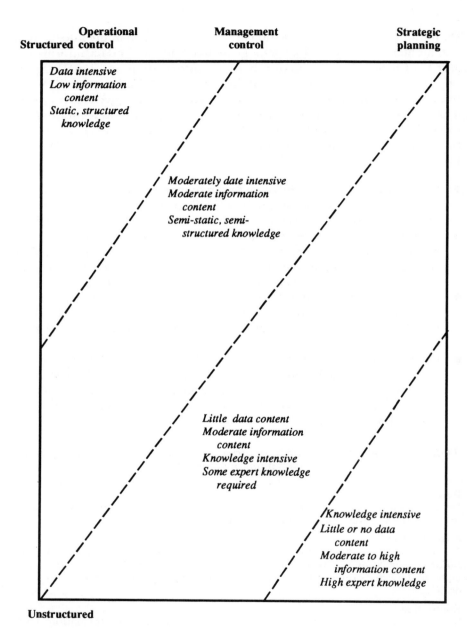

FIGURE 5.4   Integration View 2: Data/Information/Knowledge View

Knowledge, then, is how information is applied or utilized in a given task domain and the more unstructured, complex the domain is, the more the requirement for expert knowledge. The more structured and routine the task domain is implies more structured, less expert based knowledge. Knowledge, as stated before, may be a set of rules or principles, perhaps in the form of policies, procedures, requirements, conditions and so on. This type of knowledge is potentially useful for a class of decisions as indicated on Figure 5.4. This class of decisions requires data, information and knowledge about how to organize and apply the data and information. Another definition of knowledge is expert knowledge; that is, the experiences and organized knowledge structures of an expert in a particular area which can be captured and transferred to another source, such as an expert system. This type of knowledge is located on Figure 5.4 in the lower right-hand corner (unstructured, complex decision making).

One contribution of this conceptual model is the recognition of the distinction between data, information and knowledge and that there is a wide class of problems for which knowledge is desirable; especially to augment current data and information based systems. Knowledge can be applied to structured, operational decisions as well as unstructured, strategic planning decisions. The type of knowledge varies from static, structured rules for the structured task domains to more dynamic, adaptive, conceptual knowledge for the unstructured domains. Thus one type of integration summarized by View 2 is the integration of knowledge with data and information.

View 3: Decision Making View

View 1 described the problem/task/decision view. Decisions in View 1 were structured–operational, structured–management control, structured–strategic planning, semi–structured–operational, semi–structured–management control, semi–structured–strategic planning, unstructured–operational, unstructured management control, and unstructured–strategic planning. In addition to these decision areas, View 3 is concerned with individual or group judgment support (different from decision support), delegation in the decision making process, monitoring of decisions, conflict resolution, consensus building, and training/technology transfer.

Purpose of the System   Systems designed to solve a specific task or support a specific decision may also provide decision making information that can be integrated into other decision making domains. For example, in one Fortune 500 firm (TRW) with which the authors are familiar, output from a system designed to detect intruders into an MIS system proved to be quite useful in the generation of data about the clients of a database service, for marketing purposes. Another system developed by a New York bank to audit

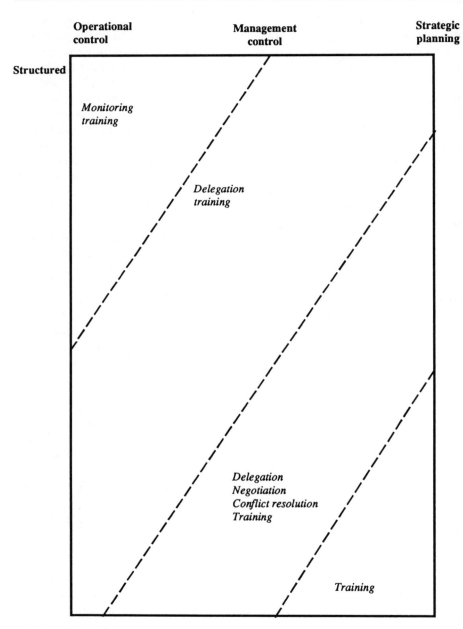

FIGURE 5.5   *Integration View 3: Decision Making View*

foreign currency trading also was found to be useful as a management tool (O'Leary and Watkins (1989a). Thus, in Figure 5.5, an operational–semi-structured decision environment provided output which then could be integrated into a system providing semi-structured–managerial control support.

Delegation   In many situations the role of delegating tasks to subordinates by managers can be replaced or augmented by appropriate integration of delegation based knowledge systems. For example, routine, semi-structured tasks may be augmented by a task delegation system where the system replaces the traditional managerial delegation task as indicated in Figure 5.5.

Monitoring   Oftentimes, monitoring is a relatively stable activity that intelligent systems can perform in an efficient manner (e.g., Denning, 1987). Accordingly, intelligent systems can be embedded in other systems in order to monitor access, examine input or output for errors, and a variety of other functions. Monitoring systems may be more appropriate at the structured–operational control level as shown in Figure 5.5.

Negotiation —Conflict Resolution   Increasingly intelligent systems offer the opportunity to computerize negotiation processes. Such approaches are beginning to be integrated into decision making processes. For example, at Westinghouse:

> With OptionFinder, each meeting participant has a small numeric key pad, with which he or she votes into the OptionFinder Software, which instantly tallies them and produces a graph of the results... *Because everyone must participate, must push their button, the tools encourage teamwork* (Wilkinson,1989).

Thus, negotiation type augmentation may be more at the semi-structured, planning level as shown in Figure 5.5.

Training   Training, although not specifically identified with decision making, can change the manner in which decisions are made and encourage more rapid and effective technology transfer by embedding appropriate training modules into existing systems. For example, in Figure 5.5, training modules can be embedded into all of the problem/task/decision supporting areas from very structured to unstructured tasks and thus provide benefits in terms of training integration. This may enhance decision making performance over time and allow managers to provide more realistic learning environments for new hires and employees who have been assigned to new tasks.

View 4: Systems View

The systems view looks at the various intelligent and conventional systems and describes their characteristics from a standalone and integrated point of view. Figure 5.6 provides a hierarchical view of conventional and intelligent information systems. This view is a non-integrated view, that is, each system is conceptualized as a standalone system. The definitions of transaction processing systems (TPS), management information systems (MIS), decision support systems (DSS) and executive support (or information) systems (ESS) are generally well known, although there may be disagreement as to the precise definition of DSS, and ESS. The definitions on Figure 5.6 are to provide a point of reference and perspective, not necessarily to argue strongly that a given definition is precise and unconditionally accepted.

Definitions of knowledge based systems (KBS), expert systems (ES), natural language (NL) and neural nets (NN) are less well known in the systems literature and are now briefly discussed. Knowledge based systems form the broad category of systems that derive from applied artificial intelligence. The argument is that much of intelligence in any system, human or machine, is based on knowledge. Knowledge based systems then may contain detailed, factual knowledge which has little or no expertise component or they may contain a great deal of expert knowledge. For this chapter, expert systems are considered to be a sub-set of knowledge based systems wherein a high level of *expert* knowledge about a given task domain is present. KBS, then, contain knowledge, but not necessarily expert knowledge. Natural language systems are well known in the systems literature and have been proposed as front ends to database systems and for user interface technologies for decision support systems. Little more will be said about these systems in this chapter. Neural nets are artificial intelligence derivatives which have application in a wide variety of settings. Of particular interest for business information systems are NN that are focused on pattern recognition of certain kinds of activities such as accounts receivable collections, or mortgage or commercial loan applications. The NN technology is based on scanning patterns of characteristics of the task over a large history file and generating a template or master pattern which can be applied to current task settings. A logical extension of NN is to interface these with other intelligent technologies such as KBS or ES for interpretation and decision making activities. In the systems view of integration, the goal is to integrate the standalone systems with each other for a particular problem/task/decision and to support the appropriate integration of data/information/knowledge. Thus various combinations of systems can be envisioned as appropriate. For example, ES-DSS, ES-MIS, ES-TPS, KBS-DSS, KBS-MIS, KBS-TPS, ES-NN-TPS, ES-NN-TPS, KBS-NN-MIS, KBS-NN-TPS and so on. The emphasis should be placed on the data/information/knowledge needs

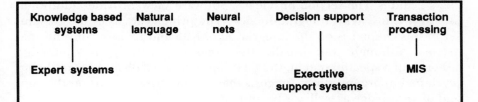

DEFINITIONS

Knowledge Based Systems: Systems which have factual, procedural and little or no *expert* knowledge for a given task or problem domain. Knowledge is represented primarily in the form of rules. Has an inference mechanism. Knowledge base may be relatively static (accounts receivable collectibility system) and need little or no maintenance or for some domains may need frequent updates (e.g. tax rules adviser).

Expert Systems: Systems whose primary type of knowledge is obtained from experts for a given problem or task domain. Knowledge may be represented in a variety of ways. Has varied inference mechanisms. Knowledge base may need modification in view of new experiences.

Neural Nets: Specialized processing networks which are adaptive based on pattern recognition of task histories. An example would be an equities trading program where the neural net looks at volumes of stock market data and correlates data patterns with probable stock market behaviors.

Transaction Processing: System oriented towards processing high volumes of transactions, e.g., bank check clearing systems.

MIS: System which focuses on generation of reports for a variety of management support activities. May be part of the transaction processing system.

DSS: Focused on supporting decision making. Key element is database and may have other components such as a models manager and so on.

ESS: Executive support system. Focus is on support for top executives and provides graphics and other presentation views for executive support. May have mail systems and dialog systems interconnected.

FIGURE 5.6   Hierarchy of intelligent and conventional systems

of View 2 within the context of the problem/task/decision domain of Views 1 and 3. The section on View 8, Software View, provides additional issues for the systems integration view. The primary focus of the remainder of this chapter is on the integration of KBS and ES into conventional systems. Although conceptually, the organizing concept is knowledge rather than a specific system, the fact that separate KBS and ES are being developed in organizations suggests that this discussion focus on the concept of knowledge as well as KBS and ES.

In Figure 5.7, the various types of systems are shown in the context of the problem/task/decision domain and the data/information/knowledge domain of Views 1 and 2.

View 5: Organization Environment View

The organization environment view may be evaluated from the perspective of Figure 5.1 where the organizational boundary encompasses the information systems activity within the organization. Theorists such as Katz and Kahn (1966, 1986) and others commonly use at least the following seven categories in discussing organizations:

- Organization structure
- Centralization/decentralization
- Leadership and power
- Organization roles
- Communications and communications flow
- Corporate culture

All of the above seven categories can have an impact on the problem/task/decision domain, the data/information/knowledge domain and the decision making domain. Much of the discussion that follows views integration in the context of standalone versus integrated or non-standalone systems.

Organization Structure   An environment where applications are integrated as opposed to standalone, requires different organizational structure. If the systems are standalone systems then this likely would encourage independent departments either to develop their own intelligent systems or to develop a department that would specialize in such systems. On the other hand, if intelligent systems are integrated into other types of information systems then the department where expertise on intelligent systems is resident is likely to be integrated with the expertise on the development of those other systems.

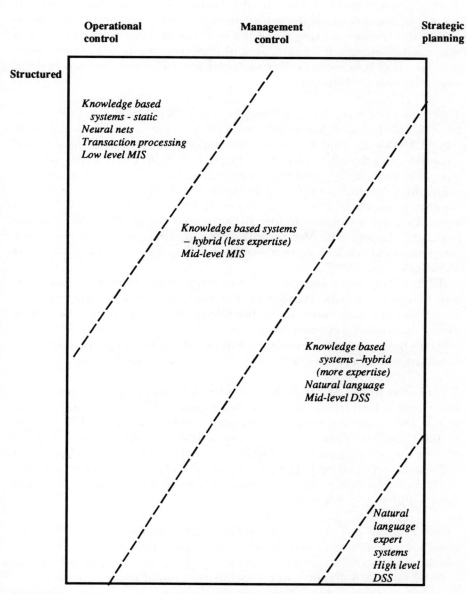

FIGURE 5.7   Integration View 4: Systems View

Centralization/Decentralization   If all knowledge and expertise is resident in only humans or standalone systems then it becomes more difficult to centralize decision making since the decision making resources are too dispersed. Similarly, if knowledge and expertise is integrated into other systems, then it becomes easier to centralize, since the decision making resources also are integrated.

Leadership and Power   Several researchers (e.g., Katz and Kahn, 1966, 1986) have noted that both leadership and power at least partially derive from expert knowledge and access to information. In standalone systems the expertise, and thus the power for expertise, remains distributed with particular individuals or groups of individuals. However, in integrated systems, the expertise is implicitly available to all. Thus, it appears that an important variable in determining the feasibility of integrating expertise into a system is the *willingness* to lose the potential power of distributing the expertise. As noted by Mowshowitz (1985, p. 102), *When real money and power are at stake the realization of a redistribution of control takes more than mere technological possibility.*

Alternatively, some may argue that by integrating intelligence into a system that power can be broadened. For example, if integrating expertise into a system means limiting the feasible set of options of the users then power of management can be increased. For example, many of the systems designed to support auditors improve the control that management would have over auditors in the field (e.g., O'Leary and Watkins, 1989a).

Organization Roles   As expert and knowledge based systems are developed, some new roles can be added to the organization. One pivotal role in stand alone expert systems is the expert system manager (O'Leary and Watkins, 1989a). This manager is responsible for monitoring and maintaining the performance of the system, as it evolves over time. However, if the system were embedded or integrated into a larger information system that role might change to one of less emphasis on a single application and more emphasis on the system.

Communications and Communications Flow   If an intelligent system is developed for a standalone environment, then clearly that system is physically accessible to only a few members of the firm and inhibits communications flow.

Integrating intelligent systems within traditional types of systems can facilitate communications. For example, a module representing expertise can provide communication from the expert to the group using the system. O'Leary and Watkins (1989b, c) discuss an integrated expert system designed to facilitate communication of technical updates. The system was integrated with a database of analyst updates issued by management to clarify changes in technology. Communication in the other direction could be facilitated by a system that tracked what was done with expertise recommended by the system.

Corporate Culture   The corporate culture also can play a critical part in the adoption of technology, such as integrating intelligent systems. In Wilkinson (1989), corporate culture is credited with being a critical part in the development of a group DSS designed to streamline meetings.

Thus, organizational environment issues can have a major effect on the integration effort and both mandate organizational structural changes as well as force technology into a particular role in order to meet organizational needs.

View 6: Design/Implementation/Support View

Integration issues arise as systems and components of systems are designed, implemented and supported through maintenance functions, security and audits. Since characteristics of intelligent systems may differ from conventional systems, care must be taken in the integration effort to insure recognition and compatibility of the differences that arise as divergent yet complementary technologies are integrated.

Requirements Determination   Prototyping is the promulgated basis of requirements determination in expert, knowledge based and decision support systems. Its use as a tool in standalone systems has been investigated by a number of authors in transaction systems (Earl, 1982), decision support systems (Henderson and Ingraham, 1982) and expert systems (O'Leary, 1988a). Jenkins and Fellers (1986) have accumulated a substantial bibliography on prototyping.

Although the use of prototyping in traditional systems has been investigated empirically by Alavi (1984), generally, more structured *top-down* or *bottom-up* approaches are used or promulgated in traditional TPS or MIS. As a result, there can be a conflict in promulgated methodologies when ES, KBS or DSS are integrated with TP or MIS. If a structured approach is used then the less structured prototyping approach may provide inadequate inputs at various points in time in the requirements determination process. Unfortunately, the potential difficulties of the integration of alternative approaches to requirements definition has received little attention.

Design/Implementation   The design and implementation of intelligent systems is somewhat different than that of conventional systems. In many cases, the problem/task/decision to be supported by intelligent systems is very narrow and thus becomes a very specialized project. One of the major difficulties

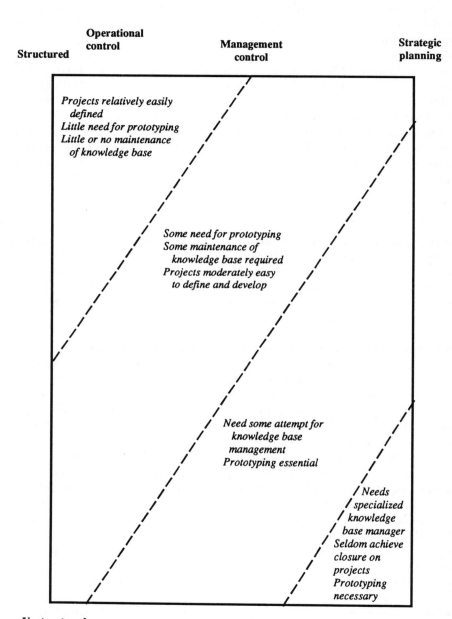

FIGURE 5.8   Integration View 6: Design/Implementation/Support /View

with the design/implementation of high-level KBS and ES is that they are seldom ever finished (Tener, 1988). That is, the knowledge base component is somewhat dynamic and requires constant maintenance and adjustment which in turn may have impact on the system. In many cases, high level intelligent systems are designed and built on a *trial and error* basis and are in a constant state of evolution and fine tuning. Thus, it may be difficult to say that closure has been achieved on a given KBS, ES project which makes it difficult for information systems management and other management to accept. Conventional information systems usually can be specified in advance with a definite and finite project development plan and timetable. High level KBS and ES can rarely be well specified in advance and timetables are rarely estimable.

KBS in support of structured tasks where there is little expert knowledge and where little maintenance of the knowledge base is required are more like conventional systems in the design phase and maintenance activity. As intelligent systems are developed in support of more unstructured tasks requiring *expertise* it tends to become less easy to completely specify the design in advance and provide reliable estimates of the development cycle.

Figure 5.8 provides some perspective for these differences in design/ implementation/maintenance for the various types of decisions supported.

Compatibility Another key issue in the integration of intelligent technology into existing technology is in the area of systems compatibility and the feasibility of the integration effort. For example, the authors are aware of a major defense contractor who is attempting to integrate advanced expert systems technology with a first generation database and is finding the task almost all but impossible given the differences between the two technologies. Thus, although integration of intelligent technologies into existing technologies may be desirable from a conceptual point of view, it may be somewhat undesirable from a technical compatibility point of view. In industry there exist many older technologies simply because of cost benefit considerations in changing to new technology, e.g., the first generation database which is very large and would have tremendous costs for conversion, upgrading to newer technology.

Support/Maintenance The support and maintenance of integrated systems may be quite different from that of conventional systems. New job descriptions may have to be created and new training methods developed for employees in these positions. For example, in high level KBS and ES, a knowledge base management position is required. Analogous in concept to a database manager, in reality the job description for a knowledge base manager may be quite different (Tener, 1988). The knowledge base manager must not only have knowledge about the contents of the knowledge base of the intelligent system but must also have expertise in the problem/task domain to which the KBS, ES is to be applied. This is because the KB manager must be able to assess the impact of changes in the knowledge base to the manner in which the problem domain will be affected when the knowledge base modifications are utilized by an end user. In addition the KB manager must know what the impact of the knowledge base changes will have on the other components of the integrated system. For example, changes in the knowledge base may affect certain assumptions that the rest of the system relied on or conversely, changes in the environments or assumptions of aspects of the conventional systems could cause major problems for the knowledge base. Thus, knowledge based management is an area that requires a great deal of expertise and attention, yet very little is known about the qualities needed for successful knowledge base management.

Security   Software engineers (e.g., Pressman [1987, p. 185]) define security as ... *the degree to which system and information access is protected...* Integrating intelligent systems into alternative computing environments can provide increased security risks or move toward mitigating security difficulties.

A recent conversation with a consultant indicated some of the security problems that can occur with the integration of expert systems into a computing environment that allows potential access to other software or databases. The consultant asked if he could examine a particular expert system. After providing the consultant with a brief introduction to the system, the consultant asked if he could *try out* the system on his own. As with many expert systems, the system had an easy-to-use-and-learn interface that allowed the experienced user to rapidly learn what was required of the user. Unfortunately, the system was so easy to use that the consultant was able to access classified database information. The system allowed the user to circumvent the security inherent in the database system. The user and the system effectively had different security levels.

Alternatively, since the law of requisite variety (Ashby, 1963) indicates that it takes equivocality to remove equivocality, this suggests that intelligent systems can be integrated into existing systems to assist in securing the system. Denning (1987) discusses such a system that is designed to detect intrusions to a computer system. As discussed in Tener (1988) intrusion-detection systems also can be integrated into a other applications.

Auditability   As noted by Weber (1988, p.1), *EDP auditing is a function that has been developed to assess whether computer systems safeguard assets, maintain data integrity, and achieve the goals of the organization.* Integrating intelligent systems into other computer-based systems can either assist in the process of auditing the resulting systems or add to original systems complexity, and thus, the audit difficulty.

The work by Hansen and Messier (1986) is an example of the first situation. EDP-Xpert is a frequently referenced knowledge based system that is designed to assist in the audit of advanced EDP systems. AY/ASQ, developed by the accounting firm Arthur Young (now Ernst and Young), is a decision support system designed to assist in the audit of transaction-based systems.

Alternatively, by embedding an intelligent system into an existing system, auditing the resulting system becomes more difficult. Since expert systems and other intelligent systems generally are designed using different software and different development methodologies, including symbolic representation of knowledge, etc., they are conceptually different than the transaction processing software in which they are embedded. As a result, if an investigator were to audit the system they would find that alternative processes likely would be required to audit the embedded system. In addition, integrating such systems into other transaction processing systems means attending to the interfaces with those systems, thus, further complicating the resulting audit.

View 7: Hardware View

Integration of intelligent systems may present special challenges from a hardware point of view. Many high level expert systems have, in the past, been developed and implemented on standalone Lisp workstations. Rather than recode the systems to run in a production code such as COBOL or C, some firms have attempted to integrate the Lisp workstations with the conventional systems hardware. In many cases the issues of hardware compatibility and integration are no different from conventional systems issues. On the other hand, hardware capabilities can provide some major difficulties in the integration effort. For example, in a microcomputer environment, either standalone or networked, end-users may have some applications that they wish integrated with KBS or ES. The capabilities of the micros may be insufficient to run the KBS or ES efficiently. On the other hand, cost benefit analysis may suggest that specialized hardware is too costly and thus compromises in efficiency have to be made which can in turn affect the decision making environment. Figure 5.9 shows the effects of this integration in the conceptual model.

View 8: Software View

KBS and ES and other intelligent technologies are, after all, software products. The issues of software integration are therefore very important and somewhat dominate the integration issues. Thus far in this chapter integration has been discussed at a non-software level. As software integration is now discussed it is useful to further refine the notion of integration.

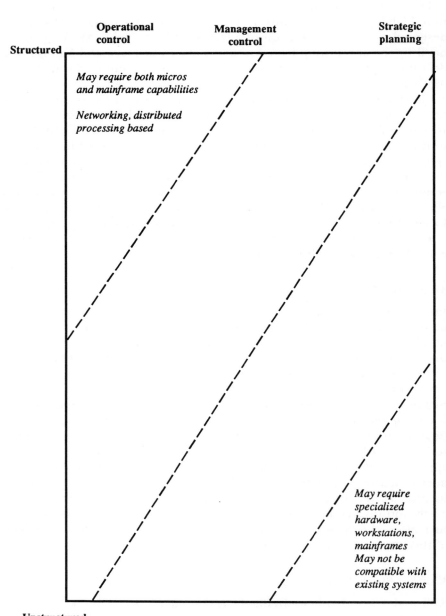

FIGURE 5.9   Integration View 7: Hardware View

Concepts of Integration   Integration of systems is a somewhat nebulous concept. For purposes of clarity, a distinction is made between integration and the embedding of systems with each other. Embedded systems are integrated systems but integrated systems are not necessarily embedded.

Embedded systems are those that generally have been considered in a top-down design approach and have been built into the system as part of the overall programming effort. Examples of these type of systems are most commonly found on standalone applications for microcomputers where the software vendor has built in, say, a rule based, KBS component to the program but where to the user the program is a more friendly, powerful program. Examples include Borland Pardox, Symantec Q & A and Lotus Agenda where KBS are embedded into the software package as a seamless, overall strategic part of the software development effort. Another example would be the embedding of ES into CASE technology programs for re-engineering COBOL code in organizations.

Integration, which may include embedded systems, may simply mean augmenting two or more diverse technologies for the overall benefit of the organization. For example, Figure 5.10 shows the integration of a KBS into a conventional information system for the diagnosis of application software and hardware problems for communications applications between terminals and workstations of the user communities and the company networked mainframes. As shown in Figure 5.10, a knowledge base, rules and an inference engine are augmented to a conventional MIS which has various database components and files. Not shown in Figure 5.10 is that the conventional system is in a networked environment shared by multiple communications consultants. To the user, the KBS component is seamless, but to the developer and maintainer of the systems, the KBS component is simply integrated and needs separate attention and maintenance and specialized attention apart from the conventional MIS component. These views of the system will be in a subsequent paragraph.

Another example of integration is where a standalone ES is hooked up to an existing MIS to analyze outputs and render judgments based on those outputs. Turban and Watkins (1986) provide several examples of this type of integration. Engart (1989) describes the need for an ES component for LAN management and numerous other examples may be found.

There seem to be varying degrees of integration of intelligent systems and TPS, MIS, DSS and ESS. At one end of the spectrum are embedded systems and at the other end are manual transfers of information from one system to another. In large, mainframe environments, embedded systems are more prevalent in TPS whereas manual or non-seamless transfers of information are made between intelligent and conventional systems at the DSS level. On the other hand, with microcomputing, the standalone, vendor supplied packages, many of which are DSS in nature, tend to have the embedded intelligent systems whereas the TPS systems, such as accounting

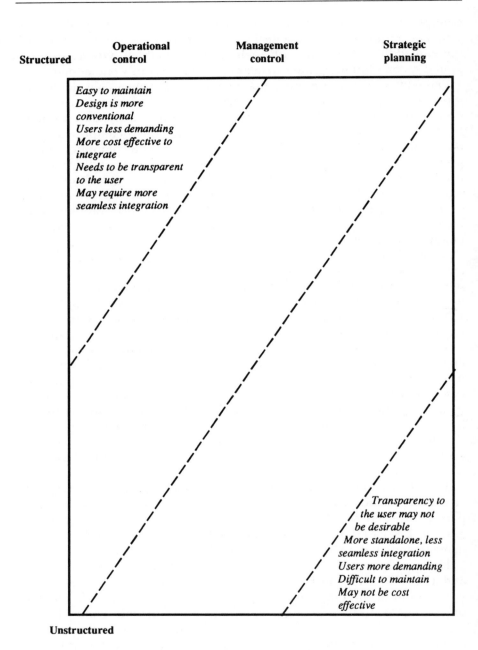

	Operational	**Management**	**Strategic**
Structured	**control**	**control**	**planning**

Easy to maintain
Design is more
conventional
Users less demanding
More cost effective to
integrate
Needs to be transparent
to the user
May require more
seamless integration

Transparency to
the user may not
be desirable
More standalone, less
seamless integration
Users more demanding
Difficult to maintain
May not be cost
effective

Unstructured

FIGURE 5.10   Integration View 8: Software View

packages, don't have embedded intelligence and require manual transfer or non-seamless transfer between them and intelligent systems.

As stated before, the focus of the integration, embedded systems activity, should be motivated and driven by the problem/task/decision considerations and the type of knowledge augmentation required in given problem/task/decision domains.

From the software integration view, several perspectives or views are worth discussing. These are the user, designer, maintainer, manager (not necessarily the user) and the developer's point of view. Each of these are now briefly described.

From the user's point of view, embedded or integrated systems are desirable if they solve a problem or make the task at hand more easily dealt with. The user wants results and the appearance of a system that solves a problem is the primary concern of the user. How the integration takes place and whether it is embedded or not is usually of no interest to the user.

The designer's point of view can vary depending on what is being designed. If a standalone intelligent application is being designed for a workstation, then the designer should be concerned with providing hooks or other means of interface to other technologies. On the other hand, the designer of a conventional application may wish to embed KBS components in the software to make the program more functional and provide more features to the user. In a large mainframe or distributed environment, designers need to provide for the possibility of a variety of software integration issues. For example, the authors are aware of a commercial software product (ES shell) for a mainframe environment that two Fortune 500 firms have been attempting to integrate into their mainframe conventional software systems. Both firms have been working on the projects for over a year now and are having major problems due to the lack of good design features in the shell which make the integration effort feasible.

The maintenance of the software may require different skills in an integrated environment. Conventional applications programmers may not have the expertise to maintain the KBS or ES components of the systems and thus a team approach may be necessary for effective maintenance. Figure 5.10 shows the maintenance effort may be a function of the type of problem/task/decision and data/information/knowledge circumstances. Structured support systems may be much easier to maintain than unstructured support systems.

The developer's view or software engineer's view may be quite different from the other views discussed. Software engineering is aimed at using engineering approaches in order to develop efficient and effective software in a cost beneficial manner. The integration of software engineering methods in information systems has been discussed in, e.g., O'Leary (1989a). In the case of software that is not complex it generally is easier to employ engineering principles in a formal manner. However, as the software becomes more complex, more *ad hoc* approaches seem to be employed. This is clearly the case with intelligent systems at one end of the spectrum, for which prototyping typically is promulgated, and transaction processing at the other end of the spectrum, for which more structured methods generally are promulgated. Unfortunately, integrating the *ad hoc* and the structured is an issue that has received little attention.

Figure 5.10 shows the impact of the problem/task/decision and data/information/knowledge views on the integration of software. For example, structured problems may be easier to integrate (e.g., accounts receivable) than unstructured tasks which are more difficult to integrate (R&D Planning). Accounts receivable inputs and outputs are stable, and thus are easier to integrate. On the other hand, activities such as R&D planning and mergers and acquisitions have less stable inputs and outputs.

Some applications may be necessary to integrate where others are less necessary to integrate. This is a function, in part, of the *closeness* of the application to the database. For example, accounts receivable provides information to a number of users, while R&D planning provides little immediate data to other users.

Applications may range from those which are embedded to those which are integrated but make knowledge transparent to user (e.g., assumptions, procedures, etc.). Because the knowledge employed in applications like accounts receivable are stable and the inputs and outputs are stable, such applications can operate with little intervention. On the other hand, even if applications such as mergers and acquisitions were integrated into an overall information system, generally, the user would be concerned about what assumptions are being made, what data is available, what kinds of reports should be prepared, and so on. (Note that this argument is for sufficiency—but it is not necessary to embed all such systems, e.g., ALDO. However, in a truly intelligent system, ALDO would be embedded, since such a system would track previous decisions, store information about those decisions in a database, be adaptive, etc.)

Another consideration is those applications which are cost effective to integrate to those which are not cost effective to integrate. Because of all these concerns it becomes less and less cost effective to integrate as you move from structured tasks in Figure 5.10 to unstructured tasks.

5.3 SUMMARY AND CONCLUSIONS

This chapter has focused on the major views of the integration of intelligent technologies into conventional information systems. As was discussed, eight views of integration were presented: problem/task/decision, data/information/knowledge, decision making, systems, organizational environments, design/implementation/support, hardware and software. Within these eight views are many sub-views and issues that were described. The fundamental theme of this paper is the conceptual model which shows that the problem/task/decision domain and the data/information/knowledge domain are the driving and principal forces in the model. That is, most integration issues can be put into perspective by considering these two domains. Other issues remain in the integration effort and subsequent research will address these issues in more detail. One effort of future research will be to look at combinations of existing systems and evaluate commonalities and differences as they apply to integration: such as DSS-ES or TPS-KBS and so on. The goal will be a comprehensive framework of integration attributes and components.

REFERENCES

Alavi, M. (1984), An Assessment of the Prototyping Approach to Information Systems Development, *Communications of the ACM*, June.

Ashby, R. (1963), *An Introduction to Cybernetics*, John Wiley, New York.

Denning, D. (1987), An Intrusion Detection Model, *IEEE Software Engineering*, Vol. **SE-14**, 3, pp. 252–261.

Earl, M. (1982), Prototyping Systems for Accounting and Control, *Accounting, Organizations and Society*, Vol. 3, No. 2, pp. 161–170.

Gorry, G. and Scott-Morton, M. (1971), A Framework for Management Information Systems, *Sloan Management Review*, Vol. 13, No. 1, pp. 55–70.

Hansen, J. and Messier, W. (1986), A Knowledge-based Expert System for Auditing Advanced Computer Systems, *European Journal of Operational Research*, September, pp. 371–379.

Henderson, J. and Ingraham (1982), Prototyping DSS: A Critical Appraisal, in (ed) M. Ginzberg, W. Reitman and E. Stohr, *Decision Support Systems*, North Holland, New York.

Jenkins, A. and Fellers, J. (1986), *An Annotated Bibliography on Prototyping*, Graduate School of Business, Indiana University.

Karlinsky, S. and O'Leary, D. (1988), A Framework for Taxation-Based Computer Decision Systems, *Expert Systems Review*, Vol. 1, No. 2, pp. 13–16.

Katz, D. and Kahn, R. (1966/1986), *The Social Psychology of Organizations*, Wiley, New York.

Ko, C. and O'Leary, D. (1987), The Impact of Culture on Expert Systems, *Proceedings of Pan-Pacific Conference IV*, Taipei, Taiwan, May.

Mowshowitz, A. (1985), On the Social Relations of Computers, *Human Systems Management*, pp. 99–110.

O'Leary, D. (1986), Expert Systems in Accounting in a Personal Computer Environment, *Georgia Journal of Accounting, Special Issue on Microcomputers*, 107–117.

O'Leary, D. (1986a), Expert Systems Prototyping as a Research Tool, in *Applied Expert Systems*, (ed) E. Turbin and P. Watkins, North Holland.

O'Leary, D. (1986b), Software Engineering and Research Issues in Accounting Information Systems, *The Journal of Information Systems*, Spring, pp. 24–38.

O'Leary, D. (1989), Security in Expert Systems, *IEEE Expert*, Forthcoming.

O'Leary, D. and Turbin, E. (1988), The Organizational Impact of Expert Systems, *Human Systems Management*, Vol. 7, pp. 11–19.

O'Leary, D. and Watkins, P. (1989a), Expert Systems in Internal Auditing, *Institute of Internal Auditors*, Altamonte Springs, Florida.

O'Leary, D. and Watkins, P. (1989b), Knowledge Acquisition for a Diagnosis-Based Task, *Under Review*, February.

O'Leary, D. and Watkins, P. (1989c), *An Integrated Expert System for Diagnosing Communications Problems*, Unpublished paper presented at the ORSA/TIMS meeting in Vancouver, May.

Pressman, R. (1987), *Software Engineering*, McGraw Hill.

Tener, W. (1988), *Integrating Expect Systems Into MIS*, paper presented at The First National Symposium on Expert Systems in Business, Finance and Accounting, September.

Turban, E. and Watkins, P.R. (1986) Integrating Expert Systems and Decision Support Systems, *MIS Quarterly*, Vol. 10, No. 2, pp. 121–138, June.

Watkins, P. and O'Leary, D. (1987), Knowledge Acquisition for Small Scale Expert Systems from Consulting Experts: A Field Study Approach, *First European Conference on Knowledge Acquisition for Knowledge Based Systems*, Reading, United Kingdom, September.

Weber, R. (1988), *EDP Auditing*, McGraw-Hill, New York.

Wilkinson, S. (1989), Decision Support Tool Streamlines Meetings, *PC Week*, February 6, p. 49 & 51.

Part II
ISSUES IN THE MODELING OF HUMAN JUDGMENT FOR EXPERT SYSTEMS

Chapter 6

THE META LOGIC OF COGNITIVELY BASED HEURISTICS

Alan J. Rowe
University of Southern California, Los Angeles, CA

6.1 INTRODUCTION

Heuristics increasingly are being used for complex problems and are able to find *good* or even optimal solutions. Heuristics are valuable especially where variables are interdependent, problems are ill defined and they have politically determined goals. As artificial intelligence and expert systems are applied to managerial decision problems, finding approaches to solving these problems will become even more important.

This chapter will examine a meta logic perspective that relates the cognitive processes to developing efficient search strategies for problem solving. Cognitive mapping, judgmental processes, composite concepts, analogical reasoning, neural networks, heuristic rule development and problem formulation will be discussed.

6.2 META LOGIC OF HEURISTICS

The meta logic approach relies on a combination of inductive logic with intuitive reasoning and creativity to find solutions to complex problems. This approach uses a combination of the analytic properties of the left hemisphere of the brain along with the intuitive ability of the right hemisphere.

Simon (1982) made it clear that, in complex real-world situations, numbers are not the name of the game but rather representational structures that permit functional reasoning, however qualitative it may be, are *required*. In sum, man constructs models to explain, analyze, diagnose the world *out there* by building constructs that leave out what he does not understand or see; that, when made operational by the insertion of *selected facts* from that same world, have omitted much of the events matrix in which the model is embedded.

Expert Systems in Business and Finance: Issues and Applications. Edited by P.R. Watkins and L.B. Eliot
© 1993 John Wiley & Sons Ltd.

Hertz (1988) describes models as process descriptions that are information-loaded. In such models, factual information has relevance only within more general frames of reference. In this sense, *definitions* of relevant facts must be made on the basis of some theoretical framework organized on a scale appropriate to the decision problems being investigated. In order to achieve meaningful solutions (analytical, diagnostic, decision-oriented), the local *relevant facts* must be distinguished in the models from the seemingly more randomly structured information (*noise*) of the world external to the decision arena. That is, the dividing line between the statistical order imposed by the model on some part of the world and the untidy rest of the world must be explicitly taken into account if the model is to be pragmatically useful. The more precisely and objectively the model organizes the factual and definitional structures, the more subjective will be the application of the end results as they are applied to actions in the meta system outside the model domain.

As pointed out by Chorafas (1987), when dealing with knowledge representation it is important to understand the concept of meta knowledge. Meta knowledge is knowledge about knowledge. The sources of knowledge at one level of abstraction transform entries at another level. Knowledge sources can operate top-down or they can explode and compound knowledge sources into their components.

Chorafas indicates that meta knowledge:

(1)   Represents objects (through schemata)

(2)   Represents function (function templates)

(3)   Reasons about strategies (by means of meta rules)

(4)   Works through inference rules (rule description).

He claims that meta knowledge avoids the rigidity of always having to apply a hierarchical structure for abstraction. It provides for flexible structures, and for that reason it can make a significant contribution to expert systems development. Alternative structures have been indicated as hybrid systems, combinations of analytic and intuitive insights, and simulation models.

Using a meta logic approach to heuristics, one incorporates the cognitive process to show how appropriate solutions can be obtained. The cognitive process involves the way the mind perceives information, formulates and evaluates problems, conceives of alternative solutions, and then uses value-based reasoning to make choices and to determine what actions will be taken to implement solutions. More importantly, the meta logic approach is more likely to gain the acceptance of managers.

6.3 DEFINING HEURISTICS

Polya (1957), Gordon (1962), Rowe and Bahr (1972), Wiest (1966), Pearl (1984) and others have described the process of heuristic decision making (from the Greek *heuriskein*: to invent, discover). Heuristic thinking does not necessarily proceed in a direct manner. It involves searching, relearning, evaluating, judging and then again searching, relearning, and reappraisal as exploring and probing takes place. The knowledge gained from success or failure at some point is fed back and modifies the search process. More often than not, it is necessary to redefine either the objectives or the problem, or to solve related or simplified problems before the primary one can be solved.

Heuristic methods have been described by Pearl (1984) based on intelligent search strategies for computer problem solving using split and prune methods, repetitive splitting, branch and bound algorithms, state space graphs, logical reasoning, and sampling.

The heuristic procedure has been described as finding rules that help to solve intermediate problems; to discover how to set up these problems for final solution by finding the most promising paths in the search for solutions; finding ways to retrieve and interpret information on each experience; and then finding the methods that lead to a computational algorithm or general solution. The term heuristic has been used to include any and all of these steps.

Thus, heuristic reasoning is not regarded as final and strict but as provisional and plausible only; its purpose is to discover an approach that will lead to a general solution. Intermediate solutions that make use of information previously learned and that are plausible are indicators of progress; while the absence of these indicators warns of blind alleys and their presence focuses on the high payoff areas. However, to interpret these indicators correctly, it takes both experience and judgment.

6.4 PROBLEM SOLVING

In complex problem solving, one either seeks relationships in the nature of the problem or imposes a certain structure on the problem. This *structuring* may entail subdividing a problem into natural components, or reducing the size of the problem into parts that appear amenable to solutions. After the problem has been identified, or defined for the purpose of analysis, one can proceed to understanding relationships.

Utilizing a meta logic approach based on the cognitive process, one can have both a logical and intuitive approach to problem solving. A major advantage of this approach to heuristics is the involvement of decision makers as experts to assist in representing their knowledge of complex problems in a structured or logical manner.

Keeney (1982) has suggested a number of factors that contribute to the complexity of decision problems.

- Multiple objectives where one simultaneously tries to minimize environmental impact, and at the same time maximize positive social impact.
- Difficulty in identifying good alternatives because of the many factors.
- Intangible factors that should be taken into account.
- Difficulty of estimating future implications.
- Need to consider many stakeholders.
- Difficulty to precisely determine risk and uncertainty.
- Interdisciplinary nature of problems makes it difficult for decision makers to be qualified in all aspects of a problem.
- Multiple decision makers makes it difficult to evaluate alternatives.
- Important decisions involve critical value tradeoffs that need to be considered.
- The sequential nature of decisions makes choices hard to evaluate.

What this list clearly indicates is that there are many factors that affect managerial decisions and lead to a level of complexity that require heuristic approaches to find meaningful solutions.

Newell and Simon (1972) suggest three general characteristics of the ill-structured problems for which heuristics have proven useful:

- Variables whose interactions are more than purely arithmetic manipulations.
- Criteria of performance leading to an acceptable solution are not readily measurable.
- Lack of algorithms leading to optimal solutions that are computationally feasible in interesting cases.

Tong (1960) has described intelligent problem-solving, whether by man or by machine as being *selective* rather than rapid response. The implication is that concern is with exploiting partial information in a problem situation where there are no assurances that the information will lead to a best solution.

Eliot (1986) defines analogy by using an example which suggests that use of prior experiences accounts for the analogical reasoning process. Referring to research in fields such as machine learning, cognitive psychology, and linguistics, Eliot claims that there is no clear distinction between the psychological phenomenon known as analogy and other types of problem-solving. However, analogies are useful for learning by example or learning by listening. He describes analogy and analogical thinking as complex phenomena that have resisted explanation by a single macroscopic theory.

Analogy and analogical thinking are viewed as interdependent and consisting of three dominant features:

- Representations for attribute knowledge vital to the analogy and analogical thinking.
- Representations for the relationship knowledge vital to the analogy and analogical thinking, and
- Operations upon attribute and relationship knowledge to perform activities that produce the analogy.

The value of heuristics becomes evident when we recognize that many decisions are made in an environment where:

- There is no feasible method that assures reaching the optimal solution or even any solution.
- Solutions need to be described in terms of acceptability rather than by optimizing rules.
- Representation of useful actions or decisions to be made is difficult.
- Problems are sufficiently large so as to make trial-and-error infeasible.

6.5 CLASSES OF HEURISTICS

Heuristics are considered as rules of discovery used to efficiently search a solution space. Where the solution space is fairly well defined, then approaches such as those described by Pearl are most appropriate. However, many managerial problems are fuzzy in nature, are ill defined, are combinatorial or involve risk and uncertainty. The traveling salesman problem, the machine assignment problem, and job shop scheduling are all examples of combinatorial problems that have been solved by heuristic methods.

As an illustration of a meta logic approach, consider the classic problem of finding the number of times one would have to weigh a set of twelve coins to determine which one was either heavier or lighter than the rest. The solution given for this problem is to weigh four coins on one side of a balance and four on the other side. This method guarantees the *different* coin will always be found in three weighings.

Using a heuristic that considers probability along with the combinatorial nature of the problem, it can be shown that one also could use a combination starting with five coins on each side of the balance. Only two weighings are required in 1/6 of the cases and four in 1/6 of the cases, thus averaging to three weighings. However, if the problem is constrained by not allowing more than three weighings, then the recommended solution is the only feasible one.

Another example is the case of ratio delay studies used to determine the amount of time that a machine is idle. Samples are taken at random to determine whether the machine is running or is idle. This situation can be described statistically by a binomial distribution. Unfortunately, if the machine is only idle 1% of the time, and one wants a 95% confidence level, then a sample size of 156 000 is required. This is a totally unreasonable number of observations for most industrial situations. If one is willing to relax the requirements, and for example say that a 1% delay can be called either zero or two, that is, one is willing to tolerate a 100% error rather than a 5% error, the sample size reduces to approximately 1500—a significant reduction from the original sample size. On the average, however, the idle time still will be recorded as 1% even with the smaller sample size.

These two examples illustrate the meta logic approach to heuristics. The solution goes beyond the original definition of the problem and takes into account other considerations besides efficiency of search.

From this perspective, we can now describe heuristics based on either the kind of problem being considered or the cognitive complexity of the decision maker. We can state problems as either fitting generic categories or fitting the number of variables that need to be considered. The generic categories can be described as follows:

- Deterministic: These problems are assumed to be well defined and not subject to variability.
- Stochastic: These problems are subject to variability and can be considered either as risk or uncertain depending on the information available.
- Combinatorial: These are ones where either the sequence or the combination of factors determines the optimum solution.
- Organizational: These cover the broad spectrum of problems that deal with people, politics, behavior, etc.

A second classification scheme which considers the number of variables in a problem is shown below:

- One variable problem: Because of its restrictiveness, this category almost always guarantees that the solution will be suboptimal.
- Two variable problem: This category covers those situations where it is possible to show a causal relationship between two variables or to compute trade-off analyses such as cost/benefit.
- Four variable problem: This class covers double balance (2×2) and represents equilibrium in a given situation. It also relates to the magic number 3 plus or minus 1.

- The N variable problem: This category covers all those problems that involve large numbers of variables that are highly interdependent and are not amenable to rigorous solution.

While any classification scheme is arbitrary, the two described above have been found useful for application of heuristic methods.

6.6 APPLICATION OF THE HEURISTIC APPROACH

Most attempts to deal with managerial problems rely on experience, intuition, judgment, creativity, inductive reasoning, brainstorming, drawing inferences, making assumptions, implicit treatment of risk, or trial and error. For example, DeBono (1967) described *lateral think* as breaking away from the deductive logic that often missed the point when attempting to find solutions to managerial problems. Synectics, nominal group technique and brainstorming attempted to find solutions by relying on the creative vision generated through human interaction. However, these attempts seldom incorporated a systematic analysis of data or adequate problem formulation.

There have been many applications of heuristics to solve physical problems, such as plant layout, warehouse location, scheduling, and inventory control. A long list of heuristic approaches (like *cutting the problem in half*, or solving the *inverse of the problem,* and such) have been identified as being useful in finding solutions.

Finding the optimum assignment of jobs to machines has been solved using linear programming. Computer programs typically require several million calculations to find the optimum solution, depending on the size of the problem. However, moderate size problems of 5 jobs and 30 machines were solved manually using a small number of calculations in little over one minute by applying a heuristic rule based on the Pareto Law. This heuristic solution involved organizing the data so that on inspection it was obvious that a small percent of the assignments were the low cost alternatives. Thus, merely looking at the problem in a logical manner, which meant recognizing that in any given problem a small number of the possible assignments are in fact the ones that are the best, was sufficient to find the optimum solution.

The heuristic approach of separating the problem into more important and less important parts, is often used by managers to find solutions. For example, managers know intuitively that a small percent of customers contribute to most of the sales. Likewise, a small percent of workers have most of the accidents, and so on. If we formalize this approach we have one of the basic building blocks for an heuristic approach to managerial problems. This approach does not rely on experience or judgment, but rather it is putting the manager's *intuitive logic* to work in a systematic manner that allows the use of heuristics to solve complex problems in a structured or logical manner.

6.7   DEVELOPMENT OF HEURISTIC RULES

There are four characteristics of heuristic reasoning that can be used as indicators of progress in solving problems. The first is perception, not in purely sensory terms, but rather as McKenney and Keen (1973) described perceiving information in terms of patterns and relationships.

A second characteristic is so-called trial and error. What is meant here is exploring to see what can be learned. It is purposeful in direction because each probe is guided by the information that has been learned from previous successful (feasible) or unsuccessful approaches. Sometimes the solution to an analogous problem is used to discover a basis for solving the problem at hand.

A third characteristic is order and notation. Confusion and repetition can be avoided by identifying variables and describing (documenting) each step and the information gained from it.

Finally, recognition of progress may involve redefinition of the problem. Problems and goals as initially perceived may have to be redefined in the light of new learning and new information.

A logical approach to heuristic rules incorporates:

- A classification scheme which introduces structure into a problem.
- Analysis of the characteristics of the problem elements.
- Rules for selecting elements from each category to achieve efficient search strategies.
- Rules for successive selections, where required.
- An objective function that is used to test the adequacy of the solution at each stage of selection or search.

The Pareto Law provides a powerful approach to the first two steps in the development of heuristics by allowing the partitioning of problems that facilitate efficient search strategies. If we divide possible solutions into two possible conditions, we can examine the expected payoff from alternate solutions as shown in Figure 6.1.

Curve B indicates that the incremental payoff for each new or additional solution is considerably less than other solutions to a given problem. Curve A, on the other hand, shows that, in a given problem, a subset of solutions have a greater payoff or are *better* than the remaining solutions.

The Pareto Law appears in many problems. Its most frequent usage has been for inventory control to describe the high, medium, and low value items. It is used to describe the relative importance of tasks performed by

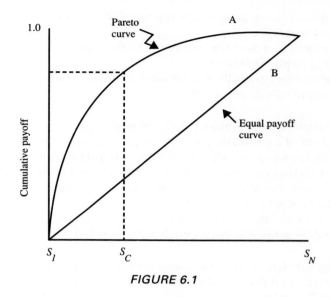

FIGURE 6.1

managers and also to describe the relative importance of the decisions they make. Because the Pareto Law describes the general behavior of a wide variety of phenomena, it provides a meaningful point of departure for developing heuristic decision rules. Decision makers or experts generally understand the characteristics of the problem being solved, and can identify the critical subset of solutions; shown as S_1 to S_c in Figure 6.1, that account for the largest payoff.

Jerome D. Weist (1966) treats the traditional enumeration procedure as a decision tree with each possible path as a branch to be evaluated by some criteria. The best alternative path is the optimal solution. The heuristic approach according to Weist, is to *prune the tree, thus eliminating from the start those branches at each decision point ... then a much smaller maze remains to be searched.*

In steps 3 and 4 above, using an efficient heuristic search algorithm, it is possible to avoid an iterative approach needed for many large combinatorial problems. What is proposed here is an approach based on a *selection* or search procedure that leads to a *good*, but not necessarily optimal solution. The advantages of such an *heuristic selection* procedure are:

● Selection often can be done with a single iteration, and is thus very efficient.
● Selection can be applied to large problems often without requiring a computer.

- If the problem can be solved using an expert system, it facilitates decision maker interaction.
- Involvement by a decision maker in the solution leads to a greater likelihood of implementation.
- *Good* solutions generally can be used as initial solutions for more formal computational procedures.

An important point to consider is the relationships that are revealed as part of the analysis of a problem. Facts are needed in order to verify what relationships exist and under what conditions. Frequently one attempts to discover what changes in relationships will produce desired results, under what conditions, and with what risks. Speculations need to be tested against what the facts may be in the future.

As an example, the branch and bound algorithm used to solve the traveling salesman problem can be described as follows:

- Intelligently structure the search of the space of all feasible solutions.
- The space of all feasible solutions is repeatedly partitioned into smaller and smaller subsets, and a lower bound is calculated for the cost of the solutions within each subset.
- After each partitioning, those subsets with a bound that exceeds the cost of a known feasible solution are excluded from all further partitions. Partitioning continues until a feasible solution is found such that its cost is no greater than the bound for each subset.
- The branch and bound algorithm requires an heuristic rule that determines which of the currently active bounding problems is to be chosen for branching, as well as the method for deriving new bounding problems.
- Branching strategies can be:

    branch from the lowest bound, or
    branch from the newest active bound

Using a meta logic approach to heuristics, the traveling salesman problem was solved with a single iteration. The result is always a *good* or the *optimum* solution. This eliminates the need to search all feasible solutions. This solution is shown in Figure 6.2 as traveling the exterior path, with no back tracking and no crossovers.

This solution demonstrates how combining the properties of the left and right hemisphere helps to find an heuristic approach to the problem. The right hemisphere has the broad vision to *look ahead* and determine which direction to pursue. The left hemisphere insures following the algorithm of no back tracking and no crossovers and no skipping of cities that are to be visited.

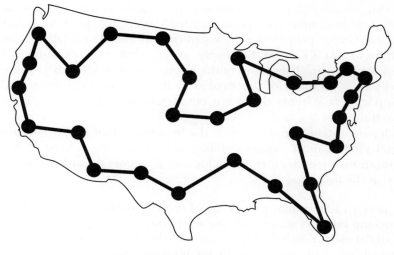

FIGURE 6.2

This application was presented to the president of a company that delivered furniture to over 30 cities in the western United States. Because there were both drop-offs and pick-ups of returns, the problem was difficult for the president to visualize. However, using a map showing where the cities were located and applying the traveling salesman heuristic described above, it was simple to show the route that should be used. The president was able to visualize the solution and readily understood the logic and had no difficulty in applying it to his problem.

6.8   COGNITION AND HEURISTICS

Researchers who have been concerned with heuristics have examined the ways in which the mind solves problems that involve discovery and judgment, especially those problems that appear to be inadequately structured in terns of precise specification and precise formulas.

Relationships appear differently to each of us depending on how we picture the problem and its various elements. In order to perceive the finer points of a problem, important elements need to be identified, how the parts are related to the whole needs to be determined, and a conceptualization that helps in solving the problem needs to be formulated. Executives are constantly creating mental images of problems that are relatively unstructured or poorly defined in terms of developing an accurate and verifiable solution. Structuring that leads to a formal statement of the problem contributes to the eventual solution.

Relying on the cognitive sciences, as contrasted to *expert systems* such as XCON for computer configurations or MYCIN for medical diagnosis, Anderson (1983) proposed a theory of cognition called Adaptive Control of Thought (ACT) or ACT-star. He argues that ACT provides a basic framework for a unified theory of the human mind. Anderson's theoretical model embodies many of the structures that are used currently in AI to develop expert systems that have characteristics similar to operational research models.

Anderson's structure is based on the hypothesis that *production rules* (an integral part of most expert systems) provide the right kind of general computational architecture for achieving a *unitary mental system*. ACT is based on the following:

- The representational properties of the knowledge structures reside in working memory along with their functional consequences.
- Careful identification of the nature of the storage process.
- Definition of the nature of the retrieval process.
- The nature of the production application which breaks down to:

  The mechanism of pattern matching.
  The process that deposits the results of pattern matching in working memory.
  The mechanisms by which production applications affect production memory.

6.9   META LOGIC AND THE BRAIN

If we distinguish among a number of the functions of the brain, we can define the meta logic of heuristics as the logic that relies on how the mind *understands* in contrast to logic that relies on *deductive reasoning*. Understanding is often equated with the cognitive process of the brain that involves operating on information that has been perceived. While differing amounts of information can be handled by individuals with varying levels of cognitive complexity, the brain uses the information input to arrive at conclusions regarding what has been perceived.

We can thus consider the following kinds of logic that the brain employs:

- Meta logic: Understanding that is a function of a person's cognitive complexity, values, beliefs, intuition and judgment. This also is referred to as inductive logic.
- Deductive logic: Reasoning that relies on analysis, formal mathematical methods or deductive approaches.
- Intuition: Applying experience, rules or procedures that are known to work, to problems at hand.

- Instinct: Relying on feeling, emotions or values as the basis for responding to informational stimuli.
- Trial and error: An approach sometimes equated with heuristics that utilizes the *right hemisphere* of the brain to do search and the *left hemisphere* to test and evaluate options.

Trial and error can be looked at in terms of how one engages in search of a problem. While in some instances, trial and error can be equated with guess work, generally it depends on past experience or intuition to determine where and how to search. For example, starting from a known solution one can readily proceed to new solutions such as is the case of the Salk vaccine for Polio that relied on known approaches for vaccination.

The brain functions in three dominant modes, the alpha, the beta and the theta mode. These can be viewed as follows:

- Alpha: The brain operates at 8 cycles per second. This mode of operation could be considered as the analysis phase that requires deep concentration and slow methodic study.
- Beta: The brain operates at 24 cycles per second. This is the typical process used during conversation or an overview of a problem that does not require the same depth of analysis as the alpha mode.
- Theta: The brain operates at its slowest speed of 4 cycles per second. This is considered the most creative mode of operation of the brain when subliminal search takes place that is able to probe beyond the cognitive limits of fully aware understanding. Both Thomas Edison and Henry Ford were supposed to have achieved their best ideas while in this mode.

Brain functions have also been described as left brain or right brain, and as reptilian or mammalian, or limbic and neocortex. If we examine the structure of the brain, it is interesting to note that there are four primary lobes: the frontal, the temporal, the occipital and the parietal. Each of these lobes appear to correspond to four basic decision types as well as to the categories of hemispheric specialization and the levels of growth or development of the human. A description of the four lobes is as follows:

- Frontal: This lobe is often associated with forward planning or logical reasoning and acts as the encoder that converts linguistic material to ideas (classification).
- Temporal: This lobe derives its name from the time orientation of the brain and is therefore associated with action or assertiveness.
- Occipital: This lobe of the brain is sometimes considered where memory is stored and where our emotions and intuition reside.

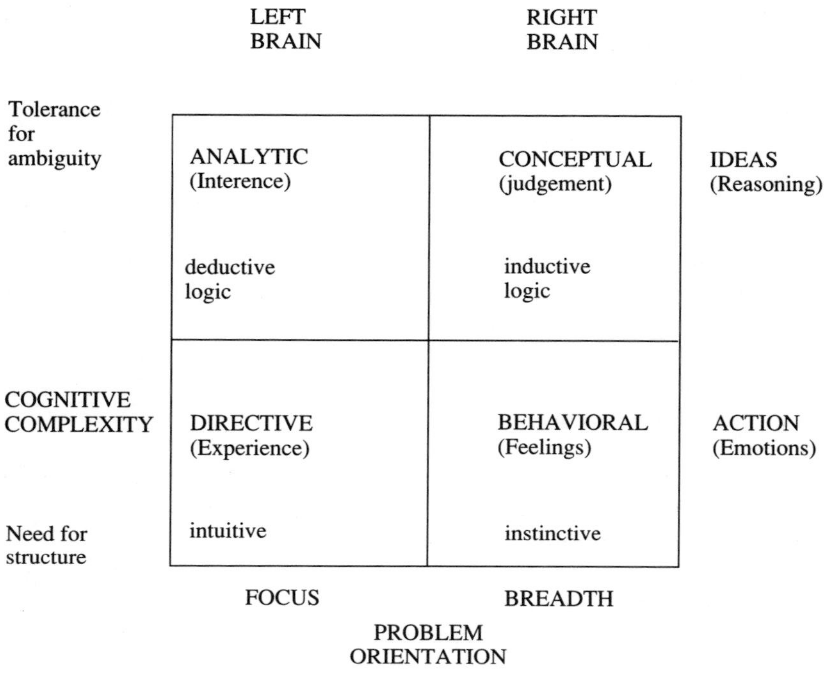

LEFT
BRAIN

RIGHT
BRAIN

Tolerance
for
ambiguity

	LEFT BRAIN	RIGHT BRAIN	
	ANALYTIC (Interence) deductive logic	CONCEPTUAL (judgement) inductive logic	IDEAS (Reasoning)
COGNITIVE COMPLEXITY	DIRECTIVE (Experience) intuitive	BEHAVIORAL (Feelings) instinctive	ACTION (Emotions)

Need for
structure

FOCUS   BREADTH

PROBLEM
ORIENTATION

FIGURE 6.3

- Parietal: This lobe operates in an overview mode that appears to associate thinking in both halves of the brain and stores memory as images or is our representational system.

Each of the lobes of the brain can be related to a basic model of decision style that uses limits of cognitive complexity on the y axis and value or functional orientation on the x axis. This model is shown in Figure 6.3.

The computational richness of the human brain come from its large number of *living neurons* that are connected to each other by a complex network or synapses. Josin (1987) describes neural-network designs that use the structure of the human brain to try and emulate the way intelligent information processing occurs within a living brain.

Jones and Hoskins (1987) describe the function of neural nets by:

- Input connections (synapses), through which the unit receives activation from other units.
- A summation function that combines the various input activations into a single activation.

- A threshold function that converts this summation of input activation into output activation (e.g., perhaps 0 output activation if the input activation falls below some threshold).
- Output connections (axonal paths) by which a unit's output activation arrives as input activation at other units in the system. In a neural network, the inter unit connections are assigned weights that modulate the activation passing through the connection. The key to understanding neural networks is the number of internodal connections and their weights. In contrast, an expert system relies on specific rules to identify conditions and actions represented by if/then pairs. The neural net can assume weights that represent learning for specific connections and activations.

A cognitive map is one way to start to build a model for a neural net. The first step is to identify the relevant factors and variables that influence a decision and can assume varying values. A cognitive map reflects the perceptions of a decision maker, and the relationships among the factors define the idiosyncrasies. These relationships reflect complexity of the net and can be used as a measure of environmental complexity.

6.10 EXERCISE OF JUDGMENT

Judgment is based on information that is perceived and processed and transformed by the human mind. Cognitive psychology has helped explain judgment as a function of perception, problem solving, thinking, memory, concept formation and information. Because judgment depends on perception, the following should be considered:

- Perception of information generally is selective.
- Information processing is done in a sequential manner.
- Humans rely on simple procedures, rules or heuristics to process information.
- People have limited memory capacity.

Combining judgment and heuristics, we can examine the rules that individuals use intuitively to solve problems. The consequences of intuitive heuristics can be seen in cases where incorrect judgments are made about chance events and data variations.

Judgment also is based on similarity or resemblance (Tversky, 1977), and can be represented as a collection of features. However, the human cognitive processes only can capture a limited number of features. Intuitively, judgments are made on the following bases:

- Whether or not an object belongs to a given category, or if several objects belong to the same category
- Predictions about prior causes based on what has been observed.

Individuals also make judgments about frequencies of events. They use heuristics to make judgments about correlations and causal relationships (Tversky and Kahneman, 1974). Typically, everyday judgments could not be made quickly and economically without heuristics.

Some of the errors that can result from the use of heuristics can be summarized as:

- Wrong coding of data
- Unable to detect covariance
- Wrong attribution of causes
- Inability to accurately predict outcomes.

Another concern related to judgment and heuristics are people's beliefs and values. Search is often selective to support existing beliefs or values and data that oppose existing beliefs will be rejected. First impressions called the "primacy effect" produce biased inferences about subsequent information. Beliefs persist even when there is discrediting of evidence on which the beliefs were based.

Because judgment and heuristics are a function of our cognitive process, it is important to recognize and deal with limitations that result from perceptual bias, strongly held beliefs, and values that are not congruent with the goals of the organization. The possible errors include:

- Preconceptions affect new information.
- Prescriptive heuristics, based on assumptions, may be inconsistent.
- Judgments may be based on inappropriate data.
- Heuristics require the test of time, and organizational acceptance.
- Heuristics do not consistently use known concepts.
- Intuitive judgments are weak in predicting chance events.
- Data may be generated improperly.
- Representativeness may be inappropriately applied in a given heuristic.
- Availability of categories or theories can be misleading in a given heuristic.
- Conceptual frameworks are needed to define the territory.
- Beliefs can be so strongly held as to be misleading.
- Judgment can preclude consideration of later facts.

- Normative inference can be more useful than intuition when coding data, covariation, attributing causes, and prediction.
- Information can easily be distorted.

6.11 PROBLEMS IN USING HEURISTICS

Geoffrion and Van Roy (1979) identifies the following shortcomings of heuristics:

- Enumeration heuristics that consider all possible combinations in practical problems can seldom be achieved.
- Sequential decision choices can fail to anticipate future consequences of each choice.
- Local improvement can short circuit the best solution because they lack a global perspective.
- Interdependencies of one part of a system can sometimes have a profound influence on the whole system.

Geoffrion and Roy maintain that common sense approaches and heuristics can fail because they are *arbitrary*. They are arbitrary in the choice of a starting point, in the sequence in which assignments or other decision choices are made, the resolution of ties, in the choice of criteria for specifying the procedure, and in the level of effort expended to demonstrate that the final solution is in fact best or very nearly so. The result is erratic and unpredictable behavior—good performance in some specific applications and bad in other.

They also expressed concern about a more profound weakness of heuristics in the planning process. It is precisely this kind of problem that requires more robust heuristics that utilize both the analytic and the intuitive capability of decision makers. They see a critical need to *solve* planning problems under several alternative sets of assumptions. Consequently, the ability to ask *What if ... ?* questions is more important than finding a so called optimum plan. The reasons are summarized as follows:

- The planning team has to come up with good recommendations, and also convincing justification to gain acceptance of the plan.
- It is important to work simultaneously with more than one set of assumptions.
- It is important to compare solutions under different sets of assumptions.

While concerns have been expressed about using heuristics, nonetheless, this is the way that managers, who are considered experts, view the world. What a Knowledge Engineer has to understand is that heuristics require a combination of right brain for insights and left brain for developing rules.

6.12   CONCLUSIONS

With the explosive growth of expert systems applications, there is a significant potential for solving complex problems. The objective in this chapter was to explore how heuristic methods could be used in expert systems. By understanding cognition and judgment as they affect knowledge representation, we are able to see that alternative representational structures can extend the boundaries of current applications. For example, Bob Dwinnell (1987) at Amphenol strongly states,

> I think model-based reasoning, that is modeling a system's structure and function and then reasoning about the models, is even more valuable as a software programming technique than the classic expert systems approach.

When modelling approaches are combined with heuristics they offer interesting new possibilities. They can be used for complex managerial problems and increase the likelihood that managers will accept solutions. Alternative schema representations using the Pareto Law, models of known phenomena, decision tables, semantic and neural networks, and so on, offer the opportunity to increase the effectiveness of knowledge representation, and thereby can enhance the value of expert systems while at the same time increasing the effectiveness of decision making and problem solving.

REFERENCES

Anderson, J.R. (1983), *The Architecture of Cognition*, Harvard University Press, Cambridge, MA.

Chorafas, D.N. (1987), *Applying Expert Systems in Business*, McGraw-Hill, New York.

DeBono, E. (1967), *New Think*, Basic Books, New York.

Dwinnell, B. (1987), "Extending Expert Systems: Model Based Reasoning," *AI Expert*, March.

Eliot, L.B. (1986), "Analogical Problem-Solving and Expert Systems," *IEEE Expert*, Vol. 1, No. 2, Summer, p. 17.

Fulton, S.P. and Pepe, C.O. (1990), An Introduction to Model-Based Reasoning, *AI Expert*, Jan., 48–56.

Gazzaniga M. (1988), *Mind Matters*, Houghton Mifflin Co., Boston, Mass., p. 63.

Geoffrion, A.M., and Van Roy, T.J. (1979), "Caution: Common Sense Planning Methods Can Be Hazardous to Your Corporate Health," *Sloan Management Review*, Summer, p. 41.

Gordon, P.J. (1962), "Heuristic Problem Solving," *Business Horizons*, Spring, p. 43.

Hertz, D.B. (1985), "That World Out There: Models and Knowledge Representation," *TIMS/ORSA Annual Meeting*, Atlanta.

Hertz, D.B. (1988), *The Executive Expert*, John Wiley & Sons, New York.

Jones, W.P. and Hoskins, J. (1987), "Back-Propagation," *BYTE*, Vol. 12, No. 11, p. 155.

Josin, G. (1987), "Neural-Network Heuristics," *BYTE*, Vol. 12, No. 11, p. 183.

Keeney, R.L. (1982), "Decision Analysis: An Overview," *Operations Research*, Sept./Oct., Vol. 30, pp. 803–838.

Keeney, R.L. and Winterfeldt, D. Von, (1989), "On the Uses of Expert Judgment of Complex Technical Problems", *IEEE Transactions*, Vol. 36, No. 2, May, pp. 83-94.

McKenney, J.L. and Keen, P. (1973)," How Manager's Minds Work," *Harvard Business Review*, Vol. 51 (4), pp. 79–90.

Newell, A. and Simon, H. (1972), *Human Problem Solving*, Englewood Cliffs, NJ: Prentice-Hall.

Pearl, J. (1984), *Heuristics*, Addison-Wesley, Reading, MA.

Penrose, R. (1989), *The Emperor's New Mind*, Oxford University Press, New York, p. 396, p. 418.

Polya, G. (1957), *How to Solve It*, Doubleday Anchor Books, Garden City, NY.

Rowe, A.J. and Bahr, F. (1972), "A Heuristic Approach to Managerial Problem Solving," *Journal of Economics and Business*, Fall, p. 159.

Simon, H. (1982), *The Science of the Artificial*, MIT Press, Cambridge, MA.

Tong, F.M. (1960), *The Use of Heuristic Programming in Management Science*, RAND Corporation Paper No. 2127.

Tversky, A. (1977), "Features of Similarity," *Psychological Review*, Vol. 84, No. 4, p. 327.

Tversky, A. and Kahneman, D. (1974), "Judgment Under Uncertainty: Heuristics and Biases," *Science*, Vol. 185, p. 1124.

Wiest, J.D. (1966), "Heuristic Programs for Decision Making," *Harvard Business Review*, October.

Chapter 7

PERFORMANCE MODELING: A COGNITIVE APPROACH TO BUILDING KNOWLEDGE-BASED SYSTEMS

Leif B. Methlie
Norwegian School of Economics and Business Administration, Bergen-Sandviken

This chapter is based on the observation that cognitive approaches to developing knowledge-based systems in practice are scarce. One reason for this is, that in building these systems, more emphasis is put on technical design than on problem analysis. Expert systems emulating human experts can only be developed by modeling real problem solving behavior—we call this performance modeling. Performance modeling, as described in this chapter, is based on theories, models, methods and techniques found in cognitive psychology. Verbal protocols and protocol analysis are central to this methodology. However, contrary to what is typically found in studies using protocol analysis methods, the methodology described in this chapter puts more emphasis on conceptual analysis and structuring. Finally, we show the methodology applied to the development of a knowledge-based system for financial advising, called SAFIR.

7.1 INTRODUCTION

7.1.1 Knowledge Engineering

When Feigenbaum and his collaborates at Stanford University were developing the first system, they coined the term knowledge engineering to describe the process of creating an expert system and the term knowledge engineer to describe an expert system developer (Feigenbaum, 1977):

> The knowledge engineer practices the art of bringing the principals and tools of AI research to bear on difficult applications problems requiring experts' knowledge for their solution. The technical issues of acquiring this knowledge representing it, and using it appropriately to construct and explain lines-of-reasoning, are important problems in the design of knowl-

Expert Systems in Business and Finance: Issues and Applications. Edited by P.R. Watkins and L.B. Eliot
© 1993 John Wiley & Sons Ltd.

edge-based systems ... The art of constructing intelligent agents is both part of and an extension of the programming art. It is the art of building complex computer programs that represent and reason with knowledge of the world.

Feigenbaum calls knowledge engineering an art. It is true that most expert systems development until now has focused on computer representations and program design. By means of very powerful development tools, so-called expert system shells, rapid prototyping has been the dominant approach. Tool-skill has been more emphasized than methodological competence in performing problem analysis. As a result, the development of a knowledge engineering methodology has been lagging behind the practice of building expert systems. Lack of concrete methods and techniques of knowledge engineering have led to the common apprehension that the performance of this task is more an art than a science (cf. the citation from Feigenbaum above). The practice of building expert systems is very similar to what is found in other areas where computers are applied to ill-structured problems, for instance, as in developing decision support systems for complex decision making. In areas where we have highly developed and functionally integrated development tools, like DSS-generators or expert system shells, the development has been very much a technology-driven process.

In a technology-driven process, the functionality of the application system grows incrementally from a preliminary specification of systems requirements. In the context of prototype systems, new ideas are generated and new opportunities are discussed in an interaction between the system builder and the user or expert. Thus, application complexity is reduced by successive redefinitions and the lack of contextual skill of the knowledge engineer is overcome by prototyping.

In a problem-driven approach, analysis is at the forefront. The problem domain is thoroughly analyzed, structured and specified. A conceptual model of problem solving (with knowledge and reasoning) is specified and implemented as a base version, from which prototyping can take over for testing, validation and growth of the knowledge-base.

A strong critique of rapid prototyping can be found in Laske (1986). He claims that *expert systems built by rapid prototyping are built on two particularly unhelpful, if not entirely wrong, assumptions.* The first assumption is that the knowledge engineer is a neutral arbiter between the expert and the development tool. The second assumption is that human experts can be tapped directly by verbal retrieval cues (e.g. questions) that force the expert to make performance-unrelated observations and comments on his solution process. This second assumption violates the methodological preconditions for achieving valid verbal reports, that is, reports that really verbalize the true performance of the expert. The latter argument is founded on the theory of human information processing theory (see Section 7.3.1). According to Laske (1986) knowledge elicitation based on some form of dialogue between the expert and the knowledge engineer (questions, retrospection, rapid prototyping, etc.) can only give knowledge about the task environment. He calls these systems competence systems. By using concurrent, verbal protocols, performance knowledge can be elicited. He calls these systems performance models of expertise.

7.1.2 What is Performance Modeling?

Expert systems, as an application field of artificial intelligence, have been indirectly influenced by cognitive aspects commonly found in cognitive psychology. By indirectly, we mean that the basic architecture of expert systems is derived from cognitive psychology, viz. that of production systems, which in turn is an outcome of research on human problem solving. This research led to the theory of human information processing (Newell and Simon, 1972) which is based on two fundamental concepts: symbols and heuristic search. The production systems which follow from this theory define memory structures, pattern matching, and control strategies. The influence of cognitive psychology is embedded in the design framework of, and development tools for, expert systems. However, so far we have seen less influence on the knowledge engineering process.

Performance modeling is an approach to knowledge engineering which utilizes models, hypotheses, methods and techniques from cognitive psychology in the building process of expert systems. Performance modeling refers to a strategy in expert system design which seeks to elicit real problem solving knowledge from human experts. This knowledge, which is in the mind of the expert, is made explicit through verbalization. This approach is also called cognitive emulation (Slatter, 1987). Performance modeling or cognitive emulation is both a descriptive concept and a prescriptive principle. As a descriptive concept, it can be argued that most expert systems incorporate—albeit unintentionally—many features characteristic of human knowledge processing. As a prescriptive principle, cognitive emulation refers to expert system work in which an explicit strategy of emulating human cognitive processes is followed (Slatter, 1987, p.10).

7.1.3 Current Status of the Cognitive Approach

We have said above that we have seen less influence of cognitive psychology on the knowledge engineering processes than on the design framework of expert systems. However, there are some early examples of cognitive approaches, for instance, INTERNIST (Pople, 1982). Also, there is a growing research to build knowledge methodologies more closely on cognitive psychology models, methods and techniques (e.g. Breuker, 1984; Boose, 1984; and Laske, 1986). However, despite the upsurge of interest, cognitive approaches in knowledge engineering are, according to Slatter (1987, p.12) more exceptions rather than the rule:

Most of the best known systems—including MYCIN (Shortliffe, 1976), PROSPECTOR (Duda *et al.* 1979), DENDRAL (Buchanan, Sutherland and Feigenbaum, 1969) and R1/XCON (McDermott, 1982)—were constructed with little or no explicit aim of modeling expert thinking. Outside of research-oriented establishments there is, if anything, even less explicit concern with cognitive emulation. In commercial applications of today's expert systems technology the emphasis is firmly on achieving expert-level performance using formal problem-solving methods. This viewpoint is expressed in the technology-based definition of expert systems offered by T. Johnson (1984, p.15): a set of computer programs which emulate human expertise by applying the techniques or logical inference to a knowledge-base.

7.1.4 What is this Chapter about?

In this chapter we shall first deal with the process of knowledge engineering from a cognitive perspective. The description of this process is in terms of what the tasks, phases, or stages are that we have to deal with or move through in order to reach a model of human problem-solving that lends itself for computer implementation within well-known expert systems architectures. This process description builds on the two basic concepts from cognitive psychology: task environment and problem space of an expert.

Next, we shall deal with performance modeling in three steps: the theoretical foundation, the methods available for eliciting knowledge, and the modeling (or analysis) of that knowledge. The theoretical foundation is based on the theory of human information processing (Newell and Simon, 1972) and the basic method of knowledge elicitation is verbalization. With respect to analysis of verbal reports, more emphasis is put on conceptual analysis in this chapter than is typically found in other studies of performance using protocol analysis (e.g. Biggs and Mock, 1983 or Bouwman *et al.*, 1987). Those studies are more focused on processes.

Finally, we demonstrate the modeling methodology on a case from financial analysis and the development of an expert system for financial advising called SAFIR.

7.2   KNOWLEDGE ENGINEERING—AN OVERVIEW OF THE PROCESS

The methodology for knowledge engineering described below presumes that the knowledge-based system to be developed is designed to emulate expert problem solving. To adequately understand and represent expertise in a conceptual model, two kinds of knowledge must be present. First is the knowledge about the task (P.E. Johnson, 1984, p.369):

> What is of interest here is the task demands, their interrelationships, the goals or criteria for task completion, and a set of rules that can accomplish the goals given some set of initial conditions"

Second is the performance knowledge about problem solving behavior. A knowledge engineering methodology must provide for both kinds of knowledge to be modeled. We shall suggest a two-stage knowledge elicitation process starting with a task analysis and followed by a performance study as shown in Figure 7.1.

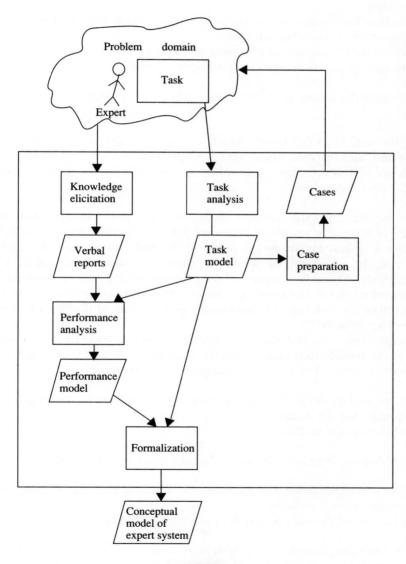

FIGURE 7.1

7.2.1 Task Analysis

The first stage is to develop a model of the task for which we want to build an expert system. The purpose of a task model is as follows:

- To prepare the setting for performance studies of expert problem-solving
- To function as an interpretative framework for protocol analysis
- To establish user characteristics
- To establish criteria for choosing an expert
- To specify performance criteria for the system.

To prepare the setting for further data collection on performance requires that:

- The task is well-defined, which means that the problem is clearly stated, and the conclusion set is well-defined
- A set of relevant cases are available containing enough information for problem solving.

To develop an interpretative framework for performance analysis, a model of the task is required. A task model is a general competence model of how a typical expert might perform the task in question. It is a first order model which will be developed further as more empirical data are available. It is the basic structure of the problem solving process involved and a general model of the reasoning steps. Thus, this task model is a decomposition of the task into sub-tasks and a specification of the flow of control between sub-tasks.

In addition to the task model an interpretative framework must consist of a general domain description, usually found in text books, or other reference documents. The domain description consists of:

- A vocabulary of the domain, i.e. what are the task-relevant terms that are specific for the domain?
- Theories and methods

Establishing the characteristics of a user involves determining:

- The competence level of the users, i.e. who are the users and with what methods are they familiar
- The role of the user in problem solving and decision making.

The final purpose of task analysis is to make an evaluation of the potential costs and benefits of a knowledge-based system for the task. Waterman has formulated some guidelines for considering expert systems development. He summarizes these guidelines as follows (Waterman, 1986, p.327):

> Consider expert systems only if expert systems development is possible, justified, and appropriate.

He develops a set of task attributes for this evaluation.

7.2.2 Performance Modeling

Performance modeling deals with the knowledge in the problem space, that is, knowledge about problem representation and problem solving in the mind of the expert. The modeling is executed in two major steps:

- Knowledge elicitation
- Performance analysis.

Using verbalization as our main method for knowledge elicitation, performance analysis starts with verbal reports (protocols) and ends with a performance model of the expert's problem solving process for each case solved. The protocols collected present detailed, step-by-step traces of the expert's problem solving behavior. We shall develop a protocol analysis methodology which is particularly suited for knowledge-based system development. The performance analysis we shall divide into the following steps:

- Conceptual identification and classification
- Conceptual structuring
- Qualifications of comparative and evaluative concepts, and
- Problem-solving strategies.

Since the rest of the chapter deals with performance modeling, each of these tasks will be dealt with in more detail below.

7.3 PERFORMANCE MODELING: THE THEORY

7.3.1 The Information Processing Theory

One approach to the study of human thinking and decision making is the information processing theory developed by Newell and Simon (1972). This theory views a human as a processor of information; and postulates that thinking, in general, and problem solving in particular, can be explained by means of an information processing theory.

Information processing in the human mind is thought of as a set of operations on mental objects (information). The question *What is the name of the capital of France?* generates a number of mental activities: identifying and understanding each word, understanding the meaning of the sentence, searching in memory for the answer, and generating the answer. In processing the question above, we have identified an orderly sequence of mental operations. When a human performs a particular cognitive task we can trace the whole set of such sequences.

Advocates of the information processing theory assert that cognitive tasks can best be understood by analogy to programmed computers. The assumptions behind this approach can be summarized as follows (Winograd and Flores, 1986, p.25):

> (1) All cognitive systems are symbol systems. They achieve their intelligence by symbolizing external and internal situations and events, and by manipulating those symbols.
> (2) All cognitive systems share a basic underlying set of symbol-manipulating processes.
> (3) A theory of cognition can be couched as a program in an appropriate symbolic formalism such that the program, when run in the appropriate environment, will produce the observed behavior.

The cognitive architecture of the human mind can be described as:

- Long-Term Memory, which for all practical purposes has unlimited capacity, permanent storage, instant retrieval times, but fairly long write times
- Short-Term Memory, or working memory, with instantaneous access and storage, but with a very limited size. Information can be processed only when it is in short-term memory (in active state)
- Mental Operations, or cognitive processor, which is a serial mechanism capable of executing only a handful of so-called elementary processes, such as retrieving symbols, comparing two symbols, etc.

The serial aspect of the cognitive processor is important for studying problem solving and decision making. As will be discussed later, the method of verbal protocols for tracing cognitive processes is based on the postulate that the performance of cognitive tasks is reflected in a person's verbalization of the processes due to the serial nature of the processor.

The long-term memory holds the domain knowledge; that is, facts, concepts and conceptual structures (relationships), and mental models (descriptive and procedural knowledge).

7.3.2 Concepts

Real world objects can be perceived at several levels of abstraction: for example, the same object can be an *asset*, a *fixed asset*, a *factory* and a *building*.

Human memory for object concepts appears to be organized in this kind of hierarchical fashion (Rosch *et al.*, 1976). Rosch *et al.* suggest that experts are capable of making finer categorical distinctions than novices, and thus have more lower level categories.

Together with this ability to make finer categorical discriminations, the expert is sensitive to more attributes of domain concepts (Murphy and Wright, 1984). Furthermore, as single attributes become less predictive of category membership, experts may place greater emphasis on the predictive value of familiar configurations of attributes (see Wittgenstein's view on concept definition based on family resemblance in Section 7.5.3). The hierarchical organization of object categories represents *is-a-kind-of* relationships.

Facts arise when objects are described by attributes, for instance, *Accounts receivable increases*. A fact is one type of a conceptual relationship. A rule is another. Look at the following excerpt of a protocol: *Accounts receivable continues to increase despite a stable sales turnover. This indicates a payment collection problem.*

This utterance can be interpreted as a result of applying the following rule:

IF   accounts receivable increases,
AND   sales turnover remains constant
THEN   this indicates a payment collection problem.

This is a heuristic rule which implicitly contains some causal relationships.

7.3.3 Mental Models

A heuristic rule may be recalled from memory. However, in performing a complex task such as financial analysis, people access some kind of mental model. Mental models help guide understanding and actions. There is a lack of agreement at present among researchers as to the exact nature of mental models. A consensus position might be that mental models are more or less definite representations embodying structural and/or functional properties of the entity modeled (Slatter, 1987).

In the protocol excerpt above, there is the following causal relationship represented:

Sales turnover+ ———> Accounts receivable+

A mental model is a collection of concept relationships concerning a specific aspect. Facts can be represented by propositions. The interconnections among propositions define a network of concepts and relationships. Further organization of knowledge in mental models can be described by schemes (structures of objects and events) or influence diagrams. In a mental model we find several kinds of relationships: numerical, logical, plausible, causal, time, etc.

7.3.4 Mental Operations

Mental operations include retrieving information from the long-term memory and processing this information in order to achieve a goal (e.g. solve a problem).

7.3.5 Fact Retrieval

Experts are far better than novices at recalling facts about a domain (Arkes and Freedman, 1984). This finding presents a challenge to the theory of inference in information retrieval from long-term memory. This theory states that inference from other information associated with a concept slows down the speed with which a fact can be retrieved. Experts' more detailed domain knowledge together with faster retrieval times than novices is the so-called *paradox of inference*.

This phenomenon is open to a number of, not necessarily mutually exclusive, explanations according to Slatter (1987):

(1) *Indexing.* Perpetual patterns in the current state of the problem solution automatically trigger the activation of relevant information. Take, for instance, the following protocol excerpt: *Financial costs are very high—let us have a look at the overdraft.* The immediate move from financial costs to the overdraft illustrates retrieval by indexing.
(2) *Integration.* Organization of knowledge in units associated with a concept (cf. mental model above) increases the activation process and reduces retrieval times.
(3) *Plausible Inference.* Experts seem able to make use of their domain knowledge to infer what correct or plausible response should be (Arkes and Freedman, 1984). Plausible inferences can be thought of as generating an explanation (also called abduction; see Charniak and McDermott, 1985).

7.4 PERFORMANCE MODELING: THE METHODOLOGY

Modeling human cognition at the level of an individual expert requires knowledge elicitation, that is, the process of acquiring knowledge from a human expert.

Several knowledge elicitation techniques exist—each one being strong in eliciting certain types of knowledge. In the following we shall give a brief discussion of some techniques.

7.4.1 Verbal Protocols

Verbal protocols are used to obtain information about the cognitive processes of a subject dealing with a problem. They are literal transcripts of the expert's verbalization as recorded on audio tape. To collect a concurrent verbal protocol the subject is asked to verbalize his/her thoughts during task performance.

Concurrent verbal protocols tap directly the successive states of heeded information in the mind of the expert. According to Ericsson and Simon (1984, p.16) this method comes closest to the reflection of the cognitive processes:

> We claim that cognitive processes are not modified by these verbal reports, and that task-directed cognitive processes determine what information is heeded and verbalized.

Most people cannot verbalize as fast as they think. People also forget to verbalize, and some repetitive cognitive processes may be automated and thus unavailable for tapping. However, for verbal reasoning tasks such as problem solving and decision making, Ericsson and Simon (1980, p.227) conclude that,

> The performance may be slowed down, and the verbalization may be incomplete, but the course and the structure of the task performance will remain largely unchanged.

Although verbal protocols provide a dense trace of cognitive behavior, and the information present is valid, some information is still unavailable, thus leaving out some details of the subject's behavior.

It is important that the setting for concurrent verbal protocol sessions come as close to the natural task environment as possible. Several preconditions have to be satisfied for a successful session to be accomplished with the expert:

(1) The sample of cases chosen is crucial. The cases must be representative for the task.
(2) The task must have a clearly defined conclusion, i.e. it must be possible to determine when the task is completed.
(3) The task must contain sufficient data for completion in one session.
(4) The data must be presented to the expert in a familiar form.
(5) The expert should be given a test case to become familiar with this experimental technique and get feedback from the knowledge engineer on the verbalization performance.

During a session, as few interruptions as possible should be made by the knowledge engineer. Only when the expert stops verbalizing should the knowledge engineer interfere.

Advantages: (1) A natural setting for problem solving where real performance knowledge can be elicited through verbalization of thought processes. (2) Richness of detail and high temporal density of oral responses. (3) Particularly useful in obtaining behavioral evidence in complex tasks (Biggs and Mock, 1983).

Disadvantages: (1) Giving protocols can interfere with task performance. (2) Protocol analysis is a skilled, difficult, and time-consuming task. (3) Transcripts can be highly ambiguous, requiring much interpretation when analyzed (Slatter, 1987).

7.4.2 Interviews

Interviews are the most familiar method in knowledge elicitation. This method is widely used because it is easy to perform. However, care has to be shown in preparing the interviews in order to obtain useful results.

We may distinguish between two types of interviews: structured and unstructured. Unstructured interviews are most akin to normal conversation. The knowledge engineer asks questions and the expert answers. The preparation for an unstructured interview is to set up a list of topics one wants to know more about. Unstructured interviews utilize addressing and probing. Topics are addressed in a breadth-first or depth-first manner, and probes are used to encourage the expert to talk, to dig deeper into a topic, to specify directions one wants to pursue, or to provide a change in view of a particular topic.

Structured interviews are more like an interrogation and are based upon a predefined set and sequence of questions. The knowledge engineer asks for clarifications, explanations, justifications, consequences, etc. The purpose of a structured interview is to get a detailed insight into the domain. It may uncover concepts and conceptual structures of the domain, qualifications of variables, justifications and explanations.

According to Welbank (1983), knowledge engineers have mainly used interviews in building expert systems.

> Interview data tends to be at the level of rules and general principles, and cannot produce the detailed context of real behavior, e.g., what setting a control knob would be put to. On the other hand, interviews are the best means of extracting background knowledge and the reason behind behavior. They are also faster than observational methods, and can cover low probability events.

Advantages: (1) Knowledge which is explicit to the expert or which can be easily probed can be elicited quickly. (2) Useful in early phases for eliciting the basic structure of the domain (task analysis), and in qualification of relationships (see Section 7.5).

Disadvantages: (1) Unsuited for eliciting expert's performance knowledge. (2) Knowledge elicited is general, inconsistent, incomprehensive and imprecise. (3) Requires careful preparation.

7.4.3 Prototyping

The importance of feedback and context has been stressed. One means of feedback is to build a prototype system once enough knowledge has been collected. This prototype can be used to further elicitate knowledge of two kinds:

(1) Test already implemented knowledge and identify missing knowledge
(2) Reveal missing patterns in the rules and fill these.

Advantages: Puts the expert in the context of using the system, thus better realizing the purpose of the knowledge engineering activities.
Disadvantages: No performance knowledge is elicited.

7.4.4 Other Methods

There exist several other methods for knowledge elicitation which we shall briefly mention here:

(1) *Observational Studies* which are similar to verbal protocols, except that there is no interference with the expert's normal task performance. Videoing, phone recording, etc. are means to perform observational studies.
(2) *Conceptual Sorting* is a well-known technique in the field of cognitive psychology. Subjects are given a set of concepts which should be sorted into several groups, identifying what each group has in common, and then combining the groups to form hierarchies.
(3) *Repertory Grid Technique* is used to identify perceived similarities and differences in a set of concepts. The basic component is the grid which when completed represents the subject's view of the world (domain). This grid is suited for analysis.

7.5   PERFORMANCE MODELING: THE PROTOCOL ANALYSIS

We shall adhere to the assumption that performance studies of expert problem solving can best be done by verbal protocols (cf. Laske, 1986 and the above discussion on methodology). The major task in information analysis, is, therefore, an analysis of verbal protocols. However, as we shall see in the next section, protocols may be complemented with interviews or other techniques, to acquire as much knowledge as possible.

7.5.1 The Protocol Methodology

The aim of the protocol methodology is to get access to the subject's problem space—that is, the internal or cognitive representation of a task. This problem space provides evidence of information processing and choice behavior of the subject. Such evidence can help to explain problem solving behavior and to explain differences among several individuals. Protocol analysis is not a uniform technique. How the analysis is done depends on the focus of the study.

In studying individual problem solving behavior, Newell and Simon's (1972) theory of human problem solving has provided the theoretical foundation for many protocol analysis studies (see for instance, Biggs and Mock, 1983 and Bouwman *et al.* 1987). The essential task of these studies has been to search for goals, operators and states of knowledge in the subject's problem space. Since the operators represent a subject's processes or actions in problem solving, they have been of primary concern in many of these studies. In the study of Biggs and Mock (1983), 14 operators were defined and classified into four general categories: task structuring, information acquisition, analytical, and action. Similarly, in the study by Bouwman *et al.* (1987), activities were defined (and coded) into 21 types and classified into the following five categories: reading and examination, reasoning, goal, memory access, and comments.

The purpose of our study is to produce the knowledge required to emulate expert behavior. We shall put emphasis on *conceptual analysis*, that is, which concepts are used by the expert, and in which relationships do they enter. After having identified the conceptual relationships we will use interviews and prototyping to qualify the relationships in terms of logical inferences, plausible inferences, numerical relationships, etc.

A first attempt to produce a rule-base for credit evaluation (a production system) by protocol analysis failed. This analysis was carried out to the level of detail of the problem behavior graphs (PBG) found in Newell and Simon (1972) and on the detailed activity levels as described in Bouwman *et al.* (1987). These findings may seem contradictory to Newell and Simon's results:

> Since our data (the PBG) are a set of correspondences between states of knowledge and the actions that resulted, the production system turns out to be a natural form for an IPS. In particular, it seems well adapted to inducing the total program from the PBG, since each production, which is an actual component of the eventual program, is introduced to handle one or more situations where certain specific information evokes given operators. The total program, then, is the collection of these individual productions, plus the ordering of the productions that resolves conflict if several conditions are satisfied concurrently.

The contradiction in our experience with the findings of Newell and Simon may be explained by differences in task complexity. In cryptarithmetic, which is the kind of problem addressed by the subjects in Newell and Simon's studies, the task is difficult but structured and the goal state is distinct and definite. In credit evaluation, task complexity is great, there is not one single, definite answer and no normative solution. The process involves evaluation and judgment. Therefore, there is not one distinct path from the initial state to the goal state.

7.5.2 The Set-up for Data Collection

Folstad (1984) has given some practical hints to the collection of verbal protocols:

> Before the protocols are collected the subject (expert) should be given an explanation what the purpose is and what the experiment is about, and what is to be expected as the outcome of the experiment. The purpose here is to motivate the subject. Next, the subject is given instructions which more specifically explain how the experiment is to be accomplished. The first part of the instructions tells the subject what the problem is, for instance, based on the given case-material make a credit evaluation of the company. Next, the subject is told how to perform the task, i.e. to think aloud: "Think, reason in a loud voice, verbalize everything that passes through your mind as you solve the problem. I am not primarily interested in your final conclusion, but in your thinking behavior, in all your attempts to find a solution, in whatever comes to your mind, no matter whether it is a good or bad idea, or a question. Don't plan what to say, or think before you speak, but rather let your thoughts speak, as though you were really thinking out loud. Don't let my presence disturb you." If the subject does pause, it is necessary to intervene and remind the subject to continue to talk.

The session must be carried out in an environment free from external disturbances and with the tape recording equipment as unobtrusive as possible for the subject. It is important to give the subject as natural a task environment as possible. A task analysis must be done prior to the protocol collection where the problems presented to the subject represent relevant cases, have sufficient information for problem solving, and have a clear problem statement.

7.5.3 Conceptual Analysis

According to Sowa (1984, p. 294) the purpose of conceptual analysis is to produce a catalog of concepts, relations, facts, and principles that make up a domain—the ontology of a domain. Concept definitions and conceptual analysis have been of concern to philosophers, linguists and psychologists for ages. The hardest concepts to analyze and describe are the ones that are closest to everyday life. For the Canadian census, data base designers found thorny problems with basic terms like building and dwelling. Since the number of possible forms for buildings were so great, they did not even attempt to give a definition (Sowa, 1984). The classical way of defining a concept is by a set of necessary and sufficient conditions. This way is used in formal treatments of mathematics and logic.

In his early philosophy, Wittgenstein adhered to this view. In his later philosophy, he (Wittgenstein, 1953) developed his view on concept definitions based on family resemblance. A word like *game* has no common properties that characterize its uses. Competition is present in ball games, but absent in solitaire. The concept GAME has no differentiae that distinguish games from all other activities. Instead, games share a sort of family resemblance. For most of the concepts of everyday life, meaning is determined not by definition, but by family resemblances or a characteristic prototype. A concept is defined by an example or prototype if an object, which is an instance of a concept *c*, resembles the characteristic prototype of *c*: more closely than the prototypes of concepts other than *c* (Smith and Medin, 1981).

> When a natural concept is expressed in a computable form, its vague boundaries and continuous shadings are replaced by sharp, precise distinctions. Although precision is usually desirable, resemblance is replaced with a concept of the same that is defined by necessary and sufficient conditions.

Sowa (1984) distinguishes between concepts that are natural types (e.g. PERSON) and others that are role types (e.g. PEDESTRIAN). Furthermore, we have concepts of the comparative type like BIG, or an evaluative type like GOOD.

We shall now describe a protocol analysis method with focus on conceptual analysis and with the purpose of producing a knowledge-base in a computable form. According to what we have said above this means to be able to express concepts and concept relations in a precise way, which for natural concepts may lead to problems. However, we shall deal with domains only where concepts to a great extent are technically defined and expressed in precise terms. For instance, in financial analysis, the vocabulary is given by accounting terminology concerning financial statements and ratio analysis.

We shall divide the task into four sub-tasks:

- Concept identification and classification
- Conceptual structuring
- Qualifications of comparative and evaluative concepts
- Problem solving strategies.

Concept Identification and Classification

Protocols contain information that reveal many aspects of the subject's concern about the task. They not only contain information about cognitive behavior, but they also reveal information about the subject's familiarity with the task, uncertainty about how to approach the task, affections, etc.

We shall only concern ourself with task-specific knowledge, knowledge which describes the subject's cognitive behavior.

We shall perform this task in three steps:

- Identification of domain concepts
- Segmentation
- Classification.

Identification of the domain concepts is done by matching terms of the protocol with theoretical concepts of the domain. In financial analysis this is done by matching terms of the protocols with accounting terminology.

For instance, the subject says: Let us use as a rule of thumb that if return on investment is between 10 and 15, then it is *slightly below satisfactory.* The object of interest here (the domain concept) is *return on investment,* a term well known in the vocabulary of financial analysis. At this stage of analysis we also have to look for synonyms. Terms identified to mean the same may be replaced by synonyms. Some care has to be exercised here in order not to lose semantic content.

Segmentation of a protocol means to split it into parts. The segmentation criterion is an identified object and everything that is said about this object in one sequence. For example:

> Let us use as a rule of thumb that if return on investment is between 10 and 15, then it is slightly below satisfactory. If it is below 10, then it is clearly less than satisfactory. I don't think it is necessary to make any steps below that. But when I see that it moves towards 11–12%, then I say, well, this starts to become fairly good.

A segment is a paragraph of the protocol concerning one object. This object is called the focus object. It is described by relations to other objects, verbs, prepositions, and adjectives. A paragraph can be split into topics, each one being a description element or argument about the focus object.

Classification of arguments can now be done on the level of a topic for each focus object. The following classifications are used: A focused object is described in terms of evaluative and comparative concepts, or in terms of explanatory concepts and type hierarchies. All of these descriptive concepts are what we call attributes of the focused object.

Evaluative Attributes are associated with absolute values and explicit norms, for instance, profitability is good. We denote evaluative attributes by the term LEVEL.

Comparative Attributes are associated with relative values and explicit differentials, for instance, profitability is improving. We shall denote comparative attributes by the term TREND.

Explanatory Attributes and type hierarchies define concept relations. We shall not at this stage define the kind of relation (causal, definitional, etc.), but only denote the relation by the name of the object which occurs in a descriptive role. For instance, we may note from the protocol: Return on investment (ROI) has improved due to faster asset turnover. We shall only identify the relation between *ROI and Asset Turnover* and carry the qualification to subsequent analysis by specifying a topic line.

A classified protocol may now look like the following:

FOCUS-OBJECT	ATTRIBUTE	TOPIC LINE	PROTOCOL REF	
ROI	TREND	A sizeable dip in 1985	Loan Off	1
ROI	LEVEL	Clearly less satisfactory	Loan Off	1
ROI	ASSET TURNOVER	Improved	Loan Off	1

Classified protocols, as shown above, can now be used to compile everything that is said about an object (the focus object) and all relational objects.

Conceptual Structuring

By compiling the set of classified protocols, we have a collection of all that is said about each object and its relations upwards (its role as an explanatory object), and downwards (its role as a focus object). Thus, we can produce a conceptual structure of the domain. This conceptual structure describes which objects are related. From this structure, knowledge about how objects are related can be specified. We shall particularly be concerned with inferential and algorithmic knowledge.

A classified protocol may look like the following:

FOCUS OBJECTS	ATTRIBUTES
PROFITABILITY	PRODUCTIVITY
PROFITABILITY	COST STRUCTURE
PRODUCTIVITY	SALES PER EMPLOYEE
PRODUCTIVITY	CONTRIBUTION MARGIN PER EMPLOYEE
COST STRUCTURE	SALES GROWTH
COST STRUCTURE	CONTRIBUTION MARGIN
COST STRUCTURE	GROWTH IN FIXED COSTS
CONTRIBUTION MARGIN	SALES
CONTRIBUTION MARGIN	CONTRIBUTION
CONTRIBUTION MARGIN	FIXED COSTS

From this, we can draw the following conceptual structure:

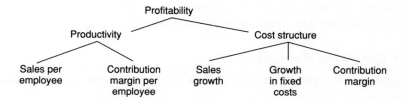

Qualifications

Descriptive attributes, on the other hand, like *level* and *trend*, must be assigned values. In human reasoning, these attributes will normally take qualitative values: good, bad, marginal, etc. This process of assigning qualitative values to attributes is called qualification.

For example:

Return on Investment   Level   Very good above 20%

Qualification implies defining a value set, also called a scale, and defining equivalence between separate scales, for instance, the equivalence between a numeric scale and a qualitative scale.

Return on investment:
very good	> 20%
satisfactory	15–20%
marginal	10–15%
very low	< 10%

For aggregated variables, like liquidity, we must relate qualitative variables on a lower level to qualitative variables on a higher level. This is done by rules.

Problem solving Strategies

How does the subject approach the problem? We describe this on two levels: the task level and the performance level. On the task level, we arrive at a general model of problem-solving. The processes identified are assumed to be common across several subjects in a domain. This model is called a task model. For financial analysis we have defined a task model consisting of the following sub-tasks: financial statements adjustments, ratio analysis, interpretation, diagnosis, and recommendation for change.

On the performance level individual behavior is identified with respect to information search and reasoning.

In this study we have taken the task model as the basis for the overall design of the expert system. However, within each sub-task, performance knowledge has been modeled and implemented. No particular problem solving strategies have been defined on this level.

7.5.4 Conceptual Model of a KBS

We have considered the process of task analysis and performance analysis above. At the end of these processes we arrive at a model of the knowledge and the reasoning process. We shall refer to this model as the *conceptual model* of a knowledge-based system. It represents the knowledge used to solve a particular problem in a domain. This knowledge should be organized in such a way that it can be implemented as a knowledge-based system on a computer. This requires that:

(1) The conclusions or results of the reasoning process are explicitly specified.
(2) Sub-problems are identified and further decomposed.
(3) The input level of observations or findings is determined.
(4) The relationships between observations and conclusions (the inference structure) are established.

The conceptual model should be free from any tool-specific terminology or representation formalism. Furthermore, the knowledge must be general enough to solve most of the problems in the domain in which the system is going to work. The performance knowledge arrived at by protocol analysis must therefore be generalized.

We can now work out a more detailed specification of what this conceptual model should contain:

Task:	Conclusions
Facts:	Input data (finding/observations)
Algorithmic knowledge:	Models, equations
Inferential knowledge:	Logic, rules
Problem solving strategies:	Chaining, conflict resolution

7.6 SAFIR—AN EXAMPLE OF THE KNOWLEDGE MODELING PROCESS

We shall use the methodology described above in discussing the development of SAFIR, a financial advisor in domains dealing with credit evaluation, corporate acquisition, financing of investments, and financial restructuring of corporations. SAFIR was developed by extensive task analysis and performance studies of a domain expert. Methods used for knowledge acquisition were interviews, verbal protocols and prototyping.

We shall look at performance modeling of an expert dealing with financial analysis problems. This section is based on a thesis by Lyngstad (1987).

7.6.1 Knowledge Elicitation

The first session with the expert was partly an interview and partly a protocol collection. The purpose of this session was to acquaint the knowledge engineer with the task and to give the expert some experience with concurrent verbal protocols. Methodological aspects about protocol collection were evaluated and the first proposal of a task model was presented.

Altogether, six sessions were performed with the expert. Protocols of eight cases were collected and three unstructured interviews were conducted. Everything said was tape-recorded, resulting in 150 pages of typewritten reports.

Session 1:	Interview: task analysis
Session 2:	Protocols of companies 1, 2 and 3
Session 3:	Protocol of company 4
	Interview about model specification
	Interview about qualitative variables and their scales
Session 4:	Interviews
	● about financial actions
	● about formalization
Session 5:	Protocols and prototyping
	● companies 5, 6 and 7
Session 6:	Protocols, prototyping and interview
	● protocol of company 8
	● review of prototype

Each of the sessions had two main objectives:
(1) To test and review knowledge representations
(2) To identify new knowledge

7.6.2 Concept Identification and Classification

We shall now perform a conceptual analysis of the following sample protocol from the SAFIR-project (translated from Norwegian):

> I notice that financing costs have gone somewhat up and down. What this means is not easy to say. I guess that they have gone up in 1985 due to the dramatic increase in the overdraft. They have gone up by 4.33 mill. (NOK). Long-term debts, I see, have increased sharply in '85, and dropped strongly in '84. Why this is so I cannot see immediately from the figures here. It does not look likely that the drop in long term debts is financed by an increase in short term debts. So, most probably it is a realization of assets.

This verbalization is a direct transcript of the tape recording of the expert's thinking aloud protocol (apart from the English translation). This protocol is now analyzed for task-relevant knowledge. By using the vocabulary from accounting and financial statements analysis, we can identify task-relevant objects, such as financing costs, overdraft, etc. We then divide the protocol into segments, each segment saying something about one particular object. In our case, the whole sample protocol says something about *financial costs*. This segment can be further divided into topic lines: statements saying something about the object in focus (properties or relations to other objects).

The protocol now looks like the following (task-relevant objects are denoted by capital letters):

SEGMENT (Focus Object): FINANCING COSTS
- Topic 1: Up and down
- Topic 2: Guess...gone up in '85 due to dramatic increase in OVERDRAFT...gone up by 4.3 mill (NOK)
- Topic 3: LONG TERM DEBTS...sharp increase in '85...strong drop in '84. Why...I cannot see immediately
- Topic 4: It doesn't look likely that the decrease in LONG TERM DEBTS is financed by increase in SHORT TERM DEBTS
- Topic 5: Probably a REALIZATION.

Editing a protocol in this way is helpful in order to obtain a better view of the task-relevant knowledge in the protocol. Classification of objects and object relations can now be done on the level of topic lines. Several protocols can now be compiled into one set, the classified set of protocols, containing everything that is said about an object.

The classification of SAFIR-protocols resulted in 440 classified statements. Table 7.1 shows all classified statements on return on investment (ROI).

7.6.3 Conceptual Structuring

Conceptual structuring is based on the compiled set of classified protocols. Implicit in the statements there is a conceptual structure of the domain. However, to make this structure explicit is not a simple task. Furthermore, taking all the relationships defined by the classified statements results in a complex network. To turn this structure into a hierarchy which can form the basis for calculations, logical deductions or plausible inferencing requires interpretations.

In structuring the domain, the task model is helpful in addition to the classified protocols. Also, it is helpful to let the expert specify the specific goal

TABLE 7.1 Classified statements

Focus	Attributes	Topic-Line	References[1]
ROI	LEVEL	13.2% – a little better	MA p 16
ROI	LEVEL	Terrible	RI p 4
ROI	LEVEL	Good, slightly below satisfactory, clearly not satisfactory	INT p 30
ROI	LEVEL	Between 14–16% – satisfactory	UJ p 2
ROI	LEVEL	Fairly good: 14.9%	KT p 8
ROI	LEVEL	High: 22.9%	BA p 36
ROI	TREND	12%	BA p 16
ROI	TREND	16.2% – managed to improve	BA p 26
ROI	FIXED ASSETS	Kept the growth down	BA p 26
ROI	ASSET TURNOVER	Decompose into asset turnover and profit margin	MJ p 2
ROI	ASSET TURNOVER	Reduced turnover rate by 50%	MJ p 9
ROI	PROFIT MARGIN	Not sufficient, satisfactory	JB p 16
ROI	INTEREST COVERAGE	Simultaneous requirements	INT p 30
ROI	HIDDEN RESERVES	Only found in stocks	BA p 26
INTEREST COVERAGE	ROI	Too high financial costs	KT p 8
INTEREST COVERAGE	ROI	Does not improve due to heavy increase in debts	UJ p 3
ROE	ROI	Reasonable relations	4/3 p 21

[1] Company identification.

states of the diagnosis. The goal states of the financial diagnosis were defined by our expert to fall into two categories: (1) operational issues which are primarily related to profitability measures, and (2) status issues which are primarily related to financing measures.

The classified protocols are now turned into the two conceptual structures shown in Figures 7.2 and 7.3, for the profitability and for the financing, respectively.

7.6.4 Qualifications

An important task in financial analysis is ratio calculations and ratio analysis. For a ratio to have any meaning it must be interpreted. Here, interpretation means to qualify numeric ratios; i.e. what does it mean that return on investment is 14.9%? Our expert interpreted this figure to be *fairly good*. But what is the equivalent qualitative scale on a numeric scale?

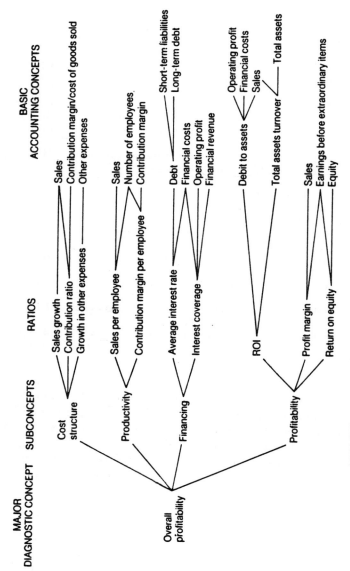

FIGURE 7.2   Profitability inference structure (from Klein, 1990)

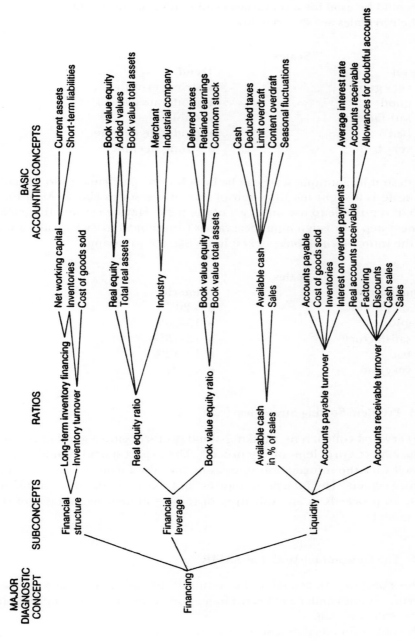

FIGURE 7.3   Financing inference structure (from Klein, 1990)

By interviewing the expert it was possible to find one qualitative scale that could be used for level-variables and one scale for trends.

The two scales are shown below:

Scales

Level	Trend
● very good	● strong growth
● good	● moderate growth
● satisfactory	● stable
● bad	● moderate decline
● very bad	● strong decline

If desirable, a unique scale can be built for one particular ratio. Usually, this scale is a slight modification of one of the scales above. Also, for a ratio, it is possible to use only part of the scale. Having created the scales, the next step is to assign numerical values (thresholds) to each qualification. For the ratio *return on investment* it looks like the following:

Scales

Qualitative	Numeric
● very good	● > 20%
● good	● 15–20%
● satisfactory	● 12–15%
● bad	● 10–12%
● very bad	● < 10%

7.6.5 Problem Solving Strategies

The very first concurrent, thinking-aloud protocol gave a good indication of the expert's problem-solving process. The expert starts by familiarizing himself with the information sources he has, the income statements and balance sheets. He interprets figures and starts to identify problems. Next, he proceeds to an evaluation of ratios followed by subtasks of the task model.

7.6.6 The Conceptual Model of SAFIR

At this point we can assemble the results of the task analysis and the performance studies under a coherent framework, called the conceptual model of the expert system.

The task is financial diagnosis of a corporation.

Diagnosis components:	• Profitability
	• Financial Structure
	• Leverage
	• Liquidity
Values of the diagnoses: LEVEL	very bad
	bad
	satisfactory
	good
	very good
TREND	strong decline
	moderate decline
	stable
	moderate growth
	strong growth

Factual Knowledge

- Input data (finding/observations) which are found in financial statements and notes. These data are mainly time series of data for the accounting periods provided.
- Derived data from the input data either by inferencing or numeric computations.

Analytical models can be formulated where causal relationships and definitional relationships can be expressed in terms of algorithms or equations. From the task model and the performance studies we have identified the need for two models:

- ratio calculations
- fund flow statement generation

Inferential knowledge is particularly present in tasks dealing with interpretation and diagnosis. Using the rule formalism, but not constrained by any computer tool syntax, we could formulate the inferential knowledge as shown in the following rule:

IF the level of return on investment is very good
AND the level of net profit margin is at least as good
THEN profitability is very good.

Problem solving Strategy

The task analysis indicated that the process starts in diagnosis, but jumps rather fast to search for problems in the input data. The search strategy formulated for SAFIR is backward chaining but with a meta rule that controls reasoning within all the subcomponents of diagnosis.

SAFIR has been built using the development tool OPTRANS EXPERT™. A printout of the diagnoses is shown in Figure 7.4.

PROFITABILITY	1984	1985
RETURN ON INVESTMENT (%)	8.3	14.9
PROFIT MARGIN (%)	0.7	1.5
INTEREST COVERAGE	1.1	1.3
AVERAGE INTEREST RATE (%)	9.1	13.7

Return on investment is satisfactory.
Profit margin is very bad.
Interest coverage is bad.
Average interest rate is high.
The company has satisfactory operational profitability, but the financing of capital is expensive. Therefore, the overall profitability is low.

FINANCIAL STRUCTURE	1984	1985
LONG-TERM INVENTORY FINANCING (%)	31.5	79.5
INVENTORY TURNOVER (days)	182.9	52.4

Long-term financing of inventories is good.
Inventory turnover is average.
The company has a satisfactory relationship between long-term debts and short-term liabilities.
Long-term financing of inventories is increasing sharply.
Inventory turnover is decreasing sharply.
Relationship between short-term liabilities and long-term debt has improved.

FINANCIAL LEVERAGE	1984	1985
REAL EQUITY RATIO (%)	18.5	16.0
ACCOUNTED EQUITY RATIO (%)	1.8	3.4

Real equity ratio is satisfactory.
Financial leverage is satisfactory, but accounted equity is rather low.
Real equity ratio is declining somewhat.
Financial leverage is weakening.

LIQUIDITY	1984	1985
AVAILABLE CASH (% OF SALES	4	14.5
ACCOUNTS RECEIVABLE TURNOVER (days)	53.5	33.5
ACCOUNTS PAYABLE TURNOVER (days)	121	101

Liquidity is good.
Accounts receivable turnover is normal.
Accounts payable turnover is very high.
Available cash is satisfactory, but accounts payable should be decreased in order to avoid interest on overdue payments.

FIGURE 7.4   *Financial diagnoses from Safir*

ACKNOWLEDGEMENTS

This paper is based on Chapter 8, Knowledge Modeling, in M. Klein and L.B. Methlie (1990), *Expert Systems. A Decision Support Approach. With Applications in Management and Finance*, by permission of Addison-Wesley Publishers Ltd, Wokingham, UK.

REFERENCES

Arkes, H.R. and M.R. Freedman (1984), Demonstration of the Cost and Benefits of Expertise in Recognition Memory, *Memory and Cognition*, **12**, pp.84–89.

Biggs, S.F. and T.J. Mock (1983), An Investigation of Auditor Decision Processes in the Evaluation of Internal Controls and Audit Scope Decisions, *Journal of Accounting Research*, Vol. 21, No.1, Spring.

Blainbridge, L. (1981), Verbal Reports as Evidence of the Process Operator's Knowledge, E.H. Mamdami and B.R. Gaines (eds.) *Fuzzy Reasoning and its Applications*, Academic Press, London.

Boose, J.H. (1984), Personal Construct Theory and the Transfer of Expertise, *Proceedings of AAAI-84* , pp.27–33.

Bouwman, M.J., P.A. Frishkoff, and P. Frishkoff (1987), How do Financial Analysts make Decisions? A Process Model of the Investment Screening Decision, *Accounting, Organization and Society*, Vol. 12, No.1.

Breuker, J.A., and B.J. Wielinga (1984), *Techniques for Knowledge Elicitation and Analysis*, Report 1.5 Esprit Project 12, University of Amsterdam.

Buchanan, B., G. Sutherland and E.A. Feigenbaum (1969), Heuristic DENDRAL: A program for Generating Explanatory Hypotheses in Organic Chemistry, in *Machine Intelligence 4*, Elsevier, New York.

Charniak, E. and D. McDermott m(1985), *Introduction to Artificial Intelligence*, Addison-Wesley Publ. Comp., Reading, MA.

Duda, R.O., J.G. Gaschnig and P.E. Hart (1979), Model Design in the Propector Consultant System for Mineral Exploration, D. Michie (ed.), *Expert Systems in the Micro-Electronic Age*, Edinburgh Press, Edinburgh.

Ericsson, K.A. and H. Simon (1980), Verbal reports as data, *Psychological Review*, Vol. 87, pp.215–251.

Ericsson, K.A. and H. Simon (1984), *Protocol Analysis*, The MIT Press, Cambridge, MA.

Feigenbaum, E. (1977), The Art of Artificial Intelligence: Themes and Case Studies of Knowledge Engineering, *Proceedings of the Fifth International Joint Conference on Artificial Intelligence*, Cambridge, MA, pp. 1014–1029.

Folstad, W. (1984), *Thinking Aloud Protocols and Protocol Analysis, An attempt to apply this to a practical case of financial analysis* (In Norwegian), Termpaper, NHH.

Hart, A. (1986), *Knowledge Acquisition for Expert Systems*, Kogan Page Ltd., London.

Johnson, P.E. (1984), The Expert Mind: A New Challenge for the Information Scientist, T.A. Bemelmans (ed.) *Beyond Productivity: Information Systems Development for Organizational Effectiveness*, Elsevier Science Publ.

Johnson, P.E. (1983), What Kind of an Expert Should a System Be? *The Journal of Medicine and Philosophy*, Vol. 8:77, 97.

Johnson, T. (1984), The Commercial Application of Expert System Technology, *Knowledge Engineering Review*, Vol. 1(1): 15–25.

Klein, M. and L.B. Methlie (1990), *Expert Systems. A Decision Support Approach*, Addison-Wesley, Wokingham, UK.

Laske, O.E. (1986), On Competence and Performance Notions in Expert Systems

Design: A Critique of Rapid Prototyping, *Proceedings of the Sixth International Workshop on Expert Systems an Their Applications*, April.

Lyngstad, P.B. (1987), *Knowledge Modeling of Expertise in Financial Diagnostics* (In Norwegian), Thesis, NHH.

McDermott, J. (1982), R1: A Rule-Based Configurer of Computer Systems, *Artificial Intelligence*, Vol. 19, pp.39–88.

Murphy, G.L. and J.C. Wright (1984), Changes in Conceptual Structure with Expertise: Differences Between Real-World Experts and Novices, *Journal of Experimental Psychology: Learning, Memory, and Cognition*, Vol. 10, pp.144–155.

Newell, A. and H. Simon (1972), *Human Problem Solving*, Prentice-Hall Inc., Englewood Cliffs, New Jersey.

Pople, H.E. (1982), Heuristic Methods for Imposing Structure on Ill-Structured Problems: The Structuring of Medical Diagnostics, P. Szolovits (ed.), *Artificial Intelligence in Medicine*, Westview, Boulder.

Rosch, E., C.B. Mervis, W.D. Gray, D.M. Johnson and P. Boyes-Braem (1976), Basic Objects in Natural Categories, *Cognitive Psychology*, Vol. 8, pp.382–439.

Shortliffe, E.H. (1976), *Computer-Based Medical Consultations: MYCIN*, Elsevier, New York.

Slatter, P.E. (1987), *Building Expert Systems: Cognitive Emulation*, John Wiley and Sons, New York.

Smith, E. and D.L. Medin (1981), *Categories and Concepts*, Harvard University Press, Cambridge, MA.

Sowa, J.F. (1984), *Conceptual Structures: Information Processing, Mind and Machine*, Addison-Wesley, Reading, MA.

Waterman, D.A. (1986), *A Guide to Expert Systems*, Addison-Wesley, Reading, MA.

Welbank, M. (1983), *A Review of Knowledge Acquisition Techniques for Expert Systems*, British Telecommunications.

Winograd, T. and F. Flores (1986), *Understanding Computers and Cognition*, Addison-Wesley, Reading, MA.

Wittgenstein, L. (1953), *Philosophical Investigations*, Basil Blackwell, Oxford.

Chapter 8

THE ARCHITECTURE OF EXPERTISE: THE AUDITOR'S GOING-CONCERN JUDGEMENT

Mallory Selfridge
Stanley F. Biggs
University of Connecticut, Storrs, CT

One approach to the development of expert systems for complex real-world applications is the use of cognitive models of human experts. One of the most important problems in building such models is the nature and content of the human expert's knowledge, since the architecture of the model and resulting expert system is founded directly on this knowledge. This chapter examines this problem in the context of the auditing domain, and describes the nature of the knowledge employed by expert auditors. It proposes that a cognitive model of the expert auditor would require knowledge in each of these domains, and that the architecture of an expert system based on such a model would be significantly different from that of a traditional expert system.

8.1 INTRODUCTION

Traditional rule-based expert systems probably are not optimal for complex real-world applications. While expert systems for physical domains may incorporate explicit domain models, there are a number of applications areas in which explicit domain models do not appear possible. Expert systems for such applications may instead embody a cognitive model of human domain experts, thus raising the question of the nature of cognitive models of human experts. This chapter considers this issue in the domain of the auditor's going-concern judgement, and proposes nine different knowledge structures organized in a particular fashion which will be required for a cognitive model of an expert auditor. Such complex organizations of different knowledge structures probably are required for high performance in a number of real-world application areas.

The going-concern judgement is rendered by auditors on all publicly-held companies to inform the public of the auditors' opinion as to whether the

Expert Systems in Business and Finance: Issues and Applications. Edited by P.R. Watkins and L.B. Eliot
© 1993 John Wiley & Sons Ltd.

company will be in business for the following year. This is important because unless a company is a 'going-concern', then its financial statements cannot be interpreted according to generally accepted accounting principles. In order to render a going-concern judgment, the auditor must (1) recognize that a problem exists, (2) understand the cause of the problem, (3) evaluate management plans to address the problem, and (4) render a judgement on the basis of whether the problems are sufficiently serious and whether management plans are judged to succeed (AICPA, 1988).

The development of an expert system to perform the auditor's going-concern judgement is important because such a system could enable the auditor to perform more thoroughly and accurately, and also because it would provide insight into how to build expert systems for other real-world applications. Since no expert systems are routinely rendering real-world going-concern judgements, the question of how such expert systems are to be constructed remains open. Of central importance in this regard is the question of the nature of the knowledge structures such an expert system should possess.

The nature of knowledge structures is not relevant within traditional expert systems, since all knowledge is encoded within rules or assertions in such systems. However, traditional expert systems break down or perform poorly when confronted with situations outside the boundaries of their domain (McCarthy, 1983; Holland, 1986; Duda and Shortliffe, 1983), lack human-level explanation and learning capabilities that characterize expert behavior (Schank and Hunter, 1985), and often do not out-perform human experts. For these reasons high-performance real-world expert systems will probably embody cognitive models of human experts, and could thus be termed "cognitive expert systems" (Selfridge *et al.*, 1987).

Development of a cognitive expert system to perform the auditor's going-concern judgement thus will require building a cognitive model of the expert auditor. In this regard, the issue of the nature of the auditor's knowledge structures is quite relevant. Specifically, two questions arise. First, what knowledge do expert auditors possess, and how should that knowledge be represented? Second, what is the organization of this knowledge? Answers to these questions are important not only to the development of expert systems for the going-concern judgement, but also for expert systems to perform other parts of the audit process, since such answers provide insight into the organization of the human mind which, in turn, will provide the basis on which cognitive expert systems will be built.

This chapter answers questions of the type and organization of the expert auditor's knowledge structures for the going-concern judgement by proposing nine different kinds of knowledge structures that auditors use to render a going-concern judgement, and by proposing that these knowledge structures are organized in a particular way. This chapter draws on prior research with the GCX system (Selfridge *et al.*, 1986; Krupka, 1987;

Selfridge and Biggs, 1988; Selfridge *et al.* [to appear]), and also extends that research toward a more comprehensive approach than is represented by GCX.

Naturally, there are a number of aspects of knowledge representation for the going-concern judgement which are beyond the scope of this chapter. For example, no mention is made of taxonomies of causal and relational linkages within knowledge structures, and such linkages are certainly part of an auditor's knowledge. Second, only passing mention is made of the reasoning and inference processes which must be used to render a going-concern knowledge, yet such processes must also be considered part of the auditor's knowledge. The decision to omit such topics from this chapter was made because this chapter is intended to address questions of knowledge structures, and linkages and processes may arguably be omitted from a discussion of structures. Krupka (1987) and Selfridge *et al.* [to appear] discuss these topics in substantial detail, though with considerably narrower scope than here.

Section 8.2 addresses the question of what knowledge auditors possess and how it should be represented. It argues that auditors possess at least nine different types of knowledge by presenting, for each type, auditor statements drawn from transcripts of interviews with a partner and manager at an international accounting firm (Transcript 1986a,b) the generation of which can be explained most plausibly by postulating the presence of that type of knowledge. After arguing that the auditor possesses a given type of knowledge, the nature and content of that knowledge is discussed, and approaches to the problem of representing that knowledge are reviewed.

Section 8.3 addresses the question of the organization of the auditor's knowledge. It does so by considering the function of each type of knowledge within the overall going-concern judgement, and inferring the connections between each type of knowledge required to perform that function. It concludes by proposing a set of connections between each type of knowledge and various other types of knowledge, and, based on inter-knowledge structure connections, proposing an overall organization of knowledge for a going-concern expert system which models the expert auditor.

8.2 THE CONTENT OF THE AUDITOR'S KNOWLEDGE

8.2.1 General Financial Knowledge

The first set of excerpts concern the auditors' ability to describe the company from a financial point of view. For example, they said:

> Current assets for the current year was 22 million and their current liabilities was 66 million. Their stockholder's deficiency in total was 19 million. (Transcript, 1986a, p.1).

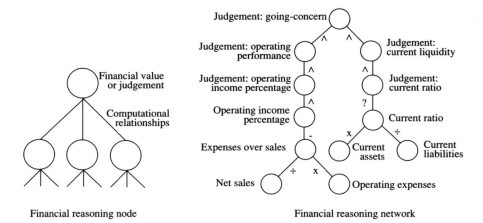

FIGURE 8.1   *Representing general financial knowledge*

...its total liabilities exceeded its total assets ... [this factor], among others, indicate that the company may not be able to continue in existence. (Transcript, 1986a, p.5).

These statements suggest that the auditors possess knowledge of measures of financial performance, such as financial ratios and trends. Implicit in these statements is the fact that the auditors know how to calculate financial measures from financial data. Consequently, statements such as these suggest that the auditors possess general financial knowledge. This general financial knowledge can be represented using a financial reasoning network, whose nodes represent financial items or judgements, and whose arcs represent the computation which produced the value of the financial item or judgement and which index the lower level financial items or judgements used by the computation. Figure 8.1 illustrates the form of the individual financial reasoning nodes which comprise the financial reasoning network, as well as the form of the network as a whole.

8.2.2 Knowledge of Actual Events

The second set of excerpts concern the auditors' ability to describe in detail events affecting or relating to the audited company and its environment. For example, they said:

The trade route that they discontinued was the Australian / New Zealand trade route. Prior to that, they discontinued the North Atlantic [trade route]. (Transcript, 1986a, p.4).

Nigeria's economy is just collapsing, their oil revenues are significantly down. (Transcript, 1986b, p.34).

From statements such as these which contain direct references to events and which indirectly express causal relationships among events, it is reasonable and straightforward to infer that the auditors possess substantial knowledge of actual events that affects the financial performance of the company. This event knowledge includes knowledge of individual events, and also knowledge of their temporal sequence and inter-event causality. Such knowledge can be represented in an event memory using semantic net techniques (Charniak and McDermott, 1985), in which each individual event is represented as a frame containing specific information about that event, and in which the causal and temporal sequences of events are represented by means of causal and temporal inter-event linkages. Figure 8.2 illustrates the form of a single node in event memory, while Figure 8.3 illustrates the overall form of event memory.

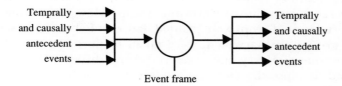

FIGURE 8.2   Representation of individual event

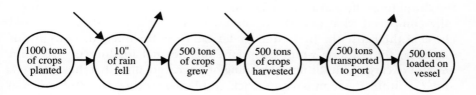

FIGURE 8.3   Representation of event memory

8.2.3 Knowledge of Normal Events

The third set of excerpts concern the auditors' knowledge of the normal course of events, the events that usually happen. Consider the following statements:

You see that there is a drought today then you know that tomorrow that drought is going to reduce the exports ... (Transcript, 1986a, p.11).

The government came in and put import quotas on the amount of beef that could be taken out of Australia ... then cargo fell off. (Transcript, 1986a, p.11).

Each statement expresses a cause-and-effect relationship between two events. It is reasonable to infer from such statements that auditors possess knowledge of events, as above. But these statements assert that one event caused another event, and this assertion must also be explained. Now, merely possessing knowledge of event sequences and causality is not enough to permit the expression of these statements of causality. This is because each event has many causal predecessors, and in order to model the auditor what must be explained is the fact that the auditor chose a particular event as "the" cause.

Examination of these and similar statements suggests that auditors chose events as causal if those events departed from the normal, or expected, sequence of events, and in fact were the first to do so. For example, normally a certain amount of crops are planted, a certain amount of rain falls, and a certain amount of crops grow, are harvested, are taken to port, and are loaded as cargo onto one of Merrytime's ships. However, during one year that same amount of crops were planted, less rain fell, and a lesser amount of crops grew, were harvested, were taken to port and were loaded as cargo onto one of Merrytime's vessels. Several different events could be considered to cause the fact that a lesser amount of crops were loaded onto one of Merrytime's ships: fewer crops were transported to the port, fewer crops were harvested, fewer crops grew, and so forth (traversing the chain of event causality backwards]. To account for the auditors' choice of the drought as the cause of the lack of cargo, we postulated that they mentally compared what actually occurred with what normally occurs, and chose as the cause the first event to deviate from the normal. Thus in this example, the auditor would compare the normal loading of a certain amount of cargo with the actual loading of less cargo, note that they differed, and continue the comparison back until discovering that the normal amount of crops were actually planted, and then choosing the first subsequent event as the cause: the drought. Since such a reasoning process appears to offer an excellent explanation of how the auditors inferred "the" cause of an event, and since such a reasoning process requires knowledge of the normal course of events in addition to the actual course of events, it is reasonable to infer that auditors possessed knowledge of normal events.

Such knowledge of the normal course of events can be represented in the same manner as actual events: a normal event memory consisting of a causal and temporal network structures comprised of normal event nodes. The general form of normal event memory is as shown in Figure 8.2, while

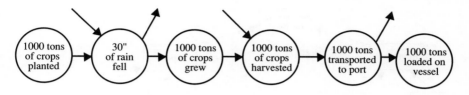

FIGURE 8.4   Knowledge of normal events

Figure 8.4 shows shows the knowledge of normal events corresponding to the actual events shown in Figure 8.3.

8.2.4 Knowledge of Company Function

The fourth set of excerpts concern the auditors' knowledge of the nature of the company's business operations. Consider the following statements:

> ...it's a simple business concept, just move cargo from this point to that point. (Transcript, 1986b, p.14).

> [The client] was going to change their business in terms of going from point to point operation, meaning from warehouse to warehouse... (Transcript, 1986b, p.18).

> The principal way the client makes money is it carries freight, in boxes, times a tariff rate ... So revenue goes up if the rates are up, or if the boxes are up. (Transcript, 1986b, p.3).

Statements such as these demonstrate that the auditors possessed detailed knowledge of the business function of the company. Specifically, they knew about both the financial and operational aspects of the company. The operational aspect of the company includes those actions and events which are carried out during the course of company business. It can be represented by means of an operational model, consisting of a causal and temporal network of those actions and events just as knowledge of normal events is represented. The financial aspect of the company includes the financial results of business actions and events, and relates those financial results to financial quantities of significance to the business. The financial aspect can be represented by means of a financial model, consisting of a tree in which nodes are financial quantities and whose arcs are the arithmetic operators used to compute financial quantities at one level from those at a lower level. The operations model and the financial model are linked into a single company model by maintaining "financial effects" (FE) links between various events and actions in the operations model and leaves of

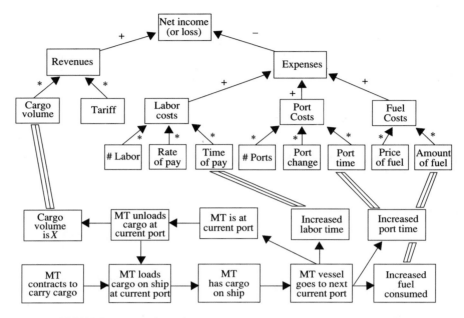

FIGURE 8.5   A fragment of a "Merrytime" company model

the financial model. Figure 8.5 illustrates a fragment of a complete company model for the company "Merrytime", containing a fragment of a financial model linked to a fragment of an operations model.

8.2.5 Knowledge of Company Markets

Statements such as the following suggest that the auditors possessed detailed knowledge of a company's market.

> The other major consideration was the business they [the client] were in. The kerosene heaters represented approximately 20% of their inventory ... and the demand for heaters was down for two reasons. One was the warm winters we have been having lately and second was the concern over their safety ... a third reason ... was the lack of public concern over the availability of other heating supplies. You don't have the public concern anymore so people aren't buying them. (Transcript, 1986a, p.12).

This knowledge includes knowledge of a number of different areas. First, the auditor possesses knowledge of the product itself: its physical description and operation of its parts, for example. Second, the auditors also possessed knowledge of product purpose. Knowing about product purpose is different from knowing about the product itself since, for example, two identical or largely identical products can be intended for two very different purposes, and two very different products can be sold for the same purpose. Third, the auditors possessed knowledge of the customer's goals. They possess knowledge of how the product's purpose fulfills the customer's needs and thus why it is of value to the customer. Finally, the auditors possess knowledge of the customer himself. This knowledge contains a description of various characteristics of the customer and his various life activities, as well as knowledge of the total number of customers and total number of potential customers.

Representing knowledge of the nature of a product, its purpose, the nature of customers, and their goals requires considerable further research. However, promising directions can be identified. Techniques for representing knowledge of the nature of a product could employ techniques being developed for representing geometric knowledge (e.g. Joskowicz, 1987) and for representing knowledge of the function of physical mechanisms (e.g.,Weld and de Kleer, 1990). Representing knowledge of the customer could be accomplished at least in part by using scripts and other higher-level abstract-event-based knowledge structures (Schank, 1982) to represent various actions and activities in which that customer engages. Representing knowledge of the purpose of a product and the goals of the customer requires representing how the product itself interacts with the customer's life activities, and different products interact different ways. However, every product has a purpose, and one approach to representing knowledge of that purpose is to use techniques for representing knowledge of the function of the product. Representing the customer's goals could be achieved using goal-based knowledge structures (Schank, 1982) in conjunction with

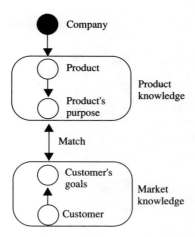

FIGURE 8.6   A company's market

knowledge of the customer's actions and activities. Finally, representing how the product satisfies the customer's goals could be achieved with a symbolic matching of the product's purpose to his goals. Figure 8.6 illustrates a representation of knowledge of a company's market in schematic form.

8.2.6 Knowledge of the Industry

Statements such as the following suggest that the auditors possessed knowledge of the industry in which a company operates, including the primary competitors, industry organizations, and their effects on the company.

> So you had 2 shipping lines competing between themselves, obviously taking cargo away from the other carriers.
> [company #1] is one of the largest, he had 43, they just dropped off significantly, the major competitor of [Merrytime] had only 3. but, when you talk of the major competitors, all 3 of those ships operated in the Med., now we are talking about fleets, then you have to talk about trade routes, there are so many different around the world, just to see where the vessels are on each of the trade routes, because that is your competition.

The auditors' knowledge of an industry involves two kinds of knowledge. First, auditors possess knowledge of the company's suppliers. They possess knowledge of the product or service provided by the supplier, the role that product or service plays in the line of business, and other characteristics of the supplier such as reliability. Second, auditors possess knowledge of the company's competitors. Generally speaking, their knowledge of competitors is essentially the same as their knowledge of the company under

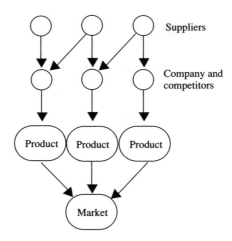

FIGURE 8.7   An industry

audit, except with less detail. That is, they know the nature of the competitor's business, its product and how it relates to the market, and its suppliers.

Since the auditor's knowledge of an industry comprises knowledge of suppliers and competitors, the techniques used to represent knowledge of the company under audit can be used to represent knowledge of those other companies. This knowledge is depicted in Figure 8.7.

8.2.7 Knowledge of Multiple Business Lines

Statements such as the following imply that auditors possess knowledge of how multiple lines of business are integrated within a single company.

> ...they got out of that line of business, they still have a TV line, they are still having difficulties, there is still a lot of competition ... this year they are importing air conditioners, on a very limited basis... (Transcript, 1986a, p.25).

They know that companies often carry out more than one independent business operation, such as manufacturing two separate product lines, which are nonetheless combined in the company, and they know how those lines are integrated within the company. This implies also that the auditors know about the markets and competitors for the company's various lines of business, as well as the suppliers to those business lines.

Representing knowledge of multiple lines of business appears to require an extension of the techniques used to represent knowledge of a single line of business. The foundation of these techniques is the representation of a single company making a single product for a single market. To represent knowledge of multiple lines of business, the knowledge of the single company must be expanded to include knowledge of the different business line operations, the different business line finances, and the overall organization which unifies the different lines into a single company. In addition,

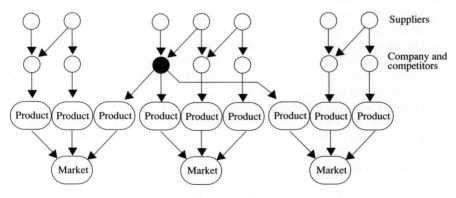

FIGURE 8.8   Multiple lines of business

knowledge of the different sets of competitors, markets, products, and suppliers must be represented using, again, the techniques used to represent knowledge of a single company. Figure 8.8 illustrates the representation of a company's different lines of business.

8.2.8 Knowledge of Changes Over Time

Statements such as the following suggest that the auditors possess knowledge not only of company operations and market and industry conditions, but also knowledge of changes in company operations and market and industry conditions over time.

> ...they got out of that line of business, they still have a TV line, they are still having difficulties, there is still a lot of competition ... this year they are importing air conditioners, on a very limited basis...

> ...you look historically, at what they have been able to do, and historically the number they have been able to achieve each year is 30% of the Med cargo they carry, approximately 30%....

This knowledge involves a number of different factors. First, auditors possess knowledge of expansions and contractions in a company's lines of business, and they possess knowledge of how those expansions or contractions depend on the company's decisions and upon its reactions to economic conditions. This can take the form of either increasing or decreasing business within a given market, entering a new market or leaving an old market, or initiating or completely eliminating a line of business altogether. Second, auditors possess knowledge of the operational and financial factors involved in each line of business, and they possess knowledge of how those factors change over time. For example, labor costs may increase, or materials costs decrease. Third, auditors possess knowledge of the decline or expansion of markets. For example, they possess knowledge of the changes in customer demand which occur over time independently of actions by the business. Fourth, auditors possess knowledge of a decline, expansion, or change in suppliers. This includes knowledge of such factors as change in financial well-being of suppliers, difficulty in producing supplies, and so on. Fifth, auditors possess knowledge of changes in a company's competitors. They know about operational and financial changes in particular competitors, and also the introduction of new competitors or departure of old competitors. Sixth, auditors possess knowledge of the changes in the relationship between a company line of business and its competitors within a given market. This knowledge includes changes in such factors as market share, product function and product quality. Figure 8.9 illustrates the auditor's knowledge of changes in company operations and market and industry conditions.

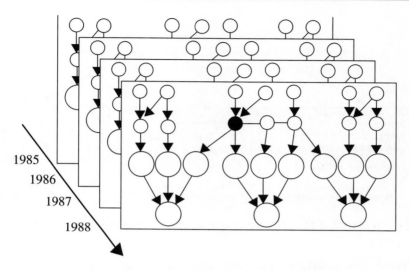

FIGURE 8.9   Knowledge of a company over time

8.2.9 Knowledge of Other Companies

Finally, statements such as the following suggest that the auditors possessed considerable knowledge of companies beyond those under audit.

> The kerosene company, they got out of that line of business, what ever they had left in inventory they had a bulk sale, ... they still have a TV line, they are still having difficulties, there is still a lot of competition ... this year they are importing air conditioners... (Transcript, 1986a, p.25).

> The reason why [Renault] made the investment in Jeep they wanted to expand their market share in the US, I guess what they didn't realize at the time was the limited share that Jeep had, and ... Jeep has two very old plants and they are out-dated... (Transcript, 1986a, p.26).

Knowledge of these other companies is acquired from a number of sources: prior audits, newspaper articles, and conversations with other auditors, and is of the same general form as knowledge of the company under audit. In order to represent this knowledge of other companies, the auditor's long-term memory must be modeled. Given a model of his long-term memory, knowledge of the individual other companies can be represented in that memory using the representational techniques used to represent knowledge of the company under audit. The question of the nature of long-term memory is currently a research issue, but Schank's [1982] "dynamic memory" approach appears a promising one. In this

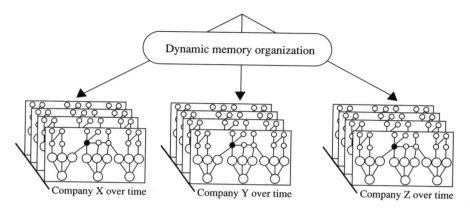

FIGURE 8.10   The auditor's memory for other companies

approach, the structure of memory is a complex one, with events indexed by multiple abstract event frameworks in order to facilitate retrieval, often in the form of "reminding". Following this approach, the auditor's knowledge of other companies would be stored within such a dynamic memory, as depicted in Figure 8.10.

8.3   THE ARCHITECTURE OF EXPERTISE

The previous section presented representative examples of auditor statements and argued on the basis of those statements that auditors possess nine different kinds of knowledge. Further, it described approaches to the problem of representing that knowledge. These types of knowledge are listed below.

- general financial knowledge
- knowledge of actual events
- knowledge of normal events
- knowledge of company function
- knowledge of company markets
- knowledge of the industry
- knowledge of multiple business line
- knowledge of changes over time
- knowledge of other companies.

The primary question which must now be addressed is *how is this knowledge organized?* This section will address this question by considering a prior question, that of the function of that knowledge. It will do so in the context of the four-step process carried out by the auditor to perform the going-concern judgement. In order to render a judgement, the auditor must (1) recognize that a problem exists, (2) understand the cause of the problem, (3) evaluate management plans to address the problem, and (4) render a judgement on the basis of whether the problems are sufficiently serious and whether management plans are judged to succeed (AICPA, 1988). The function of each type of knowledge can best be understood in terms of their role in this process. Note, however, that each type of knowledge has multiple roles, and is in fact involved in almost every aspect of the going-concern judgement.

The first phase, recognition of the existence of a going-concern problem, and the last phase, rendering an actual going-concern judgement, requires primarily general financial knowledge. This is because the nature of a going-concern problem itself is primarily financial. The result of such recognition is the identification of the financial nature of the problem, such as poor liquidity. The rendering of the actual judgement is made by applying judgemental criteria to the results of understanding the cause of the going-concern problem and evaluating management plans to solve the problem.

The second phase, understanding of the cause of the going-concern problem, can require many different types of knowledge. Consider the nature of a 'cause' of a going-concern problem: ultimately, a going-concern problem is caused by some event or action in the world, either external or internal to the company, and understanding the cause requires the identification of this event or action. In order to make such identification, the auditor must begin with the identified financial nature of the problem and reason further. This further reasoning proceeds from the general financial knowledge into the auditor's knowledge of company function: first through the financial model, to identify the financial aspects of the company which resulted in the financial problem, and then through the operations model, to identify those specific aspects of company operations responsible for the problem. Note that this requires reasoning through knowledge of the company's various lines of business. Having identified that part of company operations responsible for the problem, the auditor must then access his knowledge of real-world events to discover the instances of company operations, and reason backwards from those instances to discover the events or actions which actually caused the going-concern problem, using his knowledge of the normal course of events to infer the actual "cause". This backward reasoning will also involve knowledge of how company function has changed over time. Thus, understanding the cause of a going-concern problem requires not only general financial knowledge, but also knowledge of company function and its changes over time and knowledge of real-world events as well. Further, understanding the cause of a going-concern problem requires that general financial knowledge be connected to the financial model component of knowledge of company function, that the financial model be connected to the operations model, and that the operations model be connected to both knowledge of actual events and knowledge of normal events.

The third phase, evaluating management plans to address the problem, is a complex one, and involves knowledge in addition to that considered in this chapter, including very fundamental common sense knowledge possessed by all people. However, some aspects of the role of various kinds of knowledge can be identified within the process of evaluating management plans. Typically, management plans to address a going-concern problem involve some action with respect to the company's products. Evaluating the effect of such an action requires knowledge of the markets in which those products compete, and knowledge of the general industry which services those markets. In some instances, an evaluation can be made merely by reasoning about the results of the company's action. In other instances, however, the results cannot be determined with certainty, and the auditor must rely on more heuristic reasoning. One promising approach to such

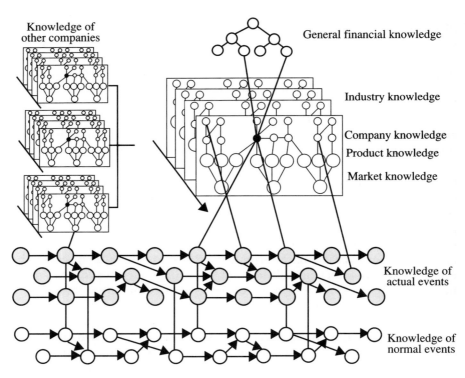

FIGURE 8.11   The architecture of expertise

heuristic reasoning is *case-based reasoning* (Riesbeck and Schank, 1989), in which the auditor would access his knowledge of other companies and recall prior situations in which those other companies had performed similar actions. He would then use his knowledge of the result of the actions of those other companies to infer the probable result of the action by the company whose plans he is evaluating.

Given this general account of the role of various knowledge structures in the process of rendering a going-concern judgement, the organization of these knowledge structures can be discerned. First, connections exist between general financial knowledge and knowledge of company operations. Second, connections exist between knowledge of company operations and knowledge of actual events which are instances of company operations. Note that these connections include connections between knowledge of the product, market and industry and knowledge of actual events as well. Further, connections exist between knowledge of actual events and knowledge of normal events, and between knowledge of company operations and knowledge of normal events. Finally, such connections exist between knowledge of actual and normal events and knowledge of the operations of other companies. This organization of these types of knowledge is required in order to account for auditors' statements and their ability to render going-concern judgements, and it thus provides an "architecture of expertise" which forms a framework for a cognitive model of an expert auditor. This organization is illustrated in Figure 8.11.

8.4 CONCLUSIONS

This chapter has argued that nine different knowledge structures are needed in order to model the auditor's performance of the going-concern judgement, and that these knowledge structures are organized according to a particular architecture. The necessity of including these structures within a model of the auditor was established by examining the auditor's statements; these structures were required in order to account for certain statements. The organization of this knowledge was established by considering the function of each type of knowledge within the process of making a going-concern judgement, and inferring the connections that must exist between the various knowledge structures. The result is a general description of the knowledge which a cognitive expert system to perform the going-concern judgement must possess.

A number of factors remain unaddressed. First, it is certain that expert auditors possess many additional types of knowledge not considered in this chapter (e.g. knowledge of economic conditions). Second, the nature and organization of the types of knowledge that were considered here will require substantial refinement prior to being incorporated within a real-world expert system. Third, no discussion of a cognitive expert system is complete without a detailed consideration of the reasoning and inference processes which access and use the various knowledge structures. Fourth, this chapter proceeded on the assumption that companies suffer from going-concern problems which are basically simple problems with a simple cause. In reality, going-concern problems are complex interactions of a number of different factors. Each such factor resembles the type of problem considered here, but their interaction in a real-world fashion will require additional research. Finally, the approach presented here must be explored within the context of other aspects of the audit process and other, non-auditing, areas.

This chapter has presented a view of the role of knowledge structures within a cognitive model of the expert auditor which is in contrast to the traditional approach to expert systems. Rather than a simple architecture consisting of a control structure, rule base, and assertion base, this chapter proposes a complex architecture of a number of different knowledge structures, used by a number of different reasoning and inference processes. Instead of attempting to force the knowledge and reasoning processes of the human expert into the mold of the traditional expert system, the most promising approach is to use the full range of artificial intelligence techniques to model that knowledge and reasoning processes as directly as possible. Such an system will be *expert* in that its performance approximates that of the expert human, and thus the cognitive modelling approach can be expected to have applicability to a variety of real-world application areas.

ACKNOWLEDGEMENTS

Substantial thanks are due to George Krupka, formerly of the Department of Computer Science and Engineering, University of Connecticut and currently at General Electric, Schenectedy, NY, for his participation in research and development of GCX and of some of the ideas in this chapter.

REFERENCES

American Institution of Certified Public Accountants (AICPA) (1988), *The Auditor's Consideration of an Entity's Ability to Continue as a Going-Concern*, Statements on Auditing Standards, #59.

Biggs, S.F. and Selfridge, M. (1986) Combining Rule-Based and Network-Based Logic in Expert Systems for Accounting, *Proceedings of the American Accounting Association Annual Meeting*, New York, August.

Charniak, E. and McDermott, D. (1985), *Introduction to Artificial Intelligence*, Addison-Wesley Publishing Co., Reading, MA.

Duda, R.O. and Shortliffe, E.H. (1983), Expert Systems Research, *Science*, Vol. 220, pp.261–268.

Holland, J.H. (1986), Escaping Brittleness: The Possibilities of a General-Purpose Learning Algorithm Applied to Parallel Rule-Based Systems, *Machine Learning*, Vol. 2, pp.593–623.

Joskowicz, L. (1987), Shape and Function in Mechanical Devices , *Proceedings of the Sixth National Conference on Artificial Intelligence*, Seattle, Washington.

Krupka, George, R. (1987), A Computational Cognitive Model of Expert Knowledge and Reasoning in the Domain of the Auditor's Going-Concern Judgement. Master's Thesis, Technical Report CSE-TR-87-42 and CSE/CARC TR-87-47, Department of Computer Science and Engineering, University of Connecticut.

McCarthy, J. (1983), Some Expert Systems Need Common Sense, Annals of the New York Academy of Sciences, Vol. 426, pp.129–137.

Riesbeck, C.K. and Schank, R.C. (1989). *Inside Case-based Reasoning*, Lawrence Erlbaum Associates, Hillsdale, NJ.

Schank, R.C. (1982), Dynamic Memory: A theory of Reminding and Learning in *Computers and People*, Cambridge University Press, Cambridge.

Schank, R.C. and Hunter, L. (1985), The Quest to Understand Thinking, *BYTE*, Vol. 10, pp.143–155.

Selfridge, M. and Biggs, S.F. (1988), GCX, A Computational Model of the Auditor's Going-Concern Judgement, *Proceedings of the Audit Judgement Symposium*, University of Southern California, Los Angeles, CA, February.

Selfridge, M., Biggs, S.F. and Krupka, G.R. (1986), *GCX: A Cognitive Expert System for Making Going-Concern Judgements*, CSE/CARC Technical Report #86-20, Department of Computer Science and Engineering, University of Connecticut.

Selfridge, M., Dickerson, D., and Biggs, S. (1987), Cognitive Expert Systems and Machine Learning: Artificial Intelligence Research at the University of Connecticut, *AI Magazine*, Vol. 8 No. 1, pp.75–79.

Selfridge, M., Biggs, S.F., and Krupka, G. (to appear). A Cognitive Model of the Auditor's Going-Concern Judgement, *International Journal of Intelligent Systems*, Vol. 7, No. 5, 1992.

Transcript with expert auditors # 1 (1986a).

Transcript with expert auditors # 2 (1986b).

Weld, D.S. and de Kleer, J. (1990), *Readings in Qualitative Reasoning about Physical Systems*, Morgan Kaurmann Publishers, Inc., San Mateo, CA.

Part III
ISSUES IN VALIDATION, AUDITABILITY AND SECURITY OF EXPERT SYSTEMS

Chapter 9

VERIFYING AND VALIDATING EXPERT SYSTEMS: A SURVEY

Daniel E. O'Leary
University of Southern California, Los Angeles, CA

Definitions of verification, validation and assessment/methods of verification/structure of validation/criterion of expertise/maintaining objectivity/reliability/impact of life cycle, special fixes and learning during validation/graphic approaches/validation methods/structuring a validation comparison/statistical models

9.1 VERIFYING AND VALIDATING EXPERT SYSTEMS: A SURVEY INTRODUCTION

The purpose of this chapter is to survey and extend the literature on verifying and validating expert systems. Accordingly, this chapter will discuss definitions for verifying and validating expert systems, provide a basic structure to meet those concerns and summarize some of the primary approaches used to verify and validate expert systems. To assist in identifying and understanding the literature, a relatively comprehensive set of references on verifying, validating and assessing expert systems is provided. Not all of the references are directly cited in this chapter.

Throughout, a fairly liberal interpretation is made of the term *expert system*. Typically, that term generates notions of *IF...THEN...* rule-based systems. However, it also will be used to refer to a broader set of systems that include other forms of knowledge representation or embed analytic tools in symbolic-based knowledge representations. For example, a number of systems (e.g., McBride *et al.*, 1989) embed an operations research technique, such as linear programming, in an object-based approach to knowledge representation.

This chapter focuses on three particular terms: validation, verification and assessment. Although these terms have met with different interpretations in the investigation of expert systems, a set of definitions based on a portion of the literature will be used as the basis of further discussion.

Expert Systems in Business and Finance: Issues and Applications. Edited by P.R. Watkins and L.B. Eliot
© 1993 John Wiley & Sons Ltd.

9.1.1 Verification

Verification is defined by Adrion *et al.* (1982, p.188) as ...*the demonstration of the consistency, completeness and correctness of the software...* As noted by O'Keefe *et al.* (1987, p.83), *verification means building the system right.* Thus, verification is aimed at eliminating errors in the implementation of the system.

Errors can occur in the rules in an expert system. For example, there may be redundant rules, conflicting rules, subsumed rules, missing rules, unreachable rules or dead-end rules (Nguyen *et al.*, 1985). Errors also can occur because the weights developed on the rules do not meet the underlying theory of the particular representation of strength of association or uncertainty.

The types of errors that can occur can be regarded, at least partially, as a function of the technology used to implement the system. For example, the paragraph immediately above and the discussion later in the chapter typically assume an *IF...THEN...* knowledge base. As a result, things such as cycles in the knowledge base must be eliminated. That is, the technology, e.g., weight scheme or knowledge representation, establishes much of the basis of verification. Different technologies likely would engender alternative approaches of verification. Further, embedding analytic techniques (linear program) into a computer program that employed a rule-based technology could require other verification approaches not recognized by the logical relationships that exist by limiting scope to rules.

9.1.2 Validation

Validation generally is regarded as a more complex task that is not dependent on the particular technology. O'Keefe *et al.* (1987, p.83) note that *validation means building the right system.* Adrion *et al.* (1982, p.188) indicates that *validation is the determination of the correctness of the final program of software produced from a development project with respect to the user needs and requirements.* The *right* system likely is to refer to the extent that an expert's activity and knowledge has been captured in the expert system. Thus, as noted by O'Leary (1987, p.468) validation refers to ...*what the system knows, does not know, or knows incorrectly.* Validation also includes determining the level of expertise of the system. Further, validation requires determining if the system is an appropriate implementation of the theory or first principles on which it is based (Davis, 1984). Finally, validation includes determining and assuring that the system functions at a certain level of reliability.

A critical issue in validating expert systems is whether the validation basis is a *specified user set of requirements,* as noted by Adrion *et al.* (1982), or an unspecified expert response. The former case is more well-defined than the latter. Expert response is unspecified because it is not known, *a priori*, how the expert will respond to interrogation.

Thus, there are reasons to assert that prespecified requirements should be used. First, if an expert system is being built for someone else (e.g., by a consultant), then there is likely to be the development of a document that functions as the specifications. Typically, this is necessary from the consultant's perspective in order to limit the scope of the system development process. Thus, this type of relationship has led to an increase in the use of specifications as the basis of comparison. Second, as the validation processes become more structured and knowledge acquisition processes become better structured, there is an increased ability to capture an expert's view of the world in a set of requirements. Third, Kolodner and Riesbeck (1986) note that memory organization is constantly changing in response to new events. The expert may alter his approach and content to the problem solving over time. Thus, if the expert is the basis of comparison then the moving target may never be hit. Fourth, in some cases a given set of knowledge acquisition tools is agreed on at some point in the knowledge acquisition process, e.g., Kelly's repertory grid. In those cases, it could be argued that the knowledge acquisition tool defines the scope of knowledge required for the system.

However, in order to capture the uniqueness of the particular expertise, that prespecification of requirements is likely to be based on a prototype expert system of the particular decision process. In addition to the prototype, that specification of requirements is likely to include addenda of various forms, including other prototypes and other agreed-to contents, based on an interaction between possible users and the developer.

9.1.3 Assessment

Although the focus of this chapter is on verification and validation, there are other issues involved with judging the *fit* between the system and the user, beyond the quality and correctness of the decisions that the system makes. These issues (Buchanan and Shortliffe, 1985) are summarized as *assessment* (O'Leary, 1987) or *evaluation* issues (Liebowitz, 1986). Under either label this includes investigation of the nature of the discourse between the system and the user, assessment of the adequacy and efficiency of the use of the hardware, quality of the implementation of the programming, the documentation of the system security and other issues.

9.1.4 Importance of Verifying and Validating Expert Systems

Verifying and validating expert systems is a critical task. Without appropriate verification and validation, the system may make costly errors or may not perform up to expectations. In either case, the decisions generated by the system can be inappropriate or wrong. If those decisions are relied on then there may be damage, such as financial loss, to the firm or decision makers. On the other hand, if the decision makers recognize the poor quality of the system then the system will not be used. In either case, the long run viability of the system may be compromised.

Sources of Validation and Verification Problems

Much of the ultimate impact of verification and validation results from errors and omissions of the expert system developer or expert. In addition, the developers and the expert may not fully understand the task or how to turn the task into a computer program.

Thus, there are a number of potential causes of limitations in the computer programs generated. First, the wrong knowledge may be gathered or keyed into the system. Second, the expert and the developer are likely to satisfice. As a result, parts of the system are likely to be just *good enough.* Unfortunately, such satisficing is likely to cascade, so that what is *good enough* for individual segments is not *good enough* when aggregated. Third, researchers have noted that humans do not think in terms of *IF...THEN...* rules (Biggs *et al.,* 1987). This finding is characteristic of a broader problem that it is not easy to capture and represent knowledge from experts. Thus, in some cases we are likely to find that what is captured is partially in error or incomplete. Fourth, there have been numerous accounts in, e.g., The *Wall Street Journal,* indicating that the expert has *held out* on the system developer. If the expert supplies inappropriate knowledge then the system will reflect that inadequate process. Fifth, typically expert systems are used to model tasks for which computer programs have not been previously developed. Since that is the case, it is likely the task is not well-understood prior to the development effort. Thus, since there often is no pre-established understanding, it can be easy to make errors in developing the system. Furthermore, the designers and the expert may not understand the structure of the problem. Thus, the resulting system may not meet the decision-making quality needs required of it. Sixth, expert systems may be integrated with other systems and technology. Such systems may assist with the generation of solutions better than those simply based on the decision-making capabilities of the expert. For example, McBride *et al.* (1989) embedded a linear programming problem in a symbolic-based expert system to solve a cash management problem. The interfaces between those systems are potential problems for both validation and verification of expert systems. Seventh, just because a system is developed does not mean that it is *done.* Changes to the systems also cause and require validation and verification.

9.1.5 Chapter Overview

This chapter proceeds as follows. Section 9.1 has provided an introduction and defined *verify*, *validate* and *assessment*. Section 9.2 discusses some of the unique characteristics of expert systems that lead to the need to consider the verification, validation and assessment of these types of systems, instead of treating them as generic computer programs. Section 9.3 examines approaches to verify expert systems. Section 9.4 provides a general structure for the validation of expert systems. Section 9.5 investigates the impact and implementation of criterion validity. Section 9.6 discusses the implementation of construct validity. Section 9.7 analyzes the manner in which objectivity can be integrated into the verification and validation of expert systems. Section 9.8 investigates the importance of reliability. Section 9.9 discusses the issues of cost and benefit. Section 9.10 reviews the impact of extraneous variance on the validation process, while Section 9.11 discusses error variance. Section 9.12 discusses the use of animation and graphics as validation methods to investigate the content validity of an expert system. Section 9.13 summarizes some of the validation methods that can be used to validate an expert system. These methods reflect criterion validity and are designed to solicit sufficient systematic variance. Section 9.14 structures the comparison to help assess content validity. Section 9.15 briefly discusses statistical models for those comparisons. Section 9.16 investigates the impact of knowledge base maintenance systems on validation efforts. Section 9.17 provides a brief summary of the chapter.

9.2 UNIQUE CHARACTERISTICS OF EXPERT SYSTEMS

Researchers have examined aspects of verification and validation for other types of systems. For example, Adrion *et al.* (1982) have examined the verification and validation of computer programs in general; Naylor and Finger (1968) have focused on verifying simulation models; Gass (1980) edited a collection on validation and assessment of energy models; and Findlay *et al.* (1988) have discussed some relationships between validating operations research models and expert systems.

However, there are a number of unique characteristics of expert systems (e.g., O'Leary, 1987). It is those unique characteristics that require unique responses in the verification and validation of those systems.

First, one of the findings in the development of expert systems and other artificial intelligence systems is that understanding the domain is critical. In many other types of programs, it is assumed that the program specifications need only be turned over to a programmer, who could then produce the code. However, generally in order to produce the computer code that is used as an expert system, the programmer must become a *near-expert* in the particular domain (e.g., Lethan and Jacobsen, 1987).

Second, another critical characteristic of expert systems is that the domain defines what are the critical aspects of an expert system developed in that domain. Reasoning and knowledge in one domain may not be the same as that in other domains.

Third, expert systems employ both numeric and symbolic information, rather than just numeric information. Because symbolic information is used, techniques typically used for the verification of numeric information are infeasible. In addition, the use of symbolic information leads to the development of new verification and validation needs, e.g., finding dead-end rules, circular reasoning, etc.

Fourth, as noted in Fox (1987), experience with knowledge representation shows that somewhat less than 10% of this knowledge escapes standard representation scheme and requires *special fixes*. Since other systems do not use knowledge representation, they do not face this problem.

Fifth, the expertise that is modeled in an expert system is generally in short supply, is expensive or is not readily available at all locations of a company. This is in contrast to other types of computer programs, such as some accounting systems, where there is substantial expertise available.

Sixth, expert systems generally are developed using a *middle-out* design, rather than a traditional top-down or bottom-up approach. A middle-out approach starts with prototype and gradually expands to meet the needs of the decision. Further, expert systems have a tendency to evolve over time, as the decisions they model become better understood.

Seventh, expert systems typically use a similar program architecture. Knowledge from the expert is stored in a knowledge base. An inference engine is used to sort through that knowledge, etc.

9.3   VERIFICATION

Verification is a function of finding errors in the implementation of the system. Such errors can occur because the weights or the knowledge does not meet the underlying theory or technological constraints on which they are based.

9.3.1   Weight Verification

Finding errors in the weights in an expert system is a process that has received limited attention. This may be because researchers have made few errors implementing different methods of uncertainty, or because errors of this type are unexpected in expert systems. In any case, at least one paper has focused on two verification issues associated with the weights in an expert system. First, O'Leary (1989b) found that a number of published papers have incorrectly developed weights, using the Bayesian-based AL/X approach to representing uncertainty. Second, O'Leary also found that a number of papers have developed AL/X-based weights that appear to have a functional relationship between the two sets of weights. Apparently, developers or experts chose one of the two weights and then developed the other weight as a function of the first. Since the two sets of weights are actually based on interlocking Bayesian analysis, the result is an *unusual* implicit underlying utility curve. Apparently, in the construction of weights, humans tend to ignore the underlying probability assumptions on which the weights are based. Thus, there is some question as to the viability of directly determining weights, rather than using underlying probability estimates to determine the resulting weights.

9.3.2 Knowledge Base Verification

TEIRESIAS (Davis, 1976) was the first program designed to automate the debugging process. TEIRESIAS investigated MYCIN rule sets. TEIRESIAS assumed that the given knowledge base was correct and that errors occurred as new knowledge was added. It provided summary investigations, including which rules were used to conclude other attributes. Whenever a new rule was added, the *IF* portion was compared to existing attributes in the model.

Errors in knowledge bases can take two primary forms: *consistency* (redundant rules, conflicting rules, subsumed rules, and circular rules) and *completeness* (unreferenced attributes, illegal attributes, unreachable rules and dead-end rules). These issues have been investigated by a number of authors including Suwa *et al.* (1982) and Nguyen *et al.* (1987), on which much of the discussion on verification of knowledge bases is based. In addition, there are many built-in verification tests in expert system shells.

9.3.3 Consistency

A useful tool in the investigation of consistency is what is known as a contingency table (O'Leary, 1988b) or a dependency chart (Nguyen *et al.*, 1987) or an incidence matrix in graph theory. This is a table with each of the possible *IF* conditions on the *y*-axis and the *THEN* conditions on the *x*-axis. Each of these different types of rules can be identified using the incidence matrix, i.e., a graphic representation of the knowledge base. Once identified the state of the rules can be brought to the attention of the developer.

Redundant Rules

As defined by Nguyen *et al.* (1987, p.70), *two rules are redundant if they succeed in the same situation and have the same conclusions.* In terms of *IF...THEN...* rules this means that the *IF* parts are the same and one or more conclusions are the same. As noted in Suwa *et al.* (1982) this primarily impacts efficiency, but does not necessarily cause logical problems. However, problems can occur in future versions of the system that change one rule but not the other.

Conflicting Rules

Conflicting rules are similar to redundant rules in that they have the same *IF* portions. However, conflicting rules come to contradictory conclusions. Determining that two rules conflict is difficult. It may be that the two conclusions each could occur probabilistically. Further, in the case of multiple conclusions it may be impossible to state that the conclusions are in contradiction.

Subsumed Rules

One rule is subsumed by another if the two rules have the same conclusions, but one contains additional constraints on the situations in which it will succeed (Nguyen *et al.* (1987, p.71). This means that there is less specificity in the subsumed rule, yet there is the same conclusion. In terms of *IF... THEN...* rules, this means that the *IF* conditions of the subsumed rule are fully contained in the conditions of some other rule that reaches the same conclusion.

Circular Rules

A set of rules contains circular reasoning if there exists a chain of reasoning that starts with some condition and then returns to that same condition. Circularity can cause an infinite loop in those cases where the system does not employ certainty factors (since each loop added to existing paths yields a *new* path); or when the system is interested in computing the largest value associated with a path, and the factors are greater than one (since each run through the loop adds value); or when the system is concerned with computing each feasible path (since each new loop makes the path without that loop a new feasible path).

9.3.4 Completeness

There is also a set of checks to examine the completeness of the knowledge. These checks are not of the type to determine that the expert has placed all the knowledge in the system necessary for an appropriate system. Instead, they are aimed at ensuring that there are no errors, because of missing data or knowledge.

Unreferenced Attributes

This situation occurs when the set of feasible *IF* conditions is not used entirely by the set of rules in the system. Thus, there is at least one condition that is not used in any rule.

Illegal Attributes

As noted by Nguyen *et al.* (1987, p.72) an illegal attribute value occurs when a rule refers to an attribute value that is not in the set of *legal values*.

Attributes are measurable conditions that can appear in either an *IF* or a *THEN* condition. Such an error can be caused by a spelling or phrasing mistake or because the set of attributes is incomplete. Some systems, such as EXSYS, eliminate this problem by having the user choose from a set of feasible options by referencing a particular rule number.

Unreachable Conclusions and Dead-end Conditions

The conclusion of a given rule should match either an *IF* condition in some other rule to allow chaining of inference from one rule to another. Otherwise, either a *THEN* conclusion will not be reached or an *IF* condition will not be initiated. Such a situation can result if the *THEN* conclusion and the *IF* condition mean the same thing to the expert, but are not the same exact verbiage so that the system can identify them as different. Alternatively, the *IF* conditions need to be feasible or else the condition will never be reached. Furthermore, the *THEN* condition needs to be a feasible goal, or it will not be investigated.

9.4 STRUCTURE OF VALIDATION EFFORTS

Since validation is ultimately concerned with the match between the system and the expert this indicates the need to establish a basis on which to proceed with the validation efforts. Unfortunately, most examinations of the validation of expert systems have been *ad hoc*. These approaches have focused on empirically or logically generated criteria to guide validation and verification efforts.

However, O'Leary (1987) developed a framework of validation based on a structure provided by research design in Kerlinger (1973). That approach has the advantage of an underlying theory that can be used to generate research issues and additional understanding.

Using research methods as the basis of a framework for expert systems, we can view the development of expert systems as experimental representations of human expertise. Kerlinger (1973, p.300) defined research design as …*the plan, structure, and strategy of investigation conceived so as to obtain answers to research questions and to control variance in that process.*

Kerlinger (1973, p.301) also stated that *research questions are invented to enable the researcher to answer research questions as validly, accurately, objectively, and economically as possible.* As he also noted, accuracy consists of reliability, systematic variance, extraneous variance, and error variance. He also indicated that there were three types of validity (content validity, criterion validity and construct validity). Benbasset and Dhaliwal (1989) presented a framework for the validation of knowledge acquisition using those same three types of validity.

The following sections address the impact of the framework, while interweaving corresponding methods to validate the resulting system.

9.5 CRITERION VALIDITY

Criterion validity is studied by comparing test or scale scores with one or more external variables or criteria, known or believed to measure the attribute under study (Kerlinger, 1973). From an expert system perspective this generally refers to ensuring that the criteria meet the needs of comparison to the system. In particular, this refers to the criteria to ascertain the level of expertise of the system. Definition of criteria that define that level of expertise is not straightforward.

9.5.1 Definition of Level of Expertise

One approach to the definition of the level of expertise is that required of human experts. For example, as was heard at one meeting, the ultimate test of my system will be to see if it passes the *Certified Public Accountant exam.* However, in general, few such *exams* exist to test the level of expertise of the system. In addition, exams such as the one just referenced are actually minimal entrance requirements into professions. An alternative approach is to evaluate the level of expertise on the level of difficulty of the problems it can solve. Moreover, the quality of the system is measured in part by the quality of the solution it produces to solve particular problems. Unfortunately, quality of the system may be as elusive a concept as the definition of expertise.

9.5.2 Measuring Quality of Expertise

An important research issue is the measurement of the level of expertise. O'Leary (1992) investigated a statistical approach to determining if experts are from the same groups, and thus, determining if there are different levels of expertise. Given a set of judgments, statistically the problem becomes one of determining if the judgments of one expert have been drawn from the same distribution as the judgments of another expert or set of experts.

9.5.3 Clarification of Evaluation Criteria

Many measures are possible. Also, different interpretations of the same measures may result. Accordingly, it is critical to establish specific and well-defined criteria prior to the validation of an expert system. In addition, it is important that there be prior agreement on those criteria before the validation efforts are initiated.

9.6 CONSTRUCT VALIDITY

Construct validity refers to the theory on which the system is based. As noted by Kerlinger (1973, p. 461), *The significant point about construct validity that sets it apart from other types of validity is its preoccupation with theory [and] theoretical constructs.*

Construct validity is a non-issue in many expert systems. This is because often the developer elicits the rules in a purely empirical manner. Rules are treated as something to be iteratively discovered, without reference to some underlying theory to guide the investigation.

This is in contrast to work by Davis who indicated that such an empirical approach is not as efficient or effective as one based on a theory or an understanding of the particular problem being investigated. As a result, he suggested that systems be developed to reason from first principles. These first principles derive from an understanding of the causality in the system being examined.

Building systems without reference to theory can be dangerous. McDermott (1986) indicated that a primary reason that many systems fail is because the systems capture knowledge, but are not based on a theory.

9.6.1 Implementation of Construct Validity

Construct validity can be investigated by focusing the subjective process of the existence of a theory: Did the development include reference to a theory? Another approach is to investigate the expertise on which the system is based. In the case of a system that generates its knowledge from multiple experts another issue needs to be examined: Are the experts from the same or different camps? Determining the theoretical consistency of different expert judgments is examined in O'Leary (1993).

9.7   MAINTAINING OBJECTIVITY

Since verification investigates aspects such as the existence of cycles in the knowledge base, the existence of dead-end rules, and other well-defined characteristics, objectivity generally is not as critical an issue as it is in validation. On the other hand, in validation, objectivity is critical because validation is a fuzzier issue. Objectivity is really a *who* issue—who will do the verification and validation. In addition, it is an *attitudinal* issue—for example, what is the attitude of the validator if it is known that there is a computer giving *expert* advice.

9.7.1 Software Features

Objectivity probably is at its highest if the validation or verification tests are built into the software. In that case particular procedures are implemented without subsequent intervention. For example, some expert system shells have a number of verification routines built into them.

9.7.2 Programmer Validation

Typically, the programmer is virtually constantly validating and verifying the system based on the level of knowledge that is brought to the system and gained in system development. However, those efforts may be less than objective depending on a number of factors. If the programmer is short on time or budget, the validation effort may be the first to be cut, since it may be seen as an overhead function. Further, if the programmer has a vested interest in the system, then letting the programmer be the only validation or verification process is somewhat analogous to letting the fox guard the henhouse. That is, there is potential for substantial violations of objectivity.

9.7.3 Independent Administration of Validation

In order to mitigate such violations, typically research methods emphasize the importance of independence of the validator. If the model builder is the only validator then there can be conflicts of interest.

9.7.4 Sponsor/End User Validation

Typically, software engineering uses an acceptance test by the sponsor/end user as the final step in the validation process. Unfortunately, if we assume that expert systems continue to evolve over time then it is not clear what is gained from such a test except further input for future changes. If the system is to change substantially then the notion of an acceptance test may be difficult to establish in expert systems. However, if we assume that there is a set of specifications, as noted earlier in the chapter, then a validation by the sponsor or end user provides evidence that at least the system accomplished what those agreed-upon specifications were to accomplish. Unfortunately, as noted in O'Leary (1987), in some cases the end user or sponsor may have insufficient expertise to validate the system.

9.7.5 Blinding Techniques to Eliminate Bias

Some researchers, e.g., Buchanan and Shortcliffe (1985), have reported that in some cases external validators may be biased in their evaluation of a system's report, if they know that the system was generated by a computer. Other biases may also influence evaluators. If a human investigator finds that a report is from an expert from *another school*, then that could impact the quality they attribute to the report. Clearly, this means that blinding techniques can be used to mitigate this type of violation to objectivity.

9.7.6 Expert v. Non-Expert

The use of an expert to validate the system may prove necessary to add new knowledge to the system. However, in many cases the use of a naive non-expert likely will provide the greatest extent of objectivity. The non-expert will not be aware of the implicit assumptions underlying the system, as an expert is likely to be. As a result, the non-expert likely will bring a different perspective to the investigation of the system.

9.8   RELIABILITY

Reliability is the accuracy of the precision of a measuring instrument (Kerlinger, 1973, p.491). In this case the measuring instrument is the expert system and the reliability refers to the reliability in the judgments of the system.

Field investigations have led to the conclusion that the reliability of the system is one of the most critical success factors for the system. Discussions with one developer of an expert system used for investigative purposes led to the finding that the continued use of the system was dependent on the system not giving wrong avenues to pursue. Erroneous system behavior could lead the user of the system to recommend erroneous paths to pursue. Such recommendations would lead the client to lose faith in the investigator's ability.

9.8.1 Analytic Model of Reliability and Validity

As noted by Kaplan (1964, p.200), *...reliability, in other words, is in turn a measure of the extent to which a measurement remains constant as it is repeated under conditions taken to be constant.* This means the extent to which the system and the expert provide the same decisions.

Based on this notion of reliability, O'Leary (1988c) developed an analytic, Bayesian model to investigate the impact of reliability on expert systems. The model treated the expert system as an intermediary source of expertise so that differences in the judgments between the system and the expert occurred because of errors or omissions in the expert system.

The model was based on a characterization of the types of risk in validation developed in O'Keefe *et al.* (1987). The model assumed that the state of the expert system is either valid or invalid, and that the action space is either accepted as valid or declared invalid. That model found that even small changes in the reliability of the system resulted in substantial changes in the probability that the system is declared invalid. Other implications also were explored in the model. Implementation of such a model could be a useful tool in the determination of the impact or reliability of the system.

9.9   COST BENEFIT ANALYSIS

Implicit and explicit cost benefit assessments permeate virtually all system development and research methods inquiries. This results in large part because in virtually every system, there are resource development or time constraints.

The survey summarized in O'Leary (1991) found that validation efforts rarely exceed budget and generally are allocated significantly less of the total system budget than is normally planned. This is consistent with *a priori* considerations that validation efforts often are driven out by the production process in the development of the system.

9.9.1 Use of the System

An important factor in examining the cost benefit of validation is the ultimate use of the system. Of the systems reported in the literature, many are research-based. As such there was not a substantial incentive to perform much of a validation effort on the system.

9.9.2 Formality of Validation

Virtually all the factors discussed in this chapter impact the cost of validation of an expert system. However, generally the formality of the validation efforts will be a major factor in the determination of the cost of the validation of an expert system. The formality has an impact on who performs the validation, when the validation is performed, and of what the validation consists.

In a formal validation, the cost of the validation likely will include the time that experts spent on the formal validation and the time spent by the sponsor of the project. A formal validation of the system is likely to take place at the conclusion of one of the major prototypes. As a result, substantial up-front effort is likely to be made to ensure that the system meets the demands placed on it. Finally, in a formal validation, the validation process is likely to require a substantial amount of interaction with the system and to include a specified sequence of tests.

9.10 EXTRANEOUS VARIANCE

As noted by Kerlinger (1973, p.309), *The control of extraneous variables means that the influences of independent variables extraneous to the purpose of the study are minimized, nullified or isolated.* O'Leary (1987) identified a number of extraneous variables that could impact quality of the system and thus, the extent of validation required.

9.10.1 Impact of Life Cycle

The importance of the location of the system in its life cycle was discussed in Shortliffe and Davis (1975). Since then, that work has been discussed in detail in Gaschnig *et al.* (1983). Recently, Benbasat and Dhaliwal (1989) have expanded the impact of location of life cycle as a substantial portion of the basis of the choice of validation methods. The impact of the life cycle is basically analogous to the *when* issue in validation as discussed in O'Keefe *et al.* (1987). In any case, there are a number of reasons that the location of the life cycle has an impact on determining the type and extent of verification and validation. First, it probably is critical to verify the knowledge-base information gathered before substantial validation efforts are begun. If validators find errors in the knowledge base due to inappropriate implementation of particular technologies then there may be substantial doubt cast upon the ability of the expert system developer to develop a correct system, let alone a system that can perform the work of an expert.

Second, some approaches to the validation of expert systems compare portions of the knowledge base at different stages of the life cycle (O'Leary and Kandelin, 1988). Then the expected relationships between that information are compared to the actual relationships in order to gauge the extent of further validation efforts. For example, in the case of interlocking sets of weights, such as those in AL/X, if one of the weights does not change from version to version of the system then it is very likely that the other set of weights should not change.

Third, verification and validation efforts required in the initial stages of development are probably different than those required later in the process. Initial efforts may concentrate on direct examination of the knowledge, while later efforts employ a test data approach to understand the system's behavior. Initial efforts likely are to investigate individual aspects of the knowledge base, while later efforts are designed to investigate the overall functioning of the system. Further, the extent of verification and validation efforts is likely to shift, depending on the life cycle stage. Early efforts are more likely to be focused on verification, while later efforts may concentrate on validation. Fourth, if the system is validated after it is able to provide reasonable assistance in decision making, then it can be run in parallel (O'Keefe *et al.*, 1987 and O'Leary, 1987).

9.10.2 Recognition of Special Fixes

As noted above, Fox (1987) indicated that one of the characteristics of knowledge representation is that roughly somewhat less than 10% of the knowledge in an expert system will require special fixes. These special fixes are a particularly difficult validation and verification problem. Since they are special fixes they are not likely to employ the same form of knowledge representation as the rest of the knowledge base. That indicates that the logical verification of the rest of the system is not likely to be the same as that required by the special fixes. Similarly, in the validation of the system, special fixes may be too situation specific. As a result, the system may not respond as well to environmental changes. Finally, since portions of the program are special fixes, those special fixes likely will require special validation efforts.

9.10.3 Learning During the Validation Process

Another critical variable that can impact the validation process is learning during the validation process. This is particularly important in those situations where a human expert is compared to a computer system. In most cases the human will continue to learn during and after any knowledge acquisition effort. In particular, the structuring of previously unstructured tasks can lead to increased understanding by the human expert. However, in most cases the system will not continue to learn. This can lead to differential understanding and difficulties when comparing the system (the way the expert used to think) to the expert (who now thinks differently).

Location of the Judges During the Testing

The contingencies of reinforcement for any decision include various factors associated with the decision-making environment. Thus, if the validation process takes possible validators out of their normal decision-making environment then some of the necessary cues of decision-making are lost. On the other hand, if decision-makers are left in their ordinary decision-making environments then ordinary distractions can impact their validation efforts. Thus, the validator must trade off on which cues have the greatest impact on the validation efforts.

9.11 ERROR VARIANCE

Kerlinger (1973, p.372) noted:

> There are a number of determinants of error variance, for instance, factors associated with individual differences among subjects. Ordinarily, we call this variance due to individual differences systematic variance. But when such variance cannot be, or is not identified and controlled, we lump it with the error variance.

Error variance is a critical, yet relatively unexplored phenomenon in the validation of expert systems. Kerlinger further suggests that error variance can be caused by random variation in the expert's responses from trial to trial, momentary inattention, guessing, temporary fatigue, lapses of memory, etc.

9.12 CONTENT VALIDITY INVESTIGATION USING GRAPHIC APPROACHES

As noted by O'Keefe *et al.* (1987), *Visual interactive validation provides visual animation of expert systems workings and allows experts to interact, altering parameters as desired.* As a result, animation or graphics has been offered as a useful tool in the validation and verification of simulation models (Bell, 1985; Sargent, 1986 and Johnson and Poorte, 1987) and knowledge-based systems (Richer and Clancey, 1985). There are likely to be at least two reasons for the potential success of animation.

First, Piaget (1973) noted that *all mathematical ideas begin by a qualitative construction before acquiring a metric character.* In addition, he noted that too rapidly moving from the qualitative to the quantitative or mathematical formulation often affects the ability to understand mathematics. Thus, since animation provides a qualitative understanding, it may be particularly prudent to initially use animation in the validation and verification of an expert system.

Second, although the system may be based on an expert, the expert is not likely to be an expert in computer programs. Thus, rather than trying to integrate the expert into the process of validation and verification using computer outputs and programs, animation may provide an alternative approach that is accessible to the expert.

9.12.1 Potential Uses of Graphics

At a general level, graphics can be used to turn a knowledge base of *IF (condition)... THEN (consequence)...* rules into a graph where arcs lead from one rule to another if the consequence is tied to some condition in another rule. In addition, the process of inferencing through a knowledge base could be used to clarify particular flows to an expert examining the system.

Furthermore, test data could be investigated using animation. The input or the output could be represented as a sequence of user friendly icons (cars, dollars, etc.), that represent the processes being modeled.

9.12.2 Implementation of Graphics for Validation and Verification

There have been some recent developments in software that could allow the development of such graphics in a cost effective manner. For example, Microsoft's Windows provides an operating environment that promulgates such developments. Unfortunately, it may be difficult or costly to develop generic approaches to using graphics to validate or verify expert systems.

However, one approach would be to design, say, software to take and input the rules from a particular expert system shell. Then the output could be graphs or flowcharts. An animation of inferencing through the graph would provide insight into the particular process.

9.13 VALIDATION METHODS

9.13.1 System v. Components

As with other systems, expert systems can be validated by examining either the individual components, such as the weights or the knowledge base, for accuracy and completeness or by testing the operation of the system as a whole. When testing the system as a whole, either the system can be treated as a black box to determine if it is making the right decisions or it can be opened up to determine if the system is making the right decision for the right reason.

9.13.2 Weights

O'Leary and Kandelin (1988) develop a number of approaches to validate the weights in an expert system. The basic assumption underlying their investigation is that the behavior of the weights can be investigated using statistical approaches. One approach is designed to investigate for the presence of outliers. Finding weights that are substantially different than the other weights is likely to indicate that those weights should be investigated further.

There are a number of different systems of weights. Many of those systems (AL/X and EMYCIN) employ a pair of weights. Generally, those pairs are related mathematically, but are generated separately. Thus, an additional issue is the relationship between the pairs of weights. O'Leary and Kandelin (1988) investigate that relationship by analyzing the correlation between the sets of weights. This process determines if the manner in which the weights have been gathered is *unusual* or that the weights have been gathered in a consistent manner.

Another issue concerns the existence of the relationship between different versions of the system. The question arises if there is a relationship between the weights in, say, the first and second versions of the system. If there is some reason to suspect that the absence or presence of a relationship, then that can be tested statistically. Such a relationship might exist because the expert on which the system is based after the first version may see that the system will work "too well." Alternatively, there may be a difference because there was a substantial revision in the system and in the understanding of the problem. Thus, the expert may change his or her approach to assigning the weights in order to impact the behavior of the system.

9.13.3 Knowledge Base

Part of the examination of criterion validity is the development of criteria by which to evaluate the quality of the knowledge base. O'Leary (1987) suggested that there were at least three such criteria: accuracy, consistency, completeness. Additionally, there is a need to assess the way in which the knowledge in the system links together.

Accuracy of Knowledge

Direct examination of the knowledge base can be used to examine its accuracy. The process of direct examination is directly facilitated by the manner in which some expert system shells and artificial intelligence languages allow the user to access the knowledge.

In some cases the knowledge bases may be too large to direct a full investigation. As a result, different approaches can be used to choose which rules are more important to examine (O'Leary, 1989b). For example, those rules that have the most costly consequences or largest profit generally could be investigated. Similarly, those rules with either the larger or smaller weights could also be examined. In the first case, those weights are on rules likely to appear in some optimal solution. In the second case, the weights are on rules unlikely to appear in some optimal solution.

Consistency

To a large extent the consistency of the knowledge base is a verification problem. For example, issues of concern to consistency include the use of the *same condition and consequence names.*

Completeness

One of the most elusive issues is that of completeness. It generally is more difficult to determine what is omitted than to find what is wrong with what is there. Techniques such as those designed to develop creativity can be particularly helpful here. However, in many cases, it may not be cost effective to have a *complete* knowledge base. As noted in O'Leary (1988b) the so-called 80–20 rule would apply. In that case, 80% of the benefit comes from 20% of the knowledge.

Completeness is both a verification and validation problem. In the first case completeness refers to completeness of logic relationships. For example, the use of a consequence indicates that it is either a final decision point or a condition for another *IF...THEN...* statement.

In the second case it refers to a generation of a knowledge base that is complete enough to make the appropriate decisions in an appropriate manner. That is, did the expert *hold out.*

Inferencing

Unfortunately, direct examination is not likely to yield information about the structure of the knowledge so that proper inferencing through the knowledge base could be developed. That is, with direct examination, it is difficult to *see* how the rules link together. In order to investigate the manner in which the rules link, approaches are needed which investigate the behavior of particular subsystems or the system as a whole.

9.13.3 System as a Whole

The classic *Turing test* uses a test data approach in order to determine the quality of the system as a whole. Based on a survey of expert system developers (O'Leary, 1991) test data seems to be the dominant method for the validation of expert systems.

Characteristics of Test Data—Systematic Variance

As noted by Kerlinger (1973, p. 308), if the independent variable does not vary substantially, there is little chance of separating its effect from the total variance of the dependent variable, so much of which is due to *chance.*

In validating expert systems, test problems need to allow the validator to differentiate the effects due to systematic variance. O'Leary (1987) elicited four different types of test problem characteristics. First, the problems to be encountered by the system should be reflected in the test problems (Chandrasekaran, 1983). Second, a sufficient number of test problems is necessary to elicit the range of parameters necessary to test the system and to be able to establish some statistical measures of significance (Chandrasekaran, 1983). Third, as noted by O'Keefe *et al.* (1987, p. 83), *the issue is ... the coverage of the test data—that is, how well they reflect the input domain.* A sufficient variation in the test problems is necessary to test the range of parameters in the model. Fourth, the nature of the problems investigated by the system also helps establish a characteristic of test data. Type I and type II errors often dictate sample test problems. For example, in the case of a system designed to investigate bankruptcy, in any one year roughly 3–5% of the firms go bankrupt. Thus, if a system was given test data in proportion to the occurrence of bankruptcy in the actual population (say, 97% not bankrupt and 3% bankrupt) the non-bankrupt firms probably would *flood* the system to result in a high success rate by the system.

Sensitivity Analysis

Sensitivity analysis provides information as to the stability of the system (Buchanan and Shortliffe, 1985). If several solutions are found by the system, given only small parameter changes, then the system may be unstable.

System as a Black Box

In a Turing test, conditions are provided to the system and the output of the system is compared to that of human experts. Ideally, the system makes the same decisions as the experts. In this case both the system and the experts are treated as black boxes, where only the output is important.

Unfortunately, human expert time can be expensive. As a result, such a comparison also can be made between the system and other models of the decision process.

Right Decision for the Right Reason

Rather than treat the system as a black box, the investigation can determine if the system made the right decision for the right reason. This can be accomplished by using the explanation facility of the system to determine if the system not only made the right decision, but also did it for the right reason.

9.14   MODELS OF EXPERT PERFORMANCE: STRUCTURING THE COMPARISON TO ASSESS CONTENT VALIDITY

As noted by Kerlinger (1973, p.459), *criterion-related validity is studied by comparing test or scale scores with one or more external variables, or criteria, known or believed to measure the attribute under study.* In terms of expert systems, this means comparing the system behavior to that of some base, say a human expert. As a result, it is easy to understand why Chandrasekaran (1983) and others have recommended the comparison of the system to an expert, i.e., a Turing test. That comparison has taken many forms, depending on the purpose of the comparison and the ultimate use of the system.

9.14.1   Human Subjects' Rating of Acceptability

Buchanan and Shortcliffe (1985, Chapter 31) have used a rating system of three alternatives: *equivalent, acceptable alternative,* or *not acceptable.* Ten cases were developed and analyzed by ten prescribers, including the system. Then those 100 case prescriptions were evaluated by eight evaluators, using those three alternatives to establish a level of performance for each of the prescriptions.

9.14.2   Human Subjects' Rating of Performance

A number of expert systems builders have compared their systems based on the rating of performance, using a larger scale for that evaluation process. For example, Meservy (1986) used a seven point scale. Using a one-hundred point scale, Hansen and Messier (1986) compared the evaluative consistency of behavior associated with the system and the human subjects.

9.14.3   Human Subjects Protocol Analysis—Structure of Activity

Meservy *et al.* (1986) derived knowledge from experts using protocol analysis. Then as part of the investigation of the performance of the system, the expert's percentage of the time spent performing specific processes, such as *cognitive processes* (e.g., assuming, conjecturing, evaluating and questioning), was compared to the system's.

9.14.4   Use of Other Models, Rather than Humans

It is clear that humans as a comparison basis are limited because of time availability and cost (e.g., Buchanan and Shortliffe, 1985). As a result, comparisons are not limited to humans. Instead, alternative models can provide a comparison basis. For example, regression analysis has been used to model a decision maker's behavior (Bowman, 1963). Unfortunately, comparison to other models may not be feasible because the symbolic nature of the decision problem may make such other model developments infeasible.

9.15   STATISTICAL MODELS

There are a number of approaches to using statistics to investigate the performance of an expert system as compared to a human expert or another model. The method used is dependent on the particular model of the expert's performance that is chosen as the basis for the comparison, as was discussed in the previous section.

O'Keefe *et al.* (1987) discusses a number of different statistical approaches. If the system produces a single result on what is equivalent to a continuous scale, then a confidence interval can be developed over which to assess the likelihood that a particular level of performance was achieved. On the other hand the system may produce multiple recommendations, as will human experts. In this case, Hotelling's one-sample T2 test can be used.

O'Keefe *et al.* (1987) also discussed measures designed to test the consistency between experts. A commonly used measure to evaluate the consistency or reliability of legal judges is to use an interclass correlation coefficient. For example, Hansen and Messier (1986) tested their system on seventeen subjects. A rating of a case study on a scale of 1–100 was obtained from each of the subjects. The ratings were applied to three categories: before using the system, the system's recommendation, and after using the system. The results were then correlated with each other and a significance level was computed. This test measured the impact of the system on the decision-making of the validators.

Alternatively, if categorical variables, such as *equivalent, acceptable* or *not acceptable* are used, then the so-called *kappa* statistic can be used (O'Keefe *et al.* (1987)). Buchanan and Shortliffe (1985) also use an *F*-test to examine this type of data.

9.16   KNOWLEDGE BASE MAINTENANCE SYSTEMS

Since expert systems evolve over time, there is a need to build the validation process into the maintenance of the system. Generally, this means that it must be the organizational responsibility of someone other than the original developer. The responsibility likely has been shifted to someone who has less technical understanding of the expert system software, but possibly more domain expertise. Since there is less system expertise, there is greater need to provide tools to assist in the process of continually verifying and validating the expert system as it evolves over time.

9.16.1 Knowledge Base Manager

In a study of the use of expert systems, (see Chapter 14), O'Leary found that at least one company employed a knowledge base manager. That manager was responsible for a particular expert system. Among the jobs of that manager were ensuring that any new knowledge added to the system was verified and validated.

In some cases the knowledge base manager will not be a sophisticated user. In other cases the system size may be too large, even for a sophisticated user. Thus, at least in these two cases, maintenance system validation capabilities are desirable.

9.16.2 Maintenance System Capabilities

Expert system maintenance systems have become increasingly important as the systems grow in size and complexity. Such systems have varying capabilities. However, verification capabilities generally are one of the primary concerns, in order to ensure that the knowledge added to the system is consistent, etc. See Shatz *et al.* (1987) for a discussion of one such maintenance system.

9.16.3 Standard Test Problems

Standard test problems may prove helpful in the revalidation process. Some limitations of standard test problems are reviewed in Gaschnig *et al.* (1983).

One of the primary concerns with using test problems in expert systems is that the system may be changed. In that case, the system may not generate answers to the standard input problem or the solutions generated may be different because substantial changes have been made. Such problems are fairly unique to expert systems.

9.17 SUMMARY

This chapter has discussed a broad range of verification and validation issues. Verification was characterized as the process of finding errors in particular implementation of different software technologies, such as uncertainty representation and knowledge representation. Validation was structured as the relationship between a constructed expert and an actual expert. It was seen as less dependent on the given technology than verification.

A large range of methods of validation and verification were discussed. Methods for both verification and validation were aimed at the weights and the knowledge. Verification methods can be made *machine-intense.* Alternatively, validation remains fuzzier and more *human-intense.*

Additional validation issues were examined based on a framework developed from research methods. This framework led to the examination of such issues as content validity, criterion validity, construct validity, objectivity, cost benefit analysis, systematic variance, extraneous variance and error variance. From this basic framework the validation issues were elicited.

REFERENCES

Adrion, W., M. Branstad, J. Cherniavsky (1982), "Validation Verification and Testing of Computer Software," *ACM Computing Surveys*, Vol. 14, No. 2, pp. 159–192.

Bachant, J. and J. McDermott (1983), R1 Revisited: Four Years in the Trenches, *AI Magazine*, Vol. 5, No. 3, pp. 21–32.

Balci, O. and R. Sargent (1981), A Methodology for Cost Risk Analysis in the Statistical Validation of Simulation Models, *Communication of the ACM*, Vol. 24, No. 4, pp. 190–197.

Balci, O. and R. Sargent (1984), Validation of Simulation Models Via Simultaneous Confidence Intervals, *American Journal of Mathematics and Management Sciences*, Vol. 4, Nos. 3 and 4, pp. 375-406.

Bell, P. (1985), Visual Interactive Modeling in Operational Research: Successes and Opportunities, *Journal of Operational Research*, Vol. 36, No. 11, pp. 975–982.

Benbasat, I. and Dhaliwal, J. (1989) A Framework for the Validation of Knowledge Acquisition *International Journal of Man-Machine Studies*, Vol. 32.

Biggs, S., W. Messier and J. Hansen (1987), A Descriptive Analysis of Computer Audit Specialists' Decision Making, *Auditing: A Journal of Theory and Practice*, Spring, Vol. 6, Number 2, pp. 1–21.

Blanning, R. (1984), Knowledge Acquisition and System Validation in Expert Systems for Management, *Human Systems Management*, Vol.4, pp. 280–285.

Bowman, E.H. (1963), Consistency and Optimality in Decision Making, *Management Science*, Vol. 9, pp. 310–321.

Buchanan, B. and E. Shortliffe (1985), *Rule-Based Expert Systems: The MYCIN Experiments of the Stanford Heuristic Project*, Addison-Wesley, Reading, MA.

Chandrasekaran, B. (1983), On Evaluating AI Systems for Medical Diagnosis, *AI Magazine*, Vol. 4, No. 2, pp. 34–37.

Cohen, J. (1968), Weighted Kappa: Nominal Scale Agreement with Provision for Scaled Disagreement or Partial Credit, *Psychological Bulletin*, Vol. 70, No. 4, pp. 213–220.

Davis, R. (1976), *Applications of Meta-Level Knowledge to the Construction, Maintenance and Use of Large Knowledge Bases*, Ph.D Dissertation, Stanford.

Davis, R. (1984) Reasoning from First Principles in Electronic Troubleshooting, *International Journal of Man-Machine Studies*, Vol. 24, pp. 347–410.

Findlay, P., G. Forsey and J. Wilson (1988), The Validation of Expert Systems—Contrasts with Traditional Methods, *Journal of Operational Research*, Vol. 39, No. 10, pp. 933–938.

Fox, M. (1987), On Inheritance in Knowledge Representation, *Sixth International Conference on Artificial Intelligence, 1979*.

Gaschnig, J. (1979), Preliminary Performance Analysis of the Prospector Consultant System for Mineral Exploration, *Sixth International Joint Conference on Artificial Intelligence*, pp. 308–310.

Gaschnig, J., P. Klahr, H. Pople, E. Shortliffe and A. Terry (1983), *Evaluation of Expert Systems: Issues and Case Studies*, in Hayes-Roth *et al.*

Gass, S., (ed.) (1980), *Validation and Assessment Issues of Energy Models*, U.S. Department of Commerce, National Bureau of Standards, February.

Grossman, J. and R. Schutz (1988) Verification and Validation of Expert Systems, *AI Expert*, February, pp. 26–33.

Hansen, J. and W. Messier (1986), A Preliminary Investigation of EDP-XPERT, *Auditing: A Journal of Theory and Practice*, Fall 1986, Vol. 6, No. 1, pp. 109–123.

Hayes-Roth, F., D.A. Waterman and D.B. Lenat (1983), *Building Expert Systems*, Addison-Wesley, Reading, Mass.

Hogarth, R. (1980) *Judgment and Choice*, New York, Wiley.

Johnson, E. and J. Poorte (1987), A Hierarchial Approach to Computer Animation in Simulation Modeling, *Simulation*, Vol. 50, No. 1, pp. 30–36.

Johnson, P. (1983), What Kind of Expert Should a System Be? *The Journal of Medicine and Philosophy*, Vol. 8, pp. 77–97.

Kaplan, A. (1964), *The Conduct of Inquiry*, Chandler Publishing, San Francisco.

Kerlinger, F. (1973), *Foundations of Behavioral Research*, New York, Holt, Reinhart & Winston.

Kolodner, J. and C. Reisbeck (1986) *Experience, Memory and Reasoning*, Lawrence Earlbaum Associates, Hillsdale, New Jersey.

Lethan, H. and H. Jacobsen (1987) ESKORT—An Expert System for Auditing VAT Accounts, *Proceedings of Expert Systems and Their Applications*, Avignon, France.

Liebowitz, J. (1986), Useful Approach for Evaluating Expert Systems, *Expert Systems*, April, Vol. 2, No. 3, pp. 86–96.

McBride, R., D. O'Leary and G. Widmeyer (1989), *A System for Supporting Cash Management Decisions*, DSS Transactions 1989, Sponsored by TIMS, San Diego, California.

McBride, R., G. Widemeyer, and D.E. O'Leary (1989), A Knowledge Based System for Cash Management with Management Science Expertise, *Annals of Operations Research*, Vol. 21, pp.301–316.

McDermott, J. (1986), Comments, *The Second Artificial Intelligence Satellite Symposium*, Texas Instruments.

Marcot, B. (1987), Testing Your Knowledge Base, *AI Expert*, July, pp. 42–47.

Meservy, R., A. Bailey and P. Johnson (1986), Internal Control Evaluation: A Computational Model of the Review Process, *Auditing: A Journal of Theory and Practice*, Fall, Vol. 6, No. 1, pp. 44–74.

Messier, W. and J. Hansen (1992), A Case Study and Field Evaluation of EDP-EXPERT, *International Journal of Intelligent Systems in Accounting, Finance and Management*, Vol. 1, No. 3, pp. 173–185.

Mingers, J. (1986), Expert Systems—Experiments with Rule Induction, *J. of the Operational Research Society*, Vol. 37, pp. 1031–1038.

Mingers, J. (1987), Expert Systems—Rule Induction with Statistical Data, *J. of the Operational Research Society*, Vol. 38, pp. 39–48.

Naylor, T. and J. Finger (1968), Verification of Computer Simulation Models, *Management Science*, Vol. 14, No. 2, pp.92–101.

Nguyen, T., W. Perkins, T. Laffery and D. Pecora (1985), Checking an Expert Systems Knowledge Base for Consistency and Completeness, *International Joint Conference on Artificial Intelligence*, pp. 374-378.

Nguyen, T., W. Perkins, T. Laffery and D. Pecora (1987), Knowledge Base Verification, *AI Magazine*, Summer, pp. 69–75.

O'Keefe, R., O. Balci and E. Smith (1987), Validating Expert System Performance, *IEEE Expert*, Winter, pp. 81–89.

O'Keefe, R. (1988), Artificial Intelligence and the Management Science Practitioner:

Expert Systems and MS/OR Methodology, *Interfaces*, November-December, Vol. 18, No. 6, pp. 105–113.

O'Leary, D. (1987), Validation of Expert Systems, *Decision Sciences*, Vol. 18, No. 3, Summer, pp. 468–486.

O'Leary, D. (1988a), Expert System Prototyping as a Research Tool, E. Turbin and P. Watkins (eds.), *Applied Expert Systems*, North-Holland, Amsterdam, pp. 17–32.

O'Leary, D. (1988b), Methods of Validating Expert Systems, *Interfaces*, Vol. 18, No. 6, pp. 72–79.

O'Leary, D. (1988c), *The Cascaded Impact of the Representation of Expertise in Expert Systems: With Applications for the Use and Validation of Expert Systems*, unpublished paper presented at the TIMS XXVIII International Conference, Paris, July.

O'Leary, D. (1988d), On the Representation and the Impact of Reliability on Expert System Weights, *International Journal of Man-Machine Studies*, Vol. 29, No. 6, pp. 637–646.

O'Leary, D. (1989), Soliciting Weights or Probabilities from Experts for Rule-Based Systems, *International Journal of Man-Machine Studies*, 1990, Vol. 32, pp. 293–301.

O'Leary, D.E. (1991), *Validating Expert Systems: A Survey of Developers*, in Validation/Verification and Testing of Knowledge Based Systems, M. Ayel and J.P. Laurent (eds.) Wiley, Chichester.

O'Leary, D. (1993), Measuring the Quality of a Computer Model Performance, *European Journal of Operational Research*, Vol. 56, pp. 319–331.

O'Leary, D. and N. Kandelin (1988), Validating the Weights in Rule-Based Expert Systems, *International Journal of Expert Systems*, Vol. 1, No. 3, pp. 253–279.

O'Leary, D. and P. Watkins (1990) *Expert Systems in Internal Auditing*, Research Monograph, Institute of Internal Auditors.

Phelps, R. (1986), Artificial Intelligence — Overview of Similarities with OR, *J. of the Operational Research Society*, Vol. 37, pp. 13–20.

Piaget, J. (1973), *To Understand is to Invent*, Grossman, New York.

Politakis, P. and S. Weiss (1984), Using Empirical Analysis to Refine Expert System Knowledge Bases, *Artificial Intelligence*, Vol. 22, pp. 23–48.

Politakis, P. (1984), *Empirical Analysis for Expert Systems*, Research Notes in Artificial Intelligence 6, Boston, Mass, Pitman Advanced Publishing Program.

Ribar, G. (1988), Expert Systems Validation: A Case Study, *Expert Systems Review*, Vol. 1, No. 3.

Richer, M. and W. Clancey (1985), Guidon-Watch: A Graphic Interface for Viewing a Knowledge-Based System, *IEEE Computer Graphics and Applications*, November, pp. 51-64.

Sargent, R. (1985), An Expository on Verification and Validation of Simulation Models, *Proceedings of the Winter Simulation Conference*, pp. 15–22.

Sargent, R. (1986), The Use of Graphical Models in Model Validation, *Proceedings of the 1986 Winter Simulation Conference*, pp. 237–241.

Shatz, H., R. Strahs and L. Campbell (1987), ExperTAX: The Issue of Long-Term Maintenance, *Proceedings of the Third International Conference on Expert Systems*, June, pp. 291-300.

Shaw, M. and J. Woodward (1988), Validation in a Knowledge Support System: Construing and Consistency with Multiple Experts, *International Journal of Man-Machine Studies*, October, pp. 329–350.

Shortliffe, E. and R. Davis (1975), *SIGART Newsletter 55*, December 1975. Paper referenced in Gaschnig *et al.* (1983).

Suwa, M., A. Scott and E. Shortliffe (1982), Completeness and Consistency in

Rule-Based Expert Systems, in Buchanan and Shortliffe (1985, Chapter 8). See also AI Magazine, Fall 1982, pp. 16–21.

Todd, P. and I. Benbasat (1987), Process Tracing Methods in Decision Support System Research: Exploring the Black Box, *MIS Quarterly*, Vol. 11, No. 4, pp. 493–512.

Turban, E. and P. Watkins (1988), *Applied Expert Systems*, North-Holland, Amsterdam.

Williams, G. (1976), Comparing the Joint Agreement of Several Raters with Another Rater, *Biometrics*, Vol. 32, No. 2, pp. 619–627.

Yu, V., B. Buchanan, E. Shortliffe, S. Wraith, R. Davis, A. Scott and S. Cohen (1979a), Evaluating the Performance of a Computer-Based Consultant, *Computer Programs in Biomedicine*, Vol. 9, No. 1, pp. 95–102.

Yu, V., L. Fagan, S. Wraith, W. Clancey, A. Scott, J. Hanigan, R. Blum, B. Buchanan and S. Cohen (1979b), Antimicrobial Selection by Computer, *J. of the American Medical Association*, Vol. 242, No. 12, pp. 1279-1282. (See also Buchanan and Shortliffe, 1985, Chapter 31).

Chapter 10

EXPERT SYSTEMS IN AUDITING

Daniel E. O'Leary
Paul R. Watkins
University of Southern California, Los Angeles, CA

This chapter provides a review of the literature on the audit environment and then focuses on the use of expert systems and decision support systems in auditing. Because of the broad nature of external and internal auditing, research and systems in many areas of auditing are described.

10.1 PURPOSES OF EXPERT SYSTEMS— TRAINING/ASSISTING/REPLACING

Different authors (e.g., O'Leary, 1986) have noted that expert systems have a number of different purposes. They can be used to assist the decision maker, replace the decision maker or train the decision maker. To date, the major advances have focused on assisting the decision maker, although this chapter also discusses systems aimed at replacing and training decision makers.

10.2 THE AUDIT ENVIRONMENT

The audit environment is a unique and highly complex decision-making environment. This implies there are sources of error and inconsistency that are unique to the audit environment. Personal computers and other changes in technology have had and will continue to have an impact on the audit environment. In addition, the audit decision-making environment is process oriented and not results oriented.

10.2.1 Complexity

The audit environment is highly complex. In a discussion of that complexity, Hansen and Messier (1982) note that the audit problem of determining control weaknesses is a *nondeterministic polynomial* problem. This indicates

Expert Systems in Business and Finance: Issues and Applications. Edited by P.R. Watkins and L.B. Eliot
© 1993 John Wiley & Sons Ltd.

that audit problems have a large number of solutions and that it is difficult to sort through those solutions, in order to choose the best one. Such problems often are solved best by using heuristic approaches to find *good*, but not necessarily *optimal* solutions. In the case of audit problems, this generally means using rules of thumb of experienced auditors. Since such rules of thumb can be included in expert systems, such systems offer an alternative and feasible solution methodology to auditing situations.

10.2.2 Sources of Error and Inconsistency

Holstrom (1984) identifies a number of different sources of error and inconsistency. Holstrom (1984, p. 1) states the following:

> Judgment errors occur when there is a departure from a generally accepted criterion. Judgment inconsistencies occur whenever there is a difference between judgments, given the same data set and objectives, regardless of whether a generally accepted criterion exists. An error in overall judgment occurs when the auditor issues an incorrect audit opinion. An inconsistency in overall audit judgments occurs when different auditors render significantly different audit opinions based upon an identical set of financial statements and an identical set of audit evidence. In the latter case, we could determine that an inconsistency has occurred, but we could not conclude which overall judgment is in error unless we know in fact whether the financial statements were materially misstated.

Research (e.g., Hogarth, 1985) has shown that computer programs, such as expert systems, can be used to improve the consistency of human responses and mitigate errors. For example, as noted by Dillard and Mutchler (1987b, p. 17) :

> Utilization of the ... (expert) ... system will lend consistency, thoroughness and verifiability to the audit opinion decision process.

10.2.3 Personal Computer Environment

One of the primary developments in computing is a shift toward a personal computer (PC) computing environment. Researchers (e.g., O'Leary, 1986) noted that the change to the PC environment can have a major impact on auditing. First, the PC allows the user to take computing power with them to various locations. As a result, expert systems can now be developed to support the auditor in the field. Second, since so much work is now done on PCs there is increased need to be able to audit in a PC environment. Expert systems can be used to bring auditing knowledge to the auditor for the audit of PC-based systems.

10.2.4 Changing Technology

Holstrom *et al.* (1987) identified ...*numerous trends that are likely to have a major impact on audit evidence, the audit process and the role of auditing in the next 10 to 15 years.* They summarized the changes in information technology in four different categories: Office Automation and Transaction Automation, Data Communications, Computer Hardware and Computer Software.

Their initial results indicate an increased use of expert systems in auditing in the future, as exemplified by some of the applications discussed later in this chapter. In addition, it is likely that expert systems will be used to mitigate some of the problems resulting from, e.g., the move toward a paperless society. For as the *Law of Requisite Variety* (e.g., Ashby, 1965) notes, it takes equivocality to remove equivocality. Accordingly, as there are changes in complexity in those four categories, the systems needed to process information from those systems also must be more complex.

As a consequence of these large-scale and rapid changes in technology there is a major impact on the training of auditors to deal with these new technologies. Since few auditors currently in the field have received formal education in these technologies, there is a substantial need for auditors to receive some kind of training or flow of information on these technologies.

10.2.5 Process Oriented—Not Results Oriented

Many problems in auditing do not have feedback mechanisms that provide for the recognition of correct or incorrect responses (Kelly *et al.*, 1987). As a result, instead of being results oriented, auditing is process oriented. The quality of the work is not judged by results, but by the record of the process as summarized in the work papers.

Expert systems can be used to promulgate a particular audit process and record work done during that process. Thus, they can provide uniform documentation of the process and act to diffuse knowledge to the auditors.

10.2.6 Organizations

There has been limited research on the organizational impact of expert systems. O'Leary and Turban (1987) examine some of the possibilities. However, there are some unique such concerns that can be critical to the audit environment. These include the following:

● The auditor has a different relationship with the rest of the organization than other groups within the organization. Auditors take on the role of auditor, consumer, developer, manager and consultant on expert systems and other computer-based technology. Often their roles as an auditor forces them to maintain an arms-length perspective.

- Since auditors rarely directly impact the production of goods, they are regarded as an overhead function. As a result, management often can be restrictive in the allocation of resources to the audit function.
- The organizational structure of an audit team is definitely hierarchical in nature. Typically, the team reports to some level of management and the team itself employs a number of levels of audit personnel.
- In addition, many of the tasks of the audit team are accomplished relatively independently by the team members. The independent activities are then assembled into the audit report. As a result, audit tasks are often *loosely coupled.*

10.3   EXPERT SYSTEMS IN AUDITING

This section describes the current state of expert systems and decision support systems in auditing. Completed or prototype expert systems and decision support systems in both external and internal auditing, including special areas of focus such as EDP auditing and governmental auditing, are described.

This section focuses on those auditing-based systems that have appeared in the literature or have been presented at a conference or of which the authors are currently aware. There may be some systems that have been developed and are in use, but are not reported here. Generally, that would be because there has been little information on those systems in the literature.

This section does not provide a general overview of expert and decision support systems. Such treatments are available from a number of sources including Hayes-Roth *et al.* (1983).

In addition, this section does not discuss or try to differentiate between expert systems and decision support systems. Both types of systems support audit decision making and thus, both are included in this chapter. The interested reader is referred to Turban and Watkins (1986) for such a discussion.

10.3.1 Previous Surveys

There have been a number of other surveys of accounting and audit-based expert systems and decision support systems in academic outlets, e.g., Amer *et al.* (1987), Bailey *et al.* (1987), Bedard *et al.* (1984), Borthick (1987), Chandler (1985), Dillard and Mutchler (1984), Messier and Hansen (1984) and O'Leary (1987a). There have also been a number of surveys of audit-based expert systems in professional outlets, e.g., Bailey *et al.* (1986), Borthick and West (1987), Elliot and Kielich (1985), Flesher and Martin (1987) and McKee (1986). However, with the exception of O'Leary and

Watkins (1990), these surveys generally have ignored intrusion detection type systems, internal auditing and governmental auditing. In addition, there has been a structural change in the development of expert systems since those papers were written. The first reports of expert systems in auditing were almost entirely from academics. Now, it seems that many of the systems that are generating the most interest are systems developed for commercial purposes.

These commercial systems differ from systems developed by academics in a number of ways. First, they are not just developed to see if such a system can be developed. They generally are designed with the idea that they ultimately will be used. Second, commercial ventures usually entail the use of greater resources then can be mustered in most academic-based expert system developments. Third, in commercial efforts, the application is dominant. Methodology issues, design issues and other research issues are the primary focus of many academic systems.

10.3.2 Review of Audit-Based Expert Systems

This section proceeds by reviewing, respectively, audit-based expert systems in EDP Auditing, External Auditing: Academic Systems, External Auditing: Commercial Systems, Governmental Auditing and Internal Auditing. Limitations of auditing-based expert systems are then discussed followed by a discussion of sources for publication and presentation of information relating to expert systems. The final section provides some summary remarks.

10.3.3 EDP Auditing

Expert systems developed for EDP auditing take two primary formats. One approach is to develop an expert system to assist the auditor in auditing the system. Another approach is to develop systems that audit use of the system, in order to determine if there has been intrusion into the system.

Auditing General EDP Systems

There is really only one system that has been developed to assist in auditing general EDP systems. That system, EDP-XPERT, has been described in two primary papers (Hansen and Messier, 1986a,b), which, respectively, describe the system and the validation efforts that were given the system.

EDP-XPERT was one of the first auditing-based expert systems on which development efforts initiated. Early discussion of that system was given in Hansen and Messier (1982) and Messier and Hansen (1984). EDP-XPERT was developed using the rule-based, expert system shell AL/X.

A sample rule from EDP-XPERT is as follows (Hansen and Messier, 1986b)

If   1) Message Control Software is Complete and Sufficient, and
      2) Recovery Measures are Adequate, and
      3) Adequate Documentation is Generated to Form a Complete Audit
         Trail,
Then There is strong suggestive evidence that controls over data loss are
      adequate.

This system demonstrates that rule-based expert systems can be used to aid the auditing of internal controls in EDP systems. However, as noted in a related inquiry, Biggs *et al.* (1987) found that EDP auditors generally do not use *if ... then...* rules of the above type. Alternatively, such rules may be constructed from knowledge acquired from those auditors.

Specific EDP-Based Applications

MIS Training Institute has developed a number of expert systems to assist internal auditors. At the time of this writing there were seven applications available, four of which are based on IBM systems. Those four systems focus on CICS (based on IBM's communications system), System/36 and Expert Auditor System/38 (two IBM minicomputers) and IMS (IBM's database environment). Three of the systems are more general and are concerned with data center reviews, disaster recovery and auditing micro-computers.

Each of the systems they have developed reflects at least three of the guidelines of a *good* expert system application (for example, O'Leary, 1986), thus providing empirical support for those theoretical observations. In particular, each system is based on a set of audit concerns about highly specific environments, each of the systems is the concern of a large number of auditors, each system operates in a PC environment and each of the applications are in areas that require a substantial amount of specific expertise.

These systems are smart questionnaire systems. Each of the systems apparently makes use of a sequence of interrelated questions.

Intrusion Detection Systems

An important aspect of auditing EDP systems is ensuring their integrity. Expert systems have been designed to provide continuing, on-line *intrusion–detection* protection of EDP systems. Such systems stay resident in the computer system, monitoring the behavior of system users.

Denning (1987) has discussed such a system. That system is based on the hypothesis that exploitation of systems involves abnormal use of the system. Thus, by detecting abnormal use of the system, security violations can be detected. There are a number of examples of such violations, including the following (Denning, 1987).

Attempted Break-in: Someone attempting to break into the system likely would generate a large number of illegal passwords.

Successful Break-in: If an illegitimate user successfully breaks into a system then they may have different location or connect time than the legitimate user on whose account they have accessed the system.

Penetration by a Legitimate User: A legitimate user interested in penetrating the security of the system might execute programs different from or in a different order than would be expected.

Leakage by a Legitimate User: A legitimate user that attempts to leak unauthorized data might employ a remote printer, not normally used, at a time of the day that also is unusual.

Virus: A virus may cause an increase in the storage used by executable files or an increase in the frequency of execution of files.

Typically, normal behavior is represented using profiles for each user or facility. Then behavior is compared to those profiles to determine if it is normal or abnormal. Abnormal behavior is then flagged.

A research area with substantial potential impact is making such systems more efficient and effective. This research requires the investigation of the efficiency of different intrusion detection strategies. Generally, this means determination of those variables that best signal intrusion and those means (for example, statistical) that best determine the levels of those variables that indicate intrusion. Further, it is unclear what the impact of context (a given firm) is on both variables and methods of investigation. In addition, it is unclear what the organizational impact is of such systems. For example, if intrusion-detection systems are used do *human detectors* continue to function or do users just say *oh, the system does that?*

10.3.4 Academic-Based External/Internal Auditing Systems

Projects of concern to internal and external auditors have received the most extensive attention. In this area there have been a number of applications, including:

Adequacy of Allowance for Bad Debts—Chandler *et al.* (1983), Dungan (1983), Dungan and Chandler (1983, 1985), Braun (1986)

Audit Planning—Kelly (1984, 1987)

Going Concern Process—Biggs and Selfridge (1986), Selfridge (1988), Selfridge and Biggs (1988a) and Dillard and Mutchler (1986, 1987a)

Internal Controls—Meservy (1984), Gal (1985), Meservy *et al.* (1986), Bailey *et al.* (1985) and Grudnitski (1986)

Materiality—Steinbart (1984, 1987)

Risk Assessment—Mock and Vertinsky (1984, 1985), Dhar *et al.* (1988) and Peters *et al.* (1988)

Adequacy of Allowance for Bad Debts

The first audit-based expert system was developed by Dungan (1983) (see also Dungan and Chandler, 1983, 1985) to analyze the problem of the adequacy of the Allowance for Bad Debts for large commercial clients, based on analyzing the accounts individually. The system, entitled AUDITOR, was developed using the rule-based expert system shell AL/X.

AUDITOR gives advice in the form of an estimate of the probability that a given account balance will prove to be uncollectable. That research study (Dungan, 1983) had as ...*its objective the creation of an expert system model of certain judgment processes of auditors.* AUDITOR employs rules acquired from expert auditors. Associated with each rule is a probability that the conclusion in the rules (the *then* part) would occur given the evidence in the rule is found to exist (the *if* part). The system then provides an estimate of the probability that the account is uncollectable, given the evidence it is provided.

A second prototype expert system, is currently being built by Braun (1986). In some respects it is an extension of AUDITOR (Chandler *et al.*, 1983). However, the emphasis of the Braun (1986) study is on the hospital industry. In addition, it also considers the combination of analytical and judgmental variables.

As noted by Dillard and Mutchler (1987b), output from systems like the one described here could be used as input to other systems in order to take advantage of development efficiencies.

Audit Planning

Kelly (1984, 1987) develop a prototype model ICE (Internal Control Evaluation) to aid in the audit planning process. ICE featured a knowledge hierarchy of three different levels. The first level included knowledge about the industry, economy, management and the audit history. The second level focused on the client environment, the organization, planning manuals and accounting procedures. The third level focused on internal control functions in the purchasing process.

ICE was developed using LISP. Unlike most expert systems, ICE made use of both frames and rules.

Going Concern Process

The going concern problem is one of the most difficult facing auditors. As noted by the AICPA (1988), in order to render a going concern judgment, the auditor must (1) recognize that a problem exists, (2) understand the cause of the problem, (3) evaluate management's plans to address the problem and (4) render a judgment on the basis of whether the problems are sufficiently serious and whether management plans are judged to succeed.

There have been at least two ongoing academic efforts to address the going concern problem. Both the work of Biggs and Selfridge and the work of Dillard and Mutchler can be traced in a series of papers describing the systems' changes over time.

Probably one of the most sophisticated accounting and auditing expert systems is GCX (Going Concern Expert) discussed in Part III of this book and in a sequence of papers by Biggs and Selfridge (1986), Selfridge (1988) and Selfridge and Biggs (1988a,b). GCX was programmed in MacScheme, a dialect of Lisp, that runs on an Apple Macintosh II. GCX was tested on five years of data from a real world company, about which the auditors who were questioned had substantial knowledge.

The research questions addressed in the development of GCX included (Selfridge and Biggs, 1988a, p. 2):

- What are the categories of expert knowledge and how are they represented?
- What are the reasoning strategies of the expert auditors and how are they represented?
- How is the knowledge and reasoning strategy organized in GCX?

In Biggs and Selfridge (1986), the system included expert knowledge in measures of financial performance, business and the business environment, and management plans. GCX had 100 financial reasoning rules and 80 business and business environment events.

Selfridge and Biggs (1988a) reported six categories of knowledge, including events, inter-event causality, company function (financial model and operations model), events/financial performance causality, measures of financial performance and going concern problems. Their model contained 140 event frames and 215 entity frames.

The Selfridge–Biggs model employs Schank's (1982) MOPs (Memory Organization Packets). For example, in the operations model there is a hierarchy of MOPs that employ successively more detailed descriptions of company operations.

In Selfridge and Biggs (1988b), that knowledge was extended to general financial knowledge, of actual events, knowledge of normal events, knowledge of company function, knowledge of company markets, knowledge of the industry, knowledge of multiple business lines, knowledge of changes over time and knowledge of other companies.

In each of the successive models the knowledge changes. As a result, the resultant auditor reasoning through that knowledge also must change. In addition, to addressing the issues specified by the authors, the sequence of papers that reflect the development of GCX allows insight into the growth and development of an expert system.

Dillard and Mutchler (1986, 1987a,b) also have done extensive work in the area of modeling the auditor's going concern opinion decision. Their system was developed on a DEC 2060 using a menu shell, XINFO. The system apparently employs approximately 450 decision frames or nodes in a decision tree. The intelligence in the system is in the decision structure and hierarchy.

The system contains *technical* knowledge about such things as basic accounting procedures, audit procedures, audit standards and the business, economic and legal environment in the context of a *task support system*. This knowledge is organized in a hierarchical branching structure with nodes representing primitive and intermediate decisions. Technical knowledge was gathered in each of seven categories: operations, financial, market, management, industry, audit and other.

The system uses an architecture that interfaces that task support system with three other components: task action system, external interface system and a guidance system. The task guidance system uses frames to provide suggestions and rules and methods for making decisions specified in the task support system. The task action system supports programs for data access, statistical analysis and other additional tools which the auditor may wish to use. Finally, the external interface system allows for the generation of documentation and audit trails.

The system does not exactly mimic expert behavior. For example, the system employs numeric rating systems which auditors are unlikely to use in going concern problems.

Internal Controls

TICOM (Bailey *et al.*, 1985) was the first auditing-based system to implement artificial intelligence techniques in the system. TICOM (The Internal Control Model) is an analytic tool that aids the auditor in modeling the internal control system and querying the model in order to aid the auditor in evaluating the internal control system. TICOM was implemented in Pascal.

Materiality

Steinbart (1984,1986) developed an audit judgment model, AUDITPLAN-NER, for the assessment of materiality. AUDITPLANNER uses six different sets of inputs to aid in the materiality decision: prior year's materiality levels, financial characteristics of the client, nonfinancial characteristics of the client, future plans of the client, nature of the audit engagement and the intended uses of the client's financial statements.

The system was built for use in profit and not-for-profit firms. The test clients included manufacturing firms, trucking firms, super markets, a school district and a Boy Scout Council.

AUDITPLANNER was built using the rule-based expert system shell, EMYCIN. The system did not include the use of certainty factors.

Risk Assessment. Substantial literature of risk assessment exists (e.g., Mock and Vertinsky, 1985). However, there are a number of problems where it is difficult to quantify risk. As a result, Dhar *et al.* (1988) describe the problem of risk assessment as knowledge-based, where knowledge about the client' history, recent events specific to the firm or industry, and knowledge about the internals of a firm are crucial in shaping the auditor's judgment about risks associated with accounts, and hence the *audit plan*. This interpretation is further enhanced by the general finding (Mock and Vertinsky, 1984, p. 1) that people are not good intuitive statisticians and therefore the craft of risk assessment is *fraught with risks*.

There is at least one paper on the use of risk assessment in auditing decision support systems (Mock and Vertinsky, 1984) and at least two papers in the use of expert systems in assessing risk (Dhar *et al.*, 1988 and Peters *et al.*, 1987).

10.3.5 External Auditing: Commerical-based Systems

Arthur Anderson

Arthur Anderson (AA) has developed expert systems for the consulting group's clients, e.g., Arthur Anderson (1985) and Mui and McCarthy (1987). However, there have been no discussions in the literature relating to internal projects to aid the AA auditing process.

Ernst & Young

Ernst & Young (EY) has taken a single product, multiple component, middle-out strategy in the development of their decision support system, AY/ASQ. AY/ASQ is software designed to automate the audit process for manufacturing environments.

AY/ASQ was developed in an Apple MacIntosh environment. The operation for each of the applications is similar to the other applications. The system consists of several modules including Decision Support, Office, Trial Balance, Time Control and Databridge.

The decision support module features the ability to reference the computer file stored documentation for the EY audit process. In addition, the system guides the audit planning process through a *smart questionnaire* approach. This smart questionnaire approach ensures that the auditor performs certain procedures. When those procedures have been followed, the computer updates the rest of the checklist.

Future enhancements likely will include the development of similar modules for different industries and the development of a module to analyze internal controls.

KPMG Peat Marwick

KPMG Peat Marwick (KPMG) apparently has taken a multiple project approach to the development of expert systems in auditing. Their best known system is LoanProbe, also known as CFILE. The development of that system is chronicled in a sequence of papers, including Kelly *et al.* (1987), Ribar (1987, 1988a,b,c). LoanProbe is a rule-based system developed using INSIGHT II (now Level V). A rule-based approach is used because of the classification nature of the problem. (Similar classification problems have been solved using a rule-based approach.) It is estimated that LoanProbe has three person-years of development time (Ribar, 1987).

LoanProbe derives its name from credit file analysis and is designed for use in bank audits loan loss evaluation. In particular, it aids the process of estimating the dollar amount of the reserve for the bank's portfolio of loans.

AUDPREX (Kelly, 1986) is a proposal to develop an expert system to aid in the design of audit programs in the area of inventory systems. Such a system would be used as an aid to determine the type, timing, nature and the amount of substantive procedures.

In contrast to LoanProbe, another system, designed to aid in interpretation of SFAS #80 on accounting futures, was developed by a single researcher within a period of several weeks (Ribar, 1987). That included the time required by the researcher to learn the expert system shell, INSIGHT II. For the SFAS-based system, the professional literature provided much of the guidance.

Price Waterhouse

There are no systems reported at Price Waterhouse (PW). However, PW recently has developed a Technology Center. At the Technology Center, PW is exploring the use of multiple technologies in auditing, including the use of decision support systems and expert systems.

10.3.6 Governmental Auditing

Governments face the problem of auditing and reviewing large volumes of tax returns and filings of various types. The large volume often means that humans are unable to process all the documents in a cost-effective manner. Alternatively, even if humans could process all the volume, often budgetary constraints limit the number and quality of persons that could be employed. As a result, the need for systems aimed at processing similar documents submitted to the government is likely to be very high. The successful development of the following systems indicates that such systems may be widespread in the near future.

Each of the following systems has been developed as either a consulting project or as an activity of an internal artificial intelligence staff.

Reviews of SEC Filings

Currently, human financial analysts use analytic review of corporate filings at the Securities and Exchange Commission (SEC) to check the correctness of the filings. Arthur Andersen & Co. (1985) (see also Mui and McCarthy 1987) developed Financial Statement Analyzer (FSA) as a LISP-based prototype to explore the possibility of using a computer program to compute and analyze ratios. FSA includes the *ability to understand* the text in the filings so that it may gather relevant information required to complete an analytic review of the return. Such a system would limit the need for human financial analysts to perform those activities and free their time for other activities.

From a research perspective, this system is one of the first functioning systems to employ the approach summarized in DeJong (1979) to read and understand natural language. Briefly, that approach reads a part of the sentence. It then predicts what will follow in the remainder of the sentence. Then it checks its prediction against what it actually finds to confirm and guide its search for meaning in the rest of the text. The system continues in this manner, predicting and substantiating while generating its understanding of the text.

Pennsylvania State Audit for Taxes

Green *et al.* (1991) address the problem of determining *which Organizations should be audited to achieve the maximum collection of monies due to the state of Pennsylvania?* Accordingly, the overall audit goal is to improve audit productivity.

Unfortunately, this problem is difficult to solve since there is little understanding about which organizations should be audited. Thus, there is little available expertise to build into the system. As a result, Hall *et al.* (1987) and Green *et al.* (1991) developed a system that would learn and develop the necessary expertise.

The general research goal is to determine how a computer program can be programmed to learn. In order to accomplish that goal they chose a genetic learning approach. Genetic algorithms learn by employing different combining rules on responses, such as inversion and mutation. For example, the system may combine the two sets of characteristics abc and cde to form abe, in its search for a better set of characteristics.

222 DANIEL E. O'LEARY AND PAUL R. WATKINS

IRS Auditing of Tax Returns

A recent publication by the Department of the Treasury (US Government, 1987) indicated that the Internal Revenue Service' new artificial intelligence lab is exploring new systems to identify likely tax returns for examination potential. Very little has been released on their efforts to-date, but summaries of activities may be found in Brown (1988), Brown and Streit (1988). However, they face a problem similar to other government activities, in that they have a number of documents to process in a short time and are subject to budgetary constraints.

Danish Customs Auditing of Value Added Tax (VAT) Accounts

Recently, Danish Customs Authorities employed a consulting firm to develop an expert system to help them audit VAT accounts (Lethan and Jacobsen, 1987). The system was designed to develop more effective VAT auditing and to improve the VAT examiner's productivity. As in other government applications, there is a great deal of work to be done and the expert system is designed to do some of the work in order to improve the productivity of the examiners.

To acquire the knowledge necessary for the system, the knowledge engineers found that they almost had to become *experts* in the VAT auditing process. Further, for the system to be used by Danish Customs officers at the sites of the companies that were being investigated the system would have to be developed for use on an IBM PC and the knowledge base would have to be in Danish.

The system is a prototype developed using the expert system shell, KEE.

Contributions and Extensions of Government Audit Systems

Each of these systems is important because they capture the knowledge of experts in their knowledge bases and allow for productivity improvements. Each of these systems is designed to allow computer processing of some human information processing activities, while allowing humans to focus on other more important issues.

However, there are additional contributions. The FSA was one of the first actual implementations of DeJong's (1979) approach to understanding text. The Pennsylvania State Tax system is the first audit system to be able to learn. The VAT system demonstrates an easy to forget capability of expert systems that the knowledge does not have to be recorded in English—the system does not care what language the knowledge is in.

Systems of this type are not limited to these applications. Instead, those situations where there are a large number of documents to process and those situations where there is interest in determining file violations are all conceptually congruent with these applications. In addition, although each of these applications is associated with a government, such applications are not limited to government but could be extended to almost any business that processes large amounts of the same kind of documents.

10.3.7 Internal Auditing

The functional area of auditing that probably has received the least attention is internal auditing. Although internal auditors will likely make use of many of the developments in each of the other categories discussed above, some applications have been aimed at the unique requirements of internal auditing.

Decision Support for Internal Audit Planning

Boritz (1983) presented an initial report on the development of a desktop decision support system for internal auditing planning. That system (Boritz, 1986a) is available to the commercial market through the Institute of Internal Auditors (IIA) as a product known as *audit MASTERPLAN* (AMP).

AMP includes two approaches to measuring risk (Based on Boritz, 1986b) and includes the IIA's Standards for Professional Practice of Internal Auditing. AMP is designed for most industries (financial, industrial, service and manufacturing). AMP has five components: Systems Management, Risk Factors Management, Audit Portfolio Management, Personnel Skills Management and Long-term Planning and Budgeting Module.

In the original report (Boritz, 1983), the research focus was on the user interface and the inclusion of knowledge into the procedures of the system rather than the storage of a separate knowledge base. Boritz and Kielstra (1987) described a methodology for the assessment of risk, using audit and inherent risk.

Price Analysis

A problem that continues to make headlines throughout the United States of America is the spending activities of the federal government, e.g., the two hundred dollar ashtray. In a sequence of at least three papers Dillard *et al.* (1987a) and Ramakrishna *et al.* (1983) proposed the development of an expert system to aid in the examination of the reasonableness of an expenditure.

Their discussion is primarily aimed at federal government acquisitions. However, as they note, price analysis is also a problem in private enterprise.

PAYPER—An Expert System to Examine Payroll and Personnel Files

Payper (Payroll–Personnel) is a prototype expert system, developed using the expert system shell EXSYS, designed to aid in the audit of payroll and personnel files. It does this by ensuring that conditions within each field of each record meet certain conditions and that the analytical relationships that hold between fields meet certain conditions. For example, not only should hours worked and pay rate meet certain constraints, but also hours worked times pay rate plus vacation pay must meet certain constraints.

The primary theoretical contribution of PAYPER is that it uses traditional expert systems, multiple conditions rules, to extend traditional EDP single field audit tests. By taking into account relations between the fields, this approach allows tighter and more comprehensive analysis of the data. In addition, it allows investigation of text data in such audit processes.

The Internal Audit Risk Assessor (TIARA)—The Equitable

There is only limited information available on TIARA as developed by Inference Corporation for The Equitable. A brief summary of the system is available (Inference Corporation, No Date) and further inquiries to Inference Corporation did not yield any additional information, except that the system was not used by The Equitable.

As originally discussed TIARA presents a methodology for assessing risk. Some of the variables used in that decision include strength/experience of the units management team, the unit's internal control consciousness, changes in the unit's basic industry/market and the length of time since their last audit. The system was designed to provide a means to enable rapid identification of high priority audits and consistent assessment of audit risk.

Coopers & Lybrand—Internal Audit Systems

Recently, Coopers & Lybrand began promoting a general internal audit system that

- Employs Audit Planning and Tracking
- Allows Automatic Sample Selection from Mainframe Data
- Automatically identifies Patterns in Sample Data
- Has Intelligent online questionnaires for policy testing and specific regulation
- Provides explanations for questions
- Records internal auditor comments during the audit

- Displays policy documents online
- Generates Work Papers
- Prints branch exception reports

Continuous Audit of Online Systems

Vasarhelyi *et al.* (1988) argue that recent advances in hardware and software technology are engendering increasingly complex information systems environments, thus, requiring increasingly complex audit approaches. However, the same technologies that increase the complexity of the information systems environment can be used to the advantage of the auditing of those systems. Not only can decision support systems be used to assist auditors, but the computer can be used to perform additional auditing. In particular, because of the large amount of data, auditors may not be able to provide an effective or efficient audit. As a result, it is desirable to build systems that continuously audit portions of the database as transactions occur.

The quality of these audit systems is dependent on the ability of the modeler to capture the expertise of auditors in the metrics and analytics used to model that expertise. Research in systems of this type needs to explore approaches that capture that expertise best.

Fraud Detection

At least two studies (Tener, 1988 and Lecot, 1988) have used expert systems to investigate the possibility of fraud as part of the internal audit function.

Tener (1988) discusses an off-line fraud detection system for deviant file use. Lecot (1988) describes an on-line system designed to determine fraudulent credit card use. In each case the focus of these systems was on determining if a user of a service of the firm is a legitimate user. Conceptually, the intrusion detection systems discussed under EDP systems and the continuous audit system discussed immediately above are similar to these systems.

The approach of each system is to first establish a profile for each of the legitimate users, that defines expected and possible behaviors. Then when that user makes use of the system, that use is compared to the profile to determine if the user is who they say they are. Those comparisons are based on the notion that *early warning symptoms* can be captured in those user profiles.

Tener (1986) suggests that audit management utilize decision support systems, management information systems and management science models to identify and project the deterioration of controls that can occur between audit engagements. Further, as firms increase in size, because of mergers and economies of scale, the quantity of auditing demands on the auditor is increasing.

10.4   DANGERS IN EXPERT SYSTEM DEVELOPMENT

One of the dangers of the current approach to most knowledge engineering projects is the preoccupation with what is, rather than what should be. On one expert system project of which the authors are aware, it was realized that a mathematical programming approach (integer programming) would provide a better solution to a subproblem in the system than using a sequence of If ... then... rules. The linear program was able to provide a better solution than simply mimicking an auditor's behavior. When optimal solution generation processes can be used to solve the problem they will provide better solutions than rule-based approaches.

Preoccupation with a given type of knowledge representation can be dangerous. For example, as Biggs and Selfridge (1986) found, auditors do not think in If ... then... rules. Turning dialogues with auditors into such rules may lead to a loss of knowledge.

In a related study, Gal and Steinbart (1986) examined the development of two expert systems for investigating the nature of audit judgment. The evidence presented in that paper indicates that refinements made to those prototype systems resulted in evaluations which *reflect more of the decision criteria actually used by the auditor.* That is, the initial systems developed may not properly represent judgment.

Another danger in the development of expert systems is that the more that computers do the less that auditors need to do. This has at least two implications. First, we must remember that expert systems are a move to automate the audit process. As with the introduction of most automation projects, the number of human workers directly involved in the production process decreases. Thus, we can expect to see a decrease in the number of auditors to accomplish the same amount of work. Second, if the system knows something then the auditor may not need to know that something. As a result, auditors may forget important information that they have learned or not learn things that are important. Reportedly, EY has tempered the inclusion of activities in AY/ASQ so as to minimize the negative implications of the system *knowing too much,* and the auditor forgetting or worse yet, not learning.

Another danger is that the auditor would blindly depend on the systems' recommendations. This could occur in at least two situations. First, if the auditor does not have the necessary base knowledge then decisions made by the system cannot be questioned. Second, if the auditor does not *interact* with the systems then the system's suggested course of action will be executed. As a result, it is important to place the responsibility for the actions on the auditor, not the system.

Further, there are security problems associated with expert systems that are different than those associated with other computer-based systems. Such security problems are discussed in O'Leary (1990).

10.5 VALIDATING EXPERT SYSTEMS

Recently, there has been considerable interest in validating expert systems. O'Leary (1987b) provided a framework for validation of expert systems. That framework is particularly useful because it elicits some of the key issues and concerns that face the validator of an expert system. Particular methods for validating expert systems are investigated and developed in O'Leary (1988b), O'Leary and Kandelin (1988) and others.

Continued development in this area is expected so that tools are developed to meet the needs of validators. Many of these issues and other issues are summarized in O'Leary (1989).

10.6 CONCLUSIONS

Recently developed audit-based expert systems have moved beyond the initial rule-based systems to include such knowledge representation schemas as frames and semantic networks. The systems went beyond just employing heuristics in the context of decision-making processes, to include developments, such as learning and natural language understanding. In addition, expert systems have moved out of academe and into commercial applications.

As summarized in this section, a wide variety of prototype and commercial systems are in operation. Thus, from an academic perspective there is no more need to build expert systems to show that they can be used to solve accounting problems.

However, expert systems remain an important tool to simulate the procedures that an auditor goes through, to test our understanding of the knowledge in a particular area of auditing and to test the use of technological developments in artificial intelligence in auditing-based expert systems.

REFERENCES

AICPA, Statements on Auditing Standards, #59 (1988), "The Auditor' Consideration of an Entity's Ability to Continue as a Going Concern."

Amer, T., Bailey, A., and De, P. (1987), "A Review of Computer Information Systems Research Related to Accounting and Auditing," *The Journal of Accounting Information Systems*, Volume 2, Number 1, pp. 3–28.

Arthur Andersen & Co. (1985), *Financial Statement Analyzer*, Unpublished report, December.

Ashby, R. (1965), *Introduction to Cybernetics*, John Wiley & Sons.

Bailey, A.D., Duke, G.L., Gerlach, J., Ko, C., Meservy, R.D., Whinston, A.B. (1985), "TICOM and the Analysis of Internal Controls," *The Accounting Review*, 60, April, pp. 186–201.

Bailey, A. D., Meservy, R., and Turner, J. (1986), "Decision Support Systems, Expert Systems, and Artificial Intelligence: Realities and Possibilities in Public Accounting," *The Ohio CPA Journal*, Spring, pp. 11–15.

Bailey, A., Meservy, R., Duke, G., Johnson, P. and Thompson, W. (1987), "Auditing, Artificial Intelligence and Expert Systems," *Decision Support Systems: Theory and Applications*, C. Holsapple and A. Whinston (eds.), Springer Verlag, Berlin.

Barbera, A. (1988), *Personal Computer and Expert System Usage by Small and Medium Sized CPA Firms*, Unpublished paper, July.

Bedard, J., Gray, G. and Mock, T.J. (1984), "Decision Support Systems and Auditing," *Advances in Accounting*, B. Schwartz (ed.), JAI Press, Greenwich, Connecticut.

Biggs, S., Messier, W. and Hansen, J. (1987), "A Descriptive Analysis of Computer Audit Specialists' Decision-Making Behavior in Advanced Computer Environments," *Auditing: A Journal of Theory and Practice*, Spring, Volume 6 Number 2, pp. 1–21

Biggs, S.F. and M. Selfridge, (1986), Combining Rule-Based and Network-Based Logic in Expert Systems for Accounting, *Proceedings of the American Accounting Association Annual Meeting*, New York, August.

Biggs, S. and Selfridge, M. (1986), "GCX: An Expert System for the Auditor's Going Concern Judgment," Unpublished presentation at the National Meeting of the American Accounting Association in New York.

Blocher, E., Krull, G., Scalf, K. and Yates, S. (1988), "Training and Performance Effects of A Knowledge-Based System for Analytical Review," Unpublished Paper Presented at the First International Symposium on Expert Systems in Business, Finance and Accounting, University of Southern California, September.

Bolc, L. and Coombs, M.J. (1988), *Expert Systems Applications,* Springer-Verlag, New York.

Boritz, J. (1983), "CAPS: The Comprehensive Audit Planning System," Unpublished Paper presented at the University of Southern California Symposium on Audit Judgment.

Boritz, J. (1986a), Audit MASTERPLAN, Audit Planning Software published by the Institute of Internal Auditors.

Boritz, J. (1986b), "Scheduling Internal Audit Activities," *Auditing: A Journal of Theory and Practice*, Fall, Volume 6, Number 1, pp. 1–19.

Boritz, J. and Kielstra, R. (1987), "A Prototype Expert System for the Assessment of Inherent Risk and Prior Probability of Error," Unpublished Paper.

Boritz, J. and Wensley (1987), "A., Structuring the Assessment of Audit Evidence—An Expert Systems Approach," December, Unpublished Paper.

Borthick, F. (1987), "Artificial Intelligence in Auditing: Assumptions and Preliminary Development," *Advances in Accounting*, pp. 179–204.

Borthick, F. and West, O. (1987), "Expert Systems—A New Tool for The Professional," *Accounting Horizons*, March, 1987, Volume 1, Number 1, pp. 9–16.

Braun, H.M. (1986), "Integrating an Expert System and Analytical Review Techniques for Making an Audit Decision," Unpublished paper presented at the ORSA/TIMS meeting in Miami, October.

Brown, C.E. (1988), Tax Expert Systems in Industry and Accounting, *Expert Systems Review for Business, Finance and Accounting*, Vol. 1, No. 3, pp.9–16.

Brown, C. and Streit, I. (1988), "A Survey of Tax Expert Systems," *Expert Systems Review*, Volume I, Number 2, pp. 6–12.

Buchanan, B.G. and Shortliffe, E.H. (1984), *Rule-Based Expert Systems*, Addison-Wesley, Reading, Massachusetts.

Chandler, J. (1985), "Expert Systems in Auditing: The State of the Art," *The Auditor's Report*, Volume 8, Number 3, Summer, pp. 1–4.

Chandler, J., Braun, H. and Dungan, C. (1983), "Expert Systems: Operational Support for Audit Decision Making," Unpublished paper presented at the University of Southern California Symposium on Audit Judgment, February.

Coopers & Lybrand (1988a), "Expert Systems Catching On With Financial Services Firms," *Executive Briefing*, May.

Coopers & Lybrand (1988b), *Expert Systems in the Financial Services Industry*, Coopers & Lybrand.

Coopers & Lybrand (1988c), *Expert Systems in the Financial Services Industry: Survey Report*, Coopers & Lybrand (Cost is $100).

David, P., Greene, D.P., Meservy, R.D. and S.F. Smith (1991), Learn Audit Selection Rules from Data: A Genetic Algorithms Approach, *in Expert Systems in Finance and Accounting*, D.E. O'Leary and P.R. Watkins (eds.) Amsterdam.

DeJong, G. (1979), *Skimming Stories in Real Time: An experiment in Integrated Understanding*, Unpublished Ph. D. Dissertation, Yale University.

Denning, D. (1987), "An Intrusion Detection Model," *IEEE Transactions on Software Engineering*, Vol. SE 13, No. 2, February, pp. 222–232.

Dhar, V., Lewis, B., and Peters, J. (1988), "A Knowledge-Based Model of Audit Risk," *AI Magazine*, Volume 9, Number 3, Fall.

Dillard, J. (1984), "Discussant's Comments on 'Expert Systems in Accounting and Auditing: A Framework and Review'" *Decision Making and Accounting: Current Research*, S. Moriarty and E. Joyce (eds.), University of Oklahoma, 1984, pp. 182–202.

Dillard, J.F. and Mutchler, J.F. (1984), "Knowledge Based Expert Systems in Auditing," Working Paper, Ohio State University, July.

Dillard, J.F. and Mutchler, J.F. (1986), "Knowledge Based Expert Computer Systems for Audit Opinion Decisions," Unpublished Paper presented at the University of Southern California Symposium on Audit Judgment.

Dillard, J.F. and Mutchler, J.F. (1987a), "A Knowledge-Based Support System for the Auditor's Going Concern Opinion Decision," Unpublished Working Paper.

Dillard, J. and Mutchler, J. (1987b), "Expertise in Assessing Solvency Problems," *Expert Systems*, August, pp. 170–178.

Dillard, J.F., Ramakrishna, K. and Chandrasekaran, B. (1983), "Expert Systems for Price Analysis: A Feasibility Study," in *Federal Acquisition Research Symposium*, U.S. Air Force, Williamsburg, Virginia, December.

Dillard, J.F., Ramakrishna, K. and Chandrasekaran, B. (1987), "Knowledge-based Decision Support Systems for Military Procurement," in Silverman, pp. 120–139.

Dungan, C. (1983), "A Model of an Audit Judgement in the Form of an Expert System," University of Illinois, Unpublished Ph.D. Dissertation.

Dungan, C. and Chandler, J. (1983), "Analysis of Audit Judgment Through an Expert System," Faculty Working Paper no. 982, University of Illinois, November.

Dungan, C. and Chandler, J. (1985), "Auditor: A Microcomputer-Based Expert System to Support Auditors in the Field," *Expert Systems*, October, pp. 210–221.

Elliot, R.K. and Kielich, J.A. (1985), "Expert Systems for Accountants," *Journal of Accountancy*, September.

Flesher, D. and Martin, C.(1987), "Artificial Intelligence," *The Internal Auditor*, February, pp. 32–36.

Gal, G. (1985), "Using Auditor Knowledge to Formulate Data Constraints: An Expert System for Internal Control Evaluation," Unpublished Ph. D. Dissertation, Michigan State University.

Gal, G. and Steinbart, P. (1986), "Knowledge Base Refinements as an Indication of Auditor Experience," Unpublished paper presented at the University of Southern California Symposium on Audit Judgment.

Gerlach, J. (1987), "Some Preliminary Notes on the Development of a General

DSS for Auditors," *Decision Support Systems: Theory and Application,* C. Holsapple and A. Whinston (eds.), Springer Verlag, Berlin.

Grudnitski, G.(1986), "A Prototype of an Internal Control System for the Sales/Accounts Receivable Application," Unpublished paper presented at the University of Southern California Symposium on Audit Judgment.

Hall, M., Meservy, R. and Nagin, D. (1987), "Audit Knowledge Acquisition by Computer Learning." Unpublished paper presented at the ORSA/TIMS Meeting, New Orleans, May.

Hansen, J.V. and Messier, W.F. (1982), "Expert Systems for Decision Support in EDP Auditing," *International Journal of Computer and Information Sciences,* 11, pp. 357–379.

Hansen, J.V. and Messier, W.F. (1986a), "A Knowledge-Based Expert System for Auditing Advanced Computer Systems," *European Journal of Operational Research,* September, pp. 371–379.

Hansen, J.V. and Messier, W.F. (1986b), "A Preliminary Investigation of EDP-XPERT," *Auditing: A Journal of Practice and Theory,* Volume 6, Number 1,Fall, pp. 109–123.

Hayes-Roth, F., Waterman, D.A., Lenat, D.B. (1983), *Building Expert Systems,* Addison-Wesley, Reading, Massachusetts.

Hogarth, R. (1985), *Judgment and Choice,* Wiley, Chichester.

Holstrom, G. (1984), "Sources of Error and Inconsistency in Audit Judgment," Working paper no. 70, School of Accounting, University of Southern California.

Holstrom, G., Mock, T. and West, R. (1987), "The Impact of Technological Events and Trends on Audit Evidence in the Year 2000: Phase I," in *Proceedings of the 1986 Touche Ross/University of Kansas Symposium on Auditing Problems,* R. Srivastava and N. Ford (eds.), School of Business, University of Kansas, Lawrence, Kansas 66045, pp. 125–146.

Inference Corporation, "The Internal Audit Risk Assessor (TIARA)—The Equitable," *ART Application Note,* Inference Corporation, Los Angeles, California.

Kelly, K.P. (1984), "Expert Problem Solving for the Audit Planning Process," Unpublished Ph. D. Dissertation, University of Pittsburgh, Pittsburgh, Pa

Kelly, K.P. (1986), "Audit Programming Expert System Project," Unpublished paper.

Kelly, K.P. (1987), "Modeling the Audit Planning Process," *Expert Systems Review,* Volume 1, Number 1.

Kelly, K.P., Ribar, G. and Willingham, J. (1987), "Interim Report on the Development of an Expert System for the Auditors Loan Loss Evaluation," in *Proceedings of the Touche Ross/University of Kansas Audit Symposium,* pp. 167–188.

Kolodner, J. (1980), *"Retrieval and Organizational Strategies in Conceptual Memory: A Computer Memory",* Unpublished Ph. D. Dissertation, Yale University.

Lecot, K. (1988), "An Expert System Approach to Fraud Prevention and Detection," *AI-88 Artificial Intelligence Conference,* Long Beach, Ca.

Lecot, K. (1988), "An Expert System Approach to Fraud Prevention and Detection," *Expert Systems Review,* Volume 1, Number 3.

Lethan, H. and Jacobsen, H. (1987), "ESKORT—An Expert System for Auditing VAT Accounts," in *Proceedings of Expert Systems and Their Applications—Avignon 87,* Avignon, France.

Lewis, B. and Dhar, V. (1985), "Development of a Knowledge-based Expert System for Auditing," Unpublished Research Proposal, University of Pittsburgh.

McKee, T. (1986), "Expert Systems: The Final Frontier?," *The CPA Journal,* July, pp. 42–46.

Meservy, R.D. (1984), "Auditing Internal Controls: A Computational Model of the Review Process," Unpublished Dissertation Proposal, University of Minnesota, October, 1984.

Meservy, R.D., Bailey, A. and Johnson, P. (1986), "Internal Control Evaluation: A Computational Model of the Review Process," *Auditing: A Journal of Theory and Practice,* Volume 6, Number 1, Fall, pp. 44–74.

Messier, W.F. and Hansen, J.V. (1984), "Expert Systems in Auditing: A Framework and Review," *Decision Making and Accounting: Current Research,* S. Moriarty and E. Joyce (eds.), University of Oklahoma, pp. 182–202.

Mock, T. and Vertinsky, I. (1984), "DSS-RAA: Design Highlights," Unpublished Paper Presented at the University of Southern California Audit Judgment Conference, February.

Mock, T. and Vertinsky, I. (1985), *Risk Assessment in Accounting and Auditing, Research Monograph Number 10,* The Canadian Certified General Accountants Research Foundation, Vancouver, British Columbia, Canada.

Moeller, R. (1987), *Artificial Intelligence — A Primer,* Institute of Internal Auditors Monograph Series.

Moeller, R. (1987), "Expert Systems: Auditability Issues," Unpublished Paper Presented at the First International Symposium on Expert Systems in Business, Finance and Accounting, University of Southern California, September 1988.

Mui, C. and McCarthy, W. (1987), "FSA: Applying AI Techniques to the Familarization Phase of Financial Decision Making," *IEEE Expert,* Vol. 2, No. 3, pp. 33–41.

O'Leary, D. (1986), "Expert Systems in a Personal Computer Environment," *Georgia Journal of Accounting,* Volume 7, Spring, pp. 107–118.

O'Leary, D. (1987a), "The Use of Artificial Intelligence in Accounting," in Silverman.

O'Leary, D. (1987b), "Validation of Expert Systems in Accounting and Business," *Decision Sciences,* Summer.

O'Leary, D. (1988a), "Expert System Prototyping as a Research Tool," in Turban and Watkins.

O'Leary, D. (1988b), "Methods of Validating Expert Systems," *Interfaces,* September–October.

O'Leary, D. (1990), "Security in Expert Systems," *IEFE Expert.*

O'Leary, D. (1989), "Validating and Assessing Expert Systems," Paper presented at the First International Symposium on Expert Systems in Business, Finance and Accounting, University of Southern California, September 1988, Chapter 9, this volume.

O'Leary, D. and Kandelin, N. (1988), "Validating the Weights in Rule-Based Expert Systems," *International Journal of Expert Systems: Research and Applications,* Volume 1, Number 4.

O'Leary, D. and Tan, M. (1987), "A Knowledge-Based System for Auditing Payroll—Personnel Files," Unpublished Paper, University of Southern California, February.

O'Leary, D.E. and Turban, E. (1987), The Organizational Impact of Expert Systems, *Human Systems Management,* Vol. 7, pp.11–19.

O'Leary, D. and P.R. Watkins (1990), *Internal Auditing and Expert Systems,* Unpublished paper.

Peat Marwick, Mitchell & Co. (1986), *Peat Marwick Foundation Research Opportunities in Auditing Program,* Interim Report.

Peters, J., Lewis, B. and Dhar, V. (1988), "Assessing Inherent Risk During Audit Planning: A Computational Model," Unpublished Paper, University of Oregon, March.

Ramakrishna, K., Dillard, J.F., Harrison, T.G. and Chandrasekaran, B. (1983), "An Intelligent Manual for Price Analysis," in *Federal Acquisition Research Symposium*, U.S. Air Force, Williamsburg, Virginia, December.

Ribar, G. (1987), "Uses of Expert Systems Technology at Peat Marwick Main," *Expert Systems Review*, Volume 1, Number 1.

Ribar, G. (1988a), "Development of an Expert System," *Expert Systems Review*, Volume 1, Number 3.

Ribar, G. (1988b), "Expert Systems Validation: A Case Study," *Expert Systems Review*, Volume 1, Number 3.

Sauers, R. (1988), "Controlling Expert Systems," in *Expert Systems Applications*, in Bolc and Coombs (1988).

Selfridge, M. (1988), "Mental Models and Memory: Expert Systems and Auditing in the Year 2000," Unpublished paper presented at the USC Audit Judgment Conference, February.

Selfridge, M. and Biggs, S. (1988a), "GCX, A Computational Model of the Auditor's Going Concern Judgment," Unpublished paper presented at the Audit Judgment Symposium, University of Southern California, February.

Selfridge, M. and Biggs, S. (1988b), "GCX: Knowledge Structures for Going Concern Structures for Going Concern Evaluations," Unpublished Paper presented at the First International Symposium on Expert Systems in Business, Finance and Accounting, University of Southern California, September.

Shank, R.C. (1982), *Dynamic Memory: A theory of Reminding and Learning in Computers and People*, Cambridge University Press, Cambridge.

Silverman, B. (ed.) (1987), *Expert Systems for Business*, Addison-Wesley, Reading, Massachusetts.

Socha, W. (1988), "Problems in Auditing Expert System Development," *EDPACS*, March, pp. 1–6.

Steinbart, P. (1984), "The Construction of an Expert System to Make Materiality Judgments", Unpublished Ph. D. Dissertation, Michigan State University.

Steinbart, P. (1987), "The Construction of a Rule-based Expert System as a Method for Studying Materiality Judgments," *Accounting Review*, January.

Tener, W. (1986), "Detection of Control Deterioration Using Decision Support Systems," *Computers and Security*, Vol. 5, pp. 290–295.

Tener, W. (1988), "Expert Systems for Computer Security," *Expert Systems Review*, Vol. 1, No. 2.

Turban, E. (1988), *Decision Support and Expert Systems*, Macmillan, New York.

Turban, E. and Watkins, P. (1986), "Integrating Expert Systems and Decision Support Systems," *Management Information Systems Quarterly*, June, pp. 121–138.

Turban, E. and Watkins, P. (1988), *Applied Expert Systems*, North-Holland, Amsterdam.

US Government, (1987) *Artificial Intelligence at the US Treasury*, Department of Treasury Report.

Vasarhelyi, M., Halper, F. and Fritz, R. (1988), "The Continuous Audit of Online Systems," Unpublished Paper presented at the University of Southern California Audit Judgment Conference and the National Meeting of the American Accounting Association.

Chapter 11

EXPERT SYSTEMS: AUDITABILITY ISSUES

Robert R. Moeller
Sears Roebuck, Chicago, IL

This chapter discusses issues facing the auditor who must understand control procedures and must assess the control risk of an expert system which is used for a financially significant application.

11.1 INTRODUCTION

In recent years, there has been an increasing number of successful implementations of expert systems within business organizations to aid them in analysis and decision-making processes. There have also been numerous expert systems developed to assist or support the auditor in both accounting issues and in forming audit opinions. Examples of these types of auditor expert systems include Coopers and Lybrand's ExperTAX, as described by Shpilberg and Graham (1986), and Hansen and Messier's (1986) experimental system to evaluate EDP controls, EDP-XPERT (1986). As the number and sophistication of these systems increases, we can potentially expect them to impact the judgment and intuitive processes of many audit professionals.

Although expert systems are found in many decision-support-related applications, they have not yet been commonly implemented as financial accounting applications which have a direct impact on the financial statements of organizations. Although the independent external auditor has an interest in the potential risks associated with the various non-financial, decision-support-related expert systems implemented in an organization being audited, a more basic concern of the auditor is the risks associated with any expert systems that might have a material effect on an organization's financial statements. Because there are today few such expert systems implemented for financially significant areas, auditors have not had to directly concern themselves with expert systems. In addition, there are only limited tools or guidance materials to help the auditor understand and assess such expert systems. However, we can probably expect, in the future, the increas-

Expert Systems in Business and Finance: Issues and Applications. Edited by P.R. Watkins and L.B. Eliot
© 1993 John Wiley & Sons Ltd.

ing use of expert systems applications in areas that directly impact financial statements. It will be necessary for auditors to be able to understand and assess these expert systems.

The chapter briefly reviews American Institute of Certified Public Accountants (AICPA) guidance materials for the review of automated systems and considers whether these materials also apply to expert-systems-based financial applications. In addition, the chapter discusses some potential procedures which the auditor might use for understanding and evaluating expert systems.

11.2   AICPA GUIDANCE MATERIALS AND EXPERT SYSTEMS

The AICPA has published a series of guidance materials through their statements of Auditing Standards (SAS) series and related audit guides to provide assistance with auditing computer systems controls. This section discusses the evolution of these guidance materials and discusses how they might apply to expert systems. In the early 1970s, public accountants realized that they had very little guidance materials covering the then growing body of computer systems which were being used for financially significant applications. This lack of specific guidance materials became evident with the Equity Funding Insurance Company failure of the early 1970s. Equity Funding failed due to a fairly pervasive fraud which included financial reports based on fraudulent computer records. This fraud, of course, was eventually detected. However, Equity Funding's fraudulent recordkeeping practices might have been detected earlier had its auditors properly analyzed the company's computer systems controls and data files.

Shortly after the Equity Funding failure, the AICPA released Statement on Auditing Standards number 3 (SAS #3) which required auditors to review data processing controls as part of their audit procedures. The AICPA's Audit Guide to the implementation of SAS #3, The Study and Evaluation of Control in EDP Systems suggested some very specific areas of EDP general and application controls for auditors to review. SAS #3 specified that the auditor was to evaluate EDP controls even if the auditor did not plan to rely on those controls.

SAS #3 was introduced in the early 1970s when data processing systems were, in many cases, unique compared to the other manual accounting systems. Over the subsequent ten years leading to the early 1980s, computerized accounting systems proliferated. Since the advent of personal microcomputers and powerful software, it has become unusual to find an organization with audited financial statements which were not produced, at least in part, by computer financial systems. In addition, many of the specific general controls which were outlined in the SAS #3 Audit Guide, such as reviewing computer center physical security access controls, no longer were very relevant for many small business computer systems.

As a replacement to SAS #3, the AICPA subsequently released SAS #48 (1984). This standard effectively said that the concepts of internal control are essentially the same whether a system is manual or computerized. EDP controls were no longer held out to be a separate issue.

SAS #48 has since been superseded by SAS #55 (1988), Consideration of the Internal Control Structure in a Financial Statement Audit, which was released in 1988 and became effective at the beginning of 1990. This standard and its related Audit Guide (1990), of the same title, discards the auditor's study and evaluation of internal control approach and replaces it with an approach where the auditor develops an understanding of the client's internal control structure and then uses that understanding to assess the level of control risk in the audit. The internal control structure is defined as having the following three elements:

- Control Environment. This includes the management style, philosophy, and control methods. It also includes the overall organization structure, personnel policies, internal audit effectiveness, and external factors influencing the organization.
- Accounting System. This element includes accounting processing as well as financial reporting procedures. The auditor should have an understanding of the classes of transactions, procedures for initiating them, and the records and documents used in the processing and reporting of transactions.
- Control Procedures. These are the policies and procedures to assure that specific objectives will be achieved. Control procedures may include such things as segregation of duties, access controls over computer programs and files, and computer system controls.

The point to consider in the above description is that the AICPA's audit standards have evolved from very specific data processing control procedures to more general statements which could include virtually any form of automated or manual system. While the standards currently contain no specific procedures covering data processing systems, examples of procedures associated with such systems are used throughout.

By extension, these existing audit standards would also cover expert systems when they are used for significant financial applications. The auditor would be expected to understand the overall accounting system which makes use of such an expert system. The auditor would also be expected to evaluate the control procedures over that expert system. These might include procedures for the authorization of transactions, the design of the system, and the controls within the expert system. An example of such controls might be the procedures for introducing new rules to the knowledge database. Although the existing overall audit standards cover such expert systems by inference, there appears to be a need for materials to allow the auditor to better understand the significant differences between an expert system and a traditional data processing application which is based on algorithmic logic. At the present time, that type of guidance material is limited in availability.

In 1987, the AICPA's EDP Technology Research Subcommittee published a special report, *An Introduction to Artificial Intelligence and Expert System*. That report was essentially a tutorial on expert systems. However, it was probably read by more practicing public accountants than similar expert systems tutorials published in other technical or specialty books and journals. The AICPA report concluded by raising the following questions on the impact of expert systems on auditing professionals as follows:

- What will be the impact upon the development of judgmental and intuitive processes and the abilities of the professional?
- What will be the impact upon engagement level quality control? What will be the impact upon audit evidence/ workpapers, engagement documentation and retention, and professional training?
- Should professional guidance be issued on auditing expert systems used by clients?

Aside from the last of these questions, all of the others addressed the auditors' use of expert systems. There has been no other guidance published to date by the AICPA on auditing expert systems. However, in early 1988, a Task Force (Artificial Intellegience: Knowledge-Based Systems) was formed by the AICPA's Computer Audit Subcommittee to investigate issues involved with auditing expert systems.

While there is a growing body of other literature covering the auditors' use of expert systems, there is very little published material on audit techniques for reviewing expert systems. For example, Messier and Hansen (1987) discusses the use of expert systems for auditing and concludes with a fairly extensive set of references. None of those references refer to auditing expert systems. Brown (1990) has also developed a fairly comprehensive bibliography of expert systems published literature; there are very few references to auditing expert systems. Moeller (1987) discusses some of the issues associated with auditing expert systems. However, these are very brief and are more oriented to the internal auditor's review of a new computer system under development. Other published works that would appear to cover the audit of expert systems from their titles often do not. For example, Sauers (1988) discusses managing the rule base of an expert system but not the audit or control issues.

The other limited material available on auditing expert systems generally discusses the potential problems associated with such reviews. For example, O'Leary (1987) discusses validation issues, Holenagel (1989) considers reliability issues and Socha (1988) discusses some of the concerns that internal auditors might face due to the constraints of expert systems design.

We will probably not see much guidance on the auditing of expert systems until more of them come into use for financially significant applications. In fact, a goal of the above mentioned AICPA Task Force was to identify the approaches practitioners are currently using for assessing expert systems. The Task Force initially tried to identify examples of expert systems used for financially significant applications. They found only examples of supporting subsystems in this limited survey. For example, an organization may use an expert system to help with certain high risk credit accounts. However, that expert system was found to be a subsystem of the main accounts receivable application that provided data to the financial statements for the organization. Since the portion of the accounts receivable balance controlled by the expert system was not material to the overall total, the auditor would have limited concerns regarding this smaller, expert system component. The Task Force, through its limited survey, found no examples of expert systems used to directly support financial statement balances. As a result the Task Force was terminated in 1988.

The AICPA will probably revisit this need for specific expert systems auditor guidance at some time in the future. At the present time, existing guidance such as SAS #55 is deemed to be sufficient. One would hope, however, that we will not have to wait for an *Equity Funding* type of event involving an expert system to provide the impetus for publishing sufficient audit guidance materials.

11.3 EXPERT SYSTEMS USED FOR FINANCIALLY SIGNIFICANT APPLICATIONS

The role of the auditor is to attest that the financial statements of an organization are fairly stated in accordance with generally accepted accounting principles. In determining that the financial statements are fairly stated, the auditor will pay particular attention to the more significant items on income statements and balance sheets. This means, for a typical organization, that the auditor will focus attention on accounts receivable, inventory, short term liabilities, and other more materially significant accounts. In a computerized environment, the auditor will often also give particular audit and review attention to those individual applications which are responsible for controlling these financial statement items.

If expert systems were being implemented to help organizations control their significant financial statement items, such as expert systems for inventory control, we probably would have already seen much more auditor attention given to audits of those expert systems. However, this has not yet been an area where significant expert systems are being developed. For example, Bartee (1988) surveys a broad variety of areas in which expert systems have been or are being currently implemented. Numerous expert system domains and applications are described. However, the financial-related applications described in this book are in areas such as insurance underwriting, insurance claims processing, banking, and securities portfolio management. There are no examples describing current expert systems applications that might directly affect financial statement balances.

This lack of expert systems in financially significant areas can, perhaps, be explained because we have already solved many financial systems control problems through conventional programming techniques. For example, a typical larger manufacturing organization today may have installed a manufacturing resource planning (MRP) system which monitors inventory levels, generates purchase orders to acquire additional inventory, and provides usage as well as production scrap reports. Although there were once considerable numbers and types of decisions required to manage such a manufacturing resource management process, many of these decision rules have been built into automated systems using conventional programming techniques. There probably is not that strong a need to develop an expert system to solve such inventory management problems. Many of the decision rules, such as when to order additional inventory parts, are relatively easy to define. Conventional MRP applications handle this task.

Many organizations today, however, are developing expert systems in areas where a large amount of human decision-making is still required. For example, the Authorizer Assistant expert system application described by Bartee (1988) was developed by American Express to improve the credit granting process for a subset of their credit card transactions which required a high level of human, objective decision-making. However, that American Express expert system works under or is part of a much larger overall Credit Authorization System, which itself is a conventionally programmed application. While audit attention has almost certainly been given to that overall authorization system, it might not necessarily be given to the Authorizer Assistant subsystem. The auditor would give consideration to that subsystem only if it controlled a material amount of the receivable balances.

Many of the expert systems being developed and implemented today seem to fall into the above general category. They are not yet replacing conventional applications in major areas. Rather, they are being implemented in areas where specialized human decision-making is required and where conventional applications have not been developed to support that decision process. For example, Baxter Healthcare has developed an expert system to analyze the exceptions generated from its conventional inventory system (Krull, 1987). Their mainframe-based inventory status system tracks 60 000 stocked units. Previously, that system generated reports flagging exception situations for a skilled employee to analyze. An expert system now is said to take care of most of this analysis.

Will expert systems eventually replace conventionally programmed applications in financially significant areas? In some instances, it may be a long time before this occurs; in other instances we may never see any significant development work. For example, the large body of established, conventionally programmed systems for inventory or material control which have been developed over recent years probably means that we will only see expert systems here in various, specialized subset areas. For most organizations, we may never see expert systems in other areas such as controlling fixed assets. Any such fixed asset expert system might only be used to help the decision-maker to decide which alternative asset to acquire and then to help decide whether to purchase or lease it. However, the financial system which calculated depreciation and records these assets for balance sheet purposes will probably continue to be a conventionally programmed application.

Despite the above disclaimer, auditors in the future will probably begin to find some expert systems used for portions of financially significant applications in areas where considerable human knowledge is now required. This will probably occur where an expert system has been used for a subset of the data or problem area and also where that expert system can be expanded to control other area functions. For example, Blue Cross/Blue Shield has reported that its MEDical CHarge Evaluation and Control (MEDCHEC) expert system (Bartee, 1988) resulted in an 80% reduction in areas where it has been deployed. Such a saving might cause such an expert system to be implemented on a much wider basis if the other conditions surrounding the system were the same.

We will probably also find expert systems developed in financially significant areas for certain specialized organizations. For example, an investment type of organization might implement an expert system to manage its portfolio of assets. This would require the auditor reviewing those financial assets to have an understanding of the accounting system and the control procedures that the expert system represents.

Even though it appears that not many examples exist today, the auditor of the near future will probably encounter an increasing number of expert systems used for financially significant applications. This is because expert systems concepts are becoming better understood, and there have been numerous success stories regarding expert systems. However, despite their increasing use and related success stories, expert systems can still be considered somewhat of an infant technology. Firdham (1988) has suggested that expert systems must move beyond a technology-driven market to a demand-driven market before they become common as basic information systems applications.

Auditors will need to develop skills and techniques to properly review these expert systems of the future. The public accountant or external auditor will need to understand the overall internal control structure and to evaluate the control risk for those financially significant expert systems. In addition, internal auditors with a control review responsibility and a reporting line to their management, will have to review, test, and evaluate expert systems implemented in a variety of financially and operationally significant areas.

11.4   AUDITING EXPERT SYSTEMS

SAS #55 directs the auditor to obtain an understanding of the internal control structure in a financial statement audit through understanding the control environment, the accounting system, and control procedures. The auditor would then document that understanding and assess the control risk. The purpose of this assessment is to determine if internal control policies and procedures are effective in preventing or detecting material misstatements in the entity's financial statements. The final step, then, in this procedure is to identify potential misstatements and to design substantive tests based on the level of assessed risk. An audit of an expert system used for recording material financial statement data would fall under the guidance of SAS #55.

Although few guidance materials regarding auditing expert systems have been published to date, many auditors will find it necessary to understand the control structure surrounding an expert system when they encounter, in practice, this type of application in a significant area. The key, perhaps, is for auditors to have a basic understanding of the unique characteristics of an expert system as well as the risks and vulnerabilities associated with such a system.

There are numerous reference sources describing the characteristics and key components of an expert system. For example, Moeller (1987) provides an introductory view while Hayes-Roth *et al.* (1983) provide the detailed background to construct such a system. While the terminology may differ somewhat from one description to another, the following describes some of the unique elements of an expert system's internal control structure:

- Reliance on a knowledge database rather than just facts. The typical application, based on classical programming techniques, relies on data to make any decisions rather than the intuitive knowledge of experts. For example, an inventory control system will flag items for reorder when inventory balance statistics indicate that they fall below a specified level. Before actually placing the order, a human expert may review the reported items and place an order based on that individual's general knowledge of conditions. In an expert system, that knowledge or rule set is built into the expert system such that the role of the external, human expert is eliminated or diminished.

- Imprecise decisions rather than predictable results. An application developed with conventional programming techniques will produce consistent results based on the data and on the programmed logic steps. An expert system may not produce a uniquely predictable set of results. If a given fact is presented slightly differently, the expert system may come to a very different conclusion.
- Ability of self-modify based on changing conditions. Expert systems can modify themselves based on new knowledge that they accumulate. That is, additional knowledge can be added to the rules database which will then create a different set of system outputs. A conventionally pro-grammed application would require a formal program logic change to allow it to yield such different results.
- Potential for diminished human review of outputs. One of the major features of an expert system is that it can capture a human expert's knowledge and make resultant decisions. The human expert, who may have reviewed an exception report from a conventional application and then made a decision, may no longer have to perform such a review because of the expert system. However, with an expert system, there is a potential risk that the system's results will be accepted without an adequate review. That is, there may be a risk of inadvertent reliance on the false results of such an expert system.

All four of the above internal control structure elements present the auditor with some unique challenges when attempting to assess an expert system. In some instances, the currently published SAS #55 guidance may even cause an auditor to always assess the level of an expert system's control risk at maximum even though that may be too high of a level of control risk. In discussing an example of a control environment weakness, SAS #55 (1988, paragraph 20) discusses as an example a budgetary reporting system that may provide adequate reports, but the *reports may not be analyzed and acted on.* An expert system budgetary reporting application, however, might be constructed such that it would not be necessary for a human expert to formally analyze those budgetary reports with the same level of attention to detail. The expert system may, itself, take many of the required actions. Even though it may not be the case, an auditor reviewing such an expert system might otherwise follow this SAS #55 guidance and place control risk at maximum. In order to properly assess such a control risk, the auditor would have to have a good understanding of how such a budget control expert system differs from a conventional application when performing such a review.

At the present, we almost certainly will not find expert systems controlling major functions in a financial accounting system. Rather, the auditor may encounter an expert system, as discussed previously, used for one or several classes of accounting transactions. If that expert system were to be used for material financial statement entries, the auditor would want to gain an understanding of the expert system. That understanding would include how the expert system generates transactions, how the data is organized and maintained, and the potential errors which could result from that expert system. In many respects, there are few differences here from the procedures the auditor would perform in working with a conventional application. The most significant difference for the auditor who is understanding an expert system accounting application is that the auditor must recognize the unique characteristics of an expert system. For example, an accounting transaction from an expert system would not be generated due to a set of fixed, programmed rules. Rather, the resultant transaction might be generated as the result of a series of *If ... then* rules embedded in the knowledge base in addition to the domain database of facts. Because traditional computer systems have been used for significant accounting systems for, perhaps, twenty years, many auditors have learned to understand the characteristics of those conventional data processing systems. The auditor may now be faced with the task of understanding the characteristics of a newer type of application, expert systems.

Because an expert system introduces some new complexities to the auditor, the auditor should place particular emphasis upon developing an understanding of control procedures when reviewing an expert system. Stated in terms of conventional application control procedures, the auditor may want to develop an understanding in the following general areas:

- Input Controls. In a conventional computerized application, the auditor is concerned that the application properly screens for errors and has batch balancing completeness checks. These controls are often not relevant for the typical expert system. However, the auditor should be concerned that the expert system receives the proper set of facts to allow it to make a proper rule based decision. The auditor may also want to determine controls to prevent incorrect interpretations of input facts. Many expert systems are constructed such that supporting facts or data are supplied to the user, at a terminal, who responds by entering queries and other data. The auditor should be concerned about this user interface. There should exist adequate documentation to support the application as well as reasonableness checks to prevent inappropriate entries.

There should also be logging facilities to allow the application to reconstruct its input activities and to determine why the application made any potentially questionable decisions.

- Processing Controls. This is the portion of an expert system where input facts, such as queries and other database items, are analyzed through the processing of the application's inference engine against its rules or knowledge database. This is perhaps the major area where an expert system differs the most from a conventional application. This is also perhaps the area where there is the greatest risk of system error. The auditor should have a good general understanding of how the knowledge database was constructed as well as the procedures used for both testing and validating it prior to implementation and on a continuing basis. Some expert systems have the ability to modify their own rule set in response to changing facts or conditions. The auditor should develop a good understanding of how such a procedure might work as well as the flags that the application raises when such a rule set modification takes place.

  The application development process for an expert system is often much more dynamic than the structured design procedures used for conventional applications. The auditor should understand these procedures. If the application was developed outside of conventional data processing functions, as is currently quite common, particular attention should be given to these system development procedures as well as to the level of system or technical documentation.

- Output Controls. For conventional applications, auditors ensured that the outputs were complete, that any rejected items were subsequently corrected, and that outputs balanced back to inputs. Auditors typically also determine that there are reasonableness checks surrounding such application outputs. While completeness and error-correction checks are still valid for an expert system, it will often be difficult to balance outputs to inputs except in the most general of manners. Reasonableness checks, however, are a particularly important type of an output control for an expert system.

  Because an expert system uses an interference mechanism to produce its output deductions, the auditor may want to give particular attention to the level of user review of the application's output results. There would appear to be a potential for a high degree of risk of inadvertent reliance on the results of an expert system. That is, the user of an expert system may initially validate the results of such an application. However, if those results appear to be correct in a series of successive validations over time, users may cease to validate or question system results, and they may place inadvertent reliance on the results of the expert system application. The auditor should take steps to determine that this is not the case.

- Access Controls. Auditors have traditionally reviewed controls over access to data and programs as part of their general review of data processing interdependent controls covering all computer applications. This area of control procedures will take a special significance when reviewing an expert system application. Many expert systems have rule databases, which may be modified over time, to improve processing results. However, an incorrect rule change could very much alter the processing results of the application. The auditor should determine that there are strong integrity controls, including both testing and authorization procedures, over updates to the rule base. Only authorized individuals should have access.

In addition to developing an understanding of the overall accounting system and the control procedures surrounding an expert system, the auditor will want to assess control risk as discussed in SAS #55. This assessment is based on obtaining and evaluating evidential matter concerning the financial statement assertions as outlined in SAS #31, Evidential Matter. These assertions are classified according to the following broad categories:

- Existence or occurrence,
- Completeness,
- Rights and obligations,
- Valuation or allocation,
- Presentation and disclosure.

Where appropriate, the auditor will want to develop tests of controls to obtain additional evidential matter for those assertions where the auditor wishes to assess control risk at less than maximum. Although it may be difficult to obtain such evidence for all of the assertions for a typical expert system, evidence can often be obtained for some of them. In particular, the auditor might probably be interested in obtaining evidence for the existence, completeness, and valuation assertions for a typical expert system which is used for a significant financial application.

SAS #55 provides some general guidance for obtaining such evidential matter and also obtaining such evidential matter for computerized systems. Unfortunately, some of that guidance will be difficult to apply to a typical expert system. For example, paragraph 49 states, in part, *evidential matter about the effectiveness of design or operation may be obtained through observation or the use of computer-assisted audit techniques to re-perform the application of relevant policies and procedures.* While observation is a valid procedure, providing the auditor has a good general understanding of expert systems, computer-assisted techniques will generally not work. The typical computer-assisted techniques and the supporting software packages used by auditors are quite effective in performing in limited areas such as recomputations and related analyses. Generally, such tests are not appropriate for an expert system.

Similarly, paragraphs 52 through 55 of SAS #55 talk about the timeliness of evidential matter. This guidance is appropriate for a conventional computer system where the auditor would determine that no changes have been made to the computer programs of the application under review. It would be much more difficult to consider such guidelines for an expert system which may be self-modifying or where changes are otherwise frequently made to the rule database.

These comments raise the question as to whether the auditor can gather sufficient evidential matter to support control risk assessments for expert systems. Certainly, as discussed in previous paragraphs, we do not have enough experience to point to actual procedures used for these expert systems. However, it would appear that a *test deck* approach as discussed by the Institute of Internal Auditors (1977) might be an appropriate method to test such an expert system. The auditor would have a fixed set of transactions or circumstances to input to a test version of the application. If the results were consistent from period to period, the auditor could assert that the application was continuing to operate as originally tested.

Certainly, other audit procedures will be developed as expert systems become more common in financially significant areas. It is also possible that some of the *expert system shell* software products will begin to be marketed with embedded audit tools as such systems become more common. During the interim, it will be necessary for auditors to develop a good understanding of expert systems operations such that they will be able to perform at least some limited procedures such as observation and inquiry.

11.5 FUTURE PROSPECTS FOR AUDITING EXPERT SYSTEMS

It is always difficult to predict the future for new technologies. However, many authors, such as Martin and Oxman (1988), give expert systems technology a bright future. We will probably see expert systems technology becoming an increasing part of existing data processing technologies. Similar to the American Express authorization described previously, the expert system will often become a component or subset of a larger conventional application.

Because expert systems will probably be initially more common in areas where we have not been able to develop good conventional applications, we may not see too many of them for significant financial accounting areas. Rather, they will continue to be developed and refined, as they are at present, in various operational areas of organizations. Quite probably, internal auditors will become quite involved in reviewing these expert systems applications. Since internal auditors often are active in reviewing new applications which are under development, they can do an effective job in understanding the risks and evaluating control characteristics of these evolving expert systems applications.

It will probably only be a matter of time before expert systems become significant subsets of applications used in significant financial accounting areas. Guidance materials and audit procedures will have to be developed for these. During the interim, the auditor should be aware of the unique characteristics of these experts systems, should understand some of the associated control risks, and should use existing audit guidance materials with these unique expert systems considerations in mind.

REFERENCES

American Institute of Certified Public Accountants (1987), *An Introduction to Artificial Intelligence and Expert Systems,* New York.

Audit Guide (1990), *Considerations of the Internal Control Structure in a Financial Statement Audit.* AICPA, New York.

Auditor's Study and Evaluation of Internal Control in EDP Systems, The (1977), New York.

Bartee, T.C. (ed.) (1988), *Expert System and Artificial Intelligence,* Howard Sams, Indianapolis.

Brown, C.E. (1990), *Accounting Expert System Bibliography,* unpublished paper by College of Business, Oregon State University.

Firdman, E.F. (1988), Expert Systems: Are You Already Behind? *Computerworld,* April 18, pp. 99–105.

Hansen, J.V. and W.F. Messier (1986), A Preliminary Investigation of EDP-EXPERT, *Auditing: A Journal of Practice and Theory,* 6:1, Fall, pp. 109–123.

Hayes-Roth, F., D.A. Waterman, and D.B. Lenat (1983), *Building Expert Systems,* Addison-Wesley, Reading, MA.

Holenagle, E. (1989), *The Reliability of Expert Systems,* Ellis Horwood, Chichester, England.

Institute of Internal Auditors (1977), *Data Processing Audit Practices Report,* Altamonte Springs, FL.

Keyes, J. (1990), AI in the Big Six, *AI Expert,* May, pp. 37–42.

Kull, D. (1987), Software Development: AI tackles the Backlog, *Computer and Communications Decisions,* Sept., pp.77–82.

Martin, J. and S. Oxman (1988), *Building Expert Systems: A Tutorial,* Prentice Hall, Englewood Cliffs, NJ.

Messier, W.F. Jr. and J.V. Hansen (1987), Expert Systems in Auditing: The State of the Art, *Auditing: A Journal of Practice & Theory,* 7:1, Fall, pp. 94–103.

Moeller, R.R. (1987), Artificial Intelligence: A Primer, *Institute of Internal Auditors Research Foundation,* Altamonte Springs, FL.

O'Leary, D. E. (1987), Validation of Expert Systems with Applications to Auditing and Accounting Expert Systems, *Decision Sciences,* Summer, 18(3), pp. 468–486.

The Effects of Computer Processing on the Examination of Financial Statements, AICPA, New York.

SAS#55 (1988), *Consideration of the Internal Control Structure in a Financial Statement Audit,* AICPA, New York.

Sauers, R. (1988), Controlling Expert Systems, *Expert Systems Applications*, Bolc, L. & Coombs M.J., eds, Springer-Verlag, New York, pp. 79–197.

Shpilberg, D. and L.E. Graham (1986), *Developing ExperTAX: An Expert System for Corporate Tax Accrual and Planning*, Auditing: A Journal of Practice and Theory, 6:1, Fall 1986, pp. 75–93.

Socha, W.A. (1988), Problems in Auditing Expert System Development, *EDPACS*, XV:9, March, pp. 1–6.

Chapter 12

PERSPECTIVES ON AUDITING OPERATIONAL KNOWLEDGE BASED SYSTEMS

Rodger Jamieson
University of New South Wales, Kensington, Australia

This chapter provides perspectives on and guidance for the auditor involved in the audit of operational knowledge based systems (KBS). An interpretation of the accounting standards and guidelines would indicate that the auditor should be involved in an audit review of the knowledge based system and it's environment where a KBS exists that impacts on, or is part of, a major financial accounting application. The chapter sets out audit objectives for the review, outlines risks in the KBS environment, and discusses internal control considerations. The final section considers gathering audit evidence and the development and use of audit tools and techniques applicable to the audit of a KBS. The conclusion discusses future issues and potential research areas.

12.1 INTRODUCTION

During the past few years knowledge based systems (KBS) or expert systems (ES) have migrated from research laboratories into many fields including the commercial and finance sectors. Many large organisations in both government and private sectors are committing considerable resources to this area in order to gain or retain their competitive advantage. Knowledge-based systems are either developed to operate in a standalone mode, built to complement an existing application, or integrated into newer products such as decision support or office automation systems.

As many of these systems will impact business operations and have significant financial influence in the future, auditors will be involved to ensure that these systems are correctly developed, secure, controllable and auditable. This need to evaluate and assess KBS is presented in order to establish the importance of these systems to organisations and auditors. To date, KBS have not been routinely built into financial accounting information systems that have a direct effect on the organisation's financial

Expert Systems in Business and Finance: Issues and Applications. Edited by P.R. Watkins and L.B. Eliot
© 1993 John Wiley & Sons Ltd.

statements. Therefore, external auditors have not been as concerned with this technology as with other information system's concerns. However, as KBS mature and their impact is felt throughout the organisation, more KBS will be developed that have a financial statement effect. Now is the time for auditors to understand and assimilate this technology (Information Technology Group ICAEW, 1989).

Auditors are more likely to be involved in normal operational audits of KBS rather than just be involved during the KBS development phase. In this area there is limited guidance for auditors when involved in these audits especially from the accounting bodies. The next sections will discuss some of the issues involved in the audit of an operational KBS, noting some of the American Auditing Standards, namely SAS #55 - Consideration of the Internal Control Structure in a Financial Statement Audit (AICPA, 1988), which took effect from 1990. These issues include recognising the risks involved in the KBS environment, understanding KBS internal controls, considering appropriate audit evidence in this environment, and thinking of new audit tools and techniques to apply to this area.

12.2   UNDERSTAND KBS COMPONENTS

If the auditor is to engage in these types of audits then a knowledge of the underlying concepts is essential. This may be obtained by reading the literature (for example Parsaye and Chignell (1988), Barrett and Beerel (1989), Waterman (1986), Harmon and King (1985), and Edwards and Connell (1989) and by discussions with those actively involved in their construction. Architecturally, an expert system may be decomposed, for simplicity, into the following components as represented in Figure 12.1. The physical and logical architecture of the KBS is dependent on the development and delivery tools involved.

The interfaces to the KBS are the knowledge acquisition sub-system which provides the knowledge engineer or expert with the ability to create and maintain the knowledge base, and the user interface which provides the user with the facility to interact with or consult the KBS.

A major contribution of KBS development in any domain is the resulting knowledge-base. This knowledge-base contains information appropriate to solving problems in the selected domain and is particular to that domain. For each consultation, a situational model is created and held in the work area of the KBS.

The workhorse of the KBS is the inference engine which determines what data and knowledge is required to solve the problem and initiates the user interface software to request this data from the user if necessary and stores it in the work area. It uses the contents of the knowledge-base to draw inferences and seek solutions to problem goals and records these inferences

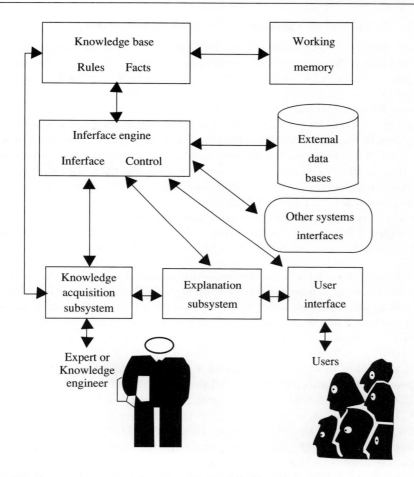

FIGURE 12.1 Expert system components (adapted from Harmon and King, 1985, p.34)

in the work area. The explanation sub-system is used to provide a help facility and explanations of the reasoning process when requested from the user. Another function is to display the results/advice from the consultation to the user along with an audit trail of the reasoning process to justify the conclusions presented.

Having gained an understanding of these fundamental concepts, the auditor will be in a stronger position from which to commence a detailed audit review of the KBS and its environment.

12.3   ACCOUNTING STANDARDS AND GUIDELINES

SAS 55 (AICPA 1988), from the AICPA in the USA, was released in 1988 to be effective at the start of 1990, and replaces SAS 48 (AICPA, 1984), which in turn replaced SAS 3 (AICPA 1977). While SAS 3 required auditors to review IS controls as part of their audits, even if they were not planning to rely on these controls, SAS 48 emphasised that internal control was no longer a separate control issue as it was the same whether a system was computer or manual. SAS 55 changes from the very specific approach of SAS 3 and 48 to a more general approach, where the auditor gains an understanding of the client's *internal control structure* and then uses that understanding to assess the level of *control risk* in the audit engagement. Moeller (1988) proposes that the general nature of these standards would cover KBS when used for significant financial transactions.

Australia's Statements of Auditing Practice AUP 4, 4-1, 4-2 (paralleling International Audit Guideline, IAG 15) AARF (1984) provide:

- that *skill and competence is required*—this means that in the KBS environment an auditor needs to have knowledge of KBS hardware, KBS software and applications in order to plan the engagement effectively, understand how KBS systems affect the evaluation of internal control in financial applications, and how to apply appropriate information systems auditing techniques.
- that *if skills are deficient,* the auditor should involve audit experts who possess the required skills, yet still should have "sufficient knowledge of EDP (KBS) to direct, supervise and review the work of assistants with EDP (KBS) skills, or to obtain reasonable assurance that the work performed by other auditors or experts with EDP (KBS) skills is adequate... and should not delegate the responsibility for forming important audit conclusions." (AARF, 1984, pp. 3048.9). Auditors, audit managers or partners with KBS skills are extremely difficult to find. This will remain a problem of appropriate IS audit education.
- that *the auditor should acquire knowledge of the accounting system that makes use of EDP (KBS)* in order to understand the control environment and the flow of transactions (inferences leading to a transaction entry). The auditor is *responsible for evaluating the control procedures* over that accounting system (KBS) and the *impact* of any EDP (KBS) environmental controls or lack of them.

A review of both American and Australian auditing practice statements indicate that the auditor should be involved in a review of the KBS and environment where a KBS exists that impacts on, or is part of, a major financial accounting application. As a result, the following sections provide a guide for the auditor commencing a review of an operational KBS.

12.4 SET AUDIT OBJECTIVES FOR THE KBS OPERATIONAL REVIEW

Prior to commencement of the review, KBS operational audit review objectives should be set. Review objectives may include:

- determining the extent of KBS use and its impact on the organisation;
- identifying personnel relevant to an audit investigation and understanding their responsibilities;
- identifying locations where the production KBS is used;
- understanding and documenting the KBS components and how they interrelate, both with each other and with other information systems technologies and systems;
- identifying risks associated with the KBS environment and system;
- identifying types of security, control and auditability mechanisms in the KBS environment;
- evaluating KBS security, controls and auditability mechanisms;
- reviewing KBS documentation and legal consideration of KBS development;
- gathering audit evidence through the use of KBS audit tools and techniques; and
- concluding evaluation after the results of compliance and substantive tests are known.

12.5 RISKS IN THE KBS ENVIRONMENT

Table 12.1 provides a selection of risks in the KBS environment that need to be taken account of by auditors.

As well as these risks the auditor should be cognisant of the control considerations applicable to the KBS environment.

12.6 INTERNAL CONTROL CONSIDERATIONS

Many of the internal control considerations have already been mentioned in the systems development section of this paper. However, other considerations associated with operational KBS are presented below and are summarised in Table 12.2.

In many organisations the trustees for KBSs are the Research and Development department. This is done in Australia in order to qualify for the 150% tax deduction incentives in this area. One emerging issue concerns the *appropriateness of the trusteeship, control and maintenance of the KBS resting with R & D*. In certain organisations this department is known for its flexibility

TABLE 12.1   Selection of risks in the KBS environment

Planning

Mismatch of KBS strategy to corporate and IS strategies
Unidentified or excessive costs especially maintenance and support
Overlooked essential KBS functionality

Accidental or intentional

Damage
Loss
Modification
Destruction
Use
to/of specialised KBS or traditional hardware used to run the system, KBS software, as well as feeder software and associated databases. Loss or incapacitation of key KBS experts, knowledge engineers, programmers, or knowledge-base maintenance personnel, is also of concern.

Fraud and computer abuse

Substitution of knowledge-base
Obscure placement of forward chaining demons within the knowledge-base
Unauthorised access to KBS or consultation histories
Modification, deletion or insertion of KBS information when passing through a network, communications or other layers of operating or support software. This includes other application software when linked or integrated with the KBS

Other exposures

Inability of imbedded KBS software to recover/restart
KBS hardware or software failure—especially real-time monitoring or imbedded systems
Lack of consultation histories (audit trails) in hardcopy and/or magnetic/optical form
Inadequate trace facilities in KBS software for debugging and KBS testing
Inadequate testing of "unknowns" options
KBS not based on expert's reasoning
Poor quantity or quality of KBS personnel
Poor management, supervision and control of the KBS application if under R & D
Inadequate training and supervision of KBS personnel
Inadequate KBS hardware/software maintenance
Legal liability for breach of software licensing for run time distribution of KBS
Legal liability for reliance on KBS opinion when that opinion caused loss of life, damage or monetary loss
Inadequate KBS documentation of tools, environment and applications

TABLE 12.2   Controls in the KBS Environment

KBS hardware

        Sensitive data access
- key locked equipment
- restricted/controlled boot up procedures
- encryption provisions

        Up-to-date documentation
        Regular audits of equipment
        Logging and follow-up of all reported faults
        Back-up
- strategy
- equipment

        Maintenance
- diagnostic aids
- documentation

        Environmental considerations
- uninterrupted power supplies or voltage regulators
- air conditioners
- physical protection barriers to restrict physical access

KBS software

        Automated procedures for KBS control
        Valid software licence agreements
        Up-to-date documentation
        KBS software integrity checks
        Appropriate KBS maintenance strategy
        KBS software upgrade controls
        Logging and follow-up of all reported faults
        KB encryption
        HOW facilities
        WHY facilities
        Help facilities
        KB integrity checking
        Restricted screen/report output
        Separate development and run time versions
        Graphical layouts of KB
        Cross reference listings
        Knowledge dictionary maintenance
        Trace facilities
        Consultation case history maintenance
        Audit trail logging of all activity
        Certified by major accounting firm

KBS development

        KBS development methodology followed
        Separate KBS development from production
        Appropriate design documentation
        Validation and testing of KBS
        Quality assurance/control review

(continued)

TABLE 12.2   Controls in the KBS Environment (continued)

Auditor involvement in development reviews
Separate development and production KB source libraries
Separate development and run time versions of KBS software

KBS applications
Systems access security (password as minimum)
Correct option setting for run time versions
Edit facilities for data input
KB encryption
Reasonableness checks
Output review by competent personnel
Hard copy or magnetic/optical collection of case histories
Management/audit review of audit trails
Good application documentation
Unauthorised copying prevention
Back-up and recovery

KBS human resources
Management commitment to KBS strategy
Assign responsibility for:
● KBS development
● KBS production operations
● disaster planning
Adequate training of KBS personnel
Supervision and management of KBS personnel
KBS Information Centre
Segregation of duties
Mandatory vacations
Personnel security checks
Maintenance supplier vetting

of approach, creativity and informality—not great attributes for implementing and enforcing strict internal controls.

As with traditional information systems processing, *systems access security* is vitally important. Unfortunately many KBS tools and environments do not provide extensive security features. The Japanese identified that KBS were currently deficient in security and reliability, and as a result are directing their efforts to KBS that explain inferences, check input and request confirmation of decisions (Gaines, 1986). Auditors working in these environments will need to specify additional security features for their clients' systems and then pressure manufacturers of expert systems shells to incorporate these features into their products. KBS software houses may also want their products certified by major accounting firms, as to the provision of reasonable security, control and auditability features in the KBS.

Traditional *input controls* such as appropriate edits, accuracy, completeness and reasonableness checking will need to be refined in the KBS environment.

Input data validation may be simple, for example a range check (numeric 1 to 20), or context-sensitive, where the validation of the input data is dependent on other information already entered into the KBS. For example, check input age of 60 years against preferred retirement age previously stated as 55. Most KBS tools provide facilities for simple data editing but fall short on context-sensitive validation. However, such facilities as *Whenever Modified* slots (in object-based KBS tools) provide for the context-sensitive style to be programmed into the KBS more easily.

Other control features include ability to retract and backtrack in a consultation to enable corrections to be made. Care is required when programming these facilities as practitioners comment that it is an area where many programming errors can be made. Also, facilities such as repeated data requests and using *Are you sure?* type questions. Many KBS provide the facilities for entering *unknown* as an answer to certain questions. These KBS require rules to deal with unknowns, although with mature KBS, unknowns would be infrequently used. From an audit perspective, we are concerned that the KBS receives a proper set of facts for the consultation under consideration, in order for it to arrive at an appropriate decision. Most interactions with KBS are via terminals where the user answers system queries by supplying numeric and symbolic facts and perhaps opinions. It is important that proper audit trails exist of the user-supplied input, which should be logged to a case history file. Currently these facilities are provided by many KBS shells and may be used at the designer's or user's discretion. More sophisticated facilities are required to mandatorily log all interactions with the KBS into a proper audit trail.

During processing, the inference engine will usually provide a combination of forward and backward chaining control mechanisms to solve the goal state and provide a decision or judgement. For both management and auditors, the importance of having adequate *trace facilities* provided by the KBS shell or processing environment is very important. These trace facilities show the consultation's questions and answers as well as the rule firing or instantiations, and the conclusions reached by the KBS. This then provides a very detailed audit trail of the inferencing process used to get to a decision or recommendation.

For *KBS outputs*, which are usually in the form of a report of the consultation and recommendation, there should be some form of reasonableness checking and knowledgeable user review prior to taking action—for example, granting a loan. Moeller (1988) points out that there is a potential high risk of inadvertent reliance on the KBS results by users. After a period of time users may not question the systems judgements. Auditors should stress to the organisation the importance of continual validation, especially in high risk applications.

It is important during development to *set correct levels of options* for use in run time versions. For example, it is important to set an option for the correct level of explanations for the system, as one insurance company removed all explanation facilities from the run time KBS in order to hide the expertise from users and competitors. If knowledge bases are of strategic importance to the organisation then *encryption* of the KB may be considered.

Legal liability may arise from the use of a KBS (Zeide and Liebowitz, 1987; Cole, 1988). It is, therefore, important not to exceed the number of run time versions of the tool that may be legally made under the software licence, nor incorrectly distribute the full development version that allows for modification of the KB. Also, be careful to caveat the decisions made by the KBS so that the organisation may not be litigated against for loss of assets or life as a result of someone acting on the system's decisions. The final responsibility must fall on a person in the organisation, not on the system. Socha (1988) observes that society expects computer systems to have a very low error rate. When a KBS fails, such as the X-ray machine's edit software resulting in the deaths of several people, then massive lawsuits may result. He also observes that this litigation is likely to include the auditor(s) who tested the KBS.

In a similar way to *controlling the amendments to source programs* for an application, KB rule changes should also be approved, correctly updated and validated, and the KB maintained in such a form that unauthorised amendments to it are impossible. This involves maintaining a secure KBS development library with versions of the KB held that are equivalent to the released production versions. Beware of KBS shells that do not provide a separate compiled or unalterable KB to be used as a delivery vehicle for production applications. This also presupposes some sort of KB development section with abilities to modify copies of the KB, fix errors and release new versions when appropriate.

Documentation is, and always will be, a perennial problem and KBS are no exception. However, with these systems there is an ever greater need to correctly document the expertise that is encapsulated in the KB and its associated design. While systems design documentation has been mentioned previously, KBS in operation should have, as a minimum, adequate on-line help facilities which are context-sensitive, a HOW facility for providing a trace of the reasons for arriving at a particular conclusion, and a WHY facility for explaining why a question is being asked or why a certain fact is requested. An exception to this guideline is for KBS imbedded within other information systems where this type of facilities may never be required. In this case, system evaluation is performed during development and at periodic intervals by quality assurance or audit. Some KBS shells do not provide adequate translation facilities (from rules to an English explanation) and, for use of the HOW or WHY facility, provide a rule chain dump for the user to unravel. An operator's or user's guide is useful as an introduction to the KBS, which could also be on-line. Some KBS shells provide excellent tutorial facilities built with their own shell. These could be very useful to developers setting up training systems for the use of particular applications. When the operational version is used for consultations, then adequate documentation of the consultation, usually in hard copy format is required, perhaps to give to the customer and to keep for statutory record purposes as proof of the business transaction or event. Optical or magnetic records may also be used to document case histories for later management or audit review. Adequate documentation of the operator's responsibilities at the end of the day is also required. This may include procedures for appropriate retention of magnetic, optical or hardcopy files and back-ups for the KBS.

Contingency planning for KBS is just as important as for traditional information systems. Alternative locations and equipment, especially for specialised AI hardware, must be found if KBS requiring this equipment are critical to the organisation. Regular off-site storage of development versions and KB production source is important for recovery purposes. Important requirements such as consultation case histories and documentation should also be stored off-site on a regular basis.

12.7 GATHERING AUDIT EVIDENCE

An important part of the audit review of the operational KBS is to document an understanding of the KBS, design and carry out compliance tests, and assess the control risk in the KBS application. If the auditor has been involved in the KBS development process then documentation of his or her understanding should be well advanced. Having identified the risks and controls in the KBS, then the auditor must gather evidential matter in the form of compliance tests of the application. Both AUP 4-1 and SAS 55 provide general guidance for gathering evidential matter. For example, paragraph 49 of SAS 55 states that "evidential matter about the effectiveness of design or operation of some control procedures performed by a computer (for example, within the KBS) may be obtained through observation or the use of computer assisted audit techniques to reperform the application of relevant policies and procedures." Moeller (1988) believes that while observation is a valid procedure for KBS, computer assisted techniques will not generally work. Certainly, traditional audit software packages may not work. However, the principles that have been developed may work. The next section focuses on KBS audit tools and techniques that may be appropriate for auditors to use when compliance or substantive testing KBS applications.

12.8 KBS AUDIT TOOLS AND TECHNIQUES

Auditors will be able to use their own expert systems, not only to assist their judgement process (refer to examples in Jamieson, 1989a), but also to audit sophisticated interacting systems including KBS. Examples of these types of systems are starting to appear. For example, Lecot (1988) discusses fraud prevention and detection at the Security Pacific National Bank. Here a proactive expert KBS was developed to search large databases looking for unusual patterns in customer transaction activities using bankcards at ATM and POS locations. The system achieved 100% accuracy on POS investigations after two months of knowledge engineering and an 85% correctness on suspicious deposit activity. This project proved so successful that a further prototype is planned to deal with fraud in commercial accounts. In these KBS, the knowledge and expertise of senior fraud investigators is made available on-line, and may front-end writing audit information to a systems control audit review file (SCARF) in a similar way to on-line auditing of traditional IS systems. Moeller (1988) reports another example where Baxter Healthcare developed a KBS to monitor and analyse the exceptions originating from its conventional inventory system, which monitored 60 000 stocked units.

In the future, expert system shells may support facilities to provide audit hooks into the knowledge base and other audit diagnostic tools, such as audit knowledge documentors, to provide for example cross-referenced knowledge dictionaries and inference hierarchies. This would provide facilities similar to spreadsheet audit utilities such as the Spread Sheet Auditor. Jansen and Compton (1989), carrying out research into knowledge dictionaries for expert systems development and maintenance, produced a knowledge dictionary prototoype in Hypercard. This system normalises knowledge, stores it in a hypercard relational database, provides graphical business, expert and technical views of the knowledge base, permits the structuring of knowledge in different representations (objects, frames, semantic nets), and provides facilities for base case testing, and if/then rule-generation. Such a product which integrity checks the knowledge base will be a powerful audit tool of the future. Currently some KBS software provides utilities for integrity checking the KB, which may be of value to the auditor during the audit.

Traditional information systems audit techniques like test decks, base case testing, audit retrieval, parallel simulation, code (rule) review, source (rule) code comparison software, may be applicable to auditing a KBS.

- *Test Decks:* The auditor may obtain actual live case histories, which may already be held on magnetic media. These cases can be added to and altered to provide a sufficiently broad spectrum of cases for audit evaluation of KBS operation and for testing key KBS security and control features. An auditor may then either run these cases against a current version of the KBS recently copied from a production machine, or have a knowledge worker, responsible for running live cases through the system, to run the test series of cases under audit control.

- *Base Case:* Here the auditor would construct a set of base cases which may be drawn from similar sources as the test deck approach. This base set may be used by the auditor to verify the integrity of the existing functionality, controls and security of key KBS following changes to the KB or, indeed, at any time. Any changes to the KBS may involve the auditor in either adding, deleting or modifying the audit base case to ensure that new variants are covered.

- *Audit Retrieval:* Traditional information systems audit uses audit retrieval software to substantively audit system results held on databases. Two different facets of audit retrieval may now be applicable. Firstly, *auditing the knowledge in the KB.* In some expert systems shells, for example M1 from Teknowledge, the KB may be retrieved and reviewed by the use of any word processor software. Other development tools have their own internal format for maintaining the KB, so that the auditor must use the KBS utilities for review of the KB. Secondly, *auditing the case histories* resulting from production use of the KBS. These case histories are the results of knowledge-based processing and will contain the judgements, decisions or advice offered by the system (such as whether to grant a loan), together with a trace of the variables requested and conclusions reached throughout the consultation (such as name, salary, employment history, credit worthiness). These trace facilities may also include explanations, justifications of conclusions reached, and the inference process gone through to arrive at the conclusions. Auditors may write extraction software to select appropriate case histories for review, based on single or multiple criteria or variables (for example, amount of loan, credit history, position of applicant, reason for loan). An example may be to extract all case histories for loans granted (*the conclusion*) over $50 000 (*amount of loan*) to government clerks (*position*) for car purchase (*reason for loan*).

- *Parallel Simulation:* For many expert systems shells a case history load, play-back and review function is available. Here the auditor can simulate an important part of the knowledge base using the auditor's own KB code to verify both the logic and inferencing process as well as the conclusions reached out of the simulated section of KB code. A trace from this section of the audit-simulated code may be automatically or manually compared to a trace from the production code, and any differences highlighted for audit review and follow up. A very high level of both audit and KBS technical expertise will be required to develop, implement and run this audit technique.

- *KB Code Review:* Auditors may use either a simple tool such as a KB listing or a more sophisticated tool such as Jansen and Compton's (1989) knowledge dictionary to review the associated KB code of a KBS.

- *KB Code Comparison Software:* KB code may be compared for security and audit purposes at both the source executable levels using currently available comparison utilities. KB source code comparisons become difficult when more sosphisticated KBS development environments are used, and the KB can no longer be presented as an ASCII text file.

- *KB Utilities:* Most KB development environments come with utilities that may be useful to the auditor. A selection of these utilities includes:

  - *Dictionary facilities* - for looking up meanings and instances of variables used in the KB together with a cross reference listing;
  - *Query facilities* - the ability to query the KB and run small consultations on sections of the KB and then examine the conclusions;
  - *What if facilities* - the ability to change the values of parameters or variables and rerun that particular consultation again to see the effect that a change in these variables makes to the conclusions reached;
  - *Check knowledge-base* - the ability to check the KB for various events, such as certain variable names and values, unused consequences in rules, missing values of variables, circular reasoning, conflicting values for variables.

Use of other independent experts by auditors to verify that lines of reasoning and results are reasonable may also be employed where systems are critical, carry a high business risk, and are of high materiality or monetary value.

12.10   CONCLUSION, FUTURE ISSUES AND RESEARCH AREAS

A special report from the AICPA's EDP Technology Research Subcommittee (AICPA, 1987) raised questions on the impact of KBS on:

- the development of auditors' judgemental and intuitive processes and abilities;
- audit engagement level quality control;
- audit evidence/workpapers, engagement documentation and retention;
- professional audit training; and
- professional guidance on the auditing of KBS used by clients.

Both Moeller (1988) and this author believe that there is sufficient scope for development of appropriate audit guidance in both the areas of audit use of KBS and the audit of KBS. Work in the USA is progressing through a task-force (Artifiical Intelligence Knowledge-Based Systems) formed in 1988 by the AICPA's Computer Audit Subcommittee to address these concerns. Holstrum *et al.* (1988) also discuss the implications of technology including expert systems on auditing when moving into the 21st century.

In the future there is a danger that auditors may abrogate their responsibilities, as an audit KBS captures human expertise and makes audit decisions.

The potential risk is that the KBS's results and reports will be accepted without adequate review, that is, with over reliance on the KBS. There must always be human judgement to provide an audit opinion.

Moeller (1988) mentions an expert system's ability to "self-modify" its rule set based on changing conditions. Currently, experiments are being conducted in AI laboratories on machine learning. However, there are currently no production KBS that provide adaptivity of the knowledge base. Any modifications to the KB must be made by a knowledge engineer or other knowledgeable person in exactly the same way as a programmer must change a line of Cobol code. In the future, hybrid semi-learning systems may be available which combine more advanced pruning inductive algorithms, such as C4 (Quinlin *et al.*, 1986), as a sophisticated front-end generator of new rules from new examples added to a case history database. This would then be tied into a rule compiler to integrity-check the new rules before releasing them in compiled mode into the production KBS. Further complications arise with integrated KBS and conventional or 4th generation applications.

An interesting consideration for the auditor is that some of the tools for developing KBS are unique, and certain firms, for example, Technowledge Inc. which develops the S1 and M1 products, have received US patents for their development software. This means that it may be difficult for an auditor, in the KBS arena, to recommend already patented elements of these systems for suggested control improvements for KBS developed using shells or environments from other KBS software houses (Socha, 1988).

Socha (1988) also believes that auditing evolving expert systems will be both a challenging and frustrating task which will create a need for a new specialisation—expert systems auditor. This may, in fact, be a new task area for information systems auditors, just as operating systems or LAN environment audits (Jamieson, 1989b) are currently performed. Certainly, there is a need for information systems auditors who are proficient and knowledgeable, in order to provide effective training and consultation in this area.

The domain of auditing expert systems, in both development and operational environments, provides the audit researcher with many potential areas for future research. A selection of areas and research questions is outlined below:

- Is an auditor's involvement in the KBS audit a useful activity? What are the benefits?
- When and where should auditors be involved in the KBS audit?
- Development and validation of an audit methodology or approach for KBS audit at the operational phase.
- What are the generic risks and their impact on the organisations operating KBS?
- What are the best set of baseline controls and security procedures for inclusion in a KBS?

- What are the best methods for validation and assessment of KBS by auditors?
- How is the KBS and its associated control environment best documented for the audit?
- How is internal control within the KBS best evaluated?
- What KBS audit tools and techniques are appropriate for gathering audit evidence in the KBS environment?
- What are the legal issues arising from use of a KBS in the audit?

These areas should provide a guide for the audit researcher starting to investigate the audit of KBS.

This chapter helps the auditor to understand the ramifications and implications of KBS technology on organisations, and to appreciate the steps and issues involved in conducting operational audits of both the KBS process and product. Relevant statements on auditing practice from Australia and the USA were reviewed to see how auditing KBS fits into their frameworks. Having determined that KBS do come under the auspices of these statements, some risks involved in KBS were presented, followed by internal control considerations that should be taken account of by auditors auditing in the KBS environment. A selection of KBS audit tools and techniques were also presented along with issues that the KBS auditor will face in the future. A guide to potential areas of KBS audit investigation for audit researchers was outlined.

If auditors neglect this challenge, then there may be many KBS in production that have inadequate documentation, are difficult or impossible to maintain, and provide the potential for abuse either unintentionally or intentionally as they operate on a daily basis. As this new KBS technology will be absorbed into the mainline information systems infrastructure and system architecture in the future, let us, as auditors, take up the challenge and be a positive force towards the operation of manageable, controllable, auditable and usable knowledge based systems.

ACKNOWLEDGEMENTS

This research was supported in part by an Australian Research Council grant and by Toshiba of Australia.

REFERENCES

American Institute of Certified Public Accountants (1977): *Audit Guide to a Statement on Auditing Standards 3, The Study and Evaluation of Control in EDP Systems,* New York.

American Institute of Certified Public Accountants (1984): *Statement on Auditing Standards 48, The Effects of Computer Processing on the Examination of Financial Standards,* New York.

American Institute of Certified Public Accountants (1987): *An Introduction to Artificial Intelligence and Expert Systems*, AICPA's EDP Technology Research Subcommittee, New York.

American Institute of Certified Public Accountants (1988): *Statement on Auditing Standards 55, Consideration of the Internal Control Structure in a Financial Statement Audit*, New York.

Australian Accounting Research Foundation, Auditing Standards Board (1984): "Statement of Auditing Practice No 4, Auditing in an EDP Environment—General Principles", March.

Barrett, M.L. and Beerel, A.C. (1989): *Expert Systems in Business: A Practical Approach*, Ellis Horwood Limited, Sussex, England.

Broad, R.D. (1986): "Audit of Systems Development Methodology", *The Internal Auditor*, June.

Coopers & Lybrand (1988): "Product Demonstrations", *Proceedings EDPAC'88*, EDP Auditors Conference, Sydney, Australia.

Coopers & Lybrand (1989): *Systems Development Audit Review Guide*, Institute of Internal Auditors, Alamonte Springs, USA.

Cole, G.S. (1988): "Legal Issues in Applied Artificial Intelligence", *The First International Symposium on Business, Finance and Accounting*, Sponsored by the Expert Systems Program, School of Accounting, University of Southern California and Peat Marwick Main Foundation, 29–30 September.

Davis, G.B. (1984): "User Developed Systems Can Be Dangerous to Your Organization", *Working Paper*, Management Information Systems Research Center, School of Management, University of Minnesota, Minneapolis, Minnesota.

EDP Auditors Foundation (1980): *Control Objectives*, EDP Auditors Foundation, Inc.

EDP Auditors Foundation (1988): "General Standards for Information Systems Auditing", EDP Auditors Foundation, Inc., Information Systems Control Foundation, January.

EDP Auditors Foundation (1989a): "Statement of Information Systems Auditing Standards Number 1—Independence: Attitude and Appearance, Organisational Relationship", EDP Auditors Foundation, Inc., Information Systems Control Foundation, April.

EDP Auditors Foundation (1989b): "Statement of Information Systems Auditing Standards Number 2—Independence: Involvement in the Systems Development Process", EDP Auditors Foundation, Inc., Information Systems Control Foundation, April.

Edwards, A. and Connell, N.A.D. (1989). Expert Systems in Accounting, Prentice-Hall (in association with The Institute of Chartered Accountants in England and Wales), London.

Gaines, B. (1986): "Sixth Generation Computing: A Conspectus of the Japanese Proposals", *Sigart Newsletter of the ACM*, January, Number 95.

Harmon, P. and King, D., (1985): *Artificial Intelligence in Business: Expert Systems*, John Wiley & Sons, Inc., New York.

Hayes-Roth, F., Waterman, D.A. and Lenat, D.B., eds., (1983): *Building Expert Systems*, Addison-Wesley Publishing Company, Reading, MA.

Holstrum, G.L., Mock, T.J., and West, R.N. (1988): *The Impact of Technology on Auditing—Moving Into the 21st Century*, The Institute of Internal Auditors Research Foundation, Altamonte Springs, Florida.

IEEE Expert (1986): "Artificial Intelligence Goes to Court", *IEEE Expert*, Vol 1 No 2, Summer, p. 101.

Information Technology Group ICAEW (1989): *IT and the Future of the Audit*, Institute of Chartered Accountants in England and Wales, London.

Jamieson, R. (1989a): "Expert Systems in Auditing: A Strategic Tool for the 1990's", *Proceedings of EDPAC '89*, EDP Auditors Association, New Zealand.

Jamieson, R. (1989b): "Security and Control Issues in Local Area Network Design", *Computers and Security*, Vol 8 No. 4, June.

Jamieson, R. and Ching, M. (1988): "Development of a Normative Model for Knowledge Based Systems Development", *Information Systems Research Report No. 35*, University of New South Wales.

Jansen, R. and Compton, P. (1989): "Data Dictionary Approach to the Maintenance of Expert Systems: The Knowledge Dictionary", *Knowledge Based Systems*, March, pp. 14-26.

Lecot, K. (1988): "Using Expert Systems in Banking: The Case of Fraud Detection and Prevention", *The First International Symposium on Business, Finance and Accounting*, Sponsored by the Expert Systems Program, School of Accounting, University of Southern California and Peat Marwick Main Foundation, 29–30 September.

Moeller, R.R. (1988): "Expert Systems: Auditability Issues", *The First International Symposium on Business, Finance and Accounting*, Sponsored by the Expert Systems Program, School of Accounting, University of Southern California and Peat Marwick Main Foundation, 29–30 September.

Montgomery, A. (1988): "GEMINI—Government Expert System Methodology Initiative", in *Research and Development in Expert Systems V* (1989), (Kelly, B. and Rector, A., Eds) Proceedings of the Expert Systems Conference of the British Computer Society, Specialist Group on Expert Systems, Brighton, 12–15 December, 14–24.

Nycum, S.H. (1985): "Artificial Intelligence and Certain Legal Issues", *The Computer Lawyer*, May, pp. 1–10.

O'Leary, D.E. (1987): "Validation of Expert Systems—with Applications to Auditing and Accounting Expert Systems", *Decision Sciences*, Vol 18.

Parsaye, K. and Chignell, M. (1988): *Expert Systems for Experts*, John Wiley & Sons, Inc., New York.

Quinlin, R., Compton, P.J., Horn, K.A. and Lazarus, L. (1986): "Inductive Knowledge Acquisition: A Case Study", *Proceedings of the Second Australian Conference on Applications of Expert Systems*, Sydney, 14–16 May.

Standards Association of Australia (1988): *Australian Standard AS 3563—Software Quality Management System*, Standards Association of Australia.

Socha, W.J. (1988): "Problems in Auditing Expert System Development", *The EDP Audit, Control and Security Newsletter*, March.

Vallabhaneni, S.R. (1988): *Information Systems Audit Process*, EDP Auditors Foundation, USA.

Waterman, D.A. (1986): *A Guide to Expert Systems*, Addison-Wesley, Massachusetts.

Zeide, J.S. and Liebowitz, J. (1987): "Using Expert Systems: The Legal Perspective", *IEEE Expert*, Spring.

Chapter 13

EXPERT SYSTEMS FOR COMPUTER SECURITY

William T. Tener
TRW Information Systems Group, Orange, CA

The data processing and telecommunications environment has undergone a major transformation during the last decade. Audit and Security Management no longer enjoy the control simplicity of a single mainframe computer without dial-up capability. Today's environment is a mix of user specific interfaces to mainframes or local area networks (LANS) through a number of communication protocols.

This chapter discusses ways in which expert systems may be used to help assure security in complex information systems environments.

13.1 INTRODUCTION

James A. Schweitzer summarizes the situation in stating *Communications are the essence of the information age.* Dial-up access enables the crossing of company as well as national boundaries. Telecommunications allow access to information anywhere in the world.

The commercial sector has distinguished itself from other data processing environments. Though the customers or users of the commercial service are not under the control of the corporation offering the service, they are often part of the security strategy. It is important that adequate controls be implemented by the corporation to maintain data security that do not depend wholly on the user.

The controls available range from the simple password to complex systems designed for federal agencies. The control specifications for any entity are contingent upon its unique requirements.

In the Information Service industry, the primary issue of user authentication is critical to the service provider, not the customer. Hackers, private investigators and criminals have found several effective methods of acquiring passwords and system access instructions. These individuals do not have to be in collusion with the authorized user. The hacker will "dumpster dive" or go through a user's trash to derive access instructions and passwords.

Expert Systems in Business and Finance: Issues and Applications. Edited by P.R. Watkins and L.B. Eliot
© 1993 John Wiley & Sons Ltd.

The private investigator will phone the custodian of the password and gain this data through subterfuge, pretending to be someone who should already have this knowledge. The criminal will use either of these means to gain access instructions and passwords.

The customer is not necessarily concerned with the service provider's security. Thus, the customer must be discounted as a part of the security program's reliability. A method of detection and prevention is required that is completely transparent to the subscriber and those individuals accessing the system.

Just about any system has the capability to lock out a *hacker* or unauthorized individual attempting to log onto a system with an invalid password. A greater challenge is to identify the impostor who has password and log-on identifier knowledge. Most illegal use of valid access codes accessing a system goes undetected, unless the condition is brought to the attention of the system manager by the legitimate system user. As a result, a monitoring mechanism to detect unauthorized use of legitimate access parameters is required.

Oscar Wilde said, *Consistency is the last refuge for the unimaginative.* It is also the hallmark of the inquiry patterns for a legitimate user. Legitimate users would be expected to have more consistent inquiry data and patterns within that data than hackers or other unauthorized individuals masquerading as legitimate users.

TRW has developed *Discovery*, an expert system to search for recurrent patterns in inquiry data and compare these patterns to daily inquiry activity to detect variances in normal user behavior. Discovery is an attempt to integrate expert systems and decision support system features to provide pattern recognition, self-learning capability, and interactive features to detect unsuspected violations.

13.2   SYSTEM DESIGN OBJECTIVES

TRW's goal is to review all daily inquiry activity and detect those inquiries made by potentially unauthorized individuals. The system processes 400 000 inquiries per day from a customer access code base of 120 000 locations. At many of these locations, several persons are authorized to access the system.

There are certain commonalities in inquiry data that constitute discriminating variables. Some of these variables are unique to our system, but many are common in most systems:

- date and time of access
- user location
- user identification

- terminal or port ID
- type of access.

The system is dynamic in its ability to detect and absorb subtle changes in user patterns over time. Inquiry data and patterns change as new services are introduced to the customer. These changes in format should not be considered as deviations to established patterns.

13.3   PROTOTYPE DEVELOPMENT

Discovery was initially prototyped on an IBM PC-XT with 60 megabytes of storage using a Bernoulli Box. The PC was equipped with a Microsoft *C* compiler.

We used coaxial mainframe access for downloading data. Recognizing that there would be a data transfer rate issue and storage limitations, we utilized stratified statistical sampling for our testing. In addition to statistical testing we processed potentially invalid access investigations in parallel with our human investigators.

The prototype provided many insights during the development phase. The results of Discovery parallel the work of our investigators. Investigative

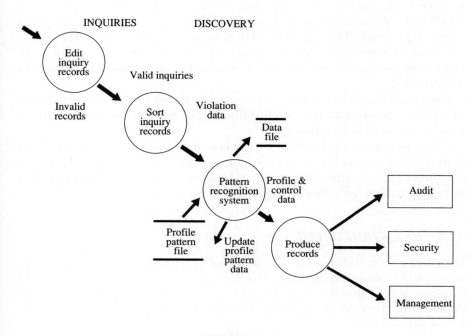

FIGURE 13.1

leads were developed in a more timely manner. The violation of the system provided additional leads in some of the cases.

The prototype findings were used to develop an IBM Model 3090-400 mainframe based COBOL application with a 3380 model 2 disk for storage. The system flow diagram in Figure 13.1 illustrates the basic characteristics of pattern recognition, self-learning profiles, dynamic databases, and statistically based thresholds. A more detailed description is discussed in the next two sections.

13.4   PATTERN DEVELOPMENT

Inquiry records are edited to eliminate invalid records. Invalid records, due to format or field errors, are extracted since they could key resulting patterns due to errors in other fields. The resulting input file consists of valid inquiries sorted on key variables in the record to identify the customer and type of access.

The system develops a *user profile* for each customer based on the type of service requested and access methodology. Each customer can vary their inquiry data based on the type of service they request.

The sorted output is processed by the pattern recognition module. The pattern is defined by an interactive choice of variables and associated thresholds. Variables exist in three forms. Data elements such as spouse initial or previous address can be isolated. Inquiry characteristics such as time of access or error rates can be delineated. Access characteristics pertaining to the geographic area accessed, or whether access was successful, are also utilized.

Each daily inquiry is analytically compared to the profile pattern. Based on defined tolerances and self-learning logic, the profile pattern file or exception data file is updated.

Three patterns exist in the current version of Discovery. A daily pattern is developed for each customer. A global pattern is developed based on accumulated daily customer patterns. In some cases we have developed an industry pattern for collection agencies or bank cards.

13.5   VIOLATION DETECTION

Inquiries with variables that fall outside of acceptable boundaries are captured in the exception data file. The boundaries or thresholds are variable dependent. The thresholds are established for each variable by the security department. Thresholds can be more restrictive for specific or suspect customer access codes.

Exception files can be created in two modes. Transaction files are created when a daily inquiry has a pattern variance to the global pattern. The second mode creates a pattern file when the customer daily pattern is in variance with the global pattern.

The system outputs an exception data file isolating the reason(s) for pattern violation. The file is in a format that permits further processing by investigators to analyze inquiry records that are outside normal inquiry patterns. The exception file enables the manipulation of only questionable data using fourth generation software.

13.6 PERFORMANCE TRENDS

Investigative leads have been developed in a more timely manner through the increased ability to detect unauthorized access. Several of the benefits we are realizing are not directly attributable to the increased level of system protection. Several deviations in customer patterns have been discovered resulting in customers changing their access methods and systems. Discovery is developing daily system usage patterns. The profile patterns provide a detailed and timely analysis of customer purchasing characteristics. The pattern illustrates what services they are buying, when they are buying these services and the transaction configuration.

An outgrowth of the purchasing pattern is the data it provides for risk analysis. Through trend analysis we can see the direction in which service access characteristics are evolving. Access mechanisms can then be put in place to provide a secure environment as our service line and access methods evolve.

13.7 SUMMARY

We wanted a method of detection and potential prevention of illegitimate access that was completely transparent to the customer. Discovery is an expert system that is meeting our expectations of isolating deviant system access. We have integrated decision support system characteristics to facilitate interactive sessions to enable fine tuning and research. These same fourth generation languages provide management with detailed marketing information.

Several lessons have been learned throughout this development process. The primary lesson is that the development of an expert system presently requires different skills. Expert systems require specific development skills of knowledge engineers. Greater user involvement is required due to the prototyping approach and analysis in the expert domain.

Both of the above issues escalate the development budget. Expert systems tend to be evolutionary,which produce additional costs. The expert system provides additional knowledge that can be enhanced within the system We are presently examining the feasibility of incorporating further investigative knowledge to analyze Discovery's output and files. O'Leary and Watkins discuss some of these efforts in the following chapter.

Chapter 14

ISSUES IN EXPERT SYSTEMS FOR SECURITY

Daniel E. O'Leary
Paul R. Watkins
University of Southern California, Los Angeles, CA

Chapter 13 described the Discovery System of TRW. This chapter focuses on some of the issues in extending the Discovery System at TRW. The Discovery System and its extensions are somewhat ususual in that they are developed and maintained within a non-MIS group, the internal audit group. Thus, this chapter suggests areas that others concerned with developing expert systems for security need to consider in their research and development efforts.

14.1 EXPERT SYSTEM APPLICATION: TRW'S DISCOVERY

One of the first and among the best known of the internal audit expert systems is TRW's *Discovery* discussed in Chapter 13.

At the time of this writing, TRW is the only credit information service company that uses software to monitor the use of the credit maintenance and reporting system. Apparently few economic incentives exist to monitor such a system. For example, if a subscribing company has an employee perform *extra transactions* then the costs of that extra use are passed back to the subscriber. However, TRW does not assess database users for the costs of monitoring transactions.

14.1.1 Knowledge Acquisition

Initially, gathering knowledge for the Discovery system was difficult. Oftentimes the experts did not know what they knew that would be appropriate for the system. For example, it was common sense to the expert that the time of the day and the day of the week were important statistics. On the other hand, the expert did not express those factors immediately to the developer as key variables to be included in the system. Thus, early versions of the system did not consider time and day in the analysis of security issues.

Expert Systems in Business and Finance: Issues and Applications. Edited by P.R. Watkins and L.B. Eliot
© 1993 John Wiley & Sons Ltd.

New knowledge is continually added to the system. The expert systems manager (ESM) (discussed below) is constantly searching out new information to add to Discovery. For example, one of the approaches to acquiring new knowledge is to periodically monitor various hacker bulletin boards to determine if information is posted on how to break into TRW's system or if generic information is posted that could be helpful to TRW.

14.1.2 Testing of the System

When the system was first developed some *false* problems were found by the system. For example, the system might indicate that there was a problem at bank Y, because it had a record of transactions from that bank on a Sunday. However, certain types of banks work on a Sunday. Thus, this knowledge had to be built into the knowledge base. Such anomalies can be used to find knowledge that needs to be added to the system.

14.1.3 Success of the System.

Discovery is able to analyze large volumes of data of client use to determine if there are any unusual patterns, in a timely manner. A human would take hours to analyze what Discovery analyzes in minutes. Discovery analyzes the data and reports anomalies the next day. Whereas, human investigators would take 30–60 days to find the problem, often too late to take remedial action.

Discovery is used because there is a high probability that if the system provides a lead then there is a security problem. The use of the system is heavily dependent on not providing incorrect information to the user. The experts do not want to be in a position of suggesting a problem exists and then having the client find no problem. Instead, the system makes them the *hero* by allowing them to state, with small probability of error, *it looks like you have a problem.*

This also suggests that one of the means of measuring the success of the system is to measure the number of leads suggested by the system that ultimately are identified as frauds.

14.2   EXPERT SYSTEM APPLICATION: DATA EDIT

TRW also uses expert systems in data edit. Subscribers provide TRW with magnetic tape summaries of, e.g., their accounts receivables. Since TRW does not require a standard input from these users, there can be a substantial effort to get the information into a standard format. Expert systems technology was chosen as a means to standardize data input tapes.

The system is integrated into the work flow of the subscriber analysis data edit process and is operational. The initial prototype of the system had approximately 10–20 rules that accounted for about 90% of the data edit problems.

The system now has about 100 rules. Many of the additional 80–90 rules are client specific.

14.2.1 Impact of the System

The process of editing client data had been a labor intensive effort requiring about 50 clerks. With the use of this expert system, the number of clerks has dropped to about 25. At this time, no measures of effectiveness or of job enrichment have been developed.

14.3 EXPERT SYSTEM APPLICATION: MAINTENANCE OF THE CREDIT DATABASE

Periodically, the credit database requires maintenance. For example, individuals may dispute the status of their account. An account may be reported to TRW as *paid* or *paid charge-off* and TRW will want to make the changes consistent. Thus, the client may indicate to TRW that they want to change a data element from x to y. However, a human expert examining the change might question the change since instead of x it should be z. This suggests that there are certain rules that are used to analyze the data for appropriateness. These rules could be the basis of another system.

14.4 ORGANIZATIONAL ISSUES

In each of the above applications, TRW found that the initial and continued success of an expert system is dependent on two unique organizational roles: expert system champion and expert system manager.

14.4.1 Expert System Champion

TRW feels that the initial success of an expert system is based in large measure with having an expert system champion (ESC). The ESC is someone willing to put himself/herself behind the development effort and the selling effort to management and the rest of the organization. TRW felt it was helpful to have an ESC in order to facilitate the development and implementation of the system.

14.4.2 Expert System Manager

With most computer programs when the system is operational and ready to go into production this means that the system will require only minimal amounts of additional programmer intervention. Programmers move on to other projects. Otherwise the system is a *flop*. However, unlike other computer programs, many expert systems need *constant care and feeding*. The knowledge base must continue to change as the environment changes. New knowledge must be put into the knowledge base as it is discovered. In the case of expert systems such constant attention is not a sign that the program is a *flop*. Instead, it is likely to indicate that the problem which the system is designed to solve is dynamic and lacks easily elicited structure.

Because expert systems continue to evolve and change over time, TRW has found need for an expert system manager (ESM) to monitor the development of the system over time. The ESM is somewhat analogous to a database manager. Although not necessarily initially a true expert in the area of the application, the ESM now is a *near expert* in the domain. The ESM has both a reactive and a proactive role in continuing the development of the expert system. The ESM can add knowledge that the user would like to be a part of the system. Further, the ESM can generate new knowledge for the system. Finally, the ESM must constantly question the system output.

14.5   KNOWLEDGE ACQUISITION

For each of the systems, one of the primary sources of knowledge and tests of the existing knowledge is the anomaly. Typically, this is something that the system cannot explain, and thus, additional knowledge must be added to allow the system to explain the problem. However, not every anomaly should be a part of the knowledge base. Some anomalies are in conflict with others.

The TRW experience also suggests that expert systems can be developed more efficiently and more rapidly if the developer also is an expert in the problem domain. This finding indicates that when putting together the expert system development team the expert needs to be actively involved in the process and the expert really needs to be a "true" expert. Too often, the team consists of available personnel, which may not be expert personnel. Further, since the expert may be active in other projects the development of the current system may receive a subordinated priority from the expert.

14.6   BENEFITS FROM EXPERT SYSTEMS

The TRW experience indicates that the benefits from implementing an expert system go beyond the direct benefits of increased output, higher quality and decreased operational personnel. TRW also experienced two additional benefits. First, TRW received extensive publicity on the system, thus, developing goodwill. Second, much of the data developed for one of the expert systems also can be used for marketing purposes.

The usage data that the system uses to determine whether or not the use of the credit database is consistent with established portfolios provides marketing information. Determining the purposes for which the client uses the database also establishes those aspects of that database which the client does not exploit. Those findings can be used to market additional use of the database.

14.7 DANGERS OF THE USE OF EXPERT SYSTEMS

There are a number of dangers with the integration of expert systems into an organization. First, if there is an expert system then there is a tendency for the human to not examine the issues with the same critical eye that would be used if the system was not there. This can lead to a decrease in the quality of results produced by the man–machine combination.

Second, after the system has been in place for a period of time a tendency exists to forget the system is there. This can prove to be a disaster if the process being examined changes, and the system does not. Similarly, if the system provides *default* values rather than requesting them from the user the presence of the system may be disguised and possible difficulties or inconsistencies in the input data may not be observed.

14.8 CONTROLS AND AUDITING EXPERT SYSTEMS

The existence of expert users of the expert system and an ESM provides a control over the knowledge in the knowledge base. Since the ESM at TRW is a near expert, the ESM provides an audit check over the information that the expert user requests which the ESM put into the system. Further, since the user is an expert, there is a check on the information placed in the system by the ESM.

Thus far, auditing of the expert systems at TRW has not proved difficult (from a perspective of understanding the process on which the system is based) because for each of the applications the audit group will audit, there is an expert in the audit group staff in that area. However, there is concern for the time when that is not the case. Then such issues as *How much do you depend on a user?* become of prime concern.

Another issue of concern at TRW is at what time do auditors get involved in the expert system design and development process. For virtually all accounting systems an auditor is involved in the design and development process at some point relatively early on, so that the appropriate controls can be built into the system.

Looking toward the future, the primary needs of the project team are the development of generic audit plans and audit tools for the audit of expert systems.

Part IV
LEGAL ISSUES, TRAINING EFFECTS AND
FINANCIAL AND RESOURCE PLANNING
APPLICATIONS OF EXPERT SYSTEMS

Chapter 15

LEGAL ISSUES IN APPLIED ARTIFICIAL INTELLIGENCE

George S. Cole
Menlo Park, CA

Artificial Intelligence and Expert Systems are moving out of the research laboratory, into the lexicon and into the marketplace. This offers fabulous opportunities to create, guide and shape the future, as well as offering new wealth or new savings to those successful at capitalizing on such knowledge—there are also the corresponding risks for failure to do so wisely. As problems arise in distributing both the penalties and the rewards, those who have been harmed, or feel that they have been rewarded inadequately, will call upon our legal system for justice. How will the law treat this broad subject matter or describe the parties who might be concerned? Can these disputes be resolved?

15.1 DEFINITIONS AND CONCERNS

15.1.1 Defining *Artificial Intelligence* and *Expert Systems* (AI and ES)

Artificial Intelligence and Expert Systems are computer programs. They may use the same hardware, supporting software, and programming languages as those used by traditional, well-established programs yet, fundamentally they are different. Furthermore, there is also a fundamental difference between any Expert System and any Artificial Intelligence program. The following definitions are based on the potential for distinct legal consequences carried by these differences:

(1) Traditional programs are algorithmic; they work entirely within a mathematical world—counting logic as mathematics. Their data is completely abstracted from its conceptual or *deep* meaning. Word processors manipulate characters, not language; spreadsheets manipulate numbers and formulae, not financial accounts; machine-tools manipulate inputs, outputs, and timing, not materials, tools, or tasks.

Expert Systems in Business and Finance: Issues and Applications. Edited by P.R. Watkins and L.B. Eliot
© 1993 John Wiley & Sons Ltd.

Theoretically, these programs are capable of proof of perfection under the rigors, and according to the constraints, of mathematics; they *never guess*. They may work with probabilities, but never with uncertainty.

(2)   Expert Systems are the first step towards heuristic programs—i.e. programs that *guess*; they work entirely within a *separable model world*. Assumptions are built into the form of the data and into the reasoning process; imperfection is recognized and traded for potential returns in efficiency, or tractability of the program, or as an inherent feature of the conceptual universe the program is manipulating. Since the data and reasoning mingles algorithmic and conceptual processing, they work within a *model* world, not the real world. Even if the Expert System is formed according to—and correctly represents—the condensed, translated knowledge and methodology which are universally accepted within its subject field, the program's basic assumptions and the form of its reasoning are not guaranteed to be correct, particularly if there are attempts to stretch beyond the model they are conceived for. A translator manipulates context and handles standard communication, but fails to interpret connotations (e.g. SHRDLU might not have understood Joseph McCarthy's reference to a *Red pyramid*); an underwriting risk analyzer manipulates future values and risk assessments with no real comprehension of human foibles beyond its built-in classifications (thus, it might issue an arson policy to Torchy LaFlame); a motor vibration analyst comprehends metals and strains, but not comfort (thus it could ignore a penetrating squeak). In order to measure a program's success or failure, Expert Systems must have their reasoning interpreted within the domain envisioned for it; they are not capable of proof of protection of its reasoning under all possible interpretations of the responses, i.e. all potential models for which the axioms are valid.

(3)   Artificial Intelligence is the second step towards heuristic programs; they guess about their inputs, and attempt to work with the *real world*. Their data and reasoning mingles algorithmic, conceptual, and perpetual processing. Voice-driven arms work with sound waves, phonemes, morphemes, sentences, and meanings to manipulate tools. Check processors work with images, handwriting, bank records, and regulations to transfer funds, but might fail to recognize a pattern of $9999.99 transfers meant to elude currency restrictions; factory robots manage complex construction tasks, but may fail to recognize other machines' failures, or the presence of the repairman. An Artificial Intelligence has its reasoning measured against the specific and limited subset of the world's activities which it was created to interpret; neither its reasoning nor its perceptions are amenable to a proof of correctness, though the effect of the former on the latter can at least be reviewed.

15.1.2 Defining Possible Parties

Many, if not everyone, will be affected in the future by some AI or ES application. The IRS and FBI have already begun work on Expert Systems whose reach extends across the country (Grady and Patil, 1987). The most obvious division lies between those who bring an AI or ES application into the marketplace and those who then use the program—the Developers are distinct from the Users. The next most obvious division lies between those who developed an AI or ES application and those who are affected by that application—the Developers are distinct from Third Parties. The last and somewhat subtler division lies between those who build the inference engine, or *reasoning* power of the AI or ES, together with those who provide the knowledge or expertise for the model or real world, and those who coordinate and market the completed combination—the Programmers are distinct from the Experts who are distinct from the Marketers. Minimizing the risk, and cost of failure or of disputes over generated wealth will require some knowledge of the disparate legal interests of each of these categories.

15.2 DEVELOPERS' LIABILITY TO USERS

15.2.1 Apportioning Liability Through Contract

Complex concerns are best handled by the more expensive and costly means of a written contract—but the unsuspecting (or unscrupulous) can attempt to bypass this process. Verbal contracts, though not favored by law, are enforceable—especially when the terms are short and memorable. A simple verbal promise of *absolute performance* or *ironclad certainty* can, if supported by the other grounds that define verbal contracts, bind the speaker to his later dissatisfaction. Short notes or exchanges of communication that one side assumes are simply *preliminary* and can be added together by the other side to make a binding agreement if the decision-maker finds the pattern of behavior coupled with industry practices to create a contract out of these incidental memoranda. In short, the Developer of an AI or ES should recognize that these relatively novel and complex wares deserve the protection afforded by the contracting process and a written expression of their agreement. A major portion of such contracts could be the definition and apportionment of liabilities, depending upon the particulars for that agreement.

Contracts are an excellent way to apportion rewards and responsibilities. Their role is improved if the contracting parties actively secure the final agreement. This is true not only because this reduces the risk of an *end-run* around the contract by an assertion that it was a contract of adhesion, but also because the process of considering and apportioning the potential risks sensitizes the parties to the potential dangers and encourages creating methods of constraining or limiting their exposure to them. The best contracting process will go as far to develop methods for reducing the cost of subsequent disagreements, or even complete failure, to both parties' advantage, since the parties will have become somewhat adjusted to the problems of reducing complex and unknowable potential concerns to present-day terms. Drafting a contract offers the opportunity to educate all persons involved about the processes involved in bringing technical details and human concerns before the law. In the event the contract must be called upon to help resolve disputes, the parties probably will have to educate the decision-maker; and in that case, they can call upon the knowledge gained and definitions attained (and discarded) during the process of drafting the contract. The parties have the right to demand that the language used be clear and not crafted out of boilerplating; the drafters have a right to insist that the hard decisions prerequisite for clarity be made. The drafter(s) of the contracts should be at least familiar with the subject-matter covered by the contract.

After the crucial and requisite elements—stating the parties to the contract, the elements of the bargain recorded (the consideration), and the date(s) of the contract—have been hammered out, the drafter and parties should address these seven principal concerns: (1) the measure of Performance (and partial performance); (2) the inclusion or exoneration of Consequential damages; (3) the definition of incidental damages; (4) the terms or limitations of Warranty; (5) the necessity (or lack thereof) and definition, of Mitigation; (6) the existence and grounds for, or lack of access to, Arbitration or other alternatives to expensive and risky litigation for resolving contractual disputes; and (7) delimitation of the operating environment for the application: for an Expert System, its domain of knowledge or model; for an Artificial Intelligence, the fractional subset of the world and the modes and limits of perception it is devised to handle. This last step is crucial, for it draws a circle around the limits of performance beyond which the Developer makes no claim of dependability or safe use, leaving those interactions subject to the intervening human judgement of those who come in contact with the application.

Of course, there are risks and problems which either cannot be prevented by a contract or that can overcome the protection of a contract, and these are discussed in the next two sections. Yet the lack of perfect behavior should not be seen as unanswerable argument against using the contractual process. Just as AI and ES applications are used because the benefits available through an imperfectible medium outweigh the alternative, perhaps unavailable approaches, the effort and expense of drafting a contract immeasurably outweigh the potentially devastating costs of not doing so. The purpose of contracts is not to avoid lawyers and courts entirely; it is to avoid being forced to use them at another's terms and timing and to avoid having to rapidly educate attorneys and judges who may know nothing of the subject matter as well as nothing of the Developer, which is the most expensive way to have Artificial Intelligence confront the law, since the Developer has to pay for all the mistakes made in haste and panic, and there is little chance to coordinate the normal business demands with those imposed by litigation.

15.2.2 Indirectly Imposing Liability Through Legal Norms

Modern courts have not been reluctant to look beyond the actual *boiler-plated* terms of standard written contracts and to include additional clauses which, though absent, reflect the societal context and concerns in which the parties operated. Too harsh an exemption, too curt a contract, too narrow a limitation, and courts and juries can decide to add liability to the extent that they deem *just*. Four general approaches support these efforts: (1) Implied Warranties; (2) the doctrine of Unconscionability; (3) the implied covenant of *Good Faith*; and (4) Equitable Estoppel for known flaws. Implied Warranties: Implied Warranties are just what the name suggests: warranties which are implied contractual provisions by law whether or not they are in the contract, and sometimes in spite of the fact that they are expressly denied in the contract. The general nature of such warranties applies to *merchantability* and *fitness* of the product underlying the contract, i.e. that the product was salable and not damaged or flawed, and that the product would serve the purpose for which it was designed.

The basis for implied warranties lies in both Federal and State legislation, while the nature and extent of the implied terms develop on a case-by-case basis. In 1975 the Magnuson–Moss Warranty Federal Trade Commission Improvement Act (Pub.L.No.93-637,88 Stat.2183;1974) came into force. Its provisions are generally more generous to Buyers than the U.C.C.; however, its effect is limited to *consumer products* [15 U.S.C. §2301(1) (1982)]. The provisions of this act apply to products that are both *consumer* and *commercial* in nature, for the presumption is to imply coverage [16 C.F.R. §700.1(a) (1984)] and provide for dual jurisdiction, but access to Federal courts is limited to situations where $50 000 or more is at issue [15 U.S.C. §2310(d)(1), 15 U.S.C. §2310(d)(3)]. A disclaimer or refusal to make any warranty whatsoever can potentially remove a product from coverage under this Act. At least nine States—Alabama, California, Kansas, Maine, Massachusetts, Minnesota, Mississippi, Vermont, Washington, and West Virginia —have enacted additional legislation (permitted by the Magnuson–Moss Act), thus further extending limits on disclaimers and modifications of warranties (Schneider, 1985). Both the Federal and State statutes are principally directed towards the consumer, that is, mass-marketed goods where there is a substantial disparity in knowledge and bargaining power between the parties. The process of negotiating a contract with specific terms concerning the reliability and methodology for measuring success or failure goes very far indeed towards establishing that an AI or ES is the focus of a *commercial* transaction, thus avoiding the impetus of these statutes. Terms of particular use for an Expert System would refer to the limits of interaction between the application and the user during a consultation and the accessibility (or lack thereof) to the person consulting the system to both the reasoning steps and the grounds for their inclusion (or exclusion), i.e. to the underlying warrant for the particular steps taken as the application moves along. Terms of particular use for an Artificial Intelligence would refer to the limits of perception and integration of the perceptions into the reasoning process of the Artificial Intelligence, as well as a clear statement of what the presumed subset of the real world the application is intended to comprehend.

Unconscionability: This doctrine is introduced by the Universal Commercial Code [U.C.C. §2-302(1); see Cal. Civil Code §1670.5 for a comparable state section] relating to transactions for the *sale of goods*. There is considerable doubt that any AI or ES program at present could be considered to be a commodity; indeed, at this time traditional, algorithmic programs are barely considered to be *goods*, though this is rapidly changing for off-the-shelf or mass-market programs. Courts considering this point will look to specific factual circumstances as well as the nature of the social and commercial environment at the time that the contract was formed, and courts will take note of the rapidity of change. In 1970, in Computer Service Centers, Inc. v. Beacon Manufacturing Company, 328 F.Supp. 653 (D.S.C. 1970), one court declined to find that a contract for data processing covered *services* and not *goods*; less than eight years later, in Triangle Underwriters, Inc.v. Honeywell, Inc. 457 F.Supp. 765 (E.D.N.Y. 1978), another court in a more sophisticated commercial environment found that a contract for a computer system (including both hardware and software prepared for the plaintiff by the defendant) was such that the computer program was a *good*:

> Although the ideas or concepts involved in the custom designed software remained Honeywell's intellectual property, Triangle was purchasing the product of those concepts. That product required efforts to produce, but it was a product nevertheless and, though intangible, is more readily characterized as *goods* than *services*. Intangibles may be *goods* within the meaning of U.C.C. (EDNY, 1987, p.769).

At present, it is uncertain whether a court would find any AI or ES application—and more particularly, its actions or results—to be a *good* under the U.C.C. Given the rapidity of development and the introduction of *expert-off-the-shelf* programs forthcoming, though, this limitation will soon fall. The question then becomes whether any contractual provision would be found to be unenforceable as *unconscionable*.

The effect of unconscionability is defined in U.C.C. §2-302:

> If the court as a matter of law finds the contract or any clause of the contract to have been unconscionable at the time it was made the court may refuse to enforce the contract, or it may enforce the remainder of the contract without the unconscionable clause, or it may so limit the application of any unconscionable clause as to avoid an unconscionable result.

But the definition of what is, or is not, unconscionable in a contract is left for a case-by-case determination. Again, the very act of mutually determining the limitations or restrictions of liability (rather than having them imposed unilaterally by the Developer), and a methodology for evaluating failures in these necessarily imperfect AI and ES programs, goes far to negate or inhibit any allegation of *unconscionability*. If the Developer of an ES application should state that it is intended solely as a tool to assist a professional and not to supplant his practice, it would not be unconscionable to prevent a recovery based on *unconscionability* for inadequately advising a layman unable to bring equally expert judgement and analysis to weigh the quality or limitations of the application. If the Developer of an AI application should state that it is not capable of distinguishing between authorized and unauthorized personnel, it would prevent a recovery based on *unconscionability* for injuring an unsuspecting trespasser into an automated factory.

Good Faith: In Communale v. Traders & General Insurance Co. 50 Cal. 2d 654[328 P.2d 198,68 A.L.R.2d883], (Sup. Ct,Cal.,1958) the California Court expounded a duty, the breach of which sounds in both contract and tort, imposed by an implied covenant of good faith and fair dealing in every contract (including insurance policies) that neither party will do anything which will injure the right of the other to receive the *benefits of the agreement*. While this concept was originally devised for insurance contracts—which are typically contracts of adhesion where a Buyer has no choice of clauses other than term and price—recently courts have been urged to extend them to banking and other industries. Again, the process of negotiating a specific contract significantly defuses this potential allegation.

Equitable Estoppel: Companies using AI or ES applications which have known limitations, that have not established sound policies for assuring that the gaps are examined, should be wary of another problem—the very provision of an allegedly flawed *tool* could leave them holding the bag when the AI or ES fails to reach a goal or result desired by the Buyer and the latter fails to pay for the program (or for further services). The doctrine known as *equitable estoppel* has been successfully invoked against an airline to prevent it from recovering from a traveler who had received a trip far beyond that which he had actually paid for, due to a flaw in its ticketing system, in Swiss Air Transport Company v. Benn 467 N.Y.S. 2d 341, 121 Misc.2d 129 (Ct. App. N.Y., 1983). This doctrine could be extended to the situation where a vendor of an AI product fails to reveal to its customers known flaws and methods to avoid or recognize potentially disastrous errors before the consequential damage ensues. Some of the actions taken to minimize this risk and to mitigate the potential exposure to, or the cost of, disasters are discussed below. The basic estoppel would arise where the Developer fails to state to the Buyer the nature and extent of the model in which the ES operates, or the nature and limitations of the perceptions used by the AI application.

All of the approaches to subvert the terms of the contract are substantially weakened whenever the parties used a negotiated, rather than a standardized, written contract. Since the nature of both AI and ES programs is such that failure to reach a desired conclusion, or failure to reach a *perfect* solution is inevitable, Developers should try to educate their customer about this inherent limitation, to devise methods of recognizing and mitigating the effect when the program is running, and to contractually provide for the methods to evaluate the relative success of the program. While including a well-drafted disclaimer for any failure may prevent statutory imposition of implied warranties, it will not prevent a court from finding alternative grounds for imposing liability if the context of the agreement was such as to contribute to the detriment of the Buyer, and the failure of the AI or ES was so basic or preventable that the court cannot, in justice, uphold the stark written terms. Moreover, in such circumstances the court may be more open to accusations which by their nature void not merely a particular term of the contract (while leaving other terms, such as those limiting damages or defining actions by the Buyer necessary to mitigate the extent of harm), but the contract as a whole. These contract-avoiding grounds for imposing liability are discussed in the next section.

15.2.3 Redirecting Apportionment of Liability In Spite of A Contract

Two legal theories hold sway in this area:(1) Fraud, and (2) Misrepresentation. The principal distinction between the two is not the extent of the missing information as much as it is the active nature of the hoaxing effect which was intended; fraud is deliberate falsification, while misrepresentation is mental misdirection, or the intended or even inadvertent omission of needed facts. Both fraud and misrepresentation can give rise to actions that lie in tort as well as in contract, leaving the door open for the potential for punitive damages—though this is difficult to establish when the misrepresentation is negligent rather than deliberate, as punitive damages generally rest on an intent to harm. Active intent may not be necessary; the phraseology differs from case to case, as no perfect formula has been found. Courts have been willing to allow punitive damages when the harm results from actions where the defendant *ought to have known better. Grossly negligent* or *Conscious disregard of risk* have been two of the phrases used in California; the characterization of conduct that will give rise to punitive damages is part of the skill of a plaintiff's counsel.

Fraud: The most potent counter to a contract is, naturally enough, fraud. If a Buyer can establish that the Seller committed fraud when the contract was being signed, then the contract can be eliminated—since it obviously does not cover the actualities of the bargain. Fraud, a charge that is difficult to establish, requires many particular points in order to be proven. (Eleven in Minnesota: 1. There must be a representation; 2. That representation must be false; 3. It must have to do with a past or present fact; 4. That fact must be material; 5. It must be susceptible of knowledge; 6. The representor must know it to be false, or in the alternative, must assert it as of his own knowledge without knowing whether it is true or false; 7. The representor must intend to have the other person induced to act, or justified in acting upon it; 8. That person must be so induced to act or so justified in acting; 9. That person's action must be in reliance upon the representation; 10. That the person must suffer damage, and 11. That damage must be attributable to the misrepresentation, that is, the statement must be the proximate cause of the injury. Davis v. Re-Trac Mfg. Corp. 276 Minn. 116, 149 N.W.2d 37 (1967); Hanson v. Ford Motor Co. 278 F.2d 586 (8th Cir. 1960); Clements v. Service Bureau Corporation, supra. (In California and other states, the number of specific elements varies but the basic concept and structure remain the same.) Yet for all the difficulty, the effect of a fraud count being sustained is so great— punitive damages are much more likely to be assessed—that efforts should be made to avoid any realistic possibility of its being found. This is an area where defensive practices should be enforced and accountability between the point of contact with the Buyer (the salesperson for the Developer) and corporate management should be constantly reviewed and, if necessary, strengthened.

Fraud requires that the Seller intentionally deceive the Buyer. Because of its inchoate nature, intent is the point an injured Buyer has the most difficulty in proving. A Developer who maintains an adequate paper trail of negotiations, including statements made to the Buyer and responses to inquiries from the Buyer, has a better chance of disproving an allegation of fraud than one who does not. When a documented trail leading up to the contract exists, there is not only a greater ability to nip any mistakes or overly exaggerated claims before the contract is signed, or to reprove and correct the sales person's error in judgement when the desire to *land* the sale outreaches the mandate to make correct statements about the capabilities (and limitations) of the product, but also a clear and convincing, well-supported disproof of fraudulent intent. This supporting trail, no less than the contract itself, must be clear of fraud and exaggerated claims. In Clements Auto Co. v. The Service Bureau, 298 F.Supp. 115 (D. Minn, 1969), at least two secondary elements to the contracting process helped to establish the defendant's liability under a fraud theory. Not only had the descriptive papers for an automated inventory control program described it as one that will provide iron-clad controls to ensure *accurate reports,* but also the defendant company had held itself out to be an expert in the field, a subsidiary of *IBM.* Neither of these phrases was contained in the contract between two sophisticated businesses, but the court found that they supported the claim of fraud and awarded major damages. There has been a great deal of *hype* concerning the potency of AI and ES applications; Developers would be wise to consider that any dubious or questionable claims for performance on the part of their applications may be grounds for a later claim of fraud or misrepresentation.

In addition to showing fraudulent intent on the part of the Developer, the Buyer must show also that his prospective reliance upon the false statements was known to the Developer. Here again, the use of a paper trail to defuse claims is recommended. General claims of reliance are not enough; courts, in an effort to control otherwise easy allegations, demand specific details—if not in the pleadings, at least at the trial. Recording and clarifying the demands or assumptions made by the Buyer—and issuing warnings if these are excessively optimistic or unreasonable—will negate this element of a fraud claim.

Misrepresentation: A lesser *cousin* of fraud is Misrepresentation; the distinction lies in the active or passive element of deceit. Statements or assurances made without support, when the vendor should have known better, can form the grounds for this type of action. The Developer should keep in mind that he may bear the liability for any mistaken assertion about the core qualities and behavior of his AI or ES application. The recommended practice is to confirm verbal assertions made to a potential Buyer with written details—an amazing amount of overstatement can be controlled by a simple insistence that the details and comments be put into writings available to the other party. This way, corrections of overstatements can be on record before any agreement is reached or contract is signed.

The courts do draw a distinction between *puffing* and *misrepresentation.* Broad claims aimed at an entire marketplace, or praise for a product which obviously represent an opinion rather than an assertion of fact, will not be grounds for an allegation of misrepresentation. Developers should be particularly wary here, however, inasmuch as there is a wide-spread perception of *hype* for AI and ES applications having gone beyond the bounds of reasonableness. Certainly, any claim for *human* quality behavior or judgement should rapidly be scotched.

The crucial concern in either a *fraud* or *misrepresentation* action—and therefore, in creating an enforcing behavior designed to defuse such allegations *ab initio*, is that unlike simple breach of contract claims, these two allegations can give rise to claims for punitive damages. Not only does the amount of possible loss mount, but also the amount which will be absorbed by the Developer directly increases dramatically, for punitive damages are not covered by insurance; in the next section, which discusses the claims which may be brought by third parties, this will be a constant cloud hovering over the Developers' heads—if the failure of, or damage wrought by, their AI or ES application is such that a third party suffers grievously, the Developer may suddenly be facing a multi-million dollar damage claim.

15.3 DEVELOPERS' LIABILITY TO THIRD PARTIES

Privity (limiting claims to the parties involved in a contract) is not entirely dead in the law—yet. Courts are increasingly willing to let persons who have dealt with the second party (the Buyer), and have been injured by a product sold by the Developer, recover directly from the Developer. Three legal theories which can support a Third Party's claim for recovery from the Developer(s) of an AI or ES application are (1) Products Liability, (2) Malpractice, and (3) Negligence.

15.3.1 Products Liability

There are many elements to any product liability for cause of action. Four, in particular, will stand out for any AI or ES application: (1) whether the application was a product or an artifact, (2) whether the plaintiff was engaged in a reasonable *use* of the product, (3) whether the product was substantially altered by the plaintiff, and (4) whether the inherent nature of Artificial Intelligence prohibits any claim for that specific injury. Taking these in turn: Was the Application a Product or Artifact? One requirement for a products liability claim is that the item used be a commercial product rather than an individually crafted artifact. This distinction barred the plaintiff's claim in LaRossa v. Scientific Design Company, Inc. 402 F.2d 937 (3d Cir. 1968), where the court based its decision on the failure of any defect to have any impact upon the public at large, and the fact that a policy reason to give rise to products liability did not exist. There is a difficulty, to the consumer, in tracing the producer–wholesaler–retailer chain. A products liability claim arises only when an element of *mass-production* has entered into the equation. Products, which are defined in their normative environments, can range from mass-produced homes [Shipper v.

Levitt & Sons, Inc., 207 A.2d 314 (New Jersey, 1965)] to water [Moody v. City of Galveston, 524 S.W. 2d 583 (Ct. App. TX, 1975)] to even electricity [Ransome v. Wisconsin Electric Power, 275 N.W.2d 641 (Sup. Ct. Wis, 1979)]. At present, AI and ES applications would be classified as *artifacts*; however, the increase of *off-the-shelf* expertise will soon see this change. An additional problem, which arises with *learning* AI systems, is discussed in the second following subsection.

Was the Use Reasonable? Courts do not look to the dictionary meaning of the word *product*, but rather, as was stated in Fluor Corp. v. Jeppesen, 170 CA 3d. 468 (Ct. App. CA, 1985), following Lowrie v. City of Evanston, 365 N.E.2d 923 (1977), they consider the item which caused the harm within the meaning of its *use*. For an AI or ES application, the Developer should establish to the court that the hardware and software environment, and the purpose of the Third Party, determines the meaning of *use*. A spreadsheet is a number-juggling product, a calendaring accessory handles dates—but both are ignorant of the *meaning* or significance of their actions. Thus an asset-valuation spreadsheet, used to draft a construction-contract bid, could not be counted on to know which elements of a bid are crucial and must be included; a legal scheduler should recognize the importance of a 71-year old party and a C.C.P §583 motion date only in California. If either were taken outside of that particular environment, the failure would be the result of that action and not the effect of any defect in the product.

What is crucial is the environment envisioned for the AI or ES—if the outputs or actions were taken by the Third Party outside the appropriate environment, then the designation of the *product* will fail and this will cause the action of collapse. The defense will attempt to establish that the plaintiff was using, or interpreting, the program outside of the environment for which it was designed. This doctrine of reasonable *use* is established in products-liability law and lends itself readily to adaptation in these new fields. Developers who limit these assumptions and express them explicitly will be far more secure against wide-ranging liability than those who never examine the underlying basis of their applications. In Arkansas, the Courts have recognized that a computer program's environment can be a deciding factor. In each of two contrasting cases, the program's output was ostensibly usurious (the face interest rate was 10%, but the computed rate was illegally higher); but the court looked to the corporate environment to determine the presence or absence of any *intent* to commit usury. In Cagle v. Boyle Mortgage Co., 549 S.W.2d 474 (Sup. Ct. Ark. 1977) the court concluded that since the defendant had extensive business and prior loans in Arkansas, and thus knew of the illegality of interest over 10%, they had committed usury; subsequently, in First American National Bank of Nashville, Tennessee v. McClure Construction Co. 581 S.W.2d 550,

(Sup. Ct. Ark., 1979), the court concluded that the defendant's scant contact with the single loan in Arkansas did not count as *intent* and therefore defendants had not committed usury.

Depending on an ES application to reason about matters not considered in its model, or to automatically include knowledge uncovered after its creation which has not yet been incorporated, would be expecting unreasonably perfect behavior. Depending on an AI application to perceive changes and reason about their impact using senses not included in the application would similarly fail. The key for a Developer would be to point to an unreasonable expectation of human adaptability and flexibility from machinery and software which basically *doesn't care*; the applications will do exactly what they are programmed to do, with the absence of common sense or concern for self-(or other-) preservation.

Was the AI or ES application substantially altered? Liability for a product exists whenever someone other than the Developer substantially alters that product; the intervening act will break the chain of liability. If the Developer sells tools, that is, an AI language or an ES shell, rather than finished applications, products liability would not apply to the programs created by these tools. They would be subject to liability only if the plaintiff had sought a tool to build an application and claimed that tool was inadequate; Greenman v. Yuba Power Co. 59 Cal.2d 57 (Sup. Ct. Cal., 1963) which discusses this point in some detail, involved a suit over a lathe lacking a proper fastening device. But that question is beyond the scope of the present discussion. At present, with most Developers selling shells and services rather than *off-the-shelf* systems, the process of creating the application counts as substantial alteration. There is a balance of expertise involved; while the maker of the shell has computer expertise, the purchaser (and joint developer) of the application has the specialized information which goes into the *knowledge base*. Right now AI and ES applications face a *bottleneck* in the lack of what are termed knowledge *engineers*, i.e. individuals trained in the design and production of AI or ES programs who are also capable of learning (or already have some knowledge of) the application discipline; this gap exists because of the need for human problem-solving capability and creativity, elements which negate the chain of causation in a products liability suit. The AI community is doing research in the automation of the transfer of knowledge as a general solution, but there have been no breakthroughs yet. Part of the problem lies in the difficulty inherent in transferring not just facts and data, but patterns of thought or the heuristics used in the field—which are simply incomprehensible to the average layperson.

Once an AI or ES program is sold that is capable of *learning* or changing its own environment or knowledge base, there arises such great scope for substantial *alteration* dependent upon the inputs and actions of Third Parties that this defense would most likely succeed. There are no cases on this topic, however, making prediction very tenuous; *learning* and the automated transfer of expertise are still very hot AI research issues.

Was the Artificial Intelligence defective or imperfect? If the nature of the domain in which the AI or ES operates is necessarily imperfect or uncertain just as the plaintiff could not recover because her VW Bus had no front end to collapse in Dreidonstok v. Volkswagen, 489 F.2d 1066 (4th Cir. 1974), the Third Party could not recover because the application acted imperfectly. If an AI or ES application performs the *wrong* action or reaches the *wrong* answer this may not be enough to establish that it is defective; it may very well be part of what the user has purchased. If the application is coping with an unpredictable, imperfect, or uncertain environment, then these results may be an *accurate* consequence.

If the buyer purchased the application, and the Third Party agreed to its use, because it was the best tool available—whether it was usually capable of producing better answers much more quickly than an algorithmic program, or capable of answering problems that an algorithmic problem could not resolve, or cheaper than using human expertise—they may not be able to recover for its lapses; they have traded speed for certainty, completeness for flexibility, or a user-friendly interface for less-competent reasoning. The question here is *What did the user pay for?* In Seattle-First National Bank v. Volkswagen, 542 P.2d 774 (Sup. Ct. WA, 1975), the court noted that the purchaser of a Volkswagen cannot reasonably expect the same degree of safety as would the buyer of the much more expensive *Cadillac.* An AI or ES program is probably more expensive than a single application of human expertise—even at today's prices—but it is an application that is designed to handle consistently difficult, and probably unverifiable, domains wherein the human resources may not be available or are too expensive for the Third Party's tastes. What he is not getting, and probably cannot get, is an algorithmically, *logically sound* program guaranteed of success. An ES application with today's rules and knowledge built in will fail every time a basic conceptual redefinition occurs; an AI application, equipped with a limited planning capacity, will not always find the optimal solution. What the user can count on is that the AI or ES application should meet the design criteria specified by the developer—i.e. if he states that the reasoning method is guaranteed to be *complete* and *correct*, then he knows that if a positive answer exists, he will find it in a delimitable amount of time, and that no inconsistencies will be introduced. He can also expect that the application will measure up to the industry standard which existed at the time of the program's creation, just as with any other product, as was stated in Ward v. Hobart Manufacturing Co., 450 F.2d 1176 (5th Cir., 1971).

At present, the most likely approach to any cause of action for products *liability* would invoke the doctrine stated in Comment K to §402(a) of the Restatement of Torts (2d):

> There are some products which, in the present state of human knowledge, are incapable of being made safe for intended and ordinary use ... Such a product, properly prepared, and accompanied by proper direction and warning, is not defective, nor is it unreasonably dangerous.

Yet this approach is not guaranteed to succeed. The AI community has already begun actively debating rules and techniques for software engineering and arguing towards minimal standards for any AI or ES application. Among the fruits of the first research phase embodied in MYCIN, PUFF, DENDRAL, and other applications, are insights into the need to consider human interaction, accessibility to the reasoning, support for that reasoning, and the design, construction, and evaluation methodologies for AI and ES applications (Jacob and Froscher, 1986; Greene, 1987). Nor will the defense that the AI or ES application used techniques standard in the *industry* always prove to be an adequate defense; if better techniques become possible, Developers will eventually be forced to use them. This rule was first enunciated in The T.J. Hooper, 60 F.2d 737 (2d Cir., 1932) and is discussed in the next section, since it may require professionals to develop and use AI or ES programs.

In summation, the individually crafted nature of present-day AI and ES applications would definitely bar a cause of action for products liability. Even when *off-the-shelf* applications become available, Developers can negate such a claim by establishing that the Third Party was injured by a use outside the environment and context assumed for the application, i.e. that the use was not *reasonable*. Plaintiffs and defendants will contest whether or not the domain of the application was such that imperfection was inevitable, and whether the techniques and methodologies used by the defendants were up to the standards of the profession at the time that the application was devised.

15.3.2 Malpractice

Computer programmers, at present, are not considered *professionals*—at least as far as the Federal Government's labor laws are concerned. Pezillo v. GTE, 414 F.Supp. 1257 (M.D. Tenn., 1976), interpreted the definition of *professionals* for whom overtime pay was not required found in 38 C.F.R. §541.302(h), Fed. Reg. Vol. 36, No.232, Dec.2, 1971, as excluding programmers precisely because they were not definable as professionals. In Triangle Underwriters, supra, the court, which was asked to create a new cause of action for computer *malpractice*, declined. This disinclination was demonstrated again three months later in Chatlos Systems Inc. v. National Cash Register Corporation, 479 F.Supp. 738 (D.C. N.J., 1979) where the court stated:

> The novel concept of a new tort called *computer malpractice* is premised upon a theory of elevated responsibility on the part of those who render computer

sales and service. Plaintiff equates the sale and servicing of computer systems with established theories of professional malpractice. Simply because an activity is technically complex and important in the business community does not mean that greater potential liability must attach. In the absence of sound precedential authority, the Court declines the invitation to create a new tort.

The difficulty will arise with the introduction of Expert Systems. (Artificial Intelligences are not considered to be even remotely close to the approaching normal, let alone expert, human in general.) Expert implies a higher standard of behavior—though it is also possible to call any program that provides expertise in the form of knowledge to a user an *Expert System*, that connotation would not be supported by a majority of the practitioners in the field. An informal survey was conducted over the national electronic Arpanet network in November, 1987; 1700 users of Expert System development shells in over 179 firms responded, identifying 160 distinct application areas. These programs' tasks ranged from *Account Business Assessment* to *When to Perform a Physical Audit*, in fields from Agriculture to Zoology. Since malpractice is a theory created by statute establishing a profession, and the profession must in turn establish minimal standards of behavior, one analyst has concluded that in the absence of any statutory support recognizing the *professional* status of the knowledge provider no cause of action for Malpractice could be extended (Christo, 1983).

The previous paragraph is scant cover, however. The programmers may not qualify as professionals—but the knowledge providers might. If the accountant who helped prepare the expert system is liable for such an answer, should he be exempted because the program did the work? If they, as individuals, are subject to malpractice claims, then there is at least the hazard that this exposure could be transmitted along with their knowledge. When an Expert System can be measured against the performance of experts in the domain and not found wanting, can the acknowledged professionals' liability be spread? Perhaps, but several substantial obstacles intervene.

First and foremost is the *idiot savant* nature of the Expert System. Too few meet the requirement stated by one noted practitioner that they *degrade gracefully* as they reach the edge of their expertise, or are applied to questions lying at the edge of the model in which they were designed to operate (Buchanan, 1985). A corporate financial advisory program may assume that all of the individuals to whom payments are made are either employees or vendors, using a *Closed-World Assumption* reasoning style (Reiter, 1982), and thus subject the company to liability for fines and penalties for inadequately handling computer consultants as employees for whom benefits must be paid as required by the IRS, simply because it was not intended to work as a tax advisor. The limitation of an Expert System to a probable subset of the domain in which the professional would be expected to act would most likely keep it from independently qualifying as a *professional*. Should that limitation keep a claim from malpractice away when a Third Party, who is unable to judge the success or failure of the *expert*, is injured? If the Expert System would not have qualified from the start as a professional, how can the standards of that profession be applied—which is the core of the malpractice doctrine.

Second is the *combined effort* nature of most Expert Systems. A great many problems arise from the incomplete coordination between the programmers and the experts. Gaps in the reasoning will be left simply because one side does not know enough about the other's domain to ask relevant questions or provide default reasoning procedures; thus, a medical expert system may attempt to diagnose a dead patient, simply because the programmers assumed the doctors could recognize the situation and the doctors never dreamed that such a basic rule would have to be included in the computer's knowledge base. In the event of failure the Third Party will have been injured by a lack for which the programmers/professionals bear as much (or as little) responsibility as he does, since they are expert in only one of the combined fields and laymen in the other, and are unable to judge the correctness or completeness of the other sides' contribution.

Third is the limited interaction inherent in any Expert System. Unlike human experts, the applications have almost no flexibility or capability of recognizing the success or failure at communicating the results to the Third Party.

Fourth is the limited ability to assess the correctness of the inputs given by the Third Party. Professionals are used to the fact that people lie, or conceal their principal interests, or have *blank spots* due to human limitations.

All of the above outline potential objections to a blanket imposition of liability based on professional standards simply because the knowledge-provider was subject to professional liability. There are far too many barriers in the transmission of knowledge between the application and the Third Party user to hold much hope that a cause of action for malpractice on the part of an Expert System would be sustainable.

Barely visible on the horizon, however, lies the day when a professional practicing without Expert System assistance will be found liable for malpractice (Willick, 1985). Several medical programs have already been measured—in their specific sub-domain of application, to be sure—against human performance and have proven to be more than adequately competent. Expert Systems offer a great increase in dependability in performing necessary but repetitive tasks or examining the *checklists* of alternatives, even though they may lack the human capacity for intuitive leaps or successfully creative problem-solving. In Golden-Eagle Distributing Corp. v. Burroughs Corp., 40 Fed.R.Serv.2d 346 (N.D. Cal, 1984) a court awarded sanctions against a law firm based in part on the failure to use LEXIS, a legal database service. (The utility and desirability of computer tools in the legal profession is also mentioned in Karl C. Wehr v. The Burroughs Corp., 619 F.2d 276 (3rd Cir. 1980); Cannon v. U.S. District Court, 564 F.Supp. 581 (D. RI, 1981).) The need to examine all possible concerns with a knowledge-supporting tool is a predictable outgrowth of the professional's *duty to warn*; how long will it be before a court finds that a physician who failed to consult a pharmaceutical-interaction advisory program is liable for malpractice when such an action would have warned against the fatal mixing of two new prescriptions (Willick, 1985)?

Courts need not wait for the professions to decide to use AI or ES tools in their practice; when development of new tools for ensuring increased safety to Third Parties has passed the experimental stage, the court can independently determine the applicability of the standard as a whole, as announced in The T.J. Hooper, supra. In Helling v. Carey, 519 P.2d 981 (Sup. Ct. WA, 1974), the Supreme Court of Washington upheld a cause of action for malpractice despite the fact that the defendant's heuristic (never testing for glaucoma if the patient is under 40 years old) was universally agreed to as the standard of his profession.

However, professionals may find themselves in a bind, particularly when the action or advice preferred by the AI or ES differs from that of their own choice. Defendants will not be able to rely solely on the fact that the *computer said so*; this line of defense was overruled by the court in Ford Motor Credit Corp. v. Swarens, 447 S.W.2d 53(Ct.App.KY,1969). Abdication of human decision-making led to an imposition of an injunction in Palmer v. Columbia Gas Co. of Ohio, 342 F. Supp.241(N.D. Ohio, 1972); see also Foggs v. Block, 722 F.2d 933 (1983). The existence, or the lack thereof, of human intervention has determined the issue of liability for unreasonable termination of disability checks in two Louisiana cases. In the first, Fredricks v. Associated Indemnity Corp., 401 So. 2d 575 (Ct.App. LA, 1981), the defendant had the opportunity to impose a human judgement, and declining to do so, was found liable, while in the second, McMillan v. Fireman's Fund, 448 So. 2d 575 (Ct. App. LA, 1984), the defendant had no opportunity to impose human judgement—and liability could not rest alone on *computer error*. A similar distinction explains the difference in results between Travelers Indemnity Co. v. Fields, 317 N.W.2d 176 (Sup. Ct. Iowa, 1982) and State Farm Mutual Insurance Co. v. Bockhorst, 453 F.2d 533 (10th Cir. 1977)—when there existed an opportunity for human intervention, failure to take it created liability. This duty applies even for the professionals, though they are not necessarily held to the standard of the *higher* expert, i.e. the application working within its presumed domain.

I suggest that the analysis used in the above cited cases, and others, which follows traditional reasoning or the existence (or absence) of a *declared profession* will not be as useful as that used by the court in Johnson v. Sears Roebuck & Co. 355 F.Supp 1065 (E.D. Wisc. 1973). In that case, the court did not disallow strict liability for the professional medical services provided by the hospital when defective, but non-negligent services had been alleged. The court noted that the hospital's service fell into two different categories:

The first consists of professional medical services and the second is made up of those mechanical and administrative services which support the first.

When the grounds for differing from the action or advice of the AI or ES arise from mechanical and *administrative* reasoning, rather than those requiring creative human judgement, interpretation, or perception, or when the human ignores the computer advice based upon its particular expertise (in that limited domain), and it is superior to his own, then a cause of action for malpractice might be supportable. Plaintiffs and defendants both will examine closely the source of the error—whether it was caused by the program, the knowledge given to the program, the inputs made available, or the design which was used. When the means to prevent a like error is *mechanical*, i.e. it could be reduced to algorithmic, rather than heuristic, processing, or when the heuristic would be such that any member of the profession would agree to its *correctness*, then the failure of such a heuristic would give rise to liability under this cause of action.

15.3.3 Negligence

Negligence is the failure to meet the *standard of reasonableness* or of the duty to act with reasonable care; it is inevitably defined on a case-by-case basis and measured in the societal context of the action or inaction which led to an injury. Stating that *reasonableness* or *duty* will have to be defined on a case-by-case basis doesn't provide much guidance; so let me suggest three possible duties and how they ought to be examined with respect to AI and ES programs, subject to a general caveat: since generations of the best jurists have failed to come up with any definition or *test of reasonable* beyond putting the question to a finder of fact, it is unjust to expect the AI or ES application to know and thus act by a general definition of *reasonableness;* the evaluation must always be made by the humans contacting the application in its envisioned environment.

Duty to Supply Information with Reasonable Care: Either an AI or ES contains in-built knowledge, both in a declarative (what it knows) and procedural (what it knows to do) fashion. The Developer who put that information in is vending information. As such, he is subject to an adaptation of the theory stated in Section 552 of the Restatement of Torts, 2d:

Information Negligently Supplied for the Guidance of Others

One who, in the course of his business, profession, or employment, or in any other transaction in which he has a pecuniary interest, supplies false information for the guidance of others in their business transactions, is subject to liability for pecuniary loss caused to them by their justifiable reliance upon the information, if he fails to exercise reasonable care in obtaining or communicating that information.

The phrase *in the course of his business* was construed narrowly in Black, Jackson and Simmons Insurance Brokerage, Inc. v. IBM, 440 N.E.2d 282 (Ill., 1982). In that case IBM had provided both hardware and *internal software* to the plaintiff to allow the brokerage to process information. The court denied a cause of action for negligence based on §552, stating that the defendant had been *selling merchandise* rather than providing information to plaintiff to guide it with regard to its behavior towards others. Since the court left several other causes of action standing, and so was not cutting off the last chance for recovery, it may have felt there was no need to extend the coverage of the law.

Yet the general meaning of this section is visible in Independent School District No. 454, Fairmont, Minnesota v. Statistical Tabulating Company 359F. Supp. 1095 (N.D. Ill., 1973). In that case the court allowed a negligence action against a third-party service bureau who had provided incorrect calculations which had led to an under-insured loss when the school burned down. The court cited five factors to be considered:

(1) the existence, if any, of a guarantee of correctness,
(2) the defendant's knowledge that the plaintiff would rely on the information,
(3) the restriction of a potential liability to a small group,
(4) the absence of proof of any correction once found being delivered to plaintiff,
(5) the undesirability of requiring an innocent plaintiff to bear the loss,
(6) and the desirability of promoting cautionary techniques among the information providers.

Developers would do well to heed these factors while constructing their applications to avoid future problems.

There have been numerous cases involving the manufacturer of aviation maps have been either incorrect or potentially misleading and the flaw was a potential factor in the crash. See Aetna Casualty & Surety Co. v. Jeppesen, 642 F.2d 339 (9th Cir. 1981); Saloomey v. Jeppesen, 707 F.2d 671 (2d Cir. 1983); Fluor Corp. v. Jeppesen, 170 Cal. App.3d 468 (Ct. App. CA, 1985). The first case did not challenge the finding that the use of different scales on the same page was misleading, but reversed on the lack of comparative negligence findings; the last case stated that the defendant was liable for the inaccurate information despite the defendant's claim that it was required by law and the Federal Government to use the incorrect information provided by the Government on its charts. Both AI and ES applications must therefore be devised with a great deal of care towards the techniques whereby they communicate with people; the *user interface*, rather than being secondary to the interface engine, perceptual algorithms, or knowledge storage, may be the single most critical element. There is much room for maneuvering here—when did the developer provide *information* as opposed to a tool to manipulate the plaintiff's information? How well does the plaintiff meet the factors suggested by the court in Independent School District v. STC, supra? And when is the symbology, terms, or user-interface used by the program *misleading* as considered in Aetna v. Jeppesen, supra? These are factual questions for the specific cases, but at least the core theoretical approach can be perceived.

Duty to Circumscribe Inputs or User Behavior: In Neal v. U.S., 402 F.Supp.678 (D. N.J., 1975) the court not only took judicial notice of the *GIGO principle*, but also stated that there existed a duty to protect against spurious errors:

> The computer is a marvelous device that can perform countless tasks at high speed and low cost, but it must be used with care. That is because it can also make errors at high speed. (Ct. Fogg v. Block, supra)

Developers should particularly emphasize any flaw arising from a less-than-accurate input device and take due consideration for human engineering factors; the plaintiff, with little or no description of the program and lacking any warning of a weakness, may presume too much and recover not based on the flaw in the product but on the failure to warn against short-comings. In Kammer v. Lambs-Grays Harbor Co., 639 P.2d 649 (Ct.App. OR, 1982), the workmen in the automated factory had turned the computer off before going to deal with a problem, but the absence of a warning about static pressure in the hydraulic system supported a finding of negligence and thus of liability. The discussions in the software field focus on the availability, and applicability, of constraining inputs to those which are *reasonable* or *even possible*—and certainly this is the easiest type of mistake to bring to the awareness and comprehension of a court. Particularly, when the *core* inputs for either an AI or ES application are involved, developers should build in constraints to ensure some checking for *reasonableness*, and methods for coping with both the norm and the extremes (as well as the unbelievables).

Duty to Avoid Design Flaws: An AI or ES application's state of design will be measured against both (1) the state of the art at the time of design; Ward v. Hobart, 450 F.2d 1176 (5th Cir. 1971); Balido v. Melody Homes Manufacturer, 589 P.2d 896 (Ct.App. AZ, 1978), and (2) the reasonableness of the manufacturer's choices; Roach v. Kononen, 525 P.2d 125 (Sup. Ct. OR, 1974). A user may complain about the *choice of depth for look-ahead*, or the density of heuristics over *algorithmic search strategy* processes; but these may have been trade-offs chosen to emphasize performance given the limits of computing speed or memory availability. If a manufacturer trades *certainty* for the use of a *time-out* on the reasoning to avoid infinite loops or unanswerable questions, or to promote efficiency, then the marketplace at the time should determine *reasonableness*—as long as the potential user is made aware of the consequences of the trade, that the AI or ES is no longer guaranteed correct or complete.

Products Liability, Malpractice, Negligence—these are the most likely avenues by which liability would be assessed against the Developer(s) of AI or ES applications. Let us briefly examine some of the issues that can arise with regard to the division, the potential for rewards and risks among the Developers, and then move on to considerations on how to *defensively* work within this burgeoning field.

15.4 DIVIDING REWARDS AND RISKS AMONG THE CREATORS

When Doug Lenat's AM discovered two theorems previously unknown in set theory, it also established a point which had been debated beforehand: AI could create *new* knowledge, and many of the applications will focus on areas where that knowledge is extremely valuable. This raises the prospect of dispute over the ownership of that new knowledge, or, rather, over the returns to be reaped as a result of its discovery.

Originally, the focus in Artificial Intelligence research was to find and implement the powerful techniques which underlay human reasoning. Repeated failures at this led to a second approach, to incorporate specialized knowledge and use weak reasoning techniques. Limits too soon reached here have caused some critical researchers, particularly those struggling with the difficulty of defining *common sense*, to question whether it is the depth and variety of generalizable knowledge and of differing levels of reasoning that foster true human intelligence (Hayes, 1985).

AI and ES applications are rarely produced by a single individual, particularly those which are or will be commercial products. More common is teamwork between the programmers who implement the inferential engine and access to databases used by the product: the experts who provide their knowledge and critical facilities in correcting and refining the product, and the knowledge engineer(s) who work with both to meld the computer to the application domain. Thus, resolving who has claimed a discovery made by the final product is not going to be a simple process. If the application is in a domain that is traditionally the preserve of a recognized profession, there may exist artificial, i.e. statutory limitations on the ability of professionals to share the rewards from their practice with non-professionals.

The courts currently assume that the sensible approach will be to trace the reasoning process by which the new discovery was made, to identify the human efforts which shared in the activity, and thereby arrange the division of the spoils. Such an approach will prove inadequate, in fact, woefully so. Developers who proscribe a division of tasks while the application is built and record the efforts and successes of the individuals involved will find this approach more feasible than those who simply build an application. However, there is some suspicion that this task, like that of devising adequate documentation, would be one of the last and least focused upon by the Developers. Two further problems are to be considered.

First, the law may be mistaken in even presuming that it will be possible to trace the reasoning process back to the individuals who supplied the particular code for the procedural reasoning or information retrieval or back to the individuals who put the substantive knowledge or interface design to the AI or ES application. Mere difficulty is no barrier—at least to the legal theory—but many applications may lack that detailed history; while able to trace their reasoning, or even the source of their reasoning, they will not contain a record as to the supplier of that effort. When the AI or ES application reaches the level of sophistication where it is able to obtain more substantive information or revise its own reasoning processes —i.e., when it is capable of learning independently—this method collapses entirely.

Second, it may be impossible to retrace the reasoning to the original starting points. If the AI or ES application should use non-monotonic reasoning principles, or include heuristics which call for strictly random analysis and reasoning in the event of mental dead-ends, and lack a recording feature of all the intermediate steps considered and discarded (which would in volume far exceed the record of the successful trace), then the application could have gone through the mathematical equivalent of a one-way street, a unidirectional transform which cannot be accurately retraced. The mirror-image of the problem arises when considering how to allocate the risks among the creators, that is further complicated by legal distinctions that can be drawn between members of a profession and laypersons. Courts have been reluctant to extend liability from one technical profession to another even when the injured party has suffered from the join of both; in Magrine v. Krasnica, 227 A.2d 539 (Ct. App. N.J., 1967), the court declined to find a dentist strictly liable for an injury that arose from a hypodermic needle breaking off in his patient's jaw, pointing out that the dentist was not a metallurgist. If malpractice is the basis for reward to the injured party then the professional canons and statutes may forbid the imposition of any joint liability to non-professional co-workers.

Considering the chaos which might arise, and the inherent difficulties of proving ownership of the benefit or the risk to be reaped from an AI or ES application, the obvious solution is to have the Developers specifically state in a written agreement how unknown and potential future rewards and risks should be divided, with specific exclusions drawn for situations there are statutory reasons relating to professional canons. Specific clauses relating to the duties and limits on indemnity, both as to amounts and time during which any claim may be made, should be included.

There is a great challenge here for jurists and practitioners. There is also a great deal of money involved. Together they are a potentially explosive combination waiting for unwary Developers who fail to give adequate forethought and preparation to their products.

15.5   PREVENTIVE, MITIGATIVE, AND CURATIVE METHODOLOGIES FOR AI AND ES DEVELOPERS

Common sense and a feel for justice both indicate that a company which takes an active approach to finding, avoiding, and mitigating harm to its customers has far less exposure to catastrophic legal action by injured purchasers or third parties affected by the company's products or actions. The maxim *an ounce of prevention is worth a pound of cure* is supported by an examination of the legal awards and settlements in computer cases; a large portion of the financial and marketing trouble experienced by Burroughs in the mid- and late-70s was the bitter fruit of adopting an extremely hard line approach towards problems caused by its products during the previous decade. An *ostrich approach* provides only increased vulnerability.

Yet merely adducing that an active program to detect and resolve problems with an AI or ES application should be implemented is sufficient; policy statements must be supported by detailed activity on all levels. Successful programs for minimizing and resolving potentially costly disputes have involved the following: First, a corporation must internally acknowledge that the inevitable risks will result in a loss to either a purchaser or a third party. Careful drafting of this acknowledgment—which will inevitably be revealed if a dispute enters litigation—can diffuse claims for gross negligence or conscious disregard of possible danger or harm to customers or third parties, but only if coupled to further actions. The disadvantage of any increase in exposure to consequential damages is more than offset by the greatly decreased exposure to uninsurable punitive damages.

The acknowledgment of the potential for failure should lead to activities designed to constantly guard against such failure. Goals should be set for periodic review of preventative procedures. Boundaries of verifiably safe behavior (which may be very small), and the description of all environments, wherein successful operation to date have been recorded, should be identified and updated. This information should be transmitted to and from the developers and vendors of the AI or ES to limit overly expensive claims as well as to maximize the opportunity of identifying the *true source* of any error that may arise.

An active process to discover the unseen assumptions buried in an AI or ES should be included as part of the design and implementation. Odd as it may seem, some of the most fruitful development will result from the interaction between the novice users and the AI or ES. Blind spots yield most readily to this interaction; the chief trouble lies in progressively introducing new novices, for novices will become less useful as they adapt in marvelous human fashion to idiosyncrasies of the AI or ES. This exposure process works to produce benefits both ways: programmers need introduction to client behavior and expectations as well as clients to programmers' limitations. The insulation of developer from user leads to unrealizable expectations or mistaken evaluation of the cost of *minor* fixes; it also makes discovering the least-cost approach to resolving problems more difficult, if not impossible, to establish. Furthermore, by identifying and delimiting the base assumptions built into the AI or ES, the developer can apply estoppel against a purchaser for problems arising from a flaw in the assumptions, and can seek joint liability or indemnity for damage assessments by third parties whose contact lay solely with a purchaser who falsely described the product's potentialities.

Priorities for resolving problems must be established by agreement, rather than by a perceived arbitrary scheduling. Assurances that work is being done are not half as useful at preventing a final collapse as perception of the work. Since problems are apt to interrelate, and are also subject to the solution with unpredictable timing, establishing an agreed-on priority scheme is important. Then any solution that occurs *out of turn* is perceived as a mutually advantageous synergetic result, rather than as a sop thrown to the maltreated party. Establishing priorities also allows accurate internal evaluation (for all parties) of the costs and benefits of continued cooperation over divisive and unrewarding litigation. A measurement methodology and procedures for review and correction should be established. Using the developing techniques of software engineering safety—and studying this fast-changing field—provides a solid defense against claims of negligence, and thus minimizes the exposure to consequential damages.

The above preventative measures will not be enough; when a problem actually arises, proper curative procedures and techniques must be implemented. These ought to be in place and practiced before any problem arises, for the single most effective cost-minimizing technique is speed of response to a complaint—and that speed depends largely in part on the possession of the skills and knowledge on the part of the individuals who will have to respond. Firefighters practice, soldiers drill; analogously, corporate managers and troubleshooters should anticipate and practice for a problem with a customer.

Active maintenance of an AI or ES is the best source of such practice. Not only does the potential exposure for negligence drastically decrease, but also the exposure to extensive consequential damages is reduced—as long as the problems and solutions uncovered are communicated to the remainder of the corporation and to its customers. Short-term and short-sighted concerns over image may argue against such communication, but having an avoidable disaster occur is a guarantee of a far more expensive disaster potentially ruinous to the company. Communication and mutual solution of any problem or disputed area is far less expensive than resolution borne entirely by the corporation. Leaving aside momentarily the transaction costs which must be added, the loss of external resources in time, knowledge, and personal interest otherwise available, means the developer must bear the burden of any solution entirely on his own. Pragmatically, communication and mutual solution is the cheapest and fastest approach for both parties. Furthermore, a mutual solution approach prevents the formation of *hard lines* and immutable demands or limits by either party which are more expensive to fulfill. The effort of working together may be great, but this is more likely to prevent emotionalism from overcoming a sober assessment of the costs and benefits of any action. Emotionalism and unreasonable demands will be subject to a dispassionate review in any litigation, and juries and judges are extremely likely to let the parties bear the costs of such activity rather than assess it as part of the reasonable damages. Lastly, communication and mutual solution minimize the longer-term frictional cost of communication in an adversarial posture, which greatly increases the expense for even the most imperfect solution.

In the long run, this approach offers a reward and return to the developer and vendor of an AI or ES. Education as to the demands and needs of his marketplace, rather than being driven and paid for by the company entirely, are partly supported by the efforts of the second and third parties. Fruitful improvements and broadening of opportunities also can arise through interesting and involving these others.

15.6 CONCLUSION

Artificial Intelligence is just reaching the commercial marketplace. Professionals, laymen, and jurists will have to exercise their own human adaptability and creativity if they wish to reap the benefits and avoid the risks of this new technology, which offers the chance to capitalize human knowledge and service efforts. The revolution, which these tools for the *mind* are bringing, rivals that which was wrought by providing tools for the *body* over the course of several centuries; yet the changes will take decades to come about.

The legal system, and the law, under which we currently live, learned to adapt to the prior revolution; and in so doing, it provided theories and techniques for such successful change. It is time to begin to consider how to apply these theories and techniques to the new revolution.

REFERENCES

Buchanan, B. (1985), *Expert Systems: Working Systems and the Research Literature*, Report No. KSL-85-37, Knowledge Systems Laboratory, Dept. of Computer Science, Stanford University.

Christo, T.K. (1983), The Applicability of Negligence and Malpractice to Data Processing Situations, I *Computer Law Reporter* 4, p. 570.

Grady, G. and Patil, R.S. (1987), An Expert System for Screening Employee Pension Plans for the Internal Revenue Service, *Proceedings of the First International Conference on Artificial Intelligence and the Law*, p. 137–154 (ACM Order #604870, ISBN 0-89791-230-6) describe the IRS's SPADES program; the FBI is reported to be working on a program to identify high-risk criminals and potential traitors titled *Big Floyd*.

Greene, C.J.R. (1987), An evolutionary Approach to Verification and Validation of Expert Systems, *Proceedings of the Fall Joint Computer Conference of the ACM*, p. 760.

Hayes, P. (1985), The Second Naive Physics Manifesto, *Readings In Knowledge Representation*, R.J. Brachman and H.J. Levesque (Eds.), Morgan Kaufman Publishers, Inc., Los Altos.

Jacob, R.J.K. and Froscher, J.N. (1986), Software Engineering for Rule-Based Systems, *Proceedings of the Fall Joint Computer Conference of the ACM*, p.185.

Reiter, R. (1982), On Closed World Data Bases, *Readings in Artificial Intelligence*, B.L. Webber and N.J. Nilsson (Eds), Tioga Press, Palo Alto, p.119.

Schneider, N. (1985), Taking the "Byte" Out of Warranty Disclaimers, *Computer Law Journal* Vol. 5 #4, p.531; see also Note (1979), Computer Programs as Goods Under the U.C.C., 77 *Mich. Law Review* 1149, 1155, 1165.

Willick, M.S. (1985), Professional Malpractice and the Unauthorized Practice of Professions: Some Legal and Ethical Aspects of the Use of Computers as Decision-Aids, in *Computing Power and Legal Reasoning*, C. Walker, (Ed.), West Publishing, p. 817.

Chapter 16

TRAINING AND PERFORMANCE EFFECTS OF A KNOWLEDGE-BASE SYSTEM FOR ANALYTICAL REVIEW

Edward Blocher
University of North Carolina, Chapel Hill, NC

George Krull, Jr.
Grant Thornton, Chicago, IL

Kenneth A. Scalf
Prentice-Hall Professional Software, Smyrna, GA

Stephen V. N. Yates
Grant Thornton, New York, NY

This chapter reports the results of a study of auditors' analytical review judgments. The results show how the auditors' risk assessments and performance in evaluating the inherent risk and bankruptcy risk of two audit cases were affected by the presence of a knowledge-based system in training and/or as a practice aid for performing analytical procedures. Though the performance results were insignificant, there was some evidence of a positive effect for the practice aid. Also, the effect on inherent risk assessments was not significant. In contrast, the practice aid had a significant effect on assessments of going concern risk.

16.1 TRAINING AND PERFORMANCE EFFECTS OF A KNOWLEDGE-BASE SYSTEM FOR ANALYTICAL REVIEW

The focus of the study described in this chapter is on the use of a knowledge-based expert system (KBES) within the context of both auditor training and auditor performance in analytical procedures. Our interest is in how a KBES might facilitate training in the performance of analytical procedures and also how it might facilitate the effective use of analytical procedures in

Expert Systems in Business and Finance: Issues and Applications. Edited by P.R. Watkins and L.B. Eliot
© 1993 John Wiley & Sons Ltd.

audit practice. This investigation was conducted using a laboratory-case study design in which 33 senior level Grant Thornton auditors participated. The KBES used in the study is the ANSWERS system which is produced by Prentice-Hall Professional Software and which is available as an engagement tool for Grant Thornton auditors.

It is important to note that our interest is not in the training of auditors to use expert systems, but rather with the use of these systems to enhance conventional training methods. Also, since the analytical review exercise in this study involves financial statement analysis, we view the task context as somewhat broad, and as having application in other areas of accounting, auditing, and management, so that the findings should be generally applicable to related KBES applications in these other areas.

16.1.1 The KBES as a Practice Aid

We use the term, practice aid, to describe any document or computer program which is used to facilitate an auditor's proper attention to a given task. We are interested in an analytical procedure involving the proper selection and interpretation of financial statement ratios for analyzing inherent risk and the risk of bankruptcy. Checklists and audit manuals are common types of practice aids, and expert systems are increasingly being used for this purpose. We use the terms *practice aid* and attention to a *given task* rather than the more common terms of *decision aid* or *judgment*, because the former are broader and more inclusive of the wide variety of auditor behaviors we are interested in. For example, a practice aid could be applicable for data acquisition, data combination and manipulation, or for a final judgment based upon the data analysis. For a more complete look at this issue, see Lewis *et al.* (1983) who presents a useful framework for thinking about the various applications of decision aids.

16.1.2 Use of The KBES in Training

There are a number of ways that expert systems can be used in training. For example, a KBES could be used simply as a benchmark for performance, much like a grading key. Alternatively, a potentially useful training exercise would be to use an expert system shell to help the students discover expert decision rules by developing an expert system as a class assignment (Dorr *et al.*, 1988). Moreover, it is likely that the involvement of teachers in using expert systems might improve training programs by drawing attention to training objectives in a new way. Perhaps rote memorization objectives would have less focus, and more attention would be given to the more analytical aspects of job performance. The context in which we are looking at training is the format now most commonly employed in staff training of auditors, that is, the use of lecture and case exercise plus discussion (hereafter, the LCED format). Thus, we will investigate how the inclusion of a KBES within the LCED format might affect subsequent auditor performance in an analytical procedures task.

16.1.3 Research Objectives

The objective of this research is to investigate, in a 2×2 analysis of covariance design, the main and interaction effects of a KBES used in training and then subsequently used as a practice aid for analytical procedures. Because of the lack of prior research for deriving a theory and expectations for our results, no research hypotheses will be tested, but rather the results will be analyzed and presented in a descriptive manner.

The task for the participants is to employ analytical procedures and to use this analysis as a basis for assessing inherent risk and bankruptcy risk for a hypothetical audit client. The covariates used in the design include audit experience, and perceptions of the value of analytical procedures in assessing inherent risk and bankruptcy risk.

16.1.4 Expected Benefits of the Research

The findings of this research are expected to be useful to those interested in the design and implementation of expert systems, and to those interested in computer-aided instruction. We observe that software developers are now producing training aids with integrated expert systems simulators (for example, Business Simulator, by Reality Software; see also, Harmon and King, 1985, Chapter 15). The integrated expert systems approach to training can be more effective and efficient than the conventional lecture, case exercise and discussion approach, since these systems can provide the students immediate expert feedback regarding the appropriateness of their decision strategies. Also, these systems can be used in a tutorial format to replace and/or reinforce the instructor's lecture. The student does case exercises using the system, thereby saving instructor time for group discussion and summary of important points.

Additionally, the results of this research are expected to have relevance for those interested in developing new approaches for using analytical procedures, in light of the new *Statement 56* on Auditing Standards (AICPA, 1988). This standard requires the use of analytical procedures at the planning and review phases of the audit. The case exercise in this study is representative of the type that an auditor could face in using analytical procedures in engagement planning.

16.2   RESEARCH DESIGN

This section describes the selection and measurement of the dependent and independent variables used in the study. The description of independent variables includes a presentation of related prior research.

16.2.1 Dependent Variables

The study examines two aspects of auditor judgement—performance in using analytical procedures, and risk assessments. We are interested in auditor performance, as it is a principal training objective. The objective of the study is to investigate how training and/or use of a KBES decision aid might influence auditor performance. Risk assessments are also important to us, as they can help to show how the auditors integrate analytical procedures into the overall audit plan.

By performance, we mean the auditor's ability to properly identify and interpret the significance of key financial statement ratios in performing a review of the summary financial data for a hypothetical audit client. The context of the review is the auditor's use of analytical procedures in planning the audit engagement. Ratio analysis is the focus of the training presented in the study because it is a commonly applied procedure for analytical review at the planning stage of the audit.

Performance is measured in the following manner. The lead author prepared a grading key for the case exercises done by the auditors, and each of the co-authors independently graded the auditors' responses using this key. To facilitate the grading of the cases, the auditors were asked to review the client data and to make judgments in each of four areas—liquidity, profitability, capital structure, and risk of bankruptcy. The grading key summarized key ratios for each of these four areas and presented a summary conclusion for each area based upon an analysis of these ratios. Auditors were graded on their ability to identify and interpret the relevant ratios. Grades were assessed on a five point scale, with one as the lowest score and five as the highest.

In addition to the ratio analysis, the auditors were asked to provide risk assessments for both the inherent risk of the client and the risk of bankruptcy. These risk assessments are important elements of the auditor's use of analytical procedures in planning. Our interest is to investigate the potential effect of a KBES training/decision aid on these risk assessments. The cases used in the study may be found at the end of this chapter.

16.2.2 First Independent Variable—Use Of The KBES As A Practice Aid

We begin this section with a consideration of the nature of the analytical procedure of focus in this study—what types of knowledge are required and what types of practice aid are most appropriate. Thus, it is useful to distinguish the four types of analytical procedures (Blocher and Willingham, 1988; Blocher, 1983):

(a) risk indicators, such as adjustments in an account in the prior year,
(b) trend analysis
(c) ratio analysis
(d) modeling, such as the reasonableness test, or regression analysis.

Blocher (1983, pp. 30–31) shows how these four types of procedures differ regarding required knowledge and suggested support aids. This thinking is summarized in Figure 16.1. Figure 16.1 attempts to provide a useful categorization of the types of analytical procedures for the purpose of considering what types of practice aids might be relevant; it is a simplified framework and not a carefully developed theoretical construct. Panel A of Figure 16.1 shows how the four types of analytical procedures differ regarding knowledge *breadth* and *depth*. In this context, breadth is used to describe the extent to which various different types of knowledge must be integrated in performing the analytical procedure. For example, trend analysis is shown to require relatively low knowledge breadth because in performing trend analysis the auditor typically reviews account balance amounts for a threshold amount or percent change, so that each reviewed item is considered separately. In contrast, the proper interpretation of a given risk indicator or financial ratio commonly requires broad knowledge of the entity and of the multiple relationships among financial and operating data for the entity. Similarly, we argue that the modeling approach requires a more in-depth level of knowledge than trend analysis because of the required mathematical and statistical concepts involved. Likewise, ratio analysis is viewed as requiring a more in-depth level of knowledge than does indicators, because of the complexity of the underlying relationships between financial and operating data.

Turning to Panel B of Figure 16.1, we argue that differences in knowledge requirements create a need for different types of practice aid. In the case of trend analysis, no aid is necessary, because of the relative simplicity of the task context. However, because of the increased depth or breadth, the indicator and modeling approaches can be supported by a checklist approach. In contrast, a carefully tailored practice aid is appropriate for the ratio analysis task—that is, one which can prompt the user for information about the specific context of the entity under examination. This is necessary because of the relative complexity of the task context. The ANSWERS system, which is used in the case exercises in this study, is a system of this type.

In the following, we explain our research question regarding the use of a KBES as a practice aid. The question has two important aspects. One is to provide a partial test of the content validity of the KBES, as described in

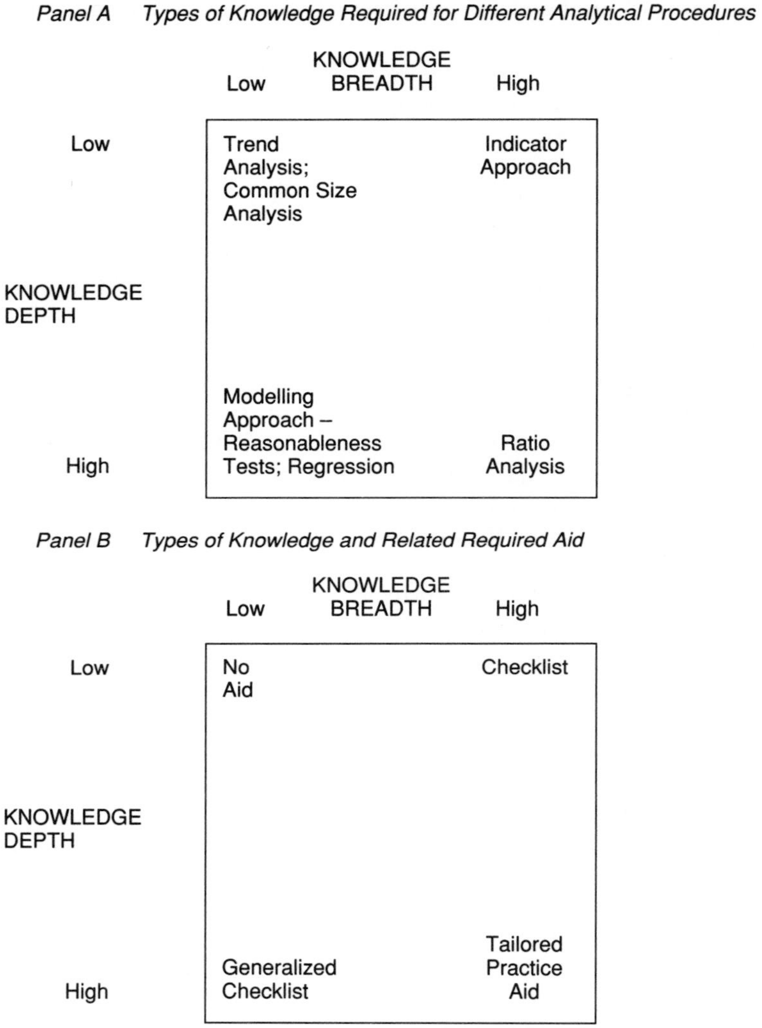

Panel A   Types of Knowledge Required for Different Analytical Procedures

KNOWLEDGE
Low   BREADTH   High

	Low	High
Low	Trend Analysis; Common Size Analysis	Indicator Approach
High	Modelling Approach – Reasonableness Tests; Regression	Ratio Analysis

KNOWLEDGE DEPTH (left axis, Low / High)

Panel B   Types of Knowledge and Related Required Aid

KNOWLEDGE
Low   BREADTH   High

	Low	High
Low	No Aid	Checklist
High	Generalized Checklist	Tailored Practice Aid

KNOWLEDGE DEPTH (left axis, Low / High)

FIGURE 16.1   A framework for an analytical procedure KBES

O'Leary (1987, pp. 472–475). Another aspect is the opportunity to compare our results with those of prior related research (Butler, 1985; Blocher and Luzi, 1987; Blocher *et al.* 1983; Cats-Baril and Huber, 1987). These studies have shown the effectiveness of a decision aid at improving some elements of decision performance. In Butler's study, auditors using the decision aid approach described by Tversky and Kahneman (1974) provided assessments of sampling risk which more closely agreed with statistically determined values. Blocher and Luzi (1987), using a well-structured analytical review task, found that guidance improved performance and decision confidence. In contrast, using a less well-structured task, Blocher *et al.* (1983) found that the auditors perceived higher risk in the presence of a checklist form of guidance. Similarly, in an ill-structured task context, Cats-Baril and Huber (1987) found that while the decision aid improved objective performance, the aid also had a negative effect on confidence, satisfaction, and attitude toward task context.

Overall, the research on decision aids suggests there will be an improvement in performance when an expert system practice aid is used together with an analytical procedures task, but the direction of the effects on other decision behaviors is not clear. Since the task context to be used in this study will be relatively ill-structured, we expect results to follow those shown by Blocher *et al.* (1983) and Cats-Baril and Huber (1987).

16.2.3 Second Independent Variable—Use Of The KBES As A Training Aid

Relatively few studies in accounting or information systems have considered the question of the effectiveness of alternative training methods. Thus, there is relatively little prior research to form a basis for expectations regarding research results. Moreover, Shanteau (1984, 1987) has argued that the process of training experts may be problematic. Shanteau (1987, p. 300) enumerated 14 important characteristics of experts, and finds that a number of these include behavioral attributes such as self-confidence and adaptability for which "... there may be little that training can do to prepare a novice to act like an expert". For such characteristics, the emphasis might best be placed on selecting novices whose behavior most closely fits the pattern associated with experts. These novices could then receive training on other, more *teachable skills.* Further confirmation of this idea is provided by Hofstedt and Dyckman (1974) who argue, in a paper on educational research methodology, that feelings, attitudes, and values are important elements of training methods and related research. These arguments appeal to us, and we find the implication of this research is to require measurement and analysis of the attitudes of the auditors performing the case exercise.

16.2.4 Expert Systems and Training

As for the entire area of educational research in accounting, relatively little has been done in business to study the effectiveness of expert systems based training aids. Harmon and King (1985, Chapter 15) provide a useful overview of the training objectives of expert systems. They describe the three objectives, how they can be achieved, and examples of expert systems which have been designed to achieve these objectives:

(a)   to perform drill and practice in a given decision domain
(b)   to help debug student performance, by explaining decision errors, etc.
(c)   to help provide for the student a *conceptual model* of the decision domain, as a basis for improving the student's expertise in the area.

Harmon and King emphasize the last approach (c)—to help develop a conceptual model—as the most effective way to train in many instances. This approach facilitates both the student's acquisition of the *task heuristics* and a better understanding of the targeted expertise by both trainer and student:

> People in training have followed the cognitive literature, and many have tried to incorporate cognitive ideas into training technology. Until recently, however, most cognitive concepts have been a little too vague or ill-defined to be applied to practical corporate training situations. This will change in the next few years. The practical techniques that have been developed by knowledge engineers are exactly the kind of specific techniques for which training technologists have been looking. (p. 245)

Harmon and King (p. 246) suggest a two-phase approach to training in which

> the trainer first performs a careful task analysis on the behavioral level, and then begins to look at the cognitive aspects of the decision domain—into successively deeper layers of knowledge...

This approach makes sense to us, though we note Kolodner's (1983, pp. 499–500) criticism; she argues that knowledge engineers focus excessively on semantic memory, and that the proper development of training aids requires a focus on episodic memory. Semantic memory can be described as the facts a person knows, while episodic memory encodes events and episodes. It seems clear that, before meaningful improvements in training technology can be made, significant additional research is needed on both the behavioral and cognitive levels.

Dorr *et al.* (1988) have performed a study which investigates the effect of the use of an expert system in training auditing students in the proper methods for evaluating internal accounting controls for payroll. Their results suggest that the students using the decision aid made decisions more similar to the decision aid than the students who did not have access to the decision aid.

Computer-assisted Instruction. While not addressing the role of the KBES directly, four recent studies have looked at the effectiveness of using the microcomputer in training accounting concepts, particularly in the intermediate accounting course.

Friedman (1981) shows the computer to have a positive impact on achievement in intermediate accounting, but noted that by the design of the study, it was possible that a type of *Hawthorne Effect* could explain the findings. Groomer (1981) used the interactive tutorial, PLATO, in a similar manner and with similar results to those of Friedman; again, there is acknowledgement of a potential *Hawthorne Effect*.

Dickens and Harper (1986) found that the use of the microcomputer in training topics of earnings per share and inter-period tax allocation had no significant effect on student performance in subsequent multiple choice questions. Finally, Fetters *et al.* (1986) found that the degree of effect for the use of the microcomputer in training depended upon the student's ability (stronger positive impact for weaker students). When viewed together, these studies suggest that the use of microcomputer software in training may not be effective, and that effectiveness may depend on the nature of the student and/or task context.

In summary, our approach in this study is to investigate for the potential performance effect of using a KBES in training. Special care is given to collecting information about the auditors' attitudes and abilities, as these might play an important role in properly interpreting the results.

16.3 METHODOLOGY

16.3.1 Subjects

The auditors participating in the study were senior level auditors attending a training course for computer audit coordinators. This training course was chosen because of the desired level of the auditors and because of the availability of microcomputers for this course. Thirty-three auditors participated in all, 16 in one course session and 17 in the next offering of the course the following week. The first group was presented training with the KBES, while the second group was presented training in the conventional LCED format only. Each group was divided for the practice aid treatment, to achieve a 2×2 between-subjects design having three cells of 8 auditors each and one cell of 9 auditors.

16.3.2 Case Exercises and Procedure

The auditors each completed two case exercises in the study. The first of the cases was used in training the auditors, and the second was used to test both training and practice aid effects. The training case was presented in the last one hour segment of training of the first day of a five day training course for computer audit specialists. The second case was presented to the auditors in the first class session the following morning. This procedure was chosen to provide a reasonable balance between recency bias and history bias which might otherwise influence the results.

The first exercise was based upon the W.T. Grant Company. The auditors were presented summary financial data and a brief description of the company and asked to analyze the inherent risk and bankruptcy risk for this hypothetical audit client. Also, they were asked to use ratio analysis to assess the liquidity, profitability, capital structure, and potential for bankruptcy for this entity. The auditors were given 30 minutes to complete the exercise. This was followed by 30 minutes of lecture and discussion to bring out the main points of the case. Under the conventional training (LCED) condition, the lecture and discussion included the use of overhead transparencies and discussion only, while in the KBES condition, the lecture and discussion portion of the training was augmented by the use of the ANSWERS system.

TRAINING

	CONVENTIONAL	COMPUTER AIDED
UNAIDED	*Training*: 1 hour of conventional LCED presentation on analytical review using W. T. Grant case.	*Training*: 1 hour of LCED training in analytical review using ANSWERS; W. T. Grant case on ANSWERS.
	Case Analysis: 1 hour of unaided exercise using Blue Water Sailboats case.	*Case Analysis*: 1 hour of unaided exercise using Blue Water Sailboats case.
CASE ANALYSIS PRACTICE AID	*Training*: 1 hour conventional training as above.	*Training*: As above.
	Case Analysis: 1 hour of case exercise using ANSWERS and Blue Water Sailboats case.	*Case Analysis*: 1 hour of case exercise using ANSWERS and the Blue Water Sailboats case.

FIGURE 16.2   Overview of experimental design

The second exercise involved a hypothetical case designed by the lead author. One hour was allowed for the completion of this case. The auditors were asked to perform the same analyses and make the same judgments as in the earlier case. In one condition, the auditors did the exercise unaided, and in the other condition, the auditors used the ANSWERS system in performing their analyses. This research design is summarized in Figure 16.2.

16.3.3 The ANSWERS System

The ANSWERS system is described in Blocher and Willingham (1988, Chapter 12) and in the *ANSWERS Users' Manual* (Prentice-Hall Professional Software, 1990). The following briefly describes the main features of the system. This is a system which works from financial data at the account or lead sheet level and selected operating data to (a) calculate specific financial ratios and relationships between financial and operating data, (b) report ratios or relationships which have exceeded a pre-determined threshold (change from prior year, change from predicted, difference from budget, difference from industry average, or difference from some specified quantity, as for example *current ratio less than one*), and (c) report specific comments related to the triggered observations in (b) above. The comments noted in (c) consist of explanations of the ratio calculation, a brief generalized interpretation of the ratios, and interpretation of the significance of the directional change or difference in the ratio, suggestions for further related audit work or investigation, suggestions for the possible cause(s) of the condition, and suggestions for improving the condition, if appropriate.

The system is intended to facilitate the financial analysis of an entity in situations wherein the data is conveniently available in microcomputer database files, at the working trial balance or lead sheet level of detail. This type of data environment describes most of the microcomputer based accounting and software systems now available and in use.

16.4 RESULTS

The data were analyzed by analysis of covariance, using the dependent and independent variables and covariates described above. Additionally, a new dependent variable was created by subtracting each auditor's score on the first case from the corresponding score on the second case. This *difference* variable represents the change in performance or risk assessment we are investigating. Additionally, this approach produces a more powerful analysis by reducing some of the variability in the auditors' responses. However, this approach introduces some biases, as explained by Borg and Gall (1979, pp. 589–593): (a) there is a confounding due to regression to the mean in repeated observations of this type (in this case, this bias should act against observing significant differences for the treatment variables), and (b) there is a *ceiling effect* that limits the amount of change in a given direction for extreme scores on the first case (this is similar to, but slightly different from, the regression bias noted above), and (c) there is an implicit assumption of linearity for the dependent variables—a given change has the same meaning across the entire width of the scale of responses. Limitations (b) and (c) above should not have an important effect on the proper interpretation of these results for the performance variables because of the limited range of these variables. However, there is a possibility that these biases will distort our measure of the auditors responses for risk assessments, as these responses varied from a low of 2% to a high of 100% for some auditors. These limitations must be kept in mind when interpreting the following results.

The results are presented in Tables 16.1 and 16.2. Table 16.1 shows the cell means and standard deviations for the dependent variables across the four treatment combinations. Selected results which include all significant ($p < 0.1$) effects for all the independent variables and covariates is shown in Table 16.2. In these tables *Performance Scores A...D* refer to the performance scores resulting from the grading of the cases by each of the four co-authors.

TABLE 16.1   *Descriptive statistics—dependent variables*

| | MEAN (SD) | | | |
| | Training Aid | | No Training Aid | |
	Practice Aid	No Practice Aid	Practice Aid	No Practice Aid
Performance Measure A	0.43 (1.40)	-0.25 (0.71)	0.33 (0.87)	-0.25 (1.04)
Performance Measure B	1.00 (0.93)	0.00 (0.76)	0.22 (1.09)	0.25 (0.707)
Performance Measure C	1.00 (1.41)	0.50 (0.53)	0.77 (1.20)	0.00 (0.93)
Performance Measure D	0.14 (1.21)	-0.375 (0.52)	0.444 (0.72)	0.25 (1.49)
Change in Inherent Risk Assessment	-3.33 (38.69)	-21.88 (33.68)	-4.16 (18.79)	-6.25 (18.66)
Change in Going Concern Risk Assessment	-2.50 35.04)	-27.50 (15.58)	1.78 (20.70)	-16.00 (16.28)
Number of Auditors	8	8	9	8

TABLE 16.2   Significance level for main, interaction and covariate effects

Independent Variable	Change in Inherent Risk	Change in Inherent Risk	Performance Measure			
			A	B	C	D
1. Practice Aid	0.93	0.02	0.20	0.04	0.16	0.49
2. Training Aid	0.25	0.35	0.71	0.17	0.30	0.08
3. Practice * Training	0.76	0.54	0.65	0.01	0.99	0.39
Covariates						
4. Perceived Value of Ratio Analysis for Inherent Risk Assessment	0.01	0.10	0.09	0.92	0.52	0.81
5. Perceived Value of Ratio Analysis for Bankruptcy Assessment	0.86	0.38	0.85	0.09	0.60	0.31
6. Months of Audit Experience	0.81	0.10	0.21	0.23	0.63	0.28

These findings can be summarized as follows. For the training manipulation, there are no significant main, interaction or covariate effects, except for one performance score main effect (Measure D) and one interaction effect (Measure B). Also, note from Table 16.1 that the main effect noted above is in the opposite direction of that expected—the KBES reduces the effectiveness of training. Since these effects occurred for only two of the four graders, we interpret this as due to chance, so that the most useful interpretation of this treatment is simply that the use of the KBES in training did not have the expected effect on subsequent performance. Possible interpretations for this are considered in the following section.

For the practice aid treatment, there appears to be a very weak positive but insignificant effect on performance. The performance effect is positive for each of the graders, and significant for one of the graders. It is not significant for the other three graders, but for two of these three graders there is some evidence of a relationship (p values of 0.16 and 0.20). This provides evidence of some performance effect, and suggests a need for further related research to clarify the nature and extent of this potential effect. This is discussed further in the following section.

The results for performance noted above are useful for considering the issue of the content validity of the KBES (O'Leary, 1987). Since the results are not conclusive, we cannot judge the content validity of the system based on this data. This remains an objective for a follow-up study with finer measures of performance.

Also, for the practice treatment, there is a strongly significant effect on the auditors' assessments of bankruptcy risk. The auditors using the practice aid set higher risk levels in the final case exercise, and similarly, they decreased their risk assessments less from the first case. The auditors' judgments followed a similar pattern for inherent risk assessments, but due in part to the relatively high variability of responses, this effect was not statistically significant.

The only significant covariate was that for the perceived usefulness of ratio and trend analysis for assessing inherent risk. This perception was significantly positively correlated with the auditors' assessments of inherent risk, and weakly significant ($p = 0.1$) for assessments of bankruptcy risk. Tests were done to determine if the four treatment groups differed for any of the three covariates, and no significant differences were noted. These results, and those noted above, are discussed in the following section.

16.5   DISCUSSION

Our overall interpretation of the results is that they indicate the need for further research. While some of the results are consistent with prior research, other aspects of the findings cannot be interpreted properly based solely upon data from this and prior research.

16.5.1   Results for the Training Treatment

The non-significance of these results is consistent with our earlier observation that the prior cited research is inconclusive with respect to the effectiveness of computer-based support aids in training. While these aids have consistently had a positive effect on attitudes, they have not been consistently effective in improving performance (Friedman 1981; Groomer 1981; Fetters *et al.*, 1986; Dickens and Harper, 1986). We observe that we neither got a performance nor an attitude effect for training in our results.

We think it is likely, as some of the authors cited above have suggested, that the effect of microcomputer-based training aids is very context specific—it is dependent on the specific type of student and task situation. This observation suggests that research in this area will be somewhat problematic, and not likely to result in useful generalizations, at least at the present time. The next step may be to investigate ways to improve the implementation of the support aid—ways that can exploit the flexibility and power of the computer most effectively.

16.5.2   Results for the Practice Aid Treatment

The tentative evidence of a positive effect of the practice aid on performance suggests the need for a follow up study which would use more precise dependent measures and perhaps richer task contexts. As noted in the studies cited earlier (Blocher *et al.*, 1983; Blocher and Luzi, 1987; Cats-Baril and Huber, 1987), task structure may have a lot to do with the appearance of a performance effect. Relatively well-structured tasks appear to be better candidates for performance improvement using this type of aid. Again, further research can provide some guidance on this issue.

16.5.3 Results for Risk Assessments

The significance of the practice aid treatment to increase the auditors' bankruptcy risk assessments (and the non-significant positive effect on inherent risk assessments) is consistent with the prior research (Blocher *et al.*, 1983, Cats-Baril and Huber, 1987) which has found that in the presence of guidance, subjects behave in a way that shows less confidence in facing the task context. In the Blocher, *et al.* study, the participating auditors who used a form of guidance in an analytical review task set higher levels of planned audit work. Also, in the Cats-Baril and Huber study, the participants using the decision aid indicated less decision confidence, a poorer attitude about the task context, and less satisfaction. These results, taken together, suggest that a practice aid such as used in this study can have the effect of creating anxiety and/or uncertainty in the participants which is then reflected in higher risk assessments. Though we did not measure time taken to complete the exercises, we observe that most of the auditors in the two practice aid groups took far longer to complete the exercise than the others. This could be attributed in part to the novelty of working with the practice aid, but we suspect that it is also due in part to a heightened sense of anxiety for the practice aid subjects, which was reflected in their greater attention to the task and higher risk assessments. This is an interesting and important issue for future research to clarify.

16.5.4 Results for the Covariate—Perception of Ratio Analysis Usefulness

The finding that the auditors who perceived greater benefit for ratio and trend analysis in assessing inherent risk also set relatively low risk assessments has some alternate interpretations. One possibility is that those most comfortable with the task (and therefore inclined to give lower risk assessments) reported higher perceptions of the benefits of the analytical procedures, in part, because of the relative easing of their task. Alternatively, the auditors with more confidence in the procedures may have felt that the risk could be assessed lower because of the perceived relatively high effectiveness of the procedures. With the data available to us, we cannot sort out these and other possible interpretations. What is needed is data which helps to explain the reasons for the perceptions—direct explanations by the auditors, or other means. The lack of the necessary data is a limitation of the study, and one which should be addressed in any follow-up work.

16.6   LIMITATIONS

There are a number of limitations to research of this type. We want to acknowledge some we think are particularly important. First, there is a potential for the Hawthorne Effect to distort the results. It could distort the performance results if the participants in the treatment groups provided greater effort than the others. It could also influence the risk assessment results, if the treatment group auditors responded in what they thought was the desired manner. We think the potential for this bias is small because of the complexity of the task and the judgments it requires, and because of our care in describing the research in an unbiased manner. However, we think the results should be read with this limitation in mind.

Second, there is a possible confounding effect between the two cases presented. Some of the auditors may have looked for those specific problem areas diagnosed in the first case, and not been attentive enough to other types of problems. It is difficult to assess the potential for bias from this limitation.

Third, there is the limitation associated with using the difference in scores in measuring our dependent variables. The nature and interpretations of these problems has been discussed earlier.

Fourth, the project suffered in unknown ways from the lack of an educational psychologist and researcher on the research team. We are more familiar with accounting and auditing research than education research *per se.*

Fifth, it would have been desirable to have more subjects so that within-cell variation could have been reduced. Because of the need to use computers, this is a difficult limitation to overcome.

REFERENCES

American Institute of Certified Public Accountants (1988), *Statement on Auditing Standards 56, Analytical Procedures*, New York.

Biggs, S.F., T.J. Mock and P.R. Watkins (1988), "A Descriptive Study of Auditor's Use of Analytical Review in Audit Program Design," *The Accounting Review* (January), pp 148–161.

Blocher, E. (1983), "Approaching Analytical Review," *The CPA Journal* (March), pp. 24–33.

Blocher, E. and A.D. Luzi (1987), "Guidance Effects on Analytical Review Decisions," *Advances in Accounting*, pp. 201–213.

Blocher, E. and J.J. Willingham (1988), *Analytical Review: A Guide to Analytical Procedures*, Shepards McGraw-Hill.

Blocher, E., R.S. Esposito, and J.J. Willingham (1983), "Auditors' Analytical Review

Judgments for Payroll Expense," *Auditing: A Journal of Practice and Theory*, Fall 1983, pp. 75–91.

Borg, W.R. and M.D. Gall (1979), *Educational Research* (Third Edition) Longman, New York.

Butler, S.A. (1985), "Application of a Decision Aid in the Judgmental Evaluation of Substantive Test Details Samples," *Journal of Accounting Research*, Autumn, pp. 513–536.

Cats-Baril, W.L. and G.P. Huber (1987), "Decision Support Systems for Ill-Structured Problems: An Empirical Study," *Decision Sciences*, Vol. 18, pp.350–372.

Dickens, T.L. and R.M. Harper (1986), "The Use of Microcomputers in Intermediate Accounting: Effects on Student Achievement and Attitudes," *Journal of Accounting Education* (Spring), pp. 127–146.

Dorr, P., M. Eining, and J.E. Groff (1988), "Developing an Accounting Expert System Decision Aid for Classroom Use," *Issues in Accounting Education* (Spring), pp. 27–41.

Fetters, M., J. McKenzie and D. Callaghan (1986), "Does the Computer Hinder Accounting Education? An Analysis of Some Empirical Data," *Issues in Accounting Education* (Spring), pp. 76–85.

Fortune, J. and B.A. Hutson (1984), "Selecting Models for Measuring Change When True Experimental Conditions Do not Exist," *Journal of Educational Research* March–April, 1984, pp. 197–206.

Friedman, M.E. (1981), "The Effect on Achievement of Using the Computer as a Problem-Solving Tool in the Intermediate Accounting Course," *The Accounting Review* (January), pp. 137–143.

Groomer, S.M. (1981), "An Experiment in Computer-Assisted Instruction for Introductory Accounting," *The Accounting Review* (October), pp. 934–941.

Harmon, P. and D. King (1985), *Expert Systems: Artificial Intelligence in Business*, Wiley.

Hofstedt, T.R. and T.R. Dyckman (1974), "Research on Teaching Innovations in Accounting," *Accounting Educations: Problems and Prospects*, (J.D. Edwards, ed.), The American Accounting Association.

Kolodner, J.L. (1983), "Towards an Understanding of the Role of Experience in the Evolution from Novice to Expert," *Journal of Man-Machine Studies*, pp. 497–518.

Lewis, B., M.D. Shields and M. Young (1983), "Evaluating Human Judgments and Decision Aids," *Journal of Accounting Research* Spring, pp. 271–285.

Messier, W.F. Jr and J.V. Hansen (1992), "A Case Study and Field Evaluation of EDP-EXPERT," *Intelligent Systems in Accounting, Finance and Management*, pp. 173–186.

O'Leary, D.E. (1987), "Validation of Expert Systems—with Applications to Auditing and Accounting Expert Systems," *Decision Sciences*, Vol. 18, pp. 468–486.

Shanteau, J. (1984), "Some Unasked Questions about the Psychology of Expert Decision Makers," M.E. Hawary (ed.) *Proceedings of the IEEE Conference on Systems, Man and Cybernetics*, New York.

Shanteau, J. (1987), "Psychological Characteristics of Expert Decision Makers," in *Expert Judgment and Expert Systems* (J.L. Mumpower, O. Renn, L.D. Philips and V.R.R. Uppuluri, eds.), Springer-Verlag, New York.

Taylor, Milton, "The Implementation and Evaluation of a Computer Simulation Game in a University Course," *Journal of Experimental Education* (Winter 1987), pp. 108–115.

Tversky, A. and D. Kahneman, "Judgments Under Uncertainty: Heuristics and Biases," *Science* (1974), pp. 1124–1131.

Zimmerman, Donald W., D.A. Andrews, David Robinson and Richard H. Williams, "A Note on Non-Parallelism of Pre-test and Post-test Measures in Assessing Change," *Journal of Experimental Education* (Summer 1985), pp. 234–236.

EXAMPLE COMPANY

Background information and selected financial data

Example company operates a chain of popular priced department stores (1208 on January 31, 1985), located in 42 states, retailing necessities and staple merchandise mainly priced at less than \$10, but selling items priced

TABLE 16.3   *Example Company: Selected Financial Data*

Account Description	(000s)					
	1980	1981	1982	1983	1984	1985
Cash	25 141	25 639	32 977	34 009	49 851	30 943
Accounts Receivable	272 4503	12 776	368 267	419 731	477 324	542 751
Prepaids	3 982	4 402	5 037	5 246	5 378	6 648
Inventories	183 722	208 623	222 128	260 492	298 696	399 533
Property & Equipment (net)	47 578	49 931	55 311	61 832	77 173	91 420
Other Assets	18 734	20 738	23 075	26 318	36 248	39 403
Total Assets	**551 607**	**622 109**	**706 795**	**807 628**	**944 670**	**1 110 698**
Accounts Payable	49 831	64 321	70 853	80 861	94 677	78 789
Accrued Expenses	86 087	102 650	113 732	131 899	143 159	164 243
Notes Payable	99 539	118 305	182 732	246 420	237 741	390 034
Long-Term Debt	62 622	43 251	35 407	32 301	128 432	126 672
Deferred Taxes Payable	7 551	7 941	8 286	8 518	9 664	11 926
Other Liabilities	5 279	5 521	5 697	5 593	5 252	4 695
Total Liabilities	**310 909**	**341 989**	**416 707**	**505 592**	**618 925**	**776 359**
Capital Stock	73 253	87 581	79 009	71 601	81 238	73 186
Retained Earnings	167 445	192 539	211 679	230 435	244 507	261 153
Total Stockholder' Equity	**240 698**	**280 120**	**290 688**	**302 036**	**325 745**	**334 339**
Total Liabilities & Equity	**551 607**	**622 109**	**706 795**	**807 628**	**944 670**	**1 110 698**
Net Sales	982 244	1 095 083	1 214 666	1 259 116	1 378 251	1 648 500
Cost of Goods Sold	669 560	739 459	817 671	843 192	931 237	1 125 261
Depreciation Expense	8 303	8 380	8 972	9 619	10 577	12 004
Interest Expense	11 248	13 146	14 919	18 874	16 562	21 128
Income Tax Expense	26 650	34 000	38 000	32 800	26 500	25 750
Dividends Paid	13 805	17 160	19 280	20 426	20 794	20 807
Net Income	**32 563**	**37 895**	**41 809**	**39 577**	**35 212**	**37 787**
Number of Common Shares Outstanding at Year End	12 817	13 714	13 728	13 684	14 023	13 993
Market Price per Share	38	43	55	65	43	31

up to $1000. Stores have 809 luncheonettes operated by the company and 1002 stores were in shopping centers. The heaviest concentration of stores is in the northeastern states including Massachusetts, Connecticut, New York, New Jersey, and Pennsylvania. It also operates five regional distribution centers located in California, Connecticut, Georgia, Indiana, and New Jersey.

Credit sales totaled $451 471 000 for the year ending January 31, 1985. At year end, there were about 2.9 million credit accounts, compared to 2.6 million the prior year. Table 16.3 shows some selected financial data for 1980–1985. The selected financial data, where appropriate, represent millions of dollars.

Exercise Questions

1. For this company, develop a one or two sentence summary of your evaluation of the following five financial statement characteristics and risk areas. Support your evaluation in each of the five areas by reference to one or more ratios, trends, or other relevant analyses.

   (a) Liquidity
   (b) Profitability
   (c) Capital structure/leverage
   (d) Risk of bankruptcy

2. After having completed step one above, and based upon your above evaluations, state quantitatively on a scale of zero to 100% your assessment of the following:

   (a) Inherent risk is the risk that an error or irregularity will be present in these financial statements prior to the action of any internal accounting controls or audit procedures.

   Inherent risk is _____ %

   (b) The risk of bankruptcy within the next two years is _____ %.

3. Indicate your view of auditing procedures as requested below:

   (a) The value of ratio and trend analyses for assessing inherent risk:

No Value				Some Value				Significant Value
1	2	3	4	5	6	7	8	9

(b) The value of ratio and trend analyses for assessing the potential for bankruptcy is:

    1   2   3   4   5   6   7   8   9

(c) The value of ratio and trend analyses the poential for management fraud is:

    1   2   3   4   5   6   7   8   9

4. Are you a CPA?   Yes   No
   Months in Public Accounting _____
   Degree   BA   MA   MBA
   Job Classification _____

BLUE WATER SAILBOATS

Blue Water Sailboats is owned by a partnership of five business people and has recently been incorporated for tax benefits and other reasons. At present, the five principal stockholders are interested in expanding the business, and you have been asked to review the financial statements.

Blue Water Sailboats sells approximately one hundred to one hundred and fifty sailboats each year, ranging from fourteen-foot dinghies to thirty-five foot cruising sailboats. The sales prices range from $2 000 to over $30 000. Blue Water has a limited inventory of boats, consisting primarily of one or two boats from each of the four manufacturers who supply Blue Water.

The company operates from one location, a large building with offices, storage, and sales for some of the smaller sailboats. The larger sailboats are in a fenced area adjacent to the main building. An ample parking area is nearby. This year Blue Water has expanded with the purchase of a boat lift, which is used for hauling boats. In addition to the revenue from these hauls, the lift has brought in revenues for boat repairs, hull painting, and related services.

The balance sheet and income statement for Blue Water Sailboats for 1980 through 1984 and the first eleven months of 1985 are attached. The increase in net fixed assets in the recent two years is due to improvements in the building, paving of the parking area, and purchase of the lift.

Blue Water obtains its debt financing from two sources. The principal source of short-term funds is a small savings and loan. An additional source of short-term loans, and the principal source of long-term debt comes from a larger, commercial bank. The terms of the loan agreement with the larger bank include certain restrictions—the current ratio must remain greater than 1.5, the debt-to-equity ratio must remain below 1.0, and the ratio of long-term debt to equity must remain less than 0.4. The loans are secured by liens on the assets of the company.

TABLE 16.4 Blue Water Sailboats: Summary Financial Data

BALANCE SHEET

						(11 Mo.)
Assets	1980	1981	1982	1983	1984	1985
Cash	23 260	21 966	18 735	28 166	43 692	31 264
Accounts Receivable	99 465	102 834	112 903	125 663	104 388	142 009
Allowance for B/D	(9 304)	(8 786)	(9 424)	(11 266)	(7 282)	(12 506)
Inventory	35 009	56 784	61 992	67 884	58 994	95 774
Other Current Assets	11 894	12 894	9 424	11 266	18 923	22 903
Total Current Assets	**$160 324**	**$185 692**	**$193 630**	**$221 713**	**$218 715**	**$279 444**
Property & Equip.	262 195	282 008	299 379	368 565	405 269	498 625
Accumulated Depr.	(65 984)	(93 442)	(122 892)	(158 099)	(187 227)	(226 307)
Total Assets	**$356 535**	**$374 258**	**$370 118**	**$432 179**	**$436 757**	**$551 762**
Liabilities and Equities						
Accounts Payable	82 635	78 127	63 346	56 256	40 189	49 545
Fed. Inc. Tax Payable	11 630	10 983	11 780	14 083	3 738	15 632
Short-term Loans	59 876	56 980	37 583	41 093	49 594	76 962
Accrued Payroll	5 227	4 598	3 649	4 224	4 775	4 779
Current Liabilities	**$159 368**	**$150 688**	**$116 358**	**$115 655**	**$98 295**	**$146 917**
Long-term Debt	41 873	55 439	61 690	74 167	80 526	105 938
Common Stock	116 300	116 950	117 800	140 830	148 945	156 320
Retained Earnings	38 994	51 182	74 270	101 526	108 991	142 588
Total Liab. & Equity	**$356 535**	**$374 258**	**$370 118**	**$432 179**	**$436 757**	**$551 763**

Income Statement

Gross Sales	$767 580	$724 878	$777 480	$929 478	$764 610	$938 857
Less Returns & Allow	$38 379	$35 645	$40 334	$45 998	$32 887	$46 380
Net Sales	$729 201	$689 233	$737 146	$883 480	$731 723	$892 477
Cost of Sales	$473 908	$441 298	$458 015	$545 778	$453 669	$530 597
Gross Margin	$255 293	$247 935	$279 131	$337 702	$278 054	$361 880
Depreciation Exp.	$29 075	$27 458	$29 450	$35 208	$29 128	$35 563
Interest Expense	$10 465	$9 857	$11 234	$9 456	$14 313	$16 229
Selling Expense						
Salaries & Wages	$81 923	$73 664	$77 846	$95 764	$92 903	$99 447
Other	$9 304	$8 786	$9 323	$11 834	$13 108	$11 380
Admin. Expense						
Salaries & Wages	$79 666	$75 234	$80 693	$96 469	$87 995	$97 441
Other	$12 630	$18 927	$15 763	$22 903	$18 934	$22 662
Pretax Income	$32 230	$34 010	$54 822	$66 069	$21 674	$79 158
Income Tax Expense	$10 776	$12 946	$23 889	$29 845	$6 453	$36 985
Net Income	**$21 454**	**$21 064**	**$30 933**	**$36 224**	**$15 221**	**$42 173**

Chapter 17

SURVEY OF EXPERT SYSTEMS FOR RESOURCE PLANNING

Carol E. Brown
Oregon State University, Corvallis, OR

Susan Athey
Colorado State University, Fort Collins, CO

This chapter describes a variety of resource planning expert systems for both manufacturing and administrative activities. The potential benefits of these expert systems for the organization are examined with attention to improving the effectiveness of resource use by managers.

17.1 INTRODUCTION

Resource planning, including both allocation and scheduling activities, is an important part of a manager's work and one with which he/she is always concerned. As the business environment becomes more complex and competitive, the ability to allocate the resources of the organization and schedule the activities of both people and equipment become increasingly important.

Inappropriate resource allocation and inefficient scheduling affect the organization from the cost of carrying inventory to the cost of excess capacity to handle emergencies to the cost of travel and meetings. Inefficient schedules and inappropriate resource allocations result in excess costs and lost opportunities, and thus reduce both profits and potential research and development funds.

Interest is high in resource planning because it entails inherently difficult tasks for humans. Many of the current techniques for resource planning include optimization algorithms which attempt to maximize or minimize an objective without violating some constraints. If the particular resource planning problem cannot be solved mathematically, an experienced human must develop the plan using many rules-of-thumb and few algorithms. Now, however, expert systems are beginning to emerge as a tool for the manager

Expert Systems in Business and Finance: Issues and Applications. Edited by P.R. Watkins and L.B. Eliot
© 1993 John Wiley & Sons Ltd.

TABLE 17.1   Expert systems for resource planning

Resource Planning Expert Systems

PLANET   Planner's Assistant   CMC - anonymous
                Resource planning   (Dhar, 1984)

Administrative Scheduling Expert Systems

NUDGE   Scheduling business meetings.   (Blanning, 1987)
ODYSSEY   Trip scheduling   Xerox PARC
                                                (Fikes, 1981)
OMEGA   Personnel scheduling   MIT
                                                (Barber, 1983)

Capital Budgeting Expert Systems

CAPITAL INVESTMENT
SYSTEM   Capital investment decisions   Texas Instruments
                regarding acquisition of equipment (Brown & Phillips, 1990)
                                                (Brown & Phillips, 1990)

Production Planning Expert Systems

ISIS   Intelligent Scheduling and   Westinghouse
                Information Systems   (Fox & Smith 1984;
                                                Fox, 1983;
                Job Shop Scheduling   Fox *et al.* 1983)
ISA   Intelligent Scheduling Assistant DEC
                Order Scheduling for Production (Orciuch, 1984;
                                                O'Connor, 1984)
IMACS   Intelligent Management Assistant DEC
                for Computer Systems   (O'Connor, 1984)
                Manufacturing
                Production and Purchase Planning
                and Scheduling.
SOJA   Système d'Ordonnancement   Alsthom-Atlantique
                Journalier d'un Atelier (French) (LePape, 1985)
                A daily workshop scheduling
                system.
GENSCHED   GENeral SCHEDuler   Georgia Tech,
                Scheduling production orders   (Semeco, 1986)
                in manufacturing.
XCON   EXpert CONfigurer   DEC
                Configuring minicomputer orders (McDermott, 1982;
                                                Soloway & Jensen 1987;
                                                Wolfgram *et al.* 1987)
DISPATCHER   Schedule orders in manufacturing DEC
                                                (Gorman, 1988)
MACHINIST   Schedules machine set-ups   NYU
                                                (Ashley, 1990)
PROD SCHED   Schedules process operations   Stone & Webster
ADVISOR   (Finn, 1990)

to use to improve the efficiency of resource plans. In addition, expert systems do not necessarily use the idea of optimizing a single objective but rather try to satisfy several objectives. If the allocation problem has an infeasible solution, then the expert system will relax the constraints based upon some predefined rules until it develops a feasible plan (Blanning, 1987). The goal is to build a plan using the same built-in heuristics an experienced human manager would use. No longer are mathematicians or very experienced personnel the only people in an organization who can build efficient and effective schedules and make difficult resource allocation decisions. The expert system allows less experienced individuals to design better plans than would be otherwise possible.

Three major areas of resource planning and scheduling are discussed in this chapter. The first is the formidable task of formulating business plans for allocating resources in large organizations. An expert system called PLANET was developed to assist managers in this area. The second planning area is scheduling the activities of people. NUDGE, ODYSSEY, and OMEGA are expert systems which assist managers in scheduling meetings, trips, and personnel assignments. The third is production planning including both scheduling and system configuration, an area in which Digital Equipment, Westinghouse, NCR, and IBM have all experimented with or implemented expert systems to handle order scheduling in a manufacturing environment (Buchanan, 1986, p.34). Each of these systems has as its objective the performance of a more efficient and effective job of planning and scheduling than the average human manager can do and, in the process, improved use of the organization's resources.

This chapter presents a review of ten of these planning and scheduling systems and examines the benefits which could accrue from using expert systems to assist in the tasks shown in Table 17.1. The need for managers to examine critically their role in the development of these systems is also discussed.

17.2 RESOURCE PLANNING EXPERT SYSTEMS

Dhar developed PLANET (Dhar, 1984) for his doctoral dissertation with the cooperation of an unnamed computer manufacturing company. A major contribution of PLANET is providing a method of resource planning that explicitly keeps track of the assumptions and rationales for various plans. When new information changes the assumptions, PLANET can consistently update the plan. This feature also allows for a type of sensitivity analysis. The underlying assumptions of the model can be systematically varied to determine the effects on the resulting resource plan.

17.3   ADMINISTRATIVE SCHEDULING EXPERT SYSTEMS

Expert systems are also operating in the administrative scheduling area. NUDGE (Blanning, 1987) is a frame-based expert system for scheduling business meetings. The knowledge used in the system includes common sense information such as types of meetings, time and location preference of the meeting organizer, and characteristics of the people asked to attend the meeting. The organizer describes the meeting requirements and interacts with NUDGE to determine the location, time, and attendees.

ODYSSEY (Fikes, 1981) performs trip scheduling for the user and can pinpoint inconsistencies and problems in a proposed trip schedule. This system handles trip planning functions such as requests for advances, flight schedules, and lodging requests. ODYSSEY assures the traveler that the dates and cities are consistent throughout the plan. As one component is changed, for example cities, the rest of the plan is updated (e.g., canceling the lodging request for that city and changing the next day's departure city). After a complete itinerary is constructed, the system will suggest an appropriate amount of money for an advance.

OMEGA (Barber, 1983) is actually a knowledge representation language designed to support an office worker's problem solving activities. It uses the ideas of goals and actions to reach those goals. Barber (1983) presents an example of OMEGA in use by determining job assignments for available Army personnel when constraints such as qualifications of available personnel, job requirements, and travel funds must be satisfied.

17.4   PRODUCTION PLANNING EXPERT SYSTEMS

The largest known expert system currently in commercial operation is XCON (Wolfgram *et al.*, 1987, pp. 32–33; Soloway and Jensen, 1987), which has been in use since January, 1980. Although this expert system is not strictly used for planning, the success of the system in terms of increases in efficiency and effectiveness requires that it be reviewed. In 1984, XCON already had about 3500 rules and had required in excess of 50 person-years of effort to develop. The system is still growing and currently has over 6 200 rules and uses a database with about 20 000 parts included.

Digital Equipment Corporation uses XCON for configuring the components of their minicomputer systems. This includes determining if a proposed order for a computer system includes all the necessary parts and if all the specified components are compatible with each other. If orders are incomplete or incompatible, XCON will suggest substitutions or additions to the order to correct the problem. In addition XCON and related programs provide a schematic layout for installing the equipment. The equipment available changes constantly, requiring changes in about

50% of the rules each year. According to DEC, this particular expert system saves them $18 to $20 million per year in manufacturing costs alone (Wolfgram *et al.*, 1987, p. 33). Obviously of financial benefit to DEC, the expert system also has such intangible benefits as improved customer satisfaction from receiving a complete package of hardware at one time and not having to wait for a missing component to arrive before the computer can be installed.

GENSCHED (Semeco *et al.*, 1986) is an order-driven general scheduling program or shell being developed at the Artificial Intelligence Branch of the Georgia Tech Research Institute. The system has been tested on proprietary data from an unnamed sponsor.

GENSCHED is a hierarchical or top-down planning system. It schedules the high level tasks first, based on an estimate of the resources required for each order. The system assumes that some way will be found to schedule the sub-tasks so that they don't interfere with one another. When a schedule is complete at one task level, then detailed scheduling begins at the sub-task level. Whenever possible, the time block allowed for the parent task includes the scheduled time for each of the subtasks.

GENSCHED uses three major information categories: tasks, resources, and orders. A hierarchy of tasks is defined. A major task is broken down into a group of sub-tasks and those sub-tasks are broken down still further until the tasks are sufficiently explicit to allow a match with equipment, people, and raw material resources.

Rules store information about a resource such as quantity on hand or model required for a particular task. Orders require specification of attributes of the order such as date-when-issued, date-when-due, part-to-make, quantity, and priority. GENSCHED allocates resources to tasks based on the priority of the order from which the task came. When resources are close to full usage the system uses a best-first search algorithm to assure that the best possible use of the resource is being made, according to the rules. The current version of GENSCHED includes only a generic rule base but a domain specific rule base is planned.

ISIS: Intelligent Scheduling and Information System (Fox and Smith, 1984; Fox 1983; Fox *et al.*, 1983) is a short-term planning and scheduling system developed by researchers at the Intelligent Systems Laboratory of the Robotics Institute of Carnegie-Mellon University along with Westinghouse Electric Corporation. This system attempts to find the best schedule for each order based on each order's own constraints. In this way, ISIS differs from most other scheduling systems which try to optimize based upon a single criterion such as order lateness or order cost. ISIS is a hierarchical system which includes tools for specifying ways to relax or give alternative values to the constraints. The constraints must also contain some measure of their relative importance. To further complicate this process, the relative importance may shift from order to order. One order may consider due date to be the most important constraint while for another order, low cost may be the most important constraint. For example, one order may have a penalty for a missed shipping date while another order went to the low cost bid. Each of these orders has a different objective for ISIS to consider in the scheduling process.

ISIS uses the idea that the scheduling activity is constraint directed. Many times, the changing environment requires relaxation of constraints during scheduling. ISIS categorizes constraints in five broad areas.

- organizational goals such as due dates, work-in-progress, personnel levels, tools, raw materials, shop stability
- physical constraints of the equipment being used
- causal constraints such as routing of orders and resource requirements
- resource constraints such as work shifts, machine down times, and maintenance schedules
- preference constraints such as machine or operation preference.

ISIS allows multi-level scheduling which produces schedules of different details. Bottleneck analysis can determine when to schedule an operation on an order to avoid unnecessary waiting and tardiness. Finally, ISIS generates a complete detailed schedule for the shop to use.

The Westinghouse Turbine Component Plant has used ISIS in a series of experiments in which 100–200 orders are in process at one time. While the results have been encouraging, especially in reducing work-in-process time, Fox and Smith (1984) warn that more work is needed.

SOJA: Système d'Ordonnancement Journalier d'un Atelier (LePape, 1985) is a daily workshop scheduling system being developed at Laboratoires de Marcoussis in France. The system has two phases: first, selecting the jobs to be scheduled and second, determining a schedule for the selected jobs that meets all the appropriate constraints. SOJA differs from ISIS by representing the constraints as rules that guide the scheduling process rather than acting directly as constraints. It constructs the schedule by building a graph. The completed graph implies a schedule.

SOJA has constraint rules and scheduling rules. The six basic categories of constraint rules used in SOJA are:

- the earliest possible start time for each job
- selection of a job phase implies that the job should be scheduled for completion before the end of the day
- precedence or ordering of job tasks
- shared resources

- timing of successive phases
- storage for waiting jobs.

The system tries to reduce costs by considering costly set-up times between operations. SOJA runs on a VAX-780 and takes five minutes to construct a schedule for 18 machines and 42 job phases for a four hour manufacturing period. When 83 job phases in an eight hour period are scheduled, SOJA requires 20 minutes to construct a schedule.

ISA: Intelligent Scheduling Assistant (Orciuch and Frost, 1984; O'Connor, 1984) is a rule-based system developed and used by Digital Equipment Company as an addition to the Corporate Common Scheduling System. ISA has been used for scheduling orders in the manufacturing area since 1982. In comparison to human schedulers who take 10–15 minutes to schedule a single order, ISA schedules many orders per second. ISA schedules orders daily. In addition to the general scheduling problems, ISA deals with problems such as an insufficient customer credit line to process the order and material shortages. ISA also handles partial shipments and suggests substitutions and speculative orders.

IMACS: Intelligent Management Assistant for Computer Systems Manufacturing (O'Connor, 1984) is an expert system also being developed by Digital Equipment Corporation to assist in the management of inventory, floor-loading, throughput, paperwork, capacity, and diagnostic selectors for computer system manufacturing. It is a rule-based system in which each rule defines a situation and the appropriate action to take in that situation. The rule base is actually a group of cooperating expert systems where each system is an expert in one aspect of the production management task. IMACS deals with a diverse set of tasks that range from keeping track of administrative details and report generation to production scheduling and alerting management to potential problems. IMACS assists in determining where and when to locate a particular computer system in the work area to begin the manufacturing process. The system also determines when to bring potential raw material shortages or surpluses to the attention of materials buyers. IMACS also points out the dates by which order administration issues must be resolved, provides several performance reports, and monitors production plans.

17.5 ADVANTAGES AND DISADVANTAGES OF EXPERT SYSTEMS

To be fair in discussing expert systems, both the advantages and disadvantages of these tools should be explored. Expert systems have many advantages over human experts. One is the permanence of expertise. Expert systems do not forget; human experts must *use it or lose it*. Another advantage is transferability or reproducibility of the knowledge in the expert system.

Expert systems are easy to copy; training new human experts is time-consuming and expensive. Expert systems are also consistent in their behavior, while the performance of human experts can vary even from one day to another. Although expert systems may be expensive to build and update, they are inexpensive to operate. Since the cost of building can be spread over many users, the overall cost can be quite reasonable when compared to expensive and scarce human experts.

Expert systems do have some disadvantages when compared to humans. In addition to possessing technical knowledge, human experts also have common sense. It is not yet known how to give expert systems common sense. When faced with a new situation, human experts can respond with creativity, but expert systems only do what their software tells them to do. Human experts automatically adapt to changing environments while expert systems must be explicitly updated. Expert systems are generally not very good at immediately recognizing that no answer exists or that the problem is outside their area of expertise. Due to these disadvantages, expert systems are most commonly and most effectively used as advisors to human experts or novices. Expert systems provide the technical knowledge and the user provides the common sense.

17.6   CONCLUSIONS

No doubt exists in the minds of most managers that the environment in which they work is more complex and competitive than it was 15 years ago. The need for timely and relevant information for decision-making becomes more important every year. Businesses can no longer afford to carry excess inventory and capacity to compensate for inaccurate estimates and inefficient operations. The cost of carrying inventory and capacity is too high. Expert systems are beginning to emerge as a tool for more efficient scheduling. While some of the expert systems reviewed focus exclusively on order scheduling (GENSCHED, ISIS, and SOJA) in a manufacturing environment, others take a more integrated approach (ISA and IMACS). ISA considers a customer's credit line in its scheduling activities. IMACS alerts managers to potential problems and provides performance reports as part of its functions. Still others have moved away from the traditional manufacturing arena of scheduling and have moved into the manager's office, recognizing that a manager's time, like inventory, is a valuable resource. NUDGE, ODYSSEY, and OMEGA are all intended to schedule time and people more effectively in administrative tasks rather than production.

In order for these scheduling expert systems to make cost-effective decisions, however, managers and other non-technical, non-computer personnel must take an active part in system development to provide information at a detail level not previously required or possible.

Planning and scheduling applications of expert systems must be examined in terms of cost and benefit. Organizations should determine the tasks which are important to the health of the company and seriously consider if expert systems can help them do their job better or more efficiently. Every day expert systems are moving from such exotic fields as internal medicine, crystallography, mineral prospecting, and oil field exploration to the less exotic ones such as scheduling, education, and auditing. The question for companies and managers, therefore, should be: *Do opportunities exist for using expert systems in non-traditional areas of the organization and, more importantly, can they be of any benefit to the organization?*

REFERENCES

Ashley, S. (1990). A MOSAIC for Machine Tools. *Mechanical Engineering.* 12 (9), pp. 38–43.

Barber, G. (1983). "Supporting Organizational Problem Solving with a Work Station." *ACM Transactions on Office Information Systems.* January. pp. 45–67.

Blanning, R.W. (1987) "A Survey of Issues in Expert Systems for Management." In B.W. Silverman (ed.), *Expert Systems For Business* Reading, MA: Addison-Wesley Publishing Company.

Brown, C.E. and Phillips, M.E. (1990). Expert Systems Solving Management Accounting Problems. *Management Accounting,* LXXI. (7), pp. 18–23.

Buchanan, B. (1986). "Expert Systems: Working Systems and the Research Literature." *Expert Systems.* 3(1), pp. 32–51.

Dhar, V.K. (1984) "PLANET: An Intelligent Decision Support System for the Formulation and Investigation of Formal Planning Models." Unpublished Doctoral Dissertation, University of Pittsburgh. Pittsburgh PA.

Fikes, R.E. (1981). "Odyssey: A Knowledge-Based Assistant". *Artificial Intelligence.* July, pp. 331–361.

Finn, G. (1990), *Expert Systems in Operation and Maintenance.* Chemical Engineering. 97(2), pp. 131–138.

Fox, M.S. (1983). "Constraint Directed Search: A Case Study in Job-Shop Scheduling." (CMU-RI-TR-83-22 CMU-CS-83-161). (The Robotics Institute: *Technical Report* Pittsburgh, PA: Carnegie-Mellon.

Fox, M.S. and Smith, S.F. (1984)." ISIS: A Knowledge Based System for Factory Scheduling." *Expert Systems.* 1(1), pp.25–48.

Fox, M.S., Allen, B.P., Smith, S.F. and Strohm, G.A. (1983). "ISIS: A Constraint-Directed Reasoning Approach to Job Shop Scheduling." (CMU-RI-TR-83-8). Pittsburgh, PA: Carnegie-Mellon University.

Gorman, H. (1988). Dispatcher Complements Material Handling System. *Manufacturing Systems.* 6(5), pp. 30–31.

LePape, C. (1985). "SOJA: A Daily Workshop Scheduling System". In Merry, M. (ed.), *Expert Systems 85: Proceedings of the Fifth Technical Conference of the British Computer Society Specialists Group on Expert Systems.* University of Warwick. (The British Computer Society Workshop Series (pp. 195–212). Cambridge, England: Cambridge University Press.

McDermott, J. (1982). "R1: A Rule Based Configurer of Computer Systems." *Artificial Intelligence.* 19, pp. 39–88.

O'Connor, D.E. (1984). "Using Expert Systems to Manage Change and Complexity in Manufacturing". In Reitman, W. (ed.), *Artificial Intelligence Applications for Business.* (pp. 149–157). Norwood, NJ: Ablex.

Orciuch, E. and Frost, J. (1984)." ISA: An Intelligent Scheduling Assistant". In *Proceedings of The First Conference on Artificial Intelligent Applications.* (pp. 314–320). IEEE Computer Society.

Semeco, A.C., Williams, B.D., Roth, S. and Gilmore, J.F. (1986). "GENSCHED - A Real World Hierarchical Planning Knowledge-Based System". In Gilmore, J.F. (Chairman/Editor), *Applications of Artificial Intelligence III.* 635. Orlando, Florida. (pp. 250–256). SPIE The International Society of Optical Engineering.

Soloway, E., Bachant, J. and Jensen, K. (1987). "Assessing the Maintainability of XCON-in-RIME: Coping with the Problems of a VERY Large Rule-Base". In AAAI87: *Proceedings of the Sixth National Conference on Artificial Intelligence. 2.* Seattle, WA. (pp. 824–829).

Wolfgram, D.D., Dear, T.J. and Galbraith, C.S. (1987). *Expert Systems for the Technical Professional.* New York, NY: Wiley.

FURTHER READING

Alexander, S. M. (1985). "Knowledge Based Expert Systems: Their Application to Production Management." *Production and Inventory Management.* Fourth Quarter, pp. 109–113.

Duchessi, P. (1987). "The Conceptual Design for a Knowledge-based System as Applied to the Production Planning Process". In Silverman, B.G. (ed.). *Expert Systems for Business.* Reading, MA: Addison-Wesley.

Ellebt, P. and Grant, T. (1986). "Knowledge Based Scheduling". In Mitra, G. (ed.), *Computer Assisted Decision Making.* (pp. 175–186). Amsterdam, The Netherlands: Elsevier Science Publishers.

Gupta, Y.P. and Ching, D.C.W. (1989). Expert Systems and Their Applications in Production and Operations Management. *Computers and Operations Research* (UK). 16 (6), pp. 567–582.

Chapter 18

A SURVEY OF EXPERT SYSTEMS USED IN THE PRACTICE OF PUBLIC ACCOUNTING

Mary Ellen Phillips
Carol E. Brown
Oregon State University, Corvallis, OR

The use of computer systems is growing rapidly in all areas of accounting. Available databases and spreadsheets are more powerful, sophisticated, user friendly, and generate reports that are more flexible and are more easily incorporated into other computer-generated documents. The judgments of the best professional experts in accounting are becoming more accessible through expert systems. Although computerized expertise has been used in accounting for several years, the use of expert systems is now growing at a phenomenal rate. Extensive research has investigated the possible applications of expert systems to the practice of public accounting (Brown, 1989; O'Leary and Watkins, 1989; Brown and Streit, 1988; Messier and Hansen, 1987).

Because of the potential for legal liability and the concerns about protecting proprietary expertise, most accounting expert systems are only for in-house use. A few systems, however, are being marketed to accounting firms and other business users. Expert systems are used in public practice for auditing, corporate tax planning and determination, individual income taxes, and personal financial planning as well as corporate accounting (Harmon, 1988). The majority of the systems used in public accounting are PC based so they can be used by auditors and other professionals in the field.

The expert systems described were selected because they demonstrate the variety of systems currently in use or development in each practice area and the approaches used by the various developers of accounting expert systems. For each of the public accounting practice areas, two or more systems are described from the more than fifty expert systems in use. For further information on corporate accounting expert systems, see Brown and Phillips (1990).

Expert Systems in Business and Finance: Issues and Applications. Edited by P.R. Watkins and L.B. Eliot
© 1993 John Wiley & Sons Ltd.

18.1   AUDITING

Expert systems are used by all the large international accounting firms as decision aids in their auditing practices, not as replacements for either auditors or their judgment. The benefits of using expert systems in the audit process are improved quality, consistency, and efficiency of decisions. A well-designed expert system increases both the structure and the efficiency of auditing methods and decisions because it imposes the structure selected by the designers of the system. System designers build into an expert system the structure that is the most efficient one based on the knowledge and experience of the firm's experts.

Although auditors often agree on internal control judgments, significant individual differences exist regarding the substantive tests to be performed and the point at which an item is considered significant enough to have a material effect on the financial statements. As auditing methods become more structured, individual auditor differences decline. In addition, as market and regulatory pressures increase the demand for quality audit services at competitive prices, accountants must become more efficient auditors.

The large public accounting firms have more than thirty different expert systems integrated into several different audit areas including audit work program development, internal control evaluation and risk analysis, technical assistance for tax related topics, technical assistance for reporting issues, and technical audit support. EY/Decision Support, Expertest, and Audit Planning Advisor are examples of expert systems that assist in the planning and development of audit programs. Risk Advisor and CCR/36 Advisor are examples of expert systems designed to identify and quantify audit risk. VATIA is an expert system for auditing a specific area and Loan Probe is used to audit a specific area in a specialized industry.

EY/Decision Support—Ernst & Young (Murphy and Brown, 1991; Brown and Murphy, 1990) is a module of Ernst & Young's Audit Automation Library support tools, that assists in preparing audit programs. The knowledge base of the system has general information about accounts such as accounts payable, other elements of the accounting system that affect those accounts such as purchase journals and cash disbursements, and related internal controls such as prenumbered purchase orders and bank reconciliations. The auditor inputs the accounts used by the client, the results of the internal control evaluation, and the degree of acceptable risk. The goal is to produce the most efficient audit program that meets all the audit objectives. The expert system helps the auditor address weaknesses in the client's system of internal controls.

EY/Decision Support provides the auditor with an audit approach plan, an audit program, and an indication of the level of comfort provided by the audit procedures. The level of comfort is the amount of risk reduction from the procedures suggested in the audit program. The system produces a table that recommends the extent to which each selected procedure in the audit program should be applied and identifies the audit assertions each procedure helps to meet. For example, purchase orders are matched with receiving slips and vendor invoices before accounts payable are paid and thus the assertion is that all goods paid for were ordered and received by the business and cash disbursements are correct.

Expertest—Coopers & Lybrand (Bickerstaff, 1988; Murphy and Brown, 1992) developed in London for junior staff use, builds audit test programs for individual clients. The knowledge base includes the experience of general practice partners and experienced audit staff personnel. The staff accountant answers questions about the structure of account balances, features of the client's accounting system, and the proposed audit approach. An optional help feature is available for each question. The help feature includes information on the effect of possible answers, where to locate additional relevant information in the audit file, and relevant examples. The auditor can review the audit program either by the timing of the tests or by the audit objective addressed, deleting or adding audit steps as needed.

Expertest designs an audit program from some or all of 19 general audit programs by using client information and an identified audit strategy. Expertest also provides a management control summary when the audit program is printed. This summary lists the answers to all questions as well as any modifications made to the audit program. Expertest prepares an audit program for a balance sheet area in approximately ten minutes that replaces a two hour manual process. Thus, Expertest allows junior staff to prepare the audit programs faster and with more independence. Junior staff as well as senior audit staff save time when Expertest is used. Coopers & Lybrand report that Expertest has increased auditor productivity, expertise, and job satisfaction.

Audit Planning Advisor—Deloitte & Touche (Murphy and Brown, 1992) is a rule-based audit planner for use by in-charge auditors. The system has over 1000 questions, both general and specific, that are grouped by audit area and are answered by the user. The system, originally developed by Touche Ross and called Micro Audit Planning System (MAPS), has been used since 1986.

Audit Planning Advisor is designed to produce a detailed first draft of an audit program. The system provides the logic that it uses in making its recommendations and a risk-task matrix that relates each audit procedure to the risks addressed. For example, Audit Planning Advisor relates the company's procedures for matching purchase orders and receiving slips to invoices with both the balance of accounts payable and cash disbursements. Audit Planning Advisor permits editing and tailoring of the audit program to special client circumstances.

Risk Advisor—Coopers & Lybrand (Murphy and Brown, 1992; Graham *et al.*, 1991) is designed to highlight and quantify potential audit issues and risk areas.

Risk Advisor has three data-gathering modules for entering a specific company's quantitative and qualitative financial information as well as information on peer companies. The system has a fourth module that organizes the information from the data-gathering modules and requests needed additional information to generate audit issues and risk areas. The fifth module formats reports for viewing or printing.

Risk Advisor has several interesting features. Specific client quantitative financial information can be entered either manually or directly from files created by other Coopers & Lybrand's software. The specific company qualitative information is gathered via the traditional question and answer method. Information on peer companies is gathered via telecommunications from other databases. More than 100 engagement team members and firm experts participated in the development of Risk Advisor over a period of several years.

CCR/36 Advisor—Ernst & Young (Murphy and Brown, 1992), formerly Computer Control Objectives Advisor or CCO Advisor, assists experienced computer auditors in assessing the internal controls in an IBM System 36 environment. The system provides management letter comments and suggestions for improving system controls. In addition, CCR/36 Advisor determines if the internal controls should or should not be relied on for audit purposes.

The system was developed using the XI shell in Paris, Brussels, and London over approximately two years by the predecessor firm of Ernst & Whinney. Twelve partners and managers from around the world made major contributions to the auditing expertise of CCR/36 Advisor. Ernst & Whinney selected this expert system application because of its anticipated significant payback. The factors contributing to the payback include:

- wide applicability—Ernst & Whinney has many clients that use an IBM System 36
- potential cost savings—audit efficiency payoffs if system controls can be relied on
- experience—many of Ernst & Whinney's knowledge engineers have a computer audit background that facilitated the development process.

VATIA—(Value Added Tax Intelligent Assistant)—Ernst & Young (Susskind and Tindall, 1988; Brown, 1988; Brown, 1991) developed by the predecessor firm of Ernst & Whinney in London, assists auditors in reviewing a client's procedures for complying with the Value Added Tax laws. In 1987, the United Kingdom began a phase-in of complex and numerous new

Value Added Tax (VAT) regulations with substantial penalties for non-compliance. The complexity of the VAT regulations, combined with the potential financial impact of failure to properly adhere to them, led Ernst & Whinney to question the adequacy of the paper checklist previously used by their auditors. VATIA was designed to help auditors interpret the VAT regulations and assist the auditor in reviewing the client's procedures for compliance with the Value Added Tax laws, thus improving the quality of service to clients and the quality of support to auditors.

A consultation, primarily through an intelligent questionnaire, takes about two hours and a record can be retained both on disk and on paper. The auditor answers questions requiring three basic types of responses: (1) "yes", "no", "don't know"; (2) menu selection; and (3) data input. VATIA is divided into seven modules relating to different aspects of the Value Added Tax regulations: registration, returns, output tax, input tax, partial exemption, records, and other matters. Relevant auditor responses and system assertions are passed among modules.

Ernst & Whinney VAT and Customs Duty Group provided the expertise for the system. The experts agreed on the content of their expertise but disagreed on the appropriate level of detail to include in the knowledge base. VATIA, written in Crystal and augmented by additional help and knowledge sharing features written in C, was designed to run on the standard computers used by Ernst & Whinney auditors. VATIA is used on all audits in the United Kingdom where computers are available.

Loan Probe—KPMG Peat Marwick (Brown and Murphy ,1990; Nielson and Brown, 1989; Willingham and Ribar, 1988; Ribar, 1988a,b, 1987) analyzes bank loans and determines the level of loan loss reserves needed. The knowledge base uses the expertise of KPMG's senior managers and partners and contain statistics and projections for more than 150 industries that are updated annually. Loan Probe is designed to arrive at a recommendation for the adequacy of the loan loss reserve for each loan being analyzed in the shortest possible time using the minimum of relevant information.

The accountant supplies information about the financial institution, the loan and its security and guarantees, the bank's access to liquid collateral and the risk associated with the collateral's valuation, and the borrower. The expert system will either suggest that no reserve is necessary, that a specific range of reserve is necessary, or that no determination can be made because of insufficient information. Loan Probe provides an explanation of the logic used in reaching the loan loss reserve recommendation, so the auditor can critique the logic, evaluate the recommendation and, if necessary, develop a different solution. Thus, the system recognizes that an auditor might encounter a lending situation beyond the system's expertise.

18.2   CORPORATE TAX PLANNING AND TAXATION

The corporate tax laws of both the United States and foreign countries are so vast and complex that an accountant cannot be an expert in all areas of the laws and their ramifications. Although the amount and timing of the income tax liability is vital to making major corporate financial and budgeting decisions and to financial reporting, the determination of the income tax effects is difficult because of the complexity and the constant revision of the various countries' income tax laws. Expert systems to assist with income tax issues are now in use at many of the major accounting firms, the Internal Revenue Service, and a number of business and consulting firms (Black *et al.*, 1990).

Expert systems provide assistance to auditors and tax professionals in data gathering and data review for tax planning, and the determination of the tax liability. These tax-planning expert systems have improved the auditor's and tax professional's information gathering process by increasing the productivity of staff accountants, improving the quality of information, and accelerating the training of staff accountants. In addition, the expertise of the systems has improved the efficiency and effectiveness of audit and tax managers.

Coopers & Lybrand's CLINTE, Price Waterhouse's International Tax Advisory System and International Tax Planning System, and Deloitte & Touche's World Tax Planner are examples of international taxation expert systems and Coopers & Lybrand's ExperTAX is an example of a United States corporate tax planning system.

A number of industries have unique or special taxation laws. Industry-specific expert systems can be developed either to complement a general, tax-planning expert system or as an independent, self-contained expert system. Industry-specific expert systems have been developed for the insurance and the oil and gas industries, and for regulated investment companies. RIC Checklist is an example of a system that deals with tax issues related to a specialized industry.

Expert systems are also developed to handle a specific area within the United States tax code. Price Waterhouse's COBRA Expert, Golden Parachutes, and Section 367 are examples of specific tax area systems (Brown, 1991). The COBRA Expert system assists the firm's auditors and their clients with properly handling employee benefits within the COBRA rules. The Golden Parachutes system assists the firm's auditors and their clients in determining if a compensation payment is subject to excise tax and suggests ways to correct the form of the transaction to avoid the tax. The Section 367 system determines the appropriate taxation of property transferred off shore under section 367 of the US tax code.

CLINTE—Coopers & Lybrand (Brown ,1991, Gleeson and West, 1988, Brown, 1988) was developed by the Knowledge Engineering and Tax Groups of Coopers & Lybrand's London office to assist auditors in quickly and easily determining the international income tax position of large multinational firms. CLINTE provides information for minimizing the present corporation's income taxes based on its income subject to tax in the various countries. The system also gives advice on the country(ies) in which to locate new subsidiaries in order to minimize future income taxes. If prepared manually, determining the tax position of multinational corporations is a time-consuming process requiring considerable expertise.

Because international income taxes are a very volatile domain, CLINTE was designed with a modular structure using "blackboard" architecture. A portion of the blackboard architecture is two basic models: the corporate model and the international model. The corporate model is a hierarchy of companies that can be viewed graphically with different symbols or "icons" used to represent different types of companies. The companies are categorized by both their position within the corporate structure, holding, parent, or subsidiary, and by the industry structure of the company, manufacturing, research and development company, stock holding, finance, and other. These categories are used because they can affect the income taxation of the corporation. CLINTE uses a set of rules to construct the corporate model. Rules for building the corporate model are divided into location rules, ownership rules, company creation rules, and control rules. The control rules are "meta rules." The meta rules define and describe when to use the location, ownership, company creation, and control rules.

The international model contains income tax law information and its applicability to multinational corporations. The income tax information for each country is stored as a separate module. The stored data include income subject to tax, income tax rates, tax offsets, and special regional benefits. The user can temporarily modify these data to incorporate the effects of proposed or possible changes in various countries' income tax laws.

CLINTE is expected to be the first module in a larger multinational corporation expert system. The full system is expected to encompass corporate loans, interest payments, geographical locations, personnel availability, markets, transportation, equities, securities and foreign exchange in addition to income taxation. Coopers & Lybrand state that the modular structure of CLINTE is successful and that this system demonstrates the usefulness of these techniques for corporate modeling, planning, and decision support.

International Tax Advisory System and International Tax Planning System—Price Waterhouse (Brown , 1988, 1991) helps the auditor recognize international tax issues. The International Tax Advisory System is currently being designed both to monitor the ongoing client situation and to assist with planning for specific client transactions.

International Tax Planning System was a "proof of concept" prototype that was completed in 1988 but no working model was developed. The prototype system is frame based and uses model-based reasoning. The system uses two models: a model of the world tax system, including rates and foreign tax credits, and a model of the companies including multinational ownership structures, countries of incorporation, and countries of operation. The rules test the models using constraint-based reasoning. The system was constructed using KEE on a Symbolics machine. The prototype has approximately 150 rules in addition to the knowledge contained in the frames based models. The system had information about 15 countries.

World Tax Planner—Deloitte & Touche (Brown 1988,1991) is an expert assistant. The system, according to some definitions, is not considered an expert system but is viewed as a very sophisticated or "intelligent" database. A large database provides information for more than 800 double tax treaties as well as tax rates and other basic tax information for 185 countries. In addition to common database search functions, the system uses brute force optimization routines that are limited to twelve critical factors for minimization of income taxes. The default values for the critical factors can be modified by the tax expert. The optimization routines rank the various paths from the corporate investor to the investee by country to minimize the amount of income taxes.

A text retrieval system provides relevant notes on all the countries where transactions occur in the routes. The system is designed to provide specialist support for mathematical calculations and text retrieval for international tax experts and thus provides advice and not decisions. The system provides advice on problems such as location of intermediate holding companies for multinationals, determining appropriate corporate structures for routing dividends and royalties from countries where revenue is generated for the parent company, and structuring international acquisitions.

The system can be run from any IBM PC or compatible microcomputer with a 2400 baud modem. In the US, the host program and database reside on a single AT computer in the Deloitte & Touche offices in Washington, D.C. Once the screen and keyboard input go over the lines all calculations are performed on the AT in Washington D.C.

ExperTAX—Coopers & Lybrand (Brown, 1988, 1991; Brown and Streit, 1988; Schatz *et al.* 1987; Shpilberg *et al.* 1986; Shpilberg and Graham, 1986) is used by auditors and tax professionals for both data gathering and data review for tax planning, tax compliance, and accounting and auditing of the income tax accrual and deferred income taxes. An intelligent questionnaire performs the data gathering function. An intelligent questionnaire asks the user a series of questions and each question asked is based on the user's answers to prior questions. ExperTAX's analysis functions, using the information gathered from the question answers, uncover and describe planning issues, provide alternative plans, evaluate the adequacy of the income tax accrual, and identify issues of income tax compliance. Coopers & Lybrand has a group of knowledge engineers and a knowledge base maintenance system for ExperTAX. The knowledge engineers are responsible for maintaining and enhancing the accuracy and completeness of ExperTAX. The knowledge base maintenance system allows the firm's tax and accounting experts, who are not computer programmers, to access and review the knowledge base. This access and review is critical to preserving and updating the system's expertise. Insurance ExperTAX and Oil & Gas ExperTAX are companions to ExperTAX for use with client companies in those industries because of the unique tax laws that apply.

RIC Checklist—Price Waterhouse (Brown and Murphy, 1990; Brown, 1988; Brown *et al.*, 1988) is an intelligent questionnaire that assists auditors in determining if a company complies with investment company regulations. The system also reviews the standard audit checklist for a mutual company and provides some assistance with the income tax accrual. RIC Checklist is integrated with a Lotus spreadsheet program. The expert system creates a file for automatic data transfer to a Lotus spreadsheet. The expert system calls up the spreadsheet and calculations are performed in the spreadsheet. The spreadsheet results are automatically returned to the expert system.

18.3   PERSONAL INCOME TAX

Expert systems for personal income taxes are often integrated into traditional, tax-preparation systems. Many of the expert systems dealing with individual income taxes are designed to cover just one area of personal tax planning and income tax liability determination. The tasks being performed by expert systems include tax return preparation assistance, tax return review, and technical assistance. The Internal Revenue Service has developed more than sixteen expert systems and currently is using several of these systems.

KPMG Peat Marwick's ALIEN (Brown, 1988, 1991), PEAT/EXPATRIATE (Brown, 1991), and Income Tax Issues of Preferred Shares (Brown, 1991) are examples of single area tax systems. ALIEN is a 150 rule-based system for the determination of resident alien status. PEAT/EXPATRIATE makes comprehensive tax calculations for 56 countries, projects the costs associated with sending employees to foreign countries, and performs "what if" analysis to evaluate different reimbursement options. Income Tax Issues of Preferred Shares assists tax professionals in Canada with determining the income tax implications of preferred shares of stock, a particularly difficult area of Canadian tax law.

Two examples of tax planning and tax preparation expert systems are KPMG Peat Marwick's Projection and Expert Analysis Tools/1040

(PEAT/1040) for use by the firm's tax professionals and Andrew Tobias' TaxCut, designed for public use.

PEAT/1040 - KPMG Peat Marwick (Brown and Phillips, 1990; Brown, 1988) is an individual Federal tax planning package with four modules. This in-house system integrates an expert system module with spreadsheet, tax preparation, and word processing software. PEAT/1040 was developed using an expert-system shell by the firm's tax professionals. If an accounting firm used KPGM's approach for developing PEAT/1040, it could create its own expert system without hiring knowledge engineers.

The system uses a spreadsheet to perform individual Federal tax calculations. In the spreadsheet, the accountant can select planning alternatives with sensitivity analysis, such as rental of a home versus purchase of a home with varying amounts of debt. The system has over 500 rules to assist in reviewing the client data for planning suggestions and input inconsistencies and completeness. The system considers only the tax questions requested by the accountant and considers only the areas that impact the taxpayer.

The conclusions are based on both the relevant client data from the spreadsheet and additional questions asked of the tax professional by the system. The suggestions, stored in a text file for use with a word processor, incorporate computed dollar amounts of expected savings and may include an in-depth review of selected income tax topics. PEAT/1040 provides the accountant with "negative assurances" for areas it analyzed but did not result in any planning suggestions.

The system produces a comprehensive diagnostic report that verifies input consistency and completeness. The diagnostic report can be prepared as part of the comprehensive planning session or run separately. The knowledge base of PEAT/1040 is deceptively small for the power of the system because the information that would be needed by the rules in a stand-alone expert system is determined by the spreadsheet module of the system. A typical session for a client can be completed in a few minutes.

The system also tracks Schedule B and passive activity items by activity basis and allocates passive loss carryovers to activities. The system has an automated bridge from the tax preparation system, Fast-Tax, to the expert planning system, PEAT/1040.

Andrew Tobias' TaxCut1 - MECA Software, Inc. (Brown, 1988) is a tax-preparation expert system designed for use by professionals in other fields or small accounting firms specializing in income taxes. The system was developed by Legal Knowledge Systems, Inc. and is marketed by MECA Software, Inc. The system sells for $89.95 and runs on a PC with at least 512K, and a hard disk is preferred. This system is available in retail stores such as Egghead.

Andrew Tobias' TaxCut is a unique tax-preparation system that integrates reproductions of commonly used 1040 tax forms with calculation features like a spreadsheet program. "Ask the Expert scratch pads" are available so the knowledge base can be applied separately to each element of a line item on the return. In addition, a feature called Shoebox allows the user to determine the correct place to enter information on the return, by identifying the data source. The unique part of this system is the on-line advisor, Expert.

Expert is a series of mini expert systems in the form of intelligent questionnaires that provide the user with tax advice about specific line items on the individual tax return. If the cursor is on a line item covered by an expert system, "Expert Available" appears at the bottom of the screen. Expert is available for most of the line items on a Form 1040 and most of the commonly used schedules. In addition, if the user selects a tax topic from a menu, an indexing feature of the system takes the user to the correct line of the tax return's schedule or form and starts the expert system covering that topic. Each Expert screen has a question, an answer space and a comment section that gives additional explanation for the question. Expert considers the previous answers, when determining the additional questions to ask the user. A hypertext glossary is available for selected words in the question. If a user does not understand a term that is highlighted an explanation can be requested.

In addition to the individual line item expert systems, an intelligent questionnaire checklist helps the user identify reportable income, deductions, and credits. The checklist specifies the tax form(s) required for each item identified. Another expert system, The Auditor, scans the completed forms for mistakes and inconsistencies, and makes tax planning suggestions. A truth-maintenance system allows the user to back up and change answers and the system will automatically retract inconsistencies.

18.4   PERSONAL FINANCING PLANNING

Personal financial planning expert systems can be classified as either comprehensive systems (Nielson *et al.*, 1991; Phillips *et al.*, 1990; Brown *et al.*, 1990; Humpert and Holly, 1988; Behan and Lecot, 1987) that provide solutions to all aspects of financial planning or specialized systems that focus on a smaller knowledge domain like income tax planning. Comprehensive personal financial planning includes investment planning, income tax planning, retirement planning, estate planning, disability income planning, cash management, and debt management.

The comprehensive personal financial planning expert systems that run on PCs are Arthur Andersen & Co.'s AAFINPLAN and Sterling Wentworth Corporation's PLANMAN. APEX's Client Profiling System, Price Waterhouse's Personal Financial Analysis, and Chase Lincoln First Bank's Personal Financial Planning System are designed to be run on mainframe computers. Personal financial planning expert systems are either proprietary or can be licensed for use by a planner at the planner's location on an annual basis or per use basis using a service bureau approach. Personal Financial Analysis and AAFINPLAN are proprietary, PLANMAN is licensed on an annual basis, and APEX's Client Profiling System and Chase Lincoln's Personal Financial Planning System can either be licensed on an annual basis or used on a per use basis.

All of the expert systems provide standardized data-gathering forms used by the client to provide both personal and financial information as well as personal goals. All provide help lines to assistant the client or planner in completing the data-gathering forms. The most complex part of the process for the client is gathering together the needed information and filling out the data-gathering forms. CPAs can help their clients with these forms by insuring that all the information is both reported and correctly entered on the forms. All of the systems have built-in parameters and can be customized. The use of planning parameters allows the system to base conclusions and recommendations on the individual planner's philosophy as well as client-specific data. The client-specific conclusions and recommendations are used to select appropriate paragraphs of information that are merged into a customized report.

All systems provide the client with a computer generated comprehensive personal financial plan or can produce modular plans for an area or areas of personal financial planning such as retirement planning and estate planning. The reports may or may not be reviewed and edited by a personal financial planner. CPAs can assist their clients by helping them interpret their expert system prepared plans and by helping them implement the plan's recommendations. Because the cost per plan prepared by an expert system is low compared to the cost of the time it would take a CPA to prepare a plan, the CPA can provide valuable advice and assistance to clients and still keep the cost of personal financial planning affordable to many clients. For additional information on all the personal financial planning expert systems see (Brown *et al.*, 1990).

PLANMAN - Sterling Wentworth Corporation (Nielson *et al.*, 1991; Phillips *et al.*, 1990; Brown *et al.*, 1990; McKell *et al.*, 1988; McKell and Jenkins, 1988) in use for several years, checks and analyzes the client's information with over 7500 decision rules built into the system and is designed for all income levels. PLANMAN can also produce proforma reports that allow the financial planner to project the long-term impact of the system's recommendations on the financial condition of the client and to do "what if" analysis. PLANMAN can be purchased for a one-time fee of $4495 with updates and unlimited phone support costing $1000 per year. The system runs on IBM compatible PCs (XT, AT, 386) with 640K and a 20 megabyte hard drive.

AAFINPLAN - Arthur Andersen & Co. is a modified version of PLANMAN available to its clients. The knowledge-base received minor modifications and the text of the recommendations had extensive modifications.

Personal Financial Analysis - Price Waterhouse (Nielson *et al.*, 1991; Phillips *et al.*, 1990; Brown *et al.*, 1990) is available to employers who are clients of the firm. The personal financial plans are for all income levels and are tailored to the client company's benefit plans. The financial plan is cross-referenced to a 350 page volume of planning information to assist the individual in implementing the plan's recommendations.

Client Profiling System - APEX (Nielson *et al.*, 1991; Phillips *et al.*, 1990; Brown *et al.*, 1990) in use since 1987, was developed for financial institutions and is for middle income clients. In 1989, APEX began offering the system on a per-use fee of $125 per plan to individual personal financial planners with volume discounts available.

Personal Financial Planning System - Chase Lincoln First Bank (Nielson *et al.*, 1991; Phillips *et al.*, 1990; Brown *et al.*, 1990; Kindle *et al.*, 1989) has been in use since 1987 and was developed over six years ago by Chase Lincoln First Bank in conjunction with the international consulting firm of Arthur D. Little, Inc. The system provides personal financial plans for all ranges of income and provides projections of the client's financial position based on the plan's recommendations. Chase Lincoln First Bank is now marketing the system to certified financial planners, other banks, and to companies for use as an employee benefit. The cost per plan is $200–$400, however, the licensing agreement requires the purchase of a minimum number of plans per year.

18.5 CONCLUSIONS

The knowledge and skill an accountant needs to perform the tasks of auditing, income tax planning and determination, personal financial planning, and corporate accounting is growing at an unbelievable rate. The ability of an accountant to master the knowledge of even one of these areas is being stretched to the limits regardless of the accountant's skill and experience. Expert system technology has expanded at a rapid rate, bringing expert system use and development into the practice of accounting.

Expert systems are assisting accountants and accounting firms in providing quality services in a cost-effective manner. Expert systems provide the needed skills and information, so the accountant can concentrate on problem solving and the exercise of professional judgment rather than routine tasks. In addition, the use of expert systems will allow the accountant to become knowledgeable and proficient in more areas of professional practice. As the complexity of practice continues, cost containment for professional services grows, and expert systems technology expands, expert system use will continue to increase in accounting.

REFERENCES

Behan, J. and Lecot, K. (1987). "Overview of Financial Applications of Expert Systems." In *Proceedings: Western Conference on Expert Systems (WESTEX-87)*. pp. 223–229.

Bickerstaff, M. (1988). "Expert Systems for the Auditor." *NIVRA Conference*. September Presentation. Paper available from Mollie Bickerstaff, Coopers & Lybrand.

Black, R.L.; Carroll, T.W. and Rex, S.K. (1990). "Expert Systems: A New Tool to Enhance a Tax Practice." *The Tax Advisor,* January, pp. 3–17.

Brown, Carol E. (June 1988). "Tax Expert Systems in Industry and Accounting." *Expert Systems Review for Business and Accounting*. 1.(3), pp. 9–16.

Brown, C.E. (1989). "Accounting Expert Systems: A Comprehensive, Annotated Bibliography." *Expert Systems Review for Business and Accounting*. II.(1&2), Spring–Summer, pp. 23–129.

Brown, C.E. (1991). "Expert Systems in Public Accounting: Current Practice and Future Directions." *Expert Systems With Applications: An International Journal*. 3(1), pp. 3–18.

Brown, C.E. and Murphy, D. (1990). "The Use of Auditing Expert Systems in Public Accounting." *The Journal of Information Systems*. 5(1), pp. 63–72.

Brown, C.E. and Phillips, M.E. (1990). "Expert Systems Solving Management Accounting Problems." *Management Accounting*. LXXI (7), pp. 18–23.

Brown, C.E. and Streit, I.K. (1988). "A Survey of Tax Expert Systems." *Expert Systems Review for Business and Accounting*. 1(2), pp. 6–12.

Brown, C.E. (ed.), Black, R., Buehler, S. and Rogers, T. (1988). "Artificial Intelligence: Application in Taxation." *Expert Systems Review for Business and Accounting*. 1(4), pp. 3–10.

Brown, C.E., Nielson, N.L. and Phillips, M.E. (1990). "Expert Systems for Personal Financial Planning." *The Journal of Personal Financial Planning*. 3(3), pp. 137–143.

Gleeson, J.F.J. and West, M.L.J. (1988). "CLINTE: Coopers & Lybrand International Tax Expert System." In Moralee, D. S. (ed.), *Research and Development in Expert Systems* IV. pp.18–31. Cambridge: Cambridge University Press.

Graham, L.E., Damens, J. and Van Ness, G. (1991). "Developing Risk Advisor: An Expert System for Risk Identification." *Auditing: A Journal of Practice & Theory*. 10(1), pp. 69–96.

Harmon, P. (1988). "Expert Systems and the Big Eight Accounting Firms." Expert Systems Strategies, 4(11), pp. 1–12.

Humpert, B. and Holly, P. (1988). "Expert Systems in Finance Planning." *Expert Systems; The International Journal of Knowledge Engineering*. 5(2), pp.78–100.

Kindle, K.W., Cann, R.S., Craig, M.R. and Martin, T.J. (1989). "PFPS - Personal Financial Planning System." Presented at *AAAI Innovative Intelligence Conference*.

McKell, L.J. and Jenkins, J.W. (1988). "Planman Structure—A Strategy for Compromise." *Expert Systems Review for Business and Accounting*. 1(4), pp. 25–29.

McKell, L.J., Jenkins, J.W. and Farr, R. (1988). *The Structure and Implementation of an Expert System for Personal Financial Planning*. Working Paper (Brigham Young University). 15 pages.

Messier, W.F. and Hansen, J.V. (1987). "Expert Systems in Auditing: The State of the Art." *Auditing: A Journal of Practice and Theory*. 7(1), pp. 94–105.

Murphy, D.S. and Brown, C.E. (1992). "The Use of Advanced Information Technology in Audit Planning." *Expert Systems Review for Business and Accounting*. 1(3), pp. 187–193.

Nielson, N.L. and Brown, C.E. (1989). "Applications of Expert Systems in Insurance Regulation." *The Journal of Insurance Regulation.* 8(1), pp. 22–35.

Nielson, N.L., Phillips, M.E. and Brown, C.E. (1991). "Expert Systems to Provide Financial Planning Benefits." *Benefits Quarterly.* 7(1), pp. 41–51.

O'Leary, D.E. and Watkins, P.R. (1989). "Review of Expert Systems in Auditing." *Expert Systems Review for Business and Accounting.* II.(1&2), pp. 3–22.

Phillips, M.E., Brown, C.E. and Nielson, N.L. (1990). "Personal Financial Planning With Expert Systems: An Expanding Employee Benefit." *Management Accounting.* LXXII.(3), pp. 29–33.

Ribar, G.S. (1987). "Expert Systems Technology at Peat Marwick Main." *Expert Systems Review for Business and Accounting.* 1(1), pp. 1,5.

Ribar, G.S. (1988a). "Development of an Audit Expert System." *Expert Systems Review for Business and Accounting.* 1(3), pp. 3–8.

Ribar, G.S. (1988b). "Expert Systems Validation: A Case Study." *Expert Systems Review for Business and Accounting.* 1(3), pp. 26–28.

Schatz, H., Strahs, R. and Campbell, L. (1987). "ExperTAX: The Issue of Long-Term Maintenance." *Proceedings of the 3rd International Conference on Expert Systems.* pp. 291–300.

Shpilberg, D. and Graham, L.E. (1986). "Developing ExperTAX: An Expert System for Corporate Tax Accrual and Planning." *Auditing: A Journal of Practice & Theory.* 6(1), pp. 75–94.

Shpilberg, D., Graham, L.E. and Schatz, H. (1986). "ExperTAX: An Expert System for Corporate Tax Planning." *Expert Systems,* 3(3), pp. 136–150.

Susskind, R. and Tindall, C. (1988). "VATIA: Ernst & Whinney's VAT Expert System." *Proceedings of IV International Conference on Expert Systems.* Learned Information.

Willingham, J.J. and Ribar, G.S. (1988). "Development of an Expert Audit System for Loan Loss Evaluation." In: *Auditor Productivity in the Year 2000: Proceedings of the 1987 Arthur Young Professors' Roundtable*; 12–14 November, Columbus, OH. Reston VA: Council of Arthur Young Professors; pp. 171–186.

FURTHER READING

Brown, C.E. and Phillips, M.E. (1991). "Expert Systems for Internal Auditing." *The Internal Auditor.* 48(4) August, pp. 23–28.

Craig, C.K. and Silhan, P.A. (1991) "Computers in Taxation: Developing Expert Decision Support Systems for Tax Applications." *The Tax Advisor,* January, pp. 50–53.

Denna, E.L., Hansen, J.V. and Meservy, R.D. (1991). "Development and Application of Expert Systems in Audit Services." *IEEE Transaction on Knowledge and Data Engineering,* Volume 3(2), pp. 172–184.

Gray, G.L., McKee, T.E. and Mock, T.J. (1991). "The Future Impact of Expert Systems and Decision Support Systems on Auditing." *Advances In Accounting.* 9, pp. 249–273.

Lehman, M.W., Malley, J.C. and Cassidy, J. (1991) "Expert Systems for Audit Planning: Strategies for Local Accounting Firms." *Woman CPA.* 53(Summer), pp. 14–17.

McCarthy, W.E., Denna, E.L., Gal, G. and Rockwell, S.R. (1992) "Expert Systems and AI-based Decision Support in Auditing: Progress and Perspectives." *International Journal of Intelligent Systems in Accounting Finance & Management.* 1(1), pp. 53–63.

Phillips, M.E. and Brown, C.E. (1991) "Need an Expert? Ask a Computer." *Journal of Accountancy.* 172(5) November, pp. 91–93.

Phillips, M.E., Nielson, N.L. and Brown, C.E. (1992) "An Evaluation of Expert Systems for Personal Financial Planning." *Financial Counseling and Planning.* 3, pp. 79–103.

Ribar, G.S., Arcoleo, F. and Hollo, D. (1991) "LOAN PROBE: Testing a BIG Expert System." *AI Expert.* 6(5), pp. 43–49.

INDEX

Note: page numbers in **bold** refer to tables; those in *italics* refer to figures.

Index compiled by Annette J. Musker